# 1776
# Census
# of
# Maryland

Bettie Stirling Carothers

HERITAGE BOOKS
2006

# HERITAGE BOOKS
*AN IMPRINT OF HERITAGE BOOKS, INC.*

### Books, CDs, and more—Worldwide

For our listing of thousands of titles see our website at
www.HeritageBooks.com

Published 2006 by
HERITAGE BOOKS, INC.
Publishing Division
65 East Main Street
Westminster, Maryland 21157-5026

Copyright © 1986 Bettie Stirling Carothers

Other books by the author:

*1783 Tax List of Baltimore County*
Robert W. Barnes and Bettie S. Carothers

*1783 Tax List of Maryland, Part I: Cecil, Talbot, Harford and Calvert Counties*

*Index to Baltimore County Wills, 1659-1850*
Robert Barnes and Bettie S. Carothers

*Maryland Oaths of Fidelity*

*Maryland Source Records: Volume 1*

All rights reserved. No part of this book may be reproduced or transmitted in any form or by any means, electronic or mechanical, including photocopying, recording or by any information storage and retrieval system without written permission from the author, except for the inclusion of brief quotations in a review.

International Standard Book Number: 978-1-58549-088-1

CONTENTS

Anne Arundel County ...................... 1

Baltimore County (Deptford Hundred ...... 32
(Middlesex Hundred, Baltimore County on page 162)

Caroline County ......................... 33

Dorchester County ....................... 38

Frederick County ........................ 54

Harford County .......................... 87

Prince George's County ................. 118

Queen Anne's County .................... 141

Talbot County .......................... 152

Baltimore County (Middlesex Hundred) ... 162

Index .................................. 164

## PREFACE

The 1776 Census of Maryland has been copied from original sources at the Hall of Records, Annapolis, Maryland. No attempt has been made to change the spelling of names as the original enumerator took them. It is suggested that every possible way of spelling is checked, since early names were often written phonetically or poorly spelled.

A name is listed in the index only once for each page on which it appears. It would be advisable to check the entire page for additional listings of the same name.

In 1814 the name of Elizabeth Town was changed to Hagerstown, which is now located in Washington County, Maryland. Records of Montgomery and Washington County families will be found in Frederick County, since they were not formed until just after the census was taken in 1776.

There could not have been a standard form used for the taking of the census and for this reason the information and method of enumeration varied from each county, and indeed, with each enumerator. However, all information available has been copied.

Part of Prince George's County (pages 120 to 140) was taken by listing the name of the head of the household, followed by the ages only, of other males living in the household. The same form is used for the females.

All Black people are included if there was a record of both a first and last name.

Every effort has been made to present these records without error; but please keep in mind how difficult it is to read some of the very old records.

## 1776 CENSUS

### ALL HALLOWS PARISH - ANNE ARUNDEL COUNTY, MARYLAND

| Head of the Household | White Males | White Females | White Children | Black Males | Black Women | Black Children | Taxables |
|---|---|---|---|---|---|---|---|
| William Read | 1 | 3 | 8 | | | | 1 |
| John Selman | 1 | 1 | 1 | | | | 1 |
| Francis Gwynn | 1 | 1 | 5 | | | | 1 |
| Richard Rawlings | 1 | 2 | 4 | | | 1 | 1 |
| Ralph Bazill | 2 | 2 | 1 | 1 | 1 | 1 | 3 |
| Joseph Williams | 2 | 4 | 4 | | | | 2 |
| Richard Jacobs | 1 | 1 | 1 | | | | 1 |
| John Jacobs | 1 | 2 | | | | | 1 |
| William Jacobs | 1 | | | | | | 1 |
| John Nicholson, Jr. | 1 | 1 | 2 | | | | 1 |
| Henry Jones | 2 | | | 1 | 2 | 3 | 5 |
| John Onion | 1 | 1 | 3 | | | | 1 |
| Capt. James Sanders | 2 | 2 | | | 2 | 2 | 4 |
| Thomas Elliott | 2 | 2 | 3 | 1 | | | 3 |
| Sarah Collings | | 2 | 1 | | | | |
| Leonard Romalls | 1 | 1 | 8 | | | | 1 |
| James Sanders | 2 | 1 | 3 | | 1 | 2 | 3 |
| Robert Walsh Elliott | 1 | 2 | 1 | | | | 1 |
| John Lee | 1 | | | | | | 1 |
| Matthew Elliott | 3 | | | | | | 3 |
| Marmaduke Morgan | 1 | 1 | 2 | | | | 1 |
| Thomas King | 1 | 1 | 1 | 1 | 2 | 4 | 4 |
| John Steel | 1 | 2 | 4 | | | | |
| John Jacobs | 1 | 1 | | | | | 1 |

| Head of the Household | White Males | White Females | White Children | Black Males | Black Women | Black Children | Taxables |
|---|---|---|---|---|---|---|---|
| Mary Jacobs | | 4 | 1 | | | | |
| Rachel Hett | | 2 | 1 | | | | |
| George Nennom | 1 | 1 | 2 | | | | 1 |
| Wm. Jiams of John | 2 | 2 | | | 1 | 3 | 3 |
| William Lockwood | 1 | 1 | 1 | | | 4 | 1 |
| John Cowman | 2 | 2 | 6 | 2 | 3 | 6 | 6 |
| Gerrard Hopkins, Jr. | 3 | 3 | 1 | 3 | 3 | 7 | 7 |
| James Phelps | 1 | 1 | 5 | | | | 1 |
| James Disney of William | 1 | 1 | 2 | 1 | | | 2 |
| William Davis, Jr. | 2 | 2 | 4 | 2 | 2 | 6 | 6 |
| Josiah Phelps | 1 | 3 | 3 | | | | 1 |
| Joseph Howard, Jr. | 1 | 1 | 2 | 5 | 1 | 7 | 6 |
| Joseph Williams of Benj. | 1 | | | 1 | 1 | 4 | 3 |
| Thomas Rutland | 2 | 1 | 2 | 6 | 2 | 6 | 10 |
| Elizabeth Williams | | 1 | | | | | |
| Denune Howard | 1 | | | | | | 1 |
| John Givens | 1 | 1 | 2 | | | | 1 |
| Benjamin Selby | 1 | 1 | 6 | 1 | 1 | 4 | 3 |
| Jonathan Selby | 1 | 3 | 1 | 2 | 1 | 1 | 2 |
| Stockett Williams | 1 | | | | | | 1 |
| Richard Elliott | 3 | 1 | 5 | | | | 2 |
| Robert Cross | 1 | 1 | 4 | | | | 1 |
| Abraham Short | 1 | 1 | 3 | | | | 1 |
| Ruth Elliott | | 3 | 1 | | | | |
| John Basil | 1 | 1 | 4 | | | | 1 |
| William Turner | 1 | 1 | 4 | | | | 1 |

| Head of the Household | White Males | White Females | White Children | Black Males | Black Women | Black Children | Taxables |
|---|---|---|---|---|---|---|---|
| Elizabeth Letton |  | 1 | 3 |  |  |  |  |
| William Ryan | 1 | 2 | 4 |  |  |  | 1 |
| John Elliott | 1 |  |  |  |  |  | 1 |
| Hester Beard |  | 3 | 6 |  |  |  |  |
| George Hurst | 1 | 1 | 2 |  |  |  | 1 |
| Richard Tydings | 1 | 1 | 9 |  |  |  | 1 |
| John Nelson Gray | 3 | 3 | 2 | 2 | 1 | 8 | 6 |
| Joseph Pearce | 1 | 1 | 6 |  |  |  | 1 |
| Jane Knighton | 1 | 3 | 3 |  | 2 |  | 3 |
| William Harwood | 1 | 1 | 1 | 3 | 3 | 7 | 7 |
| Otho French | 2 | 1 |  |  |  |  | 1 |
| William French | 1 |  |  |  |  |  | 1 |
| William Pearce | 1 | 1 | 3 |  |  |  | 1 |
| Daniel Davis | 2 | 2 | 5 | 1 | 1 | 1 | 3 |
| Benjamin Welsh | 1 | 1 | 1 |  |  |  | 1 |
| Edward Lee | 1 | 1 |  | 3 | 2 | 4 | 6 |
| Robert Welsh | 1 | 4 | 1 | 2 | 1 | 3 | 4 |
| Philip Richardson | 6 |  |  |  |  |  | 6 |
| Samuel Poole | 2 | 3 | 4 |  |  |  | 2 |
| Richard Phelps | 1 | 1 |  |  |  |  | 1 |
| Catharine Steuart | 1 | 2 | 2 |  |  |  | 1 |
| Robert Steuart | 1 |  |  |  |  |  | 1 |
| John Burgess of Wm. | 2 | 2 | 6 |  |  | 1 | 2 |
| William Anderson Jr. | 1 |  |  |  |  |  | 1 |
| James Anderson Sr. | 3 | 1 |  | 1 | 1 | 4 | 5 |
| Aaron Rawlings | 1 | 1 | 9 |  | 1 | 7 | 2 |

| Head of the Household | White Males | White Females | White Children | Black Males | Black Women | Black Children | Taxables |
|---|---|---|---|---|---|---|---|
| Matthew Beard | 1 | | | | | | 1 |
| Deborah Phelps | 1 | 3 | 2 | | | | 1 |
| Mordecai Barry | 2 | 2 | 5 | | | | 2 |
| John Basford | 1 | 1 | 3 | | | 1 | 1 |
| Thomas Bafford | 2 | 1 | 4 | | | | 2 |
| Henry Hall | 1 | 1 | | 4 | 3 | 8 | 8 |
| John Chaplain | 2 | 1 | 6 | | | | 2 |
| David Evans | 1 | 1 | 3 | 4 | 3 | 7 | 7 |
| Ann Gaither | | 1 | | | 1 | | 1 |
| Ann Stuart | 1 | 3 | 1 | | | 1 | 1 |
| Hugh Jones | 1 | 1 | 1 | | | | 1 |
| Samuel Taylor | 1 | 1 | 7 | | | | 1 |
| Mashet Howard | 1 | 1 | 7 | | | | 1 |
| Ann Taylor | | 1 | 2 | | | | |
| Benjamin Williams | 1 | 1 | 2 | 1 | | | 2 |
| Matthew Robinson | 1 | | | 1 | | | 2 |
| John Phelps | 1 | 2 | | 1 | 1 | | 2 |
| Thomas Fowler | 1 | 1 | | | | 1 | 1 |
| Thomas Francis Linthicum | 1 | 1 | 1 | | | | 1 |
| Jacob Iiams | 1 | 2 | 3 | | | | 1 |
| Eleanor Druce | | 4 | | | | | |
| Sarah Jones | 1 | 3 | 3 | 1 | | | 2 |
| George Glayden | 1 | 1 | 4 | | | | 1 |
| John Myers | 1 | 3 | | | | | 1 |
| Auther Thompson | 2 | 2 | 1 | | | | 2 |
| Burton Linthicum | 1 | 1 | | | | 1 | 1 |

| Head of the Household | White Males | White Females | White Children | Black Males | Black Females | Black Children | Taxables |
|---|---|---|---|---|---|---|---|
| William St. Lawrence | 1 | | | 1 | | | 2 |
| Eleanor St. Lawrence | | 1 | 1 | | 1 | 2 | 1 |
| Philip Brown | 1 | 1 | 3 | | | | 1 |
| Zachariah Cheney | 1 | 1 | 3 | | | | 1 |
| Edmund Wayman | 1 | 2 | 1 | 1 | | | 2 |
| Caleb Taylor | 1 | 1 | 5 | | | | 1 |
| Joseph Jones | 1 | 1 | 2 | | | | 1 |
| Susannah Phelps | 5 | 3 | 3 | | | | 5 |
| Joseph Owens | 1 | 1 | 3 | | | | 1 |
| David Stuart | 1 | 1 | 4 | 1 | 2 | 1 | 4 |
| Samuel Fowler | 1 | 1 | 2 | | | | 1 |
| Henry Onion | 1 | 1 | 3 | | | | 1 |
| Abraham Woodward's (Quarter) | | | | 2 | 2 | | 4 |
| Stephen Basford | 1 | 2 | | | 2 | 10 | 3 |
| John Connoway | 1 | 2 | 6 | | 1 | 1 | 2 |
| Thomas Orrick | 1 | 1 | | | | | 1 |
| Thomas Parsley | 1 | 1 | | | | | 1 |
| Edward Edwards | 3 | 3 | 5 | 2 | 4 | 7 | 9 |
| Philip Thomas'(Quarter) | | | | 2 | 3 | 6 | 5 |
| John Linthicum | 1 | 2 | 4 | 1 | 3 | | 5 |
| Elizabeth Linthicum | 1 | 2 | 3 | | | | 1 |
| Benjamin Talbott | 1 | 2 | 3 | 5 | 2 | 6 | 8 |
| William Andrews | 1 | 1 | 2 | | | | 1 |
| Nicholas St. Lawrence | 3 | 1 | | | | | 3 |
| Joshua Adams | 1 | 1 | 5 | | | | 1 |
| Thomas Tucker | 1 | 1 | 1 | | | | 1 |

| Head of the Household | White Males | White Females | White Children | Black Males | Black Women | Black Children | Taxables |
|---|---|---|---|---|---|---|---|
| Sarah McCauley | 1 | 6 | | | | | 1 |
| Daniel Atwell | 1 | 1 | | | | | 1 |
| Susannah Johns'(Quarter) | | | | 5 | 2 | 5 | 7 |
| Francis McCainley | 5 | 2 | 1 | 2 | 1 | 1 | 6 |
| Mary Tucker | 2 | 2 | | | | | 2 |
| William Hood | 2 | 6 | | 7 | 7 | 8 | 16 |
| John Hammond's (Quarter) | 1 | | | 3 | 1 | 2 | 5 |
| Sarah Elliott | 4 | 2 | 1 | | 1 | 4 | 5 |
| Alexander McClain | 1 | 1 | 2 | | | | 1 |
| Amos Gaither | 1 | 2 | | | 3 | 6 | 4 |
| Benjamin Cadle | 1 | 2 | 1 | | | | 1 |
| James Cadle | 1 | 2 | 6 | | | | 1 |
| Samuel Cadle | 1 | 1 | 6 | | | | 1 |
| Elizabeth Ridgely | 3 | 1 | 1 | | | | 3 |
| Cornelius Berry | 2 | 1 | 2 | | | 1 | 2 |
| Edward Gaither | 3 | 3 | | 3 | 3 | 6 | 6 |
| Cassandra Ducker | | 2 | 2 | 1 | 2 | 4 | 3 |
| Gideon Gary | 1 | 3 | 5 | 3 | 2 | 6 | 6 |
| Elijah Green | 1 | 3 | 3 | 2 | 1 | 3 | 4 |
| Thomas Fowler Basford's | 1 | 1 | 1 | | | | 1 |
| Leonard Wayman's(Quarter) | | | | 5 | 3 | 7 | 8 |
| Zachariah McCauley | 1 | 1 | | | | | 1 |
| Edward Hall's (Quarter) | | | | 4 | 2 | 2 | 6 |
| Thomas Henry Hall | 1 | 1 | 1 | 5 | 5 | 11 | 11 |
| William Hall | 1 | 1 | 1 | 3 | 1 | 5 | 5 |
| Jeremiah Crabb | 2 | 2 | 1 | 6 | 5 | 7 | 13 |

| Head of the Household | White Males | White Females | White Children | Black Males | Black Women | Black Children | Taxables |
|---|---|---|---|---|---|---|---|
| Samuel Brogden | 1 | | | 3 | 4 | 5 | 8 |
| Joseph Mayo Jr. | 1 | 1 | 5 | 1 | | | 2 |
| Thomas Philpott | 2 | 1 | 3 | | | | 2 |
| Benjamin Gravel | 1 | 2 | | | | | 1 |
| Isaac Jones | 1 | 1 | 6 | | 1 | 5 | 2 |
| Elizabeth Jones | | 1 | | 2 | 3 | 3 | 5 |
| Robert Whittaker | 1 | 1 | 7 | | | | 1 |
| John Beard | 2 | 1 | 3 | 1 | 1 | 2 | 4 |
| Joseph Watkins | 1 | 1 | 6 | 3 | 2 | 7 | 6 |
| John Iiams of John | 3 | | | 1 | | | 4 |
| Capt. John Iiams | 1 | 2 | 2 | 1 | 3 | 7 | 4 |
| Richard Beard | 2 | 1 | 7 | 2 | 1 | 4 | 5 |
| Robert John Smith | 3 | 1 | 6 | | 1 | | 4 |
| Richard Beard Sr. | 3 | 5 | | 1 | 2 | 4 | 6 |
| Richard Walker | 1 | 2 | 2 | 1 | | 1 | 2 |
| Ann Battee | 1 | 2 | 1 | 3 | 4 | 4 | 6 |
| Gassaway Watkins | 2 | 1 | 4 | 1 | 1 | 2 | 4 |
| James Elliott | 1 | 1 | 4 | | | | 1 |
| John Thomas'(Quarter) | | | | 3 | 1 | 8 | 4 |
| Mary Strachan | | | | 3 | 1 | | 4 |
| John Bishop | 1 | 1 | | | | | 1 |
| William Brown | 4 | 1 | 5 | 2 | 1 | | 7 |
| Sarah Carter | | 3 | 2 | | 1 | | 1 |
| William Thrift | 2 | 2 | 3 | | | | 2 |
| George Stolker | 2 | 1 | 1 | | | | 2 |
| Stephen Beard | 2 | 1 | 2 | 1 | 1 | 1 | 4 |

| Head of the Household | White Males | White Females | White Children | Black Males | Black Women | Black Children | Taxables |
|---|---|---|---|---|---|---|---|
| John Selman Sr. | 3 | 3 | 4 | 1 | 1 | 5 | 5 |
| Thomas Fowler of Wm. | 1 | 4 | 5 | | | | 1 |
| John Tidings | 2 | 1 | 8 | 2 | 1 | | 5 |
| John Glover | 1 | 1 | 3 | | | | |
| Lewis Lee | 1 | 2 | 2 | 2 | 1 | 4 | 4 |
| Ann Rawls | | 2 | 1 | | | | |
| Thomas Harwood's(Quarter) | 3 | | | 4 | 3 | 11 | 10 |
| Richard Burgess | 2 | 1 | 10 | 2 | 1 | 4 | 5 |
| John Cawill | 1 | 1 | 2 | 1 | | | 2 |
| Alexander Carvill | 1 | | | | 1 | | 1 |
| Stephen Rawlings | 2 | 2 | 3 | | 1 | | 2 |
| William Carvill | 1 | 1 | 1 | | 1 | | 2 |
| Thomas Phips | 2 | 1 | 1 | | | | 2 |
| Samuel Watkins | 2 | 1 | 6 | 2 | 2 | 4 | 6 |
| Ann Chambers | | 1 | | | 1 | | 1 |
| James Disney | 2 | 3 | 3 | 2 | 2 | 1 | 5 |
| William Disney | 1 | 1 | 2 | | | | 1 |
| James Davidson | 1 | | | | | | 1 |
| Mary Walsh | | 3 | 1 | | | | |
| Margaret Williams | | 3 | 3 | | | | |
| Ann Harwood | 1 | 2 | | 9 | 7 | 11 | 17 |
| Col. Richard Harwood | 1 | 1 | 5 | 4 | 6 | 5 | 11 |
| Henry Oneal Welsh | 1 | | | 8 | 7 | 13 | 16 |
| Samuel White | 1 | 1 | 2 | | | | 1 |
| William Ryan | 1 | 1 | | | | | 1 |
| Hugh Champain | 1 | | | | | | 1 |

| Head of the Household | White Males | White Females | White Children | Black Males | Black Women | Black Children | Taxables |
|---|---|---|---|---|---|---|---|
| William Powell | 1 | | | | | | 1 |
| Eleanor Butler | 1 | 1 | 3 | | | | 2 |
| John Onely | 1 | 1 | | | | | 1 |
| Samuel Jacobs | 2 | 2 | 6 | 1 | 1 | 1 | 3 |
| Daniel Pearce | 1 | 2 | 2 | | | | |
| Nicholas Maccubbin (Quarter at Beards Creek) | 1 | | | 14 | 6 | 9 | 21 |
| Plummer Iiams | 2 | 2 | 1 | 3 | 3 | 9 | 8 |
| Jeremiah Watkins | 1 | 1 | 6 | | 1 | 2 | 2 |
| Samuel Galloway's (Quarter) | | | | 6 | 5 | 12 | 11 |
| Wm. Iiams of George | 1 | 1 | 1 | 4 | 4 | 11 | 9 |
| William Davis Sr. | 2 | 2 | 2 | 1 | 1 | 2 | 4 |
| John Powell | 1 | 1 | 4 | | | | |
| Philip Chambers | 1 | 2 | 5 | | | | 1 |
| Lewis Stockett | 1 | 1 | 7 | 4 | 3 | 2 | 8 |
| Thomas Noble Stockett | 1 | 2 | 2 | 7 | 3 | 12 | 10 |
| Rachel Stockett | 1 | 1 | 3 | | 1 | 3 | 2 |
| Gassaway Rawlings | 2 | 3 | 3 | 8 | 7 | 21 | 17 |
| Joseph Cowman | 3 | 2 | 2 | 5 | 6 | 10 | 13 |
| James Owens Jr. | 1 | 1 | 3 | | | 4 | 1 |
| John Watkins of Gassoway | 1 | 1 | 4 | | | 1 | 1 |
| Wm. George McCain | 1 | 1 | 1 | | | | 1 |
| Joseph Howard Sr. | 2 | 2 | 1 | 6 | 3 | 10 | 11 |
| Rachel Sullivan | | 1 | 2 | | | | |
| Thomas Sprigg | 1 | 3 | | 23 | 16 | 29 | 40 |
| Capt. Thomas Watkins | 1 | 2 | 4 | 4 | 2 | 10 | 7 |

| Head of the Household | White Males | White Females | White Children | Black Males | Black Women | Black Children | Taxables |
|---|---|---|---|---|---|---|---|
| Richard Welsh | 1 | 2 | 2 | | | | 1 |
| Dinah Sparrow | | 2 | 1 | | | | |
| Edmund Purdy | 1 | 1 | 2 | | | | 1 |
| Richard Watkins | 1 | 2 | 4 | 1 | 1 | 1 | 3 |
| Elizabeth Brookes | 1 | 1 | | 3 | 2 | 1 | 6 |
| Ephraim Duvall | 1 | 1 | | | | | 1 |
| Thomas Gibbs | 1 | 2 | 3 | 1 | 1 | 12 | 3 |
| William Rawlings | 1 | 1 | 1 | | | | 1 |
| Charles Stewart | 2 | 2 | | 3 | 5 | 13 | 10 |
| Benjamin Burgess | 1 | 2 | 1 | 1 | | 3 | 2 |
| Sarah Burgess | | 3 | | | 1 | 4 | 1 |
| Thomas Mainear | 1 | 1 | 5 | | | | 1 |
| Jane Inch | | 2 | | | 1 | 1 | 1 |
| Capt. Thomas Walker | 1 | | | | 1 | 1 | 2 |
| Eleanor Hall | | 1 | | | | | |
| Elizabeth Buchanan | | 1 | | | 1 | | 1 |
| Joseph Gibson | 2 | 1 | 3 | | | | 2 |
| Elizabeth Scougall | | 2 | | 1 | 2 | 3 | 3 |
| Elizabeth Ferguson | | 3 | 1 | 1 | 1 | 4 | 2 |
| John Sifton | 2 | 1 | 4 | 1 | 1 | 5 | 4 |
| Sarah Mitchell | | 1 | 1 | | | | |
| William Thornton | 2 | 1 | 2 | | 2 | 4 | 4 |
| Rev Dr David Love | 1 | | | 1 | 1 | | 2 |
| Capt. Thomas Pearson | 1 | 1 | | 3 | 3 | 3 | 3 |
| Dinah Gassaway | | 4 | 2 | | 1 | 1 | 1 |
| Nicholas Gassaway | 1 | 1 | 1 | 6 | 4 | 7 | 11 |

| Head of the Household | White Males | White Females | White Children | Black Males | Black Women | Black Children | Taxables |
|---|---|---|---|---|---|---|---|
| Nathan Waters | 1 | 2 | 6 | 3 | 2 | 7 | 6 |
| Francis Linthicum | 1 | 2 | 7 | 1 | 1 | 1 | 3 |
| William Purdy | 1 | 1 | 4 | | | | 1 |
| Henry Purdy | 1 | 1 | 4 | | | | 1 |
| John Holton | 2 | 1 | 3 | 1 | | | 3 |
| William Sanders | 1 | 1 | 2 | 5 | 4 | 8 | 8 |
| Elizabeth Sanders | 1 | 1 | | 4 | 5 | 13 | 10 |
| Francis Wayman | 1 | 3 | 2 | | | | 1 |
| William Roberts | 1 | 1 | 3 | | | | 1 |
| Joseph Mayo | 3 | 3 | 5 | 8 | 2 | 7 | 16 |
| Robert Pain Davis | 1 | 7 | 3 | 3 | 4 | 6 | 8 |
| William Brewer | 1 | 1 | 5 | | 2 | 6 | 3 |
| Eleanor Brewer | 1 | 2 | 4 | 2 | 6 | 6 | 9 |
| Joseph Brewer Sr. | 1 | 1 | 5 | 1 | 2 | 3 | 4 |
| Samuel Giest | 1 | 1 | 4 | | 1 | 3 | 2 |
| Henry Brewer | 2 | 1 | | | | | 2 |
| William Jennings | 1 | 1 | 1 | | | | 1 |
| Alice Nicholson | | 2 | | 2 | 4 | 7 | 6 |
| Nicholas Maccubbin (Quarter Squirrel Neck) | | | | 11 | 11 | 25 | 22 |
| Joshua Yeates | 2 | 1 | | 1 | 2 | 3 | 5 |
| Jonathan Selman | 2 | 3 | | 7 | 3 | 7 | 12 |
| Sarah Pearce | | 1 | 1 | | | | |
| William Ward | 1 | 2 | 4 | | | | 1 |
| John Letton | 1 | 2 | 2 | | | | 1 |
| Keley Lewis | 1 | 1 | 4 | | | 1 | 1 |

| Head of the Household | White Males | White Females | White Children | Black Males | Black Women | Black Children | Taxables |
|---|---|---|---|---|---|---|---|
| John Smith | 1 | 1 | 3 | | | 1 | 1 |
| Margaret Hunter | | 2 | 1 | | | | |
| Eleanor Reed | | 1 | | 2 | | | 1 |
| William Bennett | 3 | 3 | 5 | | | | 3 |
| Benjamin Gaither | 1 | | | 5 | 3 | 8 | 9 |
| Capt. Nachel Gaither | 1 | | | | | | 1 |
| Catharine Lusby | | 1 | 2 | | | | |
| Ann Rankin | 1 | 3 | 3 | | 1 | 2 | 2 |
| Edward Steuart | 1 | 1 | 2 | 2 | 1 | 4 | 4 |
| Francis Belmear | 2 | 2 | 5 | 1 | 1 | 4 | 4 |
| William Anderson | 1 | 1 | 4 | 1 | 2 | 1 | 4 |
| Moses Donaldson | 2 | 1 | 4 | | | | 2 |
| Thomas Benson | 3 | 3 | 3 | | | | 3 |
| Samuel Cheney | 3 | 1 | 4 | | | | 3 |
| Thomas Mulliken | 1 | 2 | 6 | 3 | 4 | 13 | 8 |
| Jeremiah Mulliken | 1 | 1 | | 4 | 1 | 6 | 6 |
| Belt Mulliken | 1 | 1 | 4 | 3 | 2 | 5 | 6 |
| Absolom Anderson | 1 | 3 | 6 | 1 | 2 | 2 | 4 |
| Johns Hopkins | 3 | 1 | 8 | 6 | 12 | 25 | 23 |
| Gerrard Hopkins | 3 | 2 | | 9 | 7 | 16 | 19 |
| Joseph Hopkins | 1 | 1 | 2 | 2 | 1 | 5 | 4 |
| Rev. John Ashton's(Quarter) | | | | 2 | 2 | 6 | 4 |
| Samuel Cheney Jr. | 3 | 3 | 2 | | | | 3 |
| Joseph Cheney | 1 | 1 | 3 | | | | 1 |
| Hugh Jean Farris | 1 | | | | | | 1 |
| Mary Holliday | | 3 | 4 | 4 | 2 | 6 | 6 |

| Head of the Household | White Males | White Females | White Children | Black Males | Black Women | Black Children | Taxables |
|---|---|---|---|---|---|---|---|
| Rebecca Wilson |  | 1 | 1 |  | 1 | 2 | 1 |
| Benjamin Holliday | 1 |  |  |  | 1 |  | 1 |
| Thomas Iiames | 1 | 2 | 4 | 1 | 1 | 2 | 2 |
| John Iiames | 2 |  |  |  |  |  | 1 |
| Daniel of St.Thomas Jenifer | 2 | 1 |  | 5 | 2 | 3 | 10 |
| James Dick | 3 | 5 | 7 | 8 | 6 | 11 | 13 |
| Charles Steuart | 4 | 4 |  | 35 | 22 | 46 | 61 |
| John Nicholson | 2 | 2 | 5 | 1 | 2 |  | 5 |
| Zachariah Duvall | 1 | 1 | 3 |  |  |  | 1 |
| Samuel Galloway's(Quarter) |  |  |  | 5 | 4 | 5 | 9 |
| Capt William Brogden | 4 | 2 | 3 | 6 | 7 | 27 | 17 |
| John Brogden | 3 | 2 | 5 | 3 | 5 | 13 | 11 |
| Thomas Watkins | 2 | 1 |  | 8 | 8 | 18 | 18 |
| Elizabeth Hall | 1 | 3 | 4 | 4 | 7 | 16 | 12 |
| John Cragg | 1 |  |  |  |  |  | 1 |
| James Hunter | 1 | 1 | 4 |  |  |  | 1 |
| Anthony Stewart's (Quarter) |  |  |  | 3 | 3 | 6 | 6 |

This completes the list of inhabitants in All Hallows Parish, taken in 1776 by John Jiams.

## 1776 CENSUS

### ST. JAMES PARISH - ANNE ARUNDEL COUNTY, MARYLAND

| Head of the Household | White Women | White Boys | White Girls | Negro Men | Negro Women | Negro Boys | Negro Girls |
|---|---|---|---|---|---|---|---|
| Samuel Chew | 3 | | 2 | 26 | 26 | 20 | 33 |
| Richard Collage | | | | | | | |
| William Enness | | | | | | | |
| Lewis Scrivenor | | | | | | | |
| Francis Scrivenor | 1 | | 4 | 5 | 4 | 3 | 4 |
| Morgan Jones | 2 | 3 | 2 | 2 | 1 | 2 | 4 |
| Joseph Fraisear | 1 | 5 | 1 | 2 | 2 | | |
| William Fraisear | | | | | | | |
| Joseph Fraisear | | | | | | | |
| William Laskin | 2 | | 1 | | | | |
| Samuel Buskhad | 4 | | 5 | 3 | 6 | 6 | 5 |
| Samuel Buskhad Jr. | | | | | | | |
| Seaborn Buskhad | | | | | | | |
| Nehemiah Buskhad | 1 | | | | | | |
| Thomas H. Buskhad | | | | | | | |
| John Ried | | | | | | | |
| John Buskhad | 2 | 3 | | 2 | 1 | | 2 |
| Nehemiah Buskhad | | | | | | | |
| John Buskhad Jr. | | | | | | | |
| Francis Buskhad | | | | | | | |
| Hopeful Wood | 3 | 3 | | | | | |
| William Harris | | | | | | | |
| Robert Roughton | 1 | 1 | | | | | |
| Nehemiah Buskhad | 1 | | | 5 | 3 | 1 | 3 |

| Head of the Household | White Women | White Boys | White Girls | Negro Men | Negro Women | Negro Boys | Negro Girls |
|---|---|---|---|---|---|---|---|
| (Jo)hn Buskhad | | | | | | | |
| (Mat)thew Buskhad | | | | | | | |
| (Jo)hn Wood | 1 | 1 | 1 | | | | |
| Richard Wood | 1 | | 1 | | | | |
| Robert Ward | 3 | 1 | | 6 | 5 | | 4 |
| Sarah Wood | 1 | 4 | 1 | | | | |
| John Shinmer | 1 | | 5 | 1 | 5 | | 4 |
| Richard Randel | 2 | 1 | 4 | | | | |
| Thomas Cheyney | 1 | 1 | | | | | |
| John Ballson | 3 | 3 | 2 | 2 | | | 1 |
| John Welch | 2 | 5 | 2 | | | | |
| John Ward | 1 | | 1 | | | | |
| Robert Ward Jr. | 1 | | | | | | |
| James Tasker | 2 | | | | | | |
| James Tasker Jr. | | | | | | | |
| Daniel Sells | 1 | 1 | 2 | | | | |
| Lewis Stevens | 1 | 1 | | | | | |
| Morgan Wood | 1 | 2 | 4 | | 2 | | 1 |
| Gedean Shoemaker | 1 | | | | | | |
| William Whitington | 2 | | | | | | |
| Stephen Lambath | 1 | | | | | | |
| Joseph Warner | 1 | 1 | 1 | | | | |
| William Simmons | 2 | 2 | 3 | 1 | 3 | | |
| Samuel Morrison | 1 | | | 3 | 4 | 5 | 3 |
| Dr. Andrew Leiper | 1 | | | | 1 | | |
| William Parriott | 3 | 3 | 3 | | | | |

| Head of the Household | White Women | White Boys | White Girls | Negro Men | Negro Women | Negro Boys | Negro Girls |
|---|---|---|---|---|---|---|---|
| Thomas Parriott | 1 | 2 | 1 | | | | |
| William Devenpoto | 1 | | 2 | | | | |
| Richard Brown | 1 | 2 | 2 | 2 | | | 2 |
| Captain Thomas Smith | 1 | | | 2 | 1 | 2 | 5 |
| Richard Dowell | 1 | 2 | 2 | | | | |
| Elizabeth Lewin | | 1 | 2 | 4 | 5 | 5 | 11 |
| Samuel Lewin | 1 | | | | | | |
| (Albert) H. Smith | 1 | | 1 | 2 | 4 | 5 | 1 |
| (Joh)n Chew | 1 | 3 | | 2 | 3 | 6 | 3 |
| (Jo)hn Lane | 1 | | | 6 | 4 | 3 | |
| Thomas Shields | 1 | 1 | | | | | |
| Richard Hopkins | 1 | 3 | 2 | 1 | 1 | 1 | |
| Henry Plummer | 1 | 3 | 3 | 1 | | 1 | |
| Richard Richardson | 1 | 3 | 4 | 4 | 7 | 3 | 3 |
| Joseph Richardson | 3 | | | 5 | 9 | 7 | 10 |
| John Hall | 4 | 1 | | 2 | 8 | 17 | 5 |
| John Coal | 1 | 4 | 2 | 4 | 4 | 5 | 1 |
| Joseph Galloway | 2 | 1 | 1 | 7 | 5 | 6 | 7 |
| Jonathan Rawlings | 1 | | | | | 3 | 2 |
| Richard Rawlings | | | | | | 1 | |
| Samuel Rawlings | | | | | | | |
| Richard Harwood | | | | 7 | 4 | 6 | 5 |
| Stephen Watkins | 1 | 3 | 3 | 5 | 4 | 6 | 9 |
| Elizabeth Smith | | | | | 3 | 2 | 2 |
| Richard Wells | 1 | 1 | 2 | 3 | 3 | 3 | 1 |
| John Sullivan | | | | | | | |

| Head of the Household | White Women | White Boys | White Girls | Negro Men | Negro Women | Negro Boys | Negro Girls |
|---|---|---|---|---|---|---|---|
| Thomas Muan (?) | | | | | | | |
| Thomas Medcalf | 1 | 2 | 1 | 1 | 1 | | 1 |
| John Watkins Jr. | 1 | | 1 | 4 | 3 | 6 | 6 |
| Francis Tophouse | 1 | 2 | 3 | | | | |
| Benjamin Lane | 4 | | | 3 | 7 | 8 | 7 |
| Thomas Lane | | | | | | | |
| Gabriel Lane | | | | | | | |
| Jonas Gattwith | 3 | | 2 | | 1 | 1 | 1 |
| John Deal | | | | | | | |
| John Plummer | 2 | 2 | | 4 | 4 | 1 | 6 |
| William Barnsbury | 1 | 1 | | | | | |
| Elizabeth Taylor | | | | | | | |
| Thomas Tillard | 1 | | | 3 | 4 | 3 | 2 |
| William Dove | 3 | 3 | 1 | | | | |
| Samuel Shukells | 2 | 2 | 3 | 1 | 1 | 4 | 1 |
| Jonathan Busheard | 1 | | | 1 | | | |
| Charles Cheyney | 3 | | | 1 | 2 | 3 | 4 |
| John Curry | 1 | | 2 | | | | |
| Richard Wells | 1 | 2 | 5 | | | | |
| Richard Simmons | 2 | | | 2 | 1 | | 1 |
| Williams Simmons | 1 | 2 | | 3 | 4 | 2 | |
| Benjamin Cheyney | 4 | 2 | 2 | 1 | | | |
| Benjamin Cheyney | | | | | | | |
| James Hutton | 1 | 1 | 1 | | | | |
| Abigail Simmons | | | 4 | 3 | 4 | 6 | 5 |
| Samuel Galloway | 1 | | | 7 | 8 | 7 | 3 |

| Head of the Household | White Women | White Boys | White Girls | Negro Men | Negro Women | Negro Boys | Negro Girls |
|---|---|---|---|---|---|---|---|
| Phillip Thomas | 2 | | | 9 | 13 | 12 | 8 |
| Phillip Thomas Jr. | | | | | | | |
| Robert Welch | | | | | | | |
| Joseph Pemberton | 3 | 3 | 2 | 8 | 1 | 2 | 1 |
| George Neal | 2 | 1 | | 4 | 1 | 1 | 1 |
| John Pindell | 1 | | 1 | 1 | 1 | 1 | 1 |
| Thomas Warner | 1 | 3 | 4 | | | | |
| John Eddings | 1 | | | | | | |
| Benjamin Carr | 3 | 3 | 2 | 3 | 5 | 5 | 6 |
| Joseph Ward | 1 | 2 | 2 | 3 | 3 | 3 | 4 |
| John Welch | 3 | 2 | | | 1 | | |
| Thomas Owens | 1 | | | | | | |
| Joseph Owens | 1 | | 4 | | | | |
| Richard Sheckells | 1 | 1 | 1 | | 1 | 1 | |
| Samuel Ward | 2 | 4 | | 3 | 3 | 4 | 4 |
| Samuel Ward Jr. | | | | | | | |
| John Welch Jr. | | | | | | | |
| Mary Henwood | | 2 | 3 | | | | |
| Charles Henwood | | | | | | | |
| Solloman Story | 1 | 1 | 1 | | | | |
| Richard Deal | 1 | 1 | 1 | | | | |
| William Hutton | | | | | | | |
| Joseph Hutton Jr. | | | | | | | |
| Henry Hutton | | | | | | | |
| Daniel Armigod | 1 | 1 | 3 | | | | |
| Ann Pindel | | 4 | 2 | 5 | 7 | 9 | 10 |

| Head of the Household | White Women | White Boys | White Girls | Negro Men | Negro Women | Negro Boys | Negro Girls |
|---|---|---|---|---|---|---|---|
| Ruth Hall |  | 3 |  | 6 | 3 | 4 | 4 |
| Addam Allison | 1 |  |  |  |  | 1 | 1 |
| Ezekiel Gott | 1 | 1 | 1 | 2 | 3 | 4 | 4 |
| Ann Gott |  |  | 1 | 3 | 2 | 1 | 2 |
| John Sheckells | 1 | 3 | 5 |  |  |  |  |
| Henry Darnell | 2 |  |  | 29 | 21 | 26 | 30 |
| Richard Darnell |  |  |  |  |  |  |  |
| Phillip Darnell |  |  |  | 21 | 17 | 42 | 31 |
| E. Harrison |  |  |  | 2 | 3 | 2 | 2 |
| Phillip Hammond |  |  |  |  |  |  |  |
| Lewis Jones | 5 |  |  | 3 |  | 5 | 1 |
| Jonathan Jones |  |  |  |  |  |  |  |
| Absolom White | 1 |  | 1 |  |  |  |  |
| William Wivell |  |  |  |  |  |  |  |
| Benjamin Mungess | 1 |  |  | 4 | 2 | 2 | 3 |
| Thomas Whitington | 1 | 3 | 4 | 1 | 2 | 1 | 2 |
| Thomas Westinecoat (?) |  |  |  |  |  |  |  |
| William Armigod | 1 | 7 | 6 | 1 |  |  | 1 |
| John Wason | 1 | 1 | 2 |  |  |  |  |
| Captain John Kilty | 1 | 1 |  | 1 | 2 |  | 1 |
| Marshall Stone | 1 |  |  |  |  |  |  |
| George Ross | 1 | 1 | 1 |  |  |  |  |
| John Lambath | 1 | 3 | 2 | 1 | 1 | 1 | 1 |
| Richard Scrivanor | 1 | 1 | 3 |  |  |  |  |
| John Trott | 1 |  | 1 |  |  |  |  |
| John Trott Jr. | 1 | 4 | 2 |  |  |  |  |

| Head of the Household | White Women | White Boys | White Girls | Negro Men | Negro Women | Negro Boys | Negro Girls |
|---|---|---|---|---|---|---|---|
| Hugh Griffith | 3 | 4 | | | | | |
| Allison Ball | 1 | | | | | | |
| Susanna Wood | 2 | 1 | 1 | | | | |
| William Turner | 4 | 1 | 2 | | 1 | 1 | |
| Thomas Tucker | | | | | | | |
| Seeborn Tucker | 1 | 2 | 1 | | | | |
| Isaac Tucker | 1 | | 1 | | | | |
| John Griffith | 1 | 3 | 2 | | | | |
| John Griffith Jr. | 1 | | | | | | |
| Marshall Griffin | 1 | 2 | 1 | | | | |
| David Price | 1 | 1 | | | | | |
| H. Tarman (Female) | | 2 | | | | | |
| Benjamin French | 1 | 6 | 1 | 1 | 1 | | |
| Bazel French | | | | | | | |
| M. Hughs (Female) | | 2 | 3 | | | | |
| William Olliver | 1 | 3 | 1 | | | | |
| H. Brown | 3 | 5 | | | | | |
| William Childs | 1 | 1 | 2 | 2 | 2 | 3 | 1 |
| Henry Childs | 2 | 2 | 6 | 1 | 1 | 3 | 3 |
| Harrison Lane | 1 | 4 | 1 | | | | |
| Thomas Lane | | 2 | 1 | | | | |
| Henry Griffeth | 1 | | 2 | | | | |
| Tho'son Trott | 1 | 1 | 4 | | | | |
| Seibert Trott | 1 | 1 | | | | | |
| Richard Trott | 1 | | 1 | | | | |
| Samuel Childs | 1 | 1 | 2 | 1 | 1 | 3 | 2 |

| Head of the Household | White Women | White Boys | White Girls | Negro Men | Negro Women | Negro Boys | Negro Girls |
|---|---|---|---|---|---|---|---|
| Richard Joys | 1 | 4 | 2 | | | | |
| Nathan Hammond | | | | | | | |
| Samuel Maynard | 1 | 1 | 3 | 3 | 8 | 5 | 5 |
| James Whitington | 1 | 1 | | | | | |
| Even Roberts | 1 | 3 | | 3 | 7 | 4 | 6 |
| David Weems | 2 | 1 | | 14 | 15 | 17 | 8 |
| David Weems Jr. | 1 | 1 | | 2 | | 1 | 1 |
| William Weems | | | | | | | |
| Mary Gover | | | 2 | 3 | 2 | 4 | 1 |
| Thomas Morton | | 1 | | | | | |
| Thomas Miles | | | | | | | |
| John Dove | 1 | 2 | 4 | | | | |
| Augustis Randel | | 1 | 5 | | | | |
| John Galloway | | | | 2 | | | |
| John Williams | 1 | | 3 | | | | |
| Edward Blunt | 1 | 1 | 2 | | | | |
| Nathan Forster | 1 | 1 | 2 | | | | |
| John Chips | 1 | | 4 | | | | |
| Phillip Smith | 1 | 1 | 2 | | | | |
| Joseph Crutchley | | | | | | | |
| Samuel Osburn | 1 | | | | 1 | | |
| Benjamin Atwell | 1 | | 2 | | | | |
| John Franklin | 1 | 3 | 2 | | 2 | 3 | |
| John Dowel | | | | | | | |
| Robert Jackson | | | 2 | | | | |
| Joseph Allingins | | | | | | | |

| Head of the Household | White Women | White Boys | White Girls | Negro Men | Negro Women | Negro Boys | Negro Girls |
|---|---|---|---|---|---|---|---|
| William Sellman | | | | | | | |
| John Hewing | | | | | | | |
| Joseph Cemp | | | | | | | |
| Quinton Cemp | | | | | | | |
| William Franklain | | | | | | | |
| Joseph Allien | 1 | 2 | 3 | 4 | 5 | 10 | 3 |
| Thomas Nash | 1 | 2 | 1 | | | | |
| Thomas Dodson | | | | | | | |
| John Buskhad | | | | | | | |
| Nathaniel Phips | 1 | | 1 | | | | |
| Edward Colloson | 1 | | 1 | 2 | | 2 | 1 |
| Nathaniel Chew | 1 | | 1 | 2 | | 2 | 3 |
| William Scott | | | | | | | |
| John Carsons | | 2 | 1 | | | | |
| Thomas White | 1 | 2 | 1 | | | | |
| Thomas Laughlin | 1 | 1 | 3 | | | | |
| William Tucker | 1 | 3 | 1 | | | | |
| Peter Parrish | 1 | 4 | 3 | | | | |
| Thomas Pheps | | | | | | | |
| John Tims | 1 | 3 | 1 | | | | |
| George Gardner | | 1 | | | | | |
| Thomas Shearbert | | 2 | 1 | | | | |
| Richard Shearbert | | | | | | | |
| John Ferguson | | | | | | | |
| John Winterson | 1 | 1 | 2 | | | | |
| John Chew | 1 | | 1 | 1 | 1 | 4 | 1 |

| Head of the Household | White Women | White Boys | White Girls | Negro Men | Negro Women | Negro Boys | Negro Girls |
|---|---|---|---|---|---|---|---|
| William Easton | 1 | 1 | 1 | | | | |
| William Griffen | | | | | | | |
| Benjamin Norman | 1 | 6 | 2 | 2 | 1 | 2 | 2 |
| Thomas Norman | 2 | 4 | | 1 | | 2 | 2 |
| Griffith Collens | 1 | | 1 | | | | |
| George Crandel | 1 | 2 | | | | | |
| John Tucker | 1 | | | | | | |
| Thomas Ditty | 1 | 2 | 1 | | | | |
| Selah Tucker | 1 | 6 | 4 | | | | |
| James Tucker | | | | | | | |
| William Atwell | 1 | 3 | | | | | |
| Benjamin Atwell | 1 | 1 | 1 | 1 | 1 | | |
| Benjamin Atwell Jr. | 1 | | | | | | |
| John Attwell | 1 | 2 | 2 | | | | |
| Joseph Attwell | 1 | 1 | 1 | | | | |
| John Huet | 1 | | | | 1 | 1 | |
| Robert Atwell | 1 | 1 | | | | | |
| Joseph Tims | | | | | | | |
| Peter Tims | | | | | | | |
| John Barker | 1 | 3 | 2 | | 1 | | |
| John Barker Jr. | | | | | | | |
| William Barker | | | | | | | |
| Benjamin Bresheares | 3 | | | 3 | 5 | 2 | 5 |
| William Tillard | 1 | | | | | | |
| Samuel Wells | | | | | | | |
| James Butler | | | | | | | |

| Head of the Household | White Women | White Boys | White Girls | Negro Men | Negro Women | Negro Boys | Negro Girls |
|---|---|---|---|---|---|---|---|
| John Sheckells | | | | | | | |
| Francis Sheckells | | | | | | | |
| (Over Sear for) David Stewart | | | | ? | 4 | 2 | 6 |
| Captain Thomas Harwood | 2 | 1 | 2 | 5 | 4 | 3 | 2 |
| Isaac Simmons | 1 | 3 | 3 | | 1 | 2 | 1 |
| Joseph Owens | 1 | | 4 | | | | |
| James Cowley | | | | 1 | 2 | 2 | 1 |
| William Childs | | | | | | | |
| John Brown | 1 | 2 | 4 | | | | |
| Dowel Breshearse | | 3 | 3 | 1 | | | 1 |
| Zadock Breshearse | 1 | | 1 | | 1 | | |
| Jemima Childs | | 4 | 2 | 1 | 1 | 1 | |
| William Jenney | 1 | 2 | 5 | | | | |
| Rachel Harrison | 3 | 2 | | 10 | 10 | 13 | 14 |
| Samuel Harrison | | | | 4 | 8 | 3 | 3 |
| John Weems | 1 | | | 10 | 13 | 16 | 22 |
| Richard Harrison | | | | | | | |
| Walter Harrison | | | | | | | |
| Benjamin Ward | 2 | 3 | 1 | | | | |
| Abram Tanquain | 1 | 1 | 3 | | | | |
| John Shackall Jr. | 2 | 4 | 1 | 1 | 3 | 9 | 8 |
| John Turner | | | | | | | |
| Richard Chew | 3 | 1 | 1 | 20 | 14 | 10 | 16 |
| James Joy | 1 | 1 | 1 | | | | |
| William Scrivenor | | | | | | | |
| Joseph Hutton (Over Sear for Wm. Fitzhugh Esq.) | | | | 4 | 4 | 3 | |

| Head of the Household | White Women | White Boys | White Girls | Negro Men | Negro Women | Negro Boys | Negro Girls |
|---|---|---|---|---|---|---|---|
| Charles Drury | 1 | | 1 | 1 | | 1 | 7 |
| Mary Drury | | 2 | 2 | 4 | 3 | 2 | 6 |
| Benjamin Darnell | | | | 4 | 6 | 2 | 43 |
| William Powel | 1 | 1 | | | | | |
| William Druiry | 1 | 1 | | 1 | 1 | 3 | 1 |
| John Brown | | | | 5 | 3 | 6 | 6 |
| John Holladay | 1 | 1 | 1 | | | | |
| John Gattwood | 1 | 2 | 1 | | | | |
| Josias Parker | 2 | 2 | | | | | |
| Henry Roberts | 1 | 5 | 3 | | | | |
| Abill Hill | 1 | 1 | 1 | | 2 | 1 | 1 |
| Ann Parker | | 1 | 2 | | | | |
| John Lambath | 1 | 1 | 1 | | | | |
| Samuel Mead | 1 | 6 | 5 | 1 | 1 | | 1 |
| Rachel Ratliff | 3 | | | | | | |
| Sarah Holliday | | | | | 2 | 1 | |
| Waymark Bresheares | 1 | 3 | 1 | 1 | 1 | 4 | 1 |
| William Crandel | | | | 2 | 1 | | |
| Samuel Varnel | 1 | | 4 | | | | |
| Mary Miles | | 2 | 4 | 3 | 4 | | 1 |
| Thomas Miles | | | | | | | |
| William Miles | | | | | | | |
| John Door | 1 | 2 | 4 | | 1 | | 1 |
| John Carr | 3 | | 1 | | 1 | | 1 |
| John Carr Jr. | | | | | | | |
| John Lane Jr. | 1 | | | | | | |

| Head of the Household | White Women | White Boys | White Girls | Negro Men | Negro Women | Negro Boys | Negro Girls |
|---|---|---|---|---|---|---|---|
| Samuel Lane | 1 | 4 | 2 | 8 | 4 | 4 | 4 |
| John Richmond | | | | | | | |
| John Scrivenor | 1 | 2 | 4 | | 1 | | 1 |
| Walter Carr | 2 | 2 | 2 | | 1 | | 1 |
| Nathan Breshears | 1 | 4 | 1 | 2 | 1 | 1 | 2 |
| Gassaway Watkins | 1 | 1 | 1 | 5 | 3 | 6 | 1 |
| Zebedee Wood | | | | | | | |
| Peter Leith | | | | | | | |
| Samuel Wells | | | | | | | |
| Thomas Cowley | 1 | 3 | 1 | | | 4 | 1 |
| Ellinor Marriott | | 1 | 1 | | 1 | | 2 |
| Mary Phillips | 1 | 1 | | | | | |
| Joseph Gott | 1 | 2 | 5 | | 1 | 4 | 1 |
| Addam Crandel | | | | | | | |
| John Attwell | 1 | 2 | 1 | | | | |
| Thomas Crandel | 1 | 1 | | | | | |
| Frederick Griffin | | | | | | | |
| Joseph Crandel | 1 | 2 | 1 | 1 | | | |
| Hezekiah Orne | | | | | | | |
| Benjamin Cranford | 2 | 3 | | | | | |
| Isaac Simmons | | | | 1 | 1 | | 2 |
| John Arnold | | | | | | | |
| Richard Nowell | 2 | 1 | | | | | |
| Rachel Allison | | | 2 | | | | |
| Charles Mussy | 1 | 2 | | | | | |
| William Hayes | 1 | | 1 | 6 | 4 | 4 | 8 |

| Head of the Household | White Women | White Boys | White Girls | Negro Men | Negro Women | Negro Boys | Negro Girls |
|---|---|---|---|---|---|---|---|
| John Dority | | | | | | | |
| William Fisher | 1 | 1 | | | | | |
| Jeremiah Simmons | 1 | 4 | 2 | 1 | 2 | | |
| John Medcalf | 3 | 6 | | | | | |
| Duke Wivell | 1 | 5 | 5 | 2 | 3 | 4 | 6 |
| Captain Abram Simmons | 1 | 2 | | 1 | 3 | 4 | 5 |
| Walter Magowan | | | | 2 | 2 | 1 | 3 |
| Thomas Deal | 1 | 4 | 4 | 6 | 6 | 5 | 3 |
| James Haynes | | | | | | | |
| Moses Williams | 1 | | | | | | |
| Ann Dare | | | | 2 | 5 | 8 | 2 |
| Thomas Tongue | 1 | 3 | | 2 | 2 | 1 | 3 |
| John Pibus | 1 | | | | | | |
| Susanna Fisher | | 2 | 3 | 2 | 7 | 7 | 2 |
| Sarah Hill | 2 | | | 3 | 2 | 4 | 1 |
| Joseph Hill | 1 | | | 1 | | | 1 |
| Thomas Mackey | | | | | | | |
| Jacob Welch | 1 | 6 | 1 | | | | |
| John Stone | 2 | 1 | 1 | | | | |
| Agnes Battie | | 2 | 1 | 3 | 5 | 7 | 1 |
| William Arnold | 1 | 1 | | | | | |
| James Kendel | 1 | | | | 1 | 1 | 3 |
| Captain Richard Weems | 1 | 5 | 1 | 5 | 2 | 2 | 4 |
| Captain Henry Harrison | 1 | | | 3 | 2 | 1 | 5 |
| Mary Franklin | | | | 4 | 2 | 6 | 2 |
| Jacob Franklin | 1 | | | 3 | 3 | 4 | 6 |

| Head of the Household | White Women | White Boys | White Girls | Negro Men | Negro Women | Negro Boys | Negro Girls |
|---|---|---|---|---|---|---|---|
| Samuel Harris | | 3 | 1 | | | | |
| Robert Paniel | | | | | | | |
| David Griffiths | 1 | 1 | 1 | | | | |
| John Franklin | 2 | | | 2 | | | 1 |
| Charles Spenser | | 3 | | 2 | 3 | 5 | 3 |
| Robert Atwell | 1 | 1 | | | | | |
| John Gardener | 1 | 2 | 3 | | | | |
| Thomas Crandel | 1 | 1 | 3 | | 1 | | |
| William Deal | | | | 1 | 1 | 1 | 2 |
| Captain John Deal | 1 | 2 | 1 | 2 | | | 3 |
| Ralph Flowers | 1 | 5 | | | | | |
| John Lavie | 2 | 3 | | | | | |
| Richard Gott | 1 | 2 | 4 | | | | |
| Anthony Gott | | | 1 | 2 | 4 | 5 | 4 |
| Anthony Gott Jr | 1 | | 1 | | | | |
| Anthony Woodfield | 1 | 1 | 1 | | | | |
| William Crandel | 1 | | 1 | | | | |
| Joseph Ford | 1 | 3 | | | | | |
| Hannah Howard | | 1 | | | | | |
| John Carr | 3 | | 1 | | 1 | | 1 |
| John Carr Jr. | | | | | | | 1 |
| John Lane Jr. | 1 | | | | | | |
| Samuel Lane | 1 | 4 | 2 | 8 | 4 | 4 | 4 |
| John Richmond | | | | | | | |
| John Scrivenor | 1 | 2 | 4 | | 1 | | 1 |
| Walter Cared | 2 | 2 | 2 | | 1 | | |

28

| Head of the Household | White Women | White Boys | White Girls | Negro Men | Negro Women | Negro Boys | Negro Girls |
|---|---|---|---|---|---|---|---|
| John Marr | 2 | 2 | | | | | |
| John Marr Jr. | | | | | | | |
| Susannah Williams | | | | | | | |
| Sarah Macceni | 1 | 1 | 3 | 2 | 6 | 6 | |
| Abram Sollars | 1 | 1 | 2 | | | | |
| Richard Green | | | 10 | 4 | 11 | 10 | |
| Charles Breshearse | 1 | 2 | | | 2 | | |
| Richard Sawyer | | | | | | | |
| Wilkinson Breshearse | 1 | 3 | | 1 | 1 | | |
| George Gardner | | | | 2 | 2 | | |
| George Gardner Jr. | | | | | | | |
| James Owens | 3 | 2 | | 4 | 3 | 6 | 3 |
| Elizabeth Hopkins | 1 | 10 | 3 | 1 | 1 | 2 | 4 |
| William Hopkins | | | | | | | |
| Jarrard Hopkins | 1 | 2 | 2 | | 1 | | |
| Thomas Marriott | 1 | 3 | 2 | | | | |
| Susanna Wells | 2 | 2 | | | | | |
| John Clarke | 1 | 1 | 5 | 2 | 1 | | |
| Samuel Atwell | 2 | 1 | 1 | | | | |
| Frederick Mills | 1 | 5 | 1 | | 3 | 2 | 6 |
| Joseph Hill | 1 | 1 | 1 | 4 | 3 | 1 | 2 |
| Mary Johns | 3 | 2 | | 9 | 7 | 8 | 11 |
| Elizabeth Shearbert | | 1 | 4 | | | | |
| Thomas Shearbert | | | | | | | |
| Richard Shearbert | | | | | | | |
| Elizabeth Joys | 6 | 2 | | | | | |

| Head of the Household | White Women | White Boys | White Girls | Negro Men | Negro Women | Negro Boys | Negro Girls |
|---|---|---|---|---|---|---|---|
| Sarah Lavey | 2 | | | | | | |
| William Kinghton | 1 | 1 | 3 | | | | |
| William Shearbert | 1 | 2 | 4 | | | | |
| John Thomas | 3 | | 1 | 18 | 12 | 25 | 11 |
| William Evens | 1 | | | 2 | 1 | 1 | 2 |
| Daniel Olliver | 1 | | 4 | | | | |
| William Olliver | 1 | 5 | | | | | |
| Basel Gest | | | | | | | |
| Sarah Clark | 1 | | 1 | | | | |
| Allison or Allen Ball | 2 | 2 | 1 | | | | |
| John Bowie | 1 | 2 | 1 | | | | |
| John Simmons | | | | 1 | 1 | 2 | 3 |
| Richard Crutchley | 1 | 2 | 3 | | | | |
| Benjamin Galloway | 1 | | | | | | |
| James Weems | | | | 5 | 6 | 5 | 6 |
| Joseph Richardson (Eastern Shore) | | | | 1 | 2 | 3 | 6 |
| Steppen Steward | 3 | | | 16 | 8 | 8 | 11 |
| John Carsons | | | | | | | |
| Joseph Gilbert | | | | | | | |
| William Westly | | | | | | | |
| Thomas Neal | | | | | | | |
| Harris Harrison | | | | | | | |
| James Medcal | | | | | | | |
| William Medcal | | | | | | | |
| William Willson | | | | | | | |
| Benjamin Ward | | | | | | | |

| Head of the Household | White Women | White Boys | White Girls | Negro Men | Negro Women | Negro Boys | Negro Girls |
|---|---|---|---|---|---|---|---|
| William Spencer | | | | | | | |
| Richard Wason | | | | | | | |
| John Norris | 3 | 5 | 2 | 3 | 1 | | 1 |
| John Barker | 1 | 5 | 2 | | | | |
| Thomas Norris | 1 | 2 | 1 | 11 | 7 | 5 | 6 |
| Susannah Tucker | 1 | | | | | | |
| John Tucker | | | | | | | |
| Elizabeth Shearbert | 1 | 3 | | | | | |
| Nicholas Norman | | | | 1 | 1 | 2 | 2 |
| Thomas Roberts | 1 | 2 | 2 | | 1 | | 1 |
| Benjamin Carr Jr. | 1 | 1 | 1 | | 1 | 2 | |
| Stephen Stewart Jr. | | | | | | | |
| William Fisher | 1 | 1 | | | 5 | 5 | 4 |
| Jason Welch | | | | | | | |
| Sarah Cowley | | 1 | | 1 | 1 | | 1 |
| (Ro)ger Fips | 1 | 1 | | | | | 2 |
| (Samuel) Harrison | | | | 7 | 2 | 2 | 6 |
| John Norman | | | | 3 | | | 2 |
| William Kirby | 1 | 2 | | | | | |
| Jacob Cutler | 1 | 3 | | | | | |
| John Fips | | | | | | | |

A list of inhabitants in St. James Parish by order of Anne Arundel Committee taken by Samuel Rawlings.

# 1776 CENSUS OF DEPTFORD HUNDRED - BALTIMORE COUNTY, MARYLAND

George Patterson
Captain Elijah Lucas
Joseph Cheston
William Davis
William Hays
Mrs. Nelson
Henry Bride
Thomas Mills
John Beard
William Barker
Mrs. Button
Mrs. Vanbibber
Simon Burnes
Robert Forsyth
William Jacobs
Thomas Bagwell
Soloman Bright
Sophia Gaghin
Mrs. Hinson
Abraham Jackson
Robert Mowbery
John Morrison
Margarett Brynham
Brittingham Dickerson
Isaac V. Bibber
Ann Murphey
William Johnson
Spencer Kelly
Thomas Gray
Rowland McQuillen
Ann Kelly
Jemima Creggett
John Ziglar
William Holton
Henry Evans
William Hammond
Mrs. Moltan
George Robinson
Dandy Tull
Ann Yeoman
Robert Kirkly
Philip Smith
Arthur Kirk
William Scarff
Elizabeth Lively
Joseph Robass Rogers
Winney McCrackin
Michael Foy
Thomas Meeting
James Beard

John Cattle
John Burne
John Gibbins
Thomas Malone
John Vandevort
Doctor Colter
Christopher Burningham
James Anderson
Jacob Dawson
James Bennett
Mrs. Dunbarr
William Gozlin
Patrick Hannon
Christian Waskey
Aquillar Johns
Elizabeth Kelly
Margeritt Fowlar
Silvanus Merrill
Fargus Maccleroy
Ann Houton
Joel Hickingbottom
Henry Lawrence
Charles Chamberland
Hugh Farrell
George Lowderman
Charles Lovitt
Elizabeth Wood
Elizabeth Maloy
Mary Alexander
Ruth Moaks
Judah Cammell
Henry Elliss
Alexander Luth
Ann Simpson
John Shine
Lucey Ferguson
Ann Reese
Elizabeth Easterley
Mary Peterkin
William Williams
Abraham Gorman
Martin Judey
George Helms
Henry Bert
Jesse Wilson
John Smith
Eleanor Garvin
Frances Peters
Ann Simmons
Edward Kerns

George James
John Pine
Mary Connier
John Hayman
Thomas Connerly
William Trimble
James Conner
Isaac Brown
John Wales
Thomas Elliott
Elizabeth Aulenn
George Wells
Isaac Hall
Robert Evans
Samuel Burless
Jane Burks
Ann Larkin
Richard Allin
Thomas Craton
Samuel Sollars
Robert Evans
Thomas Morriss
Thomas Breerton
Isaac Grist
William Tinker
James Kingsbeary
Richard Clarks
John Lees
Samuel Durham
Jacob Raybolt
William Frazeer
Basil Lucas
Jesse Hollingsworth
William Nuckle
Archibald McBride
Thomas Wilkins
James Curtin
Mr. Drew (Ship Wright)
Mary Armstrong
Robert Wilson
Christian Reese
Abraham Enloes
James Hill
James Morgan
William Smith, Esquire
James Rouse

True list of the inhabitants in Deptford Hundred taken the 23rd day of August 1776 by William Aisquith

## 1776 CENSUS OF BRIDGE TOWN HUNDRED, CAROLINE COUNTY, MD.

| Head of the Household | Males under 16 | Males 16-50 | Males over 50 | Females under 16 | Females 16-50 | Females over 50 |
|---|---|---|---|---|---|---|
| Thomas Coox Stradlee | 2 | 1 | | | 1 | |
| John Walker | 1 | 1 | | 2 | 1 | |
| John Bablis Comton | | 1 | | 2 | 1 | |
| Clark Hollis | 2 | | 1 | 2 | 3 | |
| Francis Laine | 3 | 1 | | 1 | 2 | |
| Daniel Wyth | 3 | | 1 | 1 | 2 | |
| Damina Brett | 1 | | 1 | | | 1 |
| James Barwick | 2 | 1 | | 1 | 3 | |
| Grace Carrill | 1 | | | 1 | 2 | |
| Abraham Mason | 1 | 1 | | 3 | 1 | |
| Seth Hill Evett | | 1 | | 1 | 1 | |
| Capt. Thos. Smith Hill | 2 | 1 | | 1 | 1 | |
| David Cullon | 1 | 1 | | 1 | 1 | |
| Henry Wilkson | 3 | 1 | | 1 | 1 | |
| Ann Allen | | | | | 1 | 1 |
| Elijah Simson | | 1 | | 1 | 1 | |
| Owin Cooper | 2 | 2 | | 1 | 3 | 1 |
| William Rogirs | 2 | 1 | | 2 | 2 | 1 |
| Mary Baynard | | | | | 1 | |
| John Johnson | 2 | 2 | | 1 | 2 | |
| William Hamblton | | 1 | | | | |
| Henry Johnson | 2 | 1 | | 1 | 2 | |
| William Hurd | | | 1 | 3 | 1 | |
| Francis Skinner | | 2 | | | 1 | |
| Gudall Drapir | 1 | 2 | | 1 | 2 | |
| Sarah Raws | | | | 2 | 1 | |
| Solomon Willowbee | | 1 | | | 1 | |
| Absolomon Willowbee | | 1 | | | | 1 |
| Aron Chanee | 1 | 2 | | 7 | 4 | |
| John Mason | 2 | | 1 | 1 | 1 | |
| John Emery | 1 | 1 | | | 1 | |
| William Duglass | 5 | 1 | | 1 | 1 | 1 |
| William Lilley | 1 | 1 | | 1 | 1 | |
| William Cook | 2 | 1 | | 1 | 1 | 1 |
| John Rogers | 3 | 1 | | 1 | 1 | |
| Hugh Sherrived | 2 | 2 | 1 | 3 | 1 | |
| Francis Sherrived | 1 | 1 | | | 2 | |
| John Baynard | 1 | 3 | | 2 | 2 | 1 |
| John White | 2 | 2 | | 1 | 1 | |
| Parrish Garrner | 2 | 1 | | 6 | 1 | |
| Wm. Keed or Reed | | 1 | | 1 | 1 | |
| Samuel Draper | 1 | 1 | | 1 | 2 | |
| Daniel Hughs | | 1 | | 2 | 1 | |
| Robert Elaxandrio | 2 | 1 | | | 1 | |
| Charles Reed | 1 | 1 | | | 1 | |
| William More | 1 | 1 | | 1 | 1 | |
| Richard Wilighboey | 6 | 1 | | 1 | 1 | |
| Thomas Founton | 1 | 1 | | 1 | 1 | |
| Thomas Coox | 1 | 1 | | 2 | 1 | |
| James Bostick | 1 | 1 | | 2 | 2 | |

| Head of the Household | Males under 16 | Males 16-50 | Males over 50 | Females under 16 | Females 16-50 | Females over 50 |
|---|---|---|---|---|---|---|
| Samuel Founton | | | - | 1 | 1 | |
| William Owins | | 1 | | 1 | 1 | |
| Thomas Orrell | | 1 | | | | |
| Nathan Lammar | 2 | 1 | | 3 | 1 | |
| John Dickson | | 1 | | | 1 | |
| John Ingrum | 1 | 1 | | | 1 | |
| John Garroot | | 1 | | 1 | 1 | |
| Thomas Longe | 3 | 1 | 1 | 3 | 2 | |
| John Longe | 1 | 1 | | 3 | 2 | |
| William Clandin | 2 | 1 | 1 | 2 | 1 | |
| Benjamin Hariss | 2 | 1 | | 3 | 1 | |
| Edward Smith | | 1 | 1 | 1 | | |
| Richard Quinnily | | | 1 | | | 1 |
| Ann Talboy | | 2 | | | | 1 |
| Elijah Wothers | 1 | 2 | | 1 | 1 | 1 |
| William Currey | 1 | 1 | 1 | | 4 | |
| James Morgan | | 1 | | | | |
| Solomon Morgan | | 1 | | | | |
| Nathan Gladston | | 1 | | | | |
| William Hobs | | 1 | | | | |
| Thomas Lecompt | | 1 | | | | |
| Robert Wilson | | 1 | | | | |
| John Turnner | | 1 | | | | |
| Nathan Hill | | 1 | | | | |
| Benjamin Swgat | | 1 | | | | |
| Eleey Chanell | | 1 | | | | |
| Zariah Green | | 1 | | | | |
| Ruban Wothers | | 1 | | | | |
| John Wothers | 4 | 1 | | 2 | 2 | |
| Joseph Bland | | 1 | | 2 | 1 | |
| Joseph Bland Sr. | 3 | 1 | | 3 | 1 | |
| Joseph Everett | | 1 | | | | |
| George Brite | | 1 | | | | |
| William Founton | | 1 | | | | |
| Batt Jurdain | | 1 | 1 | 2 | 1 | 1 |
| Betty Black | 2 | | | 2 | | 1 |
| Preston Goodwin | 3 | 1 | | | 1 | |
| Solomon Warron | 3 | 1 | | 1 | 1 | |
| Mary Leventon | | 1 | | 1 | 1 | 1 |
| William Cahill | 1 | 1 | | 6 | 1 | |
| Larnie Porter | | 2 | | 3 | 1 | |
| Richard Thomas | | 1 | | 1 | 1 | |
| Nemiah Solsboury | 2 | 1 | | 3 | 1 | |
| Batt Fedmon | 4 | 1 | | 3 | 2 | |
| Edward Willighbouy | 4 | 1 | | 3 | 2 | |
| John Cahill | | 1 | | 2 | 1 | 1 |
| William Draper | 3 | 2 | | 2 | 2 | |
| Edward Sordinge | 3 | 1 | | 1 | 1 | |
| Isaac Paine | 5 | 2 | | 2 | 1 | |
| William Maikmahn | | 1 | | 1 | 1 | |
| William Harper | 3 | 2 | | 3 | 1 | |
| John Founton | 6 | 1 | | 1 | 1 | |
| Jonis Bright | 2 | 1 | | 3 | 1 | |

| Head of the Household | Males under 16 | Males 16-50 | Males over 50 | Females under 16 | Females 16-50 | Females over 50 |
|---|---|---|---|---|---|---|
| John Hudson |  | 1 |  |  | 1 |  |
| Robert Porter |  | 1 |  | 2 | 1 |  |
| Elijah Wilimson | 3 | 1 |  | 3 | 2 |  |
| Thomas Swegatt | 2 | 1 | 1 | 1 | 2 | 1 |
| Nemiah Draper |  | 1 |  |  |  |  |
| John Smith | 3 | 1 |  | 1 | 1 |  |
| William Munnett | 4 | 2 |  | 2 | 1 |  |
| Joshua Lister | 5 | 1 |  | 1 | 1 |  |
| Azell Stevens | 2 | 1 |  | 1 | 2 |  |
| John Bredinge | 1 | 2 |  |  | 2 | 1 |
| John Smith Sr. |  | 3 | 1 | 1 | 1 | 1 |
| Ebenezer Solsboy | 1 | 1 |  | 2 | 1 |  |
| James Solsboury | 4 | 2 |  | 1 | 4 |  |
| William Jones | 2 | 1 | 1 |  | 4 |  |
| John Simson | 1 | 1 |  | 1 | 2 |  |
| Preseller Allen |  |  |  | 2 | 2 |  |
| Elisabeth Morgan | 1 | 1 |  |  | 2 | 1 |
| Elesebeth Hoobes |  | 1 |  | 1 |  | 1 |
| James Raws |  | 1 | 1 | 1 |  | 1 |
| James Harriss | 1 | 2 |  | 1 | 1 |  |
| Joshua Smith | 2 | 2 |  | 4 | 1 |  |
| Daniel Hignuct | 1 | 1 |  | 3 | 1 |  |
| James Towirs | 2 | 1 |  | 4 | 3 |  |
| John Chilrood | 2 | 1 |  | 3 | 1 |  |
| John Dillion | 6 | 2 |  | 2 | 2 |  |
| Joseph Foster | 1 | 2 |  | 3 | 1 |  |
| Elsibeth Harriss | 1 |  |  |  | 2 |  |
| Peter Shinnee |  | 1 |  |  | 2 |  |
| Rose Mathers |  |  |  | 1 | 2 |  |
| John Solsboury | 1 | 3 |  | 2 | 1 |  |
| Oliie Solsboury | 2 | 1 |  | 1 | 2 |  |
| James Swegatt |  | 2 |  | 1 | 2 |  |
| Jamis Hamblton | 1 | 2 |  | 2 | 1 |  |
| Robert Collilis | 1 | 1 | 1 | 3 | 1 | 1 |
| Abraham Fisher | 1 | 1 |  | 2 | 1 |  |
| James Horney |  | 1 |  |  |  |  |
| Robert Porter Sr. | 2 |  | 1 | 1 | 2 | 1 |
| John Chafinch | 3 | 1 | 1 | 3 | 1 |  |
| Mary Counton | 2 |  |  | 3 | 1 |  |
| Mary Perrey | 2 | 1 |  | 1 | 1 |  |
| Joseph Howard | 2 |  | 1 | 3 | 1 |  |
| Jesa Connelly |  | 1 |  | 1 | 1 | 1 |
| William Connely | 1 | 1 | 1 |  |  | 1 |
| Smith Rumbly | 1 | 1 |  |  | 1 |  |
| Larrence Durell(Dunell?) | 1 | 1 |  | 1 | 1 |  |
| Thomas Smith |  | 1 |  | 1 | 1 |  |
| Alaxandreo Holbrook | 3 |  | 1 | 1 | 1 |  |
| Leblun Hoobs | 3 | 1 |  | 2 | 1 |  |
| Jiffery Horney |  | 3 | 1 | 2 | 1 | 2 |
| Aaron Withers | 2 | 1 |  |  | 1 |  |
| Richard Kinord |  | 1 |  |  | 1 |  |
| Batt Killey | 1 | 1 |  | 1 | 1 |  |

| Head of the Household | Males under 16 | Males 16-50 | Males over 50 | Females under 16 | Females 16-50 | Females over 50 | Negroes |
|---|---|---|---|---|---|---|---|
| Edward Greene | 4 | 2 | | 2 | 1 | | |
| John Griffind | 1 | 1 | | 3 | 3 | | |
| Solomon Withers | 1 | 1 | | 1 | 1 | | |
| John Staford | 4 | 2 | | 1 | 2 | | |
| Richard Chaniee | | 1 | | | 1 | | |
| Henry Swegott | 4 | 3 | | 3 | 2 | | |
| John Richardson | 2 | 1 | | 3 | 1 | | |
| William Stevens | 2 | 1 | | 3 | 2 | | |
| Robart Bushoope | 4 | 1 | | 1 | 1 | | |
| William Bushope | 2 | 1 | | 1 | 1 | 1 | |
| Leaven Smith | | 1 | | 1 | 2 | | |
| Arron Moberey | 1 | 1 | | 2 | 1 | | |
| William Harriss | 2 | 1 | | 5 | 2 | | |
| Mary Ward | | 1 | | | 2 | 1 | |
| Margrett Barwick | 1 | | | 3 | 1 | | |
| Johnathan Grenholt | 3 | 1 | | | 1 | | |
| Darby Marthers | | 1 | | 1 | 1 | | |
| Thomas Row | 1 | 4 | | 5 | 2 | | |
| Emmillis Earvin | 2 | | | 1 | 1 | | |
| Edward Parson | 3 | 1 | | 2 | 2 | | |
| Leavin Barnard | 2 | 1 | | 2 | 1 | | |
| Mark Cooper | 4 | 2 | | 3 | 3 | | |
| Mathew Driver | 1 | 2 | | 3 | | | 21 |
| Charles Hindson | 1 | | 1 | 1 | 3 | | 5 |
| Christopher Driver | 1 | 3 | | 1 | 2 | 1 | 7 |
| Thomas Cook | 3 | 1 | 1 | 4 | 2 | | 2 |
| Gedion Baynard | 1 | 1 | 1 | 5 | 3 | | 1 |
| Obadiah Dickson | 1 | 1 | 1 | 2 | 2 | 1 | 10 |
| Isaac Merrick | | 4 | | 1 | 1 | | 3 |
| Peter Rich | | 2 | | 2 | 1 | | 6 |
| Abigail Smith | 1 | 1 | | | | 1 | 6 |
| William Smith Jr. | 1 | 2 | | 1 | 1 | | 5 |
| Cathrine White | | | | | | 1 | 1 |
| Jeremiah Roodes | 6 | 1 | | 1 | 1 | | 16 |
| John Lucais | | 1 | | | 2 | | 2 |
| Robet Poselwatte | 2 | 1 | | 1 | 1 | | 3 |
| Benjmon Dixon | 2 | 3 | | 1 | 1 | | 1 |
| Jacob Rumbley | 2 | 1 | | 2 | 3 | 1 | 7 |
| Jonathan Wilson | 3 | 1 | 1 | 4 | 2 | | 3 |
| William Shaw | 3 | 1 | 1 | 1 | 4 | | 6 |
| Joshua Barwick | 1 | 1 | | | 2 | | 3 |
| Samuel Whitee | 1 | 1 | | 5 | 2 | | 1 |
| James Hughins | 2 | 1 | | 3 | 1 | | 9 |
| George Stockley | | 1 | | 3 | 1 | | 11 |
| Thomas Onell | | 1 | | 1 | 1 | | 1 |
| Francis Clemmer | | 1 | | | 1 | | 1 |
| Edger Rumbley | 3 | 1 | | 5 | 3 | | 1 |
| James Barwick | 4 | 3 | | 2 | 3 | | 1 |
| John Cooper | | 1 | | | 1 | | 2 |
| William Hasleitt | 1 | 2 | | 2 | 1 | | 3 |
| Michill Lucais | 6 | 2 | | 1 | 2 | | 6 |

| Head of the Household | Males under 16 | Males 16-50 | Males over 50 | Females under 16 | Females 16-50 | Females over 50 | Negroes |
|---|---|---|---|---|---|---|---|
| Sarah Swording | | | | | | 1 | 1 |
| Joseph Garrner | 1 | 1 | | | 2 | | 4 |
| Christopher Wilson | 3 | 1 | | 2 | 1 | | 1 |
| Samuel Willowbeey | | 1 | | 2 | 1 | | 3 |
| Daniel Hinds | 2 | 4 | | | | 1 | 2 |
| William Dillehay | | 1 | | 1 | 1 | | 1 |
| Thomas Founton | 1 | 2 | 1 | | 1 | | 1 |
| William Cooben | 1 | 1 | | 2 | 2 | | 1 |
| John Orill (Oniel?) | 2 | | 1 | 1 | 2 | | 6 |
| John Stevens | 1 | 1 | 1 | 1 | 2 | | 14 |
| Ebennezer Vaulx | | | 1 | | | | 2 |
| John White | 5 | 1 | 1 | 2 | 1 | | 12 |
| Andrew Founton | 3 | 3 | | 3 | 1 | | 7 |
| Merey Founton | | 2 | 1 | | | 1 | 12 |
| James Lecompt | 4 | 2 | | | 3 | | 4 |
| James Lecompt Sr. | 1 | 4 | 1 | | 2 | | 5 |
| Charles Lecompt | | 2 | | | | | 1 |
| William Juvel | 1 | 1 | 1 | 1 | 1 | 1 | 1 |
| William Rich | | 3 | | 4 | 1 | | 3 |
| John Willson | | 1 | | 4 | 2 | | 5 |
| John Scoot | | 1 | | 4 | 2 | | 7 |
| James Scoot | | 1 | | | | | 1 |
| Thomas Baynard | (no ages given) | | | | | | 2 |
| William Wheatly | 1 | 2 | | 1 | | 1 | 14 |
| Robert Dixon | (no age given) | | | | | | 3 |
| James Peterkin | | | 1(?) | | | 1 | 9 |
| Benson Stanton | | 1 | | 1 | 1 | | 25 |

January 6, 1777 - Preston Goodwin being appointed by this committee to assertain the number of inhabitants in Bridge Town Hundred, made Oath that the within and above list contains the whole of the inhabitants in Hundred.

Signed by order,

Benson Stanton, Chan.

## 1776 CENSUS OF NANTACOAKE HUNDRED, DORCHESTER COUNTY, MARYLAND

| Head of the Household | MALES -10 | 10 to 16 | 16 to 21 | 21 to 30 | 30 to 40 | 40 to 50 | 50 to 60 | 60 to 70 | FEMALES -10 | 10 to 16 | 16 to 21 | 21 to 30 | 30 to 40 | 40 to 50 | 50 to 60 | 60 to 70 | Negroes |
|---|---|---|---|---|---|---|---|---|---|---|---|---|---|---|---|---|---|
| Sarah Abet | 2 | | | | | | | | 1 | | 1 | | | | | | |
| McNamar Adams | 1 | | | 1 | | | | | 1 | 1 | | 1 | 1 | | | | |
| Phillep Ackman | 2 | | | 1 | | | | | 2 | 1 | | 1 | | | | | |
| Thomas Abbet | 2 | | | 1 | | | | | | 2 | 1 | 1 | | | | | |
| William Angel | | | | | 1 | | | | | | 2 | 2 | | 1 (1 White male 70-80) | | | |
| Rachel Adkins | 1 | 2 | | | | | | | | | | | 1 | | | | |
| Arter Atterson | 2 | | | 1 | | 1 | | | 4 | | | 1 | 1 | | | | |
| William Adley | | | | | 1 | | | | 2 | | 1 | 1 | | | | | |
| Alexander Alexson | | 1 | | 1 | | 1 | | | 2 | 2 | 1 | | | 1 | | | |
| Patrick Browhon | 1 | | | | 1 | | | | 1 | 1 | 1 | 1 | | | | | 6 |
| Levins Bramble | 2 | 2 | 1 | | | | | | 1 | 1 | 1 | | | 1 | | | |
| Christopher Badley | | 1 | | | | 1 | | | 1 | | 1 | | | 1 | | | |
| Richard Badley | | | 1 | | | | | | | | 1 | | | | | | |
| John Baker | 1 | | | 1 | | | | | 2 | | 1 | | | | | | |
| George Bonewill | 1 | 1 | | 1 | | | | | 1 | 1 | | | | | | | 4 |
| Sarah Brown | 1 | | | | | | | | 1 | | | | 2 | | | | 3 |
| Priscilla Ball | 1 | 1 | 1 | 1 | | | | | 2 | 2 | | | | 1 | | | 25 |
| McKeel Bonersill | | | 1 | | | | | | 2 | | | 1 | | | | | |
| William Bestpitch | 1 | | | 1 | | | | | 1 | | | 1 | | | | | |
| Edmon Bramble | | 1 | 1 | | | 1 | | | 1 | 1 | | | 1 | | | | |
| William Blesset | | 1 | | 1 | | | | | 1 | | | | | 1 | 1 | | |
| Ann Bancks | 1 | | | | | | | | | | | | | | | | 3 |
| Sarah Broks | 1 | | | | | | | | | | 2 | 3 | 1 | | 1 | | 9 |
| John Beard | | 1 | | | | 1 | | | | 1 | | 2 | | | | 1 | 8 |
| Benjamin Batey | | | 1 | . 1 lived in Somerset | | | | | | | | | | | | | |
| Thomas Beard | 1 | 1 | | | 1 | | | | 2 | 1 | 1 | | 1 | | | | 3 |
| John Beard | 1 | | | 1 | | | | | 1 | | 1 | 1 | 1 | | | | 1 |
| Levin Bestpitch | 3 | 1 | | 1 | | | | | | | 2 | | | 1 | | | 4 |
| Georg Beard | | | 1 | | | | | | | 1 | | | | | | | |
| Ezekal Badley | 3 | | | 1 | | | | | 1 | 1 | | 1 | | | | | |
| Georg Brown | 2 | | 1 | | 1 | | | | 3 | 1 | | 1 | | | | | 2 |
| Benjamin Ball | | | 1 | 1 | | | | | 3 | 1 | | 1 | 1 | | | | 12 |
| Isaac Cantar | 2 | | | 1 | | | | | | | | 1 | | | | | |
| Peter Cohon | | | | 1 | | | | | 1 | | 1 | | | | | | |
| Zacharas Cammel | 1 | | 1 | 1 | | | | | 4 | | | | 2 | | | | 13 |
| Sarah Canter | | 1 | | 1 | | 1 | | | | | | | | | | | |
| Elesabeth Cook | | 1 | | 1 | | | | | | | 1 | | 1 | | | | 1 |
| Charles Levi Craft | 1 | | 1 | | | | | | | | | | 1 | | | | 2 |
| Jonathan Coap | 1 | | | 1 | | | | | 2 | | 1 | 1 | | 1 | | | |
| James Clark | | | 1 | | | | | | 1 | | | | | | | | |
| William Callendar | | | 1 | | | | | | | | 1 | | | | | | |
| Charls John Craft | 1 | | 1 | | | | | | | | | | 1 | | | | |
| Mary Coap | 2 | 2 | 1 | | | | | | 1 | 2 | | | | 1 | | | |
| John Coap | | 1 | | | 1 | | | | | 2 | 2 | | | | | | |
| Joseph Cox | 1 | | | 1 | | | | | 3 | 1 | | | | 1 | | | |
| Sarah Cane | 1 | 1 | | | | | | | 1 | | 1 | 1 | | 1 | | | |
| Abraham Church | | | | | | | | | | | | | | | | | 2 |
| Joseph Coap | | 1 | 1 | 1 | | | | | 2 | | | | | | | | |

| Head of Household | 10 to -10 | 16 to 16 | 21 to 21 | 30 to 30 | 40 to 40 | 50 to 50 | 60 to 60 | 10 to -10 | 16 to 16 | 21 to 21 | 30 to 30 | 40 to 40 | 50 to 50 | 60 to 60 | Negroes |
|---|---|---|---|---|---|---|---|---|---|---|---|---|---|---|---|
| Charles John Craft | 2 | 1 | | 1 | | | | | | 1 | 1 | | | | 1 |
| Charles John Craft Sr. | | 1 | | | | 1 | | | | | 1 | | | | 1 |
| Charles Thomas Craft | 1 | | | | | | | | 1 | | 1 | 1 | | | |
| Aleas Craft | 3 | | | | | | | | | 1 | | 1 | | | |
| Jonathan Craft | | | | 1 | | | | | | | 1 | | | | |
| Sarah Craft | | | 1 | | | | | | | | | | 1 | | |
| Ezekel Dorroty | 1 | | | | 1 | | | | 3 | 1 | 1 | 1 | | | |
| Aleas Deudney | | 1 | 1 | | | | | | 1 | 2 | | 1 | | | |
| Charls Deen | | | | 1 | | | | | | | | | | | |
| Henry Deen | | | | 1 | | | | | 1 | | 1 | | | | |
| Joseph Daffin | | | | | | | | | | | | | | | 20 |
| John Daniel Sr. | 2 | | | | 1 | | | | 1 | | 1 | 1 | | | |
| John Daniel | 1 | | 1 | | | | | | | | 1 | | | | 2 |
| John Elett | 2 | 1 | | | 1 | | | | 3 | | | 1 | | | 15 |
| Thomas Ellett | 4 | 1 | | | 1 | | | | 1 | 1 | | | 1 | | |
| William Elburd | | | | | | | | | | | | 1 | | | 7 |
| Mary Evins | 1 | 1 | | | | | | | 1 | 1 | 1 | | | | |
| Thomas Ellett | | | | 1 | | | | | 3 | 2 | | 1 | | | 1 |
| Henry Fisher Evins | | | 1 | | 1 | | | | 1 | 1 | | | | | |
| John Ellett | 4 | | | 1 | | | | | 1 | 1 | | 1 | 1 | | 3 |
| Henry Ennales | | | | | | | | | | | | | | | 27 |
| Jesse Furrough | | | | 1 | | | | | | | | | | | Black Man |
| John Fisher | | | | 1 | | | | | 1 | | 1 | | | | |
| Elesabeth Foster | 1 | | | | | | | | | 1 | 1 | 1 | | 1 | Female 70-80 |
| Sarah Gambell | | 1 | | | | | | | | 2 | 2 | | 1 | | |
| Richard Green | 1 | | | 1 | | | | | | | 1 | | | | |
| Shadrick Goute | 2 | 1 | | 1 | | | | | 2 | | | 2 | | | 4 |
| Sophiah Goute | 1 | | | | | | | | 1 | | 1 | | | | |
| Joseph Griffin | | | 2 | | | | | | | | 2 | | | | 17 |
| Christopher Gardif | 1 | 2 | | | | | 1 | | 4 | | 1 | 1 | | | 2 |
| George Goute | 1 | 1 | 1 | | | | | | 3 | | 1 | | | | |
| James Gordon | 2 | 1 | 1 | | | | | | | | 1 | 1 | | | 4 |
| Archable Gray | | | 1 | | | | | | 1 | | 1 | | | | |
| Ann Grinnan | 3 | | | | | | | | 1 | | | 1 | | | |
| John Graham | 3 | 2 | | 1 | | | | | 1 | 1 | | 1 | | | |
| John Gambell | 2 | | | 1 | | | | | | | | | 1 | | |
| John Harper | 2 | | 1 | 1 | 1 | | | | 2 | 1 | | 1 | | | 2 |
| Ezekel Harper | 2 | | 1 | | 1 | | | | 3 | 2 | | 1 | | | 5 |
| Thomas Hodson | 3 | 1 | | 1 | 1 | | | | 1 | 2 | 1 | | 1 | | 7 |
| Ann Hodson | | | | | | | | | 3 | 3 | | 2 | | | 2 |
| Mary Hambleton | 1 | 1 | | | | | | | 1 | | | | 1 | | 3 |
| Lilley Hambleton | | | | | | | | | | | | | | | 4 |
| Thomas Hicks | 1 | 2 | 1 | | 1 | | | | | 2 | | | 1 | | 17 |
| Mary Hicks | 2 | | | | | | | | | | | 1 | | 1 | 13 |
| Rasmis Holland | 1 | | | | | | | | 3 | | 1 | (also 1 White Female70-80) |
| Thomas Hincks | 2 | 1 | | 1 | 1 | | | | 2 | 1 | | 1 | 1 | | 2 |
| Tabitha Hicks | 1 | | | | | | | | | | | 1 | | | |
| Sarah Higgins | 1 | 3 | | | | | | | | 1 | | | 1 | | |
| Precilla Hughs | | | | | | | | | 2 | 1 | 1 | 2 | | | |
| John Hopkins | | | | 1 | | | | | 1 | | 1 | | | | 3 |
| Mary Dudney | 4 | 1 | | | | | | | 3 | | | 1 | | 1 | |

| Head of the Household | MALES | | | | | | | FEMALES | | | | | | | Negroes |
|---|---|---|---|---|---|---|---|---|---|---|---|---|---|---|---|
| | -10 | 10 to 16 | 16 to 21 | 21_30 | 30 to 40 | 40 to 50 | 50 to 60 | 60 to 70 | -10 | 10 to 16 | 16 to 21 | 21 to 30 | 30 to 40 | 40 to 50 | 50 to 60 | 60 to 70 | |
| William Harvey | 3 | | 1 | | | | | | | | 1 | | | | | | |
| Samuel Hust | | | 1 | | | | | | 1 | 1 | 1 | | | | | | |
| Archabel Hust | 3 | 1 | | 1 | | | | | 2 | .1 | 1 | | | | | | |
| Edward Hurley | | 1 | | | | 1 | | | 1 | | | | 2 | | | | |
| James Hust | 2 | 2 | | 1 | | | | | 1 | | 3 | | 1 | | | | |
| Humphra Hubbard | 1 | | | | | | | | 1 | 1 | 1 | 1 | | 1 | | | |
| Henry Hoppar | | | | | | | | | | | | | | | | | 11 |
| James Hughs (Black Man) | | | | 1 | | | | | | | | | | | | | |
| John Henry | | 3 | 1 | 1 | | 1 | | | 1 | 2 | 1 | 1 | | 2 | | | 55 |
| William Hammon | | | | | 1 | | | | | | | 1 | | | | | |
| Edmon Hughs | 2 | | 1 | 1 | | 1 | | | 2 | | 1 | | 1 | | | | |
| John Horsman | 1 | 1 | | | | 1 | | | 1 | 1 | | | 1 | | | | |
| Luke Horsman | 2 | 1 | | | | 1 | | | 2 | 1 | | | 1 | | | | |
| Matthew Hurley | 1 | | | 1 | | | | | 2 | 1 | | 1 | | | | | |
| Jan Hurley | 1 | 1 | | | | | | | | | 1 | | | | | | |
| Jacob Hurley | 1 | 1 | | | | | | | 2 | | 1 | 1 | | | | | |
| Hezekiah Hugins | | 1 | | | | | | | 3 | | 1 | 1 | | | | | |
| Moses Hurley | | | 1 | | | | | | | 1 | | | | | | | |
| Sophiah Hurley | | | | | | | | | | 1 | 1 | | 1 | | | | 2 |
| John Hurley | 2 | 3 | | | 1 | | 2 | | 1 | | 1 | | | | | | 3 |
| Henry Horsman | 1 | 1 | (also 1 Wh.Female 70-80) | | | | | | | .1 | | | | | | | |
| Durbey Hurley | 2 | 3 | | | 1 | | | | | | | 1 | | | | | |
| John Hurley | | 2 | | | 1 | | | | 3 | 2 | | | | | | | 1 |
| Thomas Hurley | 1 | 1 | 1 | | | | | | | 1 | | | | | | | |
| Elijah Hurley | 4 | | | 1 | | | | | 1 | | 1 | | | | | | |
| Connar Hollan | | | 1 | | | | | | | 1 | | | | | | | |
| Michal Hollan | | 2 | | | 1 | | | | | 1 | | 1 | | | | | |
| John Hughe | | | | | 1 | | | | | | | | | | | | |
| David Harper | | 1 | | | 1 | | | | 2 | 2 | 1 | 1 | | | | | 7 |
| Joseph Hust | | | 1 | | | | | | | | | | | | | | |
| John Huffington | | | | 1 | | | | | | | 1 | | | | | | |
| Constantine Hurley | 2 | | | 1 | | | | | 1 | | 1 | | | | | | |
| Larance Haddan (1 leg off) | | | | | | | | | | 1 | | | | | | | |
| Connar Hollan | | | 1 | | | | | | | 1 | | | | | | | |
| Michal Hollan | | 2 | | | 1 | | | | | 1 | | 1 | | | | | |
| John Hughe | | | | | 1 | | | | | | | | | | | | |
| David Harper | | 1 | | . | 1 | | | | 2 | 2 | 1 | 1 | | | | | 7 |
| Joseph Hust | | | 1 | | | | | | | | | | | | | | |
| John Huffington | | | | 1 | | | | | | | 1 | | | | | | |
| Constantine Hurley | 2 | | | 1 | | | | | 1 | 1 | | | | | | | |
| William Jones | 1 | 2 | 1 | | 1 | | | | 2 | 1 | | 1 | 1 | | | | 3 |
| Levin Jones | 1 | 2 | | 1 | | | | | 3 | 1 | 1 | 1 | | | | | 8 |
| Mary Jones | 1 | | | | | | | | 1 | | 1 | | | | | | |
| Levin Jones | 2 | 1 | | 1 | 1 | | | | | 1 | 1 | 1 | | | | | |
| Sarah Jones | | | | | | | | | 3 | | | 1 | | | | | |
| Joseph Johnson | | 1 | | | | | | | 2 | 1 | | | 1 | | 1 | | 5 |
| James Jones | 2 | 3 | 1 | | 1 | | | | 3 | 1 | | 1 | | | | | 4 |
| William Jones | 1 | | | 1 | | | | | 1 | | 1 | | | | | | |
| Nathan Johnson | | 1 | | 1 | | | | | 2 | | | 1 | | | | | 1 |
| William Jones | 4 | | 1 | | 1 | | | | 1 | 1 | | 1 | | | | | |

|  | MALES | | | | | | | | FEMALES | | | | | | | | Negroes |
|---|---|---|---|---|---|---|---|---|---|---|---|---|---|---|---|---|---|
| Head of the Household | -10 | 10 to 16 | 16 to 21 | 21 to 30 | 30 to 40 | 40 to 50 | 50 to 60 | 60 to 70 | -10 | 10 to 16 | 16 to 21 | 21 to 30 | 30 to 40 | 40 to 50 | 50 to 60 | 60 to 70 |  |
| Levin Jones |  |  | 1 |  |  |  |  |  |  |  | 1 |  |  |  |  |  |  |
| Isaac Jones |  | 1 | 1 |  |  |  |  |  | 2 | 1 | 1 |  |  |  |  |  |  |
| Frances Jones |  | 1 | 1 |  |  |  |  |  | 1 |  | 1 | 1 |  |  |  |  |  |
| Levin Kirkman | 3 |  |  | 1 |  |  |  |  | 1 |  |  | 1 |  |  |  |  | 10 |
| Georg Kirkman |  |  |  |  | 1 |  | 1 |  |  |  |  |  |  |  |  |  | 9 |
| Elisha Kirkman |  |  | 1 |  |  |  |  |  | 1 |  | 1 |  |  |  |  |  |  |
| Henry Kimmey | 3 |  |  |  |  | 1 |  |  | 2 |  | 1 |  |  |  |  |  |  |
| John Killener |  | 2 |  | 1 |  |  |  |  |  |  |  |  |  | 1 |  |  |  |
| Glod Lewis | 1 |  | 1 | 1 |  |  |  |  |  |  |  |  |  | 1 |  |  |  |
| Frances Langfitt |  | 1 | 1 |  |  |  |  |  | 1 | 1 |  | 1 |  |  | 1 |  |  |
| Cornelus Lines |  |  |  | 1 |  |  |  |  | 1 |  |  | 1 |  |  |  |  |  |
| Jarvis Langfitt |  | 1 | 1 |  |  |  |  |  |  |  |  |  |  |  | 1 |  |  |
| William Langfitt |  |  |  |  |  |  |  |  |  |  |  |  | 2 |  |  |  | 1(1male 70-80) |
| John Langfitt | 2 |  |  | 1 |  |  |  |  | 1 | 1 | 1 |  |  |  |  | 1 | 10 |
| Levin Langfitt |  | 1 |  | 1 |  |  |  |  | 1 | 1 | 1 | 1 |  |  | 1 |  |  |
| Levin Lewis | 1 |  | 1 | 1 |  | 1 |  |  |  |  |  |  |  | 1 |  | 1 | 1 |
| William Langurl | 1 | 1 |  | 1 |  |  |  |  | 1 |  |  | 2 |  |  |  |  | 4 |
| James Lingart |  |  | 1 |  |  |  |  |  |  |  |  |  | 1 | 1 |  |  | 1(1 Wh.Man 80-90) |
| William Lingurl | 3 |  | 1 | 1 |  |  |  |  |  |  | 1 | 1 |  |  |  |  | 11 |
| James Laton | 1 | 2 |  | 1 |  |  |  |  | 2 | 1 |  | 1 |  |  |  |  |  |
| Daniel Laton |  |  | 1 | 1 |  |  |  |  | 4 |  |  | 1 |  |  |  |  | 1 |
| William McCallester | 1 | 1 |  | 1 | 1 |  |  |  | 1 | 1 | 1 |  |  | 1 |  |  |  |
| Easter McCallester |  |  |  |  |  |  |  |  | 1 |  |  | 1 |  |  |  |  |  |
| Sarah McCallester | 1 |  |  |  |  |  |  |  |  |  |  |  |  | 1 |  |  | 2 |
| Mary Marcy | 1 |  |  |  |  |  |  |  |  |  |  |  |  | 1 |  |  |  |
| Elesabeth Minish | 3 | 1 | 1 | 1 |  |  |  |  | 1 | 1 | 1 |  |  | 1 |  |  | 17 |
| James Muir | 1 |  | 1 | 1 |  | 1 |  |  |  |  | 1 | 1 |  |  | 1 |  | 7 |
| Hugh McBrid(lived in Somerset) |  |  |  | 3 | 1 | 1 |  |  |  |  |  |  | 1 |  |  |  |  |
| Fisher Mears | 3 | 1 |  |  | 1 |  |  |  |  |  |  |  | 1 |  |  |  |  |
| John Miars |  |  | 1 | 1 |  |  |  |  | 1 | 1 | 1 |  |  |  | 1 |  | 1 |
| Angel Marign | 5 |  | 1 |  |  |  |  |  |  |  | 1 |  |  |  |  |  | 5 |
| Thomas McKell |  |  |  |  | 1 |  |  |  |  |  |  |  | 1 |  |  |  |  |
| Elijah Moor | 1 | 1 |  | 1 |  |  |  |  | 3 |  |  |  | 1 |  |  |  |  |
| John McCallister |  | 1 | 1 |  |  |  |  |  |  |  | 1 |  | 1 |  | 1 |  |  |
| Andrew McCallester | 1 | 1 | 1 |  | 1 |  |  |  | 2 | 2 | 1 |  | 1 |  |  |  |  |
| James Messack | 2 | 1 |  |  |  |  |  |  |  |  |  | 2 |  |  |  |  |  |
| Alceabeth McCallster |  |  | 2 |  |  |  |  |  |  |  |  | 1 |  |  |  | 1 |  |
| William Morgan | 1 | 2 |  | 2 |  | 1 |  |  | 3 | 3 |  |  |  | 1 |  |  | 3 |
| Charls Muir | 2 | 1 |  |  |  | 1 |  |  | 1 | 1 |  |  | 1 | 1 |  |  | 29 |
| Major Levin | 2 |  |  | 1 |  |  |  |  | 1 |  | 1 |  |  | 1 |  |  |  |
| Sarah McCrary | 1 | 1 | 1 |  |  |  |  |  | 1 |  |  |  |  |  | 1 (lived in Somerset) | |  |
| Thomas Moor | 1 |  |  | 1 |  |  |  |  | 1 |  |  | 1 | 1 |  |  |  |  |
| Thomas Meddis | 2 | 1 |  |  |  |  |  |  | 1 |  |  |  |  |  |  |  |  |
| Sarah Millar |  |  |  |  |  |  |  |  | 1 | 1 |  |  | 1 |  |  |  |  |
| Tabtha McCollester | 1 | 1 |  |  |  |  |  |  | 1 |  |  | 1 |  |  |  |  |  |
| John Mabra |  |  |  |  | 1 (arised - enter in Queen Annes) | | | | | | | | | | | | |
| Christophar Norman | 2 |  |  |  |  |  |  |  |  | 1 | 1 | 1 |  | 1 |  |  |  |
| James Neel |  |  |  | 1 |  |  |  |  | 2 |  | 1 |  |  |  |  |  |  |
| Levi Oram | 2 | 1 |  | 1 |  |  |  |  | 2 |  |  | 2 |  |  |  |  | 1 |
| John Philleps | 1 | 1 |  | 1 |  |  |  |  | 1 |  |  | 1 | 1 |  |  |  | 1 |

|  | MALES | | | | | | | | FEMALES | | | | | | | | |
|---|---|---|---|---|---|---|---|---|---|---|---|---|---|---|---|---|---|
| Head of the Household | -10 | 10 to 16 | 16 to 21 | 21 to 30 | 30 to 40 | 40 to 50 | 50 to 60 | 60 to 70 | -10 | 10 to 16 | 16 to 21 | 21 to 30 | 30 to 40 | 40 to 50 | 50 to 60 | 60 to 70 | Negroes |
| William Phillips |  |  |  | 1 |  |  |  |  | 1 |  |  |  |  |  |  |  |  |
| Comfort Parris | 1 |  |  |  |  |  |  |  |  |  | 1 |  |  | 1 |  |  | 2 |
| John Parrish |  |  | 1 |  |  |  |  |  | 4 |  | 1 |  |  |  |  |  |  |
| William Pely | 2 |  |  | 1 |  |  |  |  |  |  | 1 |  |  |  |  |  |  |
| John Roberson | 1 |  | 1 |  |  |  |  |  |  |  | 1 |  |  |  |  |  |  |
| James Rawley | 2 |  | 1 |  |  |  |  |  | 1 |  | 1 | 1 |  |  |  |  |  |
| James Rawley | 2 |  | 1 |  |  |  |  |  |  |  |  | 1 |  |  |  |  |  |
| Ann Richards |  | 2 |  | 1 |  |  |  |  |  | 1 |  |  | 1 |  | 1 |  | 1 |
| Andrew Ragg |  |  | 1 | 1 |  |  |  |  | 1 | 1 |  |  |  |  |  |  | 5 |
| Tabitha Régin | 1 |  |  |  |  |  |  |  |  |  | 1 |  |  |  |  |  |  |
| John Rawley | 2 |  |  | 1 |  |  |  |  |  |  | 1 |  | 1 |  |  |  |  |
| Edward Riggin | 1 |  | 1 | 1 |  |  |  |  |  |  | 1 |  |  |  |  |  | 1 |
| James Rawley |  | 1 |  |  | 1 |  |  |  | 1 |  |  |  | 1 |  |  |  |  |
| Joshua Reed | 1 |  | 1 | 1 |  |  |  |  |  |  | 1 |  |  |  |  |  |  |
| Thomas Staintors | 1 | 4 |  | 1 |  |  |  |  | 2 |  |  | 1 |  |  |  |  | 5 |
| Vollintin Stoaks | 3 | 2 |  |  |  | 1 |  |  | 2 |  |  |  |  | 1 |  |  |  |
| Samuel Stinson |  | 2 |  | 1 |  |  |  |  | 3 |  |  |  |  | 1 |  |  |  |
| James Shaw | 2 |  | 2 |  |  |  |  |  |  |  |  | 1 |  | 1 |  |  | 4 |
| John Sandars |  |  |  |  |  |  |  |  |  |  |  |  | 1 |  |  |  | 4 |
| Jacob Staton | 2 | 2 |  | 1 |  |  |  |  | 2 | 1 |  | 1 |  |  |  |  | 2 |
| Richard Sweeting |  |  | 1 |  |  |  |  |  |  |  |  |  |  |  |  |  |  |
| Daniel Sasorson | 1 |  |  | 1 |  |  |  |  | 2 |  | 1 | 1 |  |  |  |  |  |
| James Sturd | 1 |  |  | 1 |  |  |  |  |  | 1 |  | 1 |  |  |  |  |  |
| Peter Sward | 1 |  |  | 1 |  |  |  |  |  | 1 | 1 |  |  | 1 |  |  |  |
| James Sturd |  |  |  | 1 |  |  |  |  | 1 |  |  | 1 |  |  |  |  | 1 |
| Henry Steele | 2 | 1 | 1 |  | 1 |  |  |  | 1 |  |  |  | 1 |  |  |  | 91 |
| John Sackel | 2 |  |  | 1 | 1 |  |  |  | 2 |  |  | 1 |  |  |  |  | 1 |
| Abner Shanks | 2 | 1 |  | 1 |  |  |  |  | 1 |  |  | 1 |  |  |  |  |  |
| Niell Sulivan (Nicll) | 2 | 2 |  |  |  |  |  |  |  |  |  | 1 |  |  |  |  |  |
| Peter Sears | 1 |  | 1 |  | 1 |  |  |  | 1 |  | 1 | 1 |  |  |  |  | 4 |
| John Hicks Travers | 2 | 1 |  |  | 1 |  |  |  |  |  |  |  |  |  |  |  | 9 |
| William Tickel |  | 2 |  |  |  | 1 |  |  | 1 | 2 |  | 1 |  |  | 1 |  |  |
| David Fletcher Tickel |  |  | 1 |  |  |  |  |  | 1 |  | 1 |  |  |  |  |  |  |
| Vinson Batson Tanar | 1 |  |  | 1 |  |  |  |  | 1 |  | 1 |  |  |  |  |  |  |
| Edwards Thompson | 2 |  |  |  | 1 |  |  |  | 1 |  | 1 |  | 3 |  |  |  | 6 |
| Levin Travers |  |  |  |  |  |  |  |  |  |  |  |  |  |  |  |  | 4 |
| Elijah Tilghman |  |  |  |  |  |  |  |  |  |  |  |  |  |  |  |  | 4 |
| John Tommas |  |  |  |  | 1 |  |  |  |  | 1 | 1 |  |  | 1 |  |  |  |
| Matthew Travers | 4 | 1 |  |  | 1 |  |  |  | 3 | 1 |  | 1 |  |  |  |  |  |
| Joseph Thompson | 1 |  | 1 |  | 1 |  |  |  |  |  | 1 |  | 1 |  |  |  | 2 |
| John Nickels Thompson | 2 | 1 |  |  |  |  |  |  |  |  |  |  |  |  |  |  | 1 |
| James Talor |  |  |  | 1 |  |  |  |  |  |  | 1 | 1 |  |  |  |  | 1 |
| Elesabeth Tommas |  |  | 1 |  |  |  |  |  |  |  |  |  |  |  | 1 |  |  |
| Joseph Tommas | 1 |  |  | 1 |  |  |  |  |  |  |  | 1 |  |  |  |  |  |
| Soloman Vickars |  |  |  | 3 |  |  |  |  |  |  |  |  |  | 1 |  | 1 |  |
| Henry Vain | 1 | 1 |  |  |  | 1 |  |  | 2 | 3 | 1 |  | 1 |  |  |  |  |
| John Vinson |  |  |  | 1 |  |  |  |  | 2 | 1 |  | 1 |  |  |  |  |  |
| John Wallas |  |  |  |  |  | 1 |  |  |  | 1 |  |  |  |  |  | 1 | 80-90-1 F. |
| William Wallas |  |  | 1 |  |  |  |  |  | 3 |  |  |  | 1 | 1 |  |  |  |
| Charles Windom | 3 |  | 1 |  | 1 |  |  |  | 3 | 1 | 1 |  |  |  | 1 |  |  |

|  | MALES | | | | | | | FEMALES | | | | | | | |
|---|---|---|---|---|---|---|---|---|---|---|---|---|---|---|---|
| Head of the Household | -10 | 10 to 16 | 16 to 21 | 21 to 30 | 30 to 40 | 40 to 50 | 50 to 60 | 60 to 70 | -10 | 10 to 16 | 16 to 21 | 21 to 30 | 30 to 40 | 40 to 50 | 50 to 60 | 60 to 70 | Negroes |
| Benjamin Woodards |  |  |  | 1 |  |  |  |  |  | 1 | 1 |  |  |  |  |  |  |
| John Wheelar | 1 | 1 |  |  |  | 1 |  |  | 1 |  | 2 | 1 |  |  |  |  |  |
| Levin William |  | 1 | 1 |  | 1 |  |  |  | 4 | 1 |  | 4 |  |  |  |  |  |
| Michal Willcox | 1 | 1 |  | 1 |  |  |  |  | 3 |  | 1 | 1 |  | 1 |  |  |  |
| Jon Whalend |  | 1 | 1 |  |  |  |  |  |  |  | 1 |  |  |  | 1 |  | 8 |
| Pritch Wille | 2 | 1 |  | 1 | 1 |  |  |  | 1 | 1 |  | 2 |  |  |  |  | 5 |
| John White |  |  |  | 1 |  |  |  |  |  |  |  | 1 |  |  |  |  | 6 |
| Zebulon Winget | 1 |  |  | 1 |  |  |  |  |  |  | 1 |  |  |  |  | 1 | 3 |
| Daniel Walter | 1 | 2 |  |  | 1 |  |  |  | 4 | 2 |  | 1 |  |  | 1 |  |  |
| Sarah White | 1 |  |  |  |  |  |  |  | 1 | 1 |  | 1 |  | 1 |  |  | 12 |
| Catron Webster | 1 | 1 |  |  |  |  |  |  |  |  | 2 |  |  | 1 |  |  |  |
| Robert Williams | 1 | 1 | 2 |  |  | 1 |  |  |  | 2 | 1 |  |  | 1 | 1 |  |  |
| Thomas Williams |  |  |  | 1 |  |  |  |  |  |  |  |  |  |  |  |  |  |
| Mary White |  | 1 | 1 |  |  |  |  |  | 1 |  | 1 |  |  |  | 1 |  | 5 |
| Thomas White |  |  |  | 1 |  |  |  |  |  | 1 |  |  |  |  |  |  |  |
| John White | 2 |  |  |  | 1 |  |  |  | 1 |  |  | 1 |  |  |  |  |  |
| John Wale | 2 |  | 1 |  |  |  |  |  |  |  |  | 1 |  |  |  |  |  |
| Evins Winwright | 1 |  |  | 1 |  |  | 1 |  | 3 | 1 |  | 1(White Male 70-80) |  |  |  |  |  |

The 1776 Census of Nantacoake Hundred was taken by Peter Sears and completed by September 16, 1776. Sworn before John C. Harrison, Clerk

### STRAIGHT'S HUNDRED, DORCHESTER COUNTY, MD.

| Head of the Household | -10 | 10 to 16 | 16 to 21 | 21 to 30 | 30 to 40 | 40 to 50 | 50 to 60 | 60 to 70 | -10 | 10 to 16 | 16 to 21 | 21 to 30 | 30 to 40 | 40 to 50 | 50 to 60 | 60 to 70 | Negroes |
|---|---|---|---|---|---|---|---|---|---|---|---|---|---|---|---|---|---|
| Mark Mookin | 1 | 1 |  | 1 |  |  |  |  |  |  | 1 |  | 1 |  |  |  |  |
| Mary Mookin | 2 |  |  |  |  |  |  |  | 1 |  |  |  | 1 |  |  |  |  |
| Ezekie Johnson | 2 |  | 1 |  |  |  |  |  |  |  | 1 |  |  |  |  |  |  |
| William Johnson | 3 | 2 |  |  | 1 |  |  |  | 3 |  |  |  | 1 |  |  |  |  |
| John Wells |  |  |  |  | 1 |  |  |  |  |  |  |  | 1 |  |  |  |  |
| William Tigner |  |  |  | 1 |  |  |  |  |  |  |  |  |  |  |  |  |  |
| Lewes Griffith | 1 | 1 | 1 |  | 1 |  |  |  | 3 |  | 2 |  |  | 1 |  |  |  |
| John Foxwell | 3 |  |  |  |  |  |  |  | 1 |  |  | 1 |  |  |  |  |  |
| Levin Hart | 1 |  | 1 |  |  |  |  |  |  |  |  | 1 |  |  |  |  |  |
| John Woodling | 3 |  |  | 1 |  |  |  |  |  |  | 1 | 1 |  |  |  |  |  |
| John Holmes | 1 | 2 | 2 | 1 |  |  |  |  | 2 | 1 |  |  | 1 |  |  |  |  |
| Richard Woodling | 2 |  |  |  | 1 |  |  |  | 2 | 3 |  |  | 1 |  |  |  |  |
| John Coward | 2 |  |  |  | 1 |  |  |  | 1 |  |  | 1 |  |  |  |  |  |
| Edward Pearson | 1 |  |  | 1 |  |  |  |  | 2 |  |  | 1 |  |  |  |  |  |
| David Tyler | 3 |  |  | 1 |  |  |  |  |  |  | 1 | 1 | 1 |  |  |  |  |
| James Johnson | 1 |  |  | 1 |  |  |  |  | 1 |  |  |  |  | 1 |  |  |  |
| Rachel Foxwell |  |  | 1 |  |  | 1 |  |  | 1 | 1 | 1 |  |  |  | 1 |  |  |
| Elizabeth Foxwell |  |  |  |  |  | 1 |  |  |  |  |  |  |  |  | 1 |  |  |
| James Hughs | 1 |  |  | 1 |  |  |  |  | 2 |  |  |  | 1 |  |  |  |  |
| John Tyler |  | 1 |  |  |  | 1 |  |  |  | 3 | 1 |  |  |  |  |  |  |
| John Carman |  |  |  |  |  | 1 |  |  |  | 1 |  | 1 |  |  |  |  |  |
| Charles Graham | 1 |  | 1 | 1 |  |  |  |  |  |  |  | 1 | 1 |  |  |  |  |
| John M. Nemara | 1 | 1 | 1 | 1 |  | 1 |  |  |  | 2 | 1 |  |  |  |  |  |  |
| James Barkley |  | 1 | 1 | 1 |  |  |  |  | 1 |  |  | 1 |  |  |  |  |  |
| William Merideth |  |  |  | 1 |  | 1 |  |  |  |  | 1 |  |  | 1 |  |  |  |
| John Merideth | 2 | 1 | 1 |  | 1 |  |  |  |  | 2 |  | 1 |  |  |  |  |  |

| Head of the Household | Males -10 | 10 to 16 | 16 to 21 | 21 to 30 | 30 to 40 | 40 to 50 | 50 to 60 | 60 to 70 | Females -10 | 10 to 16 | 16 to 21 | 21 to 30 | 30 to 40 | 40 to 50 | 50 to 60 | 60 to 70 | Negroes |
|---|---|---|---|---|---|---|---|---|---|---|---|---|---|---|---|---|---|
| Rebecca Merideth | 1 | | | 1 | | | | | 2 | | | 1 | | | | | |
| Elijah Starling | 1 | 1 | | | 1 | | | | | 1 | | | 1 | | | | |
| Thomas Wooten | | | | 1 | 1 | | 1 | | | | | | | | | 1 | |
| Hager Wooten | | 1 | | | 1 | | | | 3 | 1 | | | 1 | | | | |
| Salathal Adames | 1 | | | | 1 | | | | 2 | | | 1 | | | | | |
| Prissilla Wooten | | | 1 | | | | | | | 1 | | 1 | | | | | |
| Henry Starling | | | 1 | | | 1 | | | | | 1 | | | | | | |
| John Woodling | 1 | | 1 | | | 1 | | | 1 | | | | | | | | |
| John Todd | 2 | | | 1 | | | | | 2 | | 1 | | | | | | |
| Solomon Woodling | 3 | 1 | | 1 | | | | | | 2 | | | 1 | | | | |
| Abraham Misler | | 1 | 1 | | | 1 | | | | 1 | | | | | 1 | | |
| John Parks | 3 | 2 | | 1 | | 1 | | | 2 | 2 | | | | 1 | | | |
| Thomas Adames | 2 | | | 1 | | | | | 3 | | 1 | | | | | | |
| Thomas Whitley | 1 | 2 | | | 1 | 1 | | | 2 | 1 | | | | | | | |
| Thomas Wooten | 3 | 1 | 1 | 1 | | 1 | | | 1 | 1 | | | 1 | | | | |
| Priss Wooten | 2 | | 1 | | | | | | 2 | 1 | | | | | | | |
| Thomas Adames | 1 | 1 | 1 | | | 1 | | | 2 | | | 1 | | | 1 | | |
| John Parks | 2 | | 1 | | | | | | 2 | | | 1 | | | | | |
| William Shorter | 2 | | | 1 | | | | | 2 | | | 1 | | | | | |
| John Mesick | 2 | 1 | | | | 1 | | | 3 | 1 | | | | | 1 | | |
| Henry Lake | 3 | | | 1 | | | | | 2 | 1 | | | 1 | | | | |
| Bridget Whitley | 1 | 1 | | | 1 | 1 | | | 1 | | | 1 | 4 | 1 | | | |
| Jacob Paul | 2 | | | | 1 | | | | 1 | | | | | | 1 | | |
| Peter Adames | | | 1 | | | | | | | | 1 | | | | | | |
| Bettey Insley | | 1 | 1 | | | | | | | | | | | | | 1 | |
| Mary Paul | | | | | | | | | | | | | | | | 1 | |
| Peter Simpson | | | | | 1 | | | | | | | | | | | | |
| Prissillah Wooton | | | 1 | | | | | | 1 | | 1 | 1 | | | | | |
| Mary Wooton | 1 | | 1 | | | | | | 2 | | 1 | | | | | | |
| Robert Ross | | 2 | 1 | | | | | | | | 1 | | | | | 1 | |
| Thomas Ross | 2 | 1 | | 1 | 1 | | | | 3 | 2 | 1 | | 1 | | | | |
| Angelo Wingate | 1 | 1 | | | | 1 | | | 1 | | | | 1 | | | | |
| Joseph Andrews | 5 | 2 | 1 | | 1 | | | | 1 | | | 1 | | | | | |
| Sarah Shors | 1 | | | | | | | | | | 1 | | | | | | |
| Molley Wildey | 1 | 1 | | 1 | 1 | | | | 1 | | 1 | 1 | | | | | |
| Benjamin Todd | 2 | 1 | 2 | 2 | 1 | 1 | | | | 1 | | | 1 | 1 | | | |
| David Todd | | | | | 1 | | | | | | | | | | | 1 | |
| Sarah Drane | | | | | | | | | | | | | | 1 | 1 | | |
| Levin Sanders | 2 | | | 1 | | | | | 1 | | | 1 | | | | 1 | |
| Vallintine Insley | 2 | 3 | 1 | | | 1 | | | 2 | | | | 1 | | | | |
| Michael Todd | 2 | | | | 1 | | | | 2 | 1 | | | | | | | |
| Robert Scott | 1 | 1 | | 1 | | 1 | | | | 1 | 1 | | 1 | | | | |
| Molley Wingate | 1 | | | 1 | | 1 | | | | 1 | 2 | 1 | | 1 | | | |
| John Wingate | 2 | | | 1 | | | | | 2 | | | | 1 | | | | |
| William Wingate | | | 1 | | 1 | | | | | 2 | | | 1 | | | | |
| Robert Wingate | | | | | 1 | | | | 1 | | | 1 | | | | | |
| Timothey McNamara | 3 | | 1 | | | | | | 1 | | | 1 | | | | | |
| Shadrick Lewis | 1 | | 1 | | | | | | | | 1 | 1 | | | | | |
| Jacob Insley | 1 | 1 | 1 | | | 1 | | | 4 | | 1 | | | | | | |
| Job Tobb (Todd) | 2 | | | 1 | | | | | 2 | 1 | 1 | | | | | | |

|  | MALES | | | | | | | FEMALES | | | | | | | Negroes |
|---|---|---|---|---|---|---|---|---|---|---|---|---|---|---|---|
| Head of the Household | -10 | 10 to 16 | 16 to 21 | 21 to 30 | 30 to 40 | 40 to 50 | 50 to 60 | 60 to 70 | -10 | 10 to 16 | 16 to 21 | 21 to 30 | 30 to 40 | 40 to 50 | 50 to 60 | 60 to 70 | |
| Jonathan Todd |  | 1 | 1 |  |  |  |  |  |  |  |  |  |  | 1 |  |  |  |
| Thomas Moore |  | 1 | 1 |  |  |  |  |  |  | 1 |  |  |  | 1 |  |  |  |
| John Robinson | 1 |  | 1 |  |  |  |  |  |  |  |  |  |  |  |  |  |  |
| Andrew Robinson | 1 |  | 2 |  | 1 |  |  |  | 2 | 1 |  |  |  | 1 |  |  |  |
| Lake Robinson | 1 |  |  | 1 |  |  |  |  | 4 | 1 | 1 |  | 1 |  |  |  |  |
| Bettey Cannon |  |  | 1 |  | 1 |  |  |  |  | 1 |  | 1 |  |  |  |  |  |
| Levi Johnson | 2 |  | 1 |  |  |  |  |  | 1 |  | 1 |  |  |  |  |  |  |
| Susannah Cannon | 1 | 1 |  |  |  |  |  |  |  | 1 |  |  |  |  |  |  |  |
| Molley Robinson |  |  | 1 |  | 1 |  |  |  |  | 1 |  |  |  |  |  |  |  |
| Jacob Jones | 4 |  | 1 | 1 |  |  |  |  |  |  | 1 | 1 |  |  |  |  |  |
| Levin McNamara | 2 | 1 |  |  |  |  |  |  |  | 1 |  |  |  |  |  |  |  |
| John Bramble | 1 |  | 1 |  |  |  |  |  | 1 |  | 1 |  |  |  |  |  |  |
| Lewis Bramble |  | 1 | 3 | 1 | 1 |  |  |  | 1 |  |  |  | 1 |  |  |  |  |
| Henry Johnson | 1 |  |  |  | 1 |  |  |  | 1 | 1 |  | 1 |  |  |  |  |  |
| James Cannon | 2 | 1 | 1 | 1 |  |  |  |  | 3 |  |  | 1 |  | 1 |  |  |  |
| William Cannon |  | 1 | 1 |  | 1 |  |  |  | 1 | 2 |  | 2 |  |  | 1 |  |  |
| Elizabeth Cannon |  | 1 |  | 1 |  |  |  |  |  | 2 | 2 | 4 |  |  | 1 |  |  |
| John Tyler | 1 |  |  | 1 |  |  |  |  | 3 |  | 1 |  |  |  |  |  |  |
| Jobe Todd | 1 |  | 1 | 1 |  |  |  |  | 2 |  |  | 1 |  |  |  |  |  |
| Zebulon Pritchett | 2 |  | 1 |  |  |  |  |  |  |  | 1 |  |  |  |  |  |  |
| John Rumble |  | 1 | 1 |  | 1 |  |  |  | 1 |  |  | 1 |  |  |  |  |  |
| Daniel Follen | 1 |  | 1 |  |  |  |  |  | 3 |  | 1 |  |  | 1 |  |  |  |
| Thomas Pritchett | 2 |  | 1 |  |  |  |  |  | 1 |  | 2 |  |  |  |  |  |  |
| Jobis Pritchett |  |  | 1 |  |  |  |  |  |  | 1 |  |  |  |  |  |  |  |
| Moses Horner | 1 | 1 | 1 | 1 |  | 1 |  |  | 1 | 2 |  | 1 |  | 1 |  |  |  |
| Sarah Cope | 4 | 6 |  | 3 | 2 | 1 | 2 |  | 2 | 2 | 3 | 4 |  | 1 | 2 |  |  |
| Joseph Whaland | 1 |  |  | 1 |  | 1 |  |  | 1 | 1 |  | 1 |  | 1 |  |  |  |
| William Hopkins |  |  |  |  |  | 1 |  |  |  |  | 1 | 1 |  |  | 1 |  |  |
| John Rumble | 2 | 1 | 1 |  |  | 1 |  | . | 1 | 1 |  | 1 |  |  |  |  |  |
| Levi Willen | 1 |  |  | 1 |  |  |  |  | 3 |  | . | 2 |  |  |  |  |  |
| Henry Johnson |  |  |  | 1 |  |  |  |  | 1 |  |  | 1 |  |  |  |  |  |
| John Murphey | 1 |  | 1 |  | 1 |  |  |  | 1 | 1 |  |  |  | 1 |  |  |  |
| Robert Bloodsworth | 1 |  |  | 1 | 1 |  |  |  | 1 |  | 1 |  |  |  |  |  |  |
| Arthur Pritchett | 4 | 1 |  |  | 1 |  |  |  | 1 | 1 | 1 |  |  |  | 1 |  |  |
| Jobe Willson | 1 | 2 |  | 1 |  |  |  |  | 2 |  |  | 1 |  |  |  |  |  |
| Barnebay Follen | 1 |  | 2 |  |  | 1 |  |  |  |  |  | 1 |  |  |  |  |  |
| John McNemara | 2 |  |  | 1 |  |  |  |  |  |  |  | 1 |  | 1 |  |  |  |
| Bettey Insley |  |  |  | 1 |  |  |  |  | 5 |  |  |  | 1 |  |  |  |  |
| James Deane |  |  |  | 1 |  |  |  |  | 1 |  | 1 |  |  |  |  |  |  |
| Henry Deane |  | 1 | 1 |  | 1 |  |  |  | 1 | 2 | 1 |  |  |  |  |  |  |
| Naboth Hart | 2 | 2 | 1 |  |  |  |  |  | 2 |  |  |  | 1 | 1 | 1 |  |  |
| Gabril Insley |  | 1 | 1 | 1 |  |  |  |  |  |  |  |  |  |  |  |  |  |
| Joseph Insley | 1 | 1 | 2 |  |  |  |  |  |  | 1 |  |  |  |  |  |  |  |
| Levi Foxwell |  |  |  | 1 |  |  |  |  | 1 |  | 1 |  |  |  |  |  |  |
| Thomas Street | 1 |  |  | 1 |  |  |  |  | 1 |  | 1 |  |  |  |  |  |  |
| Roger Foxwell | 4 | 1 |  |  | 1 |  |  |  | 1 | 1 |  |  | 1 |  |  |  |  |
| Henry Hart | 1 | 1 | 1 |  |  |  |  |  |  |  |  | 1 |  | 1 |  |  |  |
| Andrew Insley |  |  | 1 |  | 1 |  | 1 |  |  |  |  | 1 | 1 |  |  |  |  |
| Isaac Andrews |  |  | 2 |  | 1 |  |  |  | 1 | 3 |  |  |  |  |  |  |  |

| Head of the Household | Males -10 | 10 to 16 | 16 to 21 | 21 to 30 | 30 to 40 | 40 to 50 | 50 to 60 | 60 to 70 | Females -10 | 10 to 16 | 16 to 21 | 21 to 30 | 30 to 40 | 40 to 50 | 50 to 60 | 60 to 70 | Negroes |
|---|---|---|---|---|---|---|---|---|---|---|---|---|---|---|---|---|---|
| Keziah Andrews |  |  |  | 1 |  |  |  |  | 1 | 1 | 1 |  |  |  |  |  |  |
| Nellie Willey | 1 | 1 |  |  |  |  |  |  | 2 |  |  |  |  | 1 |  |  |  |
| Jane Willey (Jeane?) | 2 | 2 |  | 1 |  |  |  |  | 4 |  |  |  |  | 1 |  |  |  |
| Bettey Ferguson |  |  |  |  |  |  |  |  | 1 |  |  | 1 |  |  |  |  |  |
| Nathal Andrews |  | 1 |  |  | 1 | 1 |  |  |  |  | 3 |  |  |  |  |  |  |
| Indey Willey | 1 |  | 1 | 1 |  |  |  |  | 2 |  |  | 1 |  |  | 1 |  |  |
| Rubin Andrews |  |  | 1 | 1 |  |  |  |  |  |  |  | 1 |  |  |  |  |  |
| William Willey | 3 | 2 |  | 1 |  |  |  |  |  |  |  | 1 |  |  | 1 |  |  |
| Elizabeth Insley |  |  |  |  |  |  |  |  |  |  |  |  |  |  | 1 |  |  |
| Rachel Phillips |  |  |  |  |  |  |  |  | 2 |  |  |  |  |  | 1 |  |  |
| Susannah Moore | 2 |  |  |  |  |  | 1 |  | 3 | 2 |  |  |  |  | 1 |  |  |
| John Smith | 1 |  |  | 1 |  |  |  |  | 2 |  |  |  |  |  | 1 |  |  |
| Arthur Smith | 1 | 1 |  |  |  | 1 |  |  |  |  |  |  |  |  |  | 1 |  |
| Ezekiel Mookins | 2 |  |  | 1 |  |  |  |  |  |  |  |  |  | 1 |  |  |  |
| Arthur Hart | 1 |  |  | 2 |  |  |  |  |  |  |  | 1 |  | 1 |  |  |  |
| Samuel Moors | 1 |  | 1 | 1 |  |  |  |  |  |  |  |  |  | 1 |  |  |  |
| William Smith | 1 | 1 | 1 |  |  |  |  |  |  |  |  |  | 1 |  |  |  |  |
| Ezekiel Willey | 1 | 1 | 1 |  | 1 |  |  |  | 1 | 1 | 1 |  |  |  | 1 |  |  |
| George Sharom (?) |  |  |  |  | 1 | 1 |  |  |  |  |  |  |  |  | 1 | 1 |  |
| Richard Deane | 2 |  |  | 1 |  |  |  |  | 2 | 1 |  |  |  | 1 |  |  |  |
| Job Sharom (?) | 2 | 1 | 3 | 1 |  | 1 |  |  |  | 1 | 1 | 1 |  | 1 |  |  |  |
| Jeane Phillips |  | 2 |  |  |  |  |  |  | 2 | 1 |  |  |  | 1 |  |  |  |
| John Gotee |  |  | 1 | 1 |  | 1 |  |  |  | 3 |  |  |  | 1 |  |  |  |
| Samuel Denike | 2 |  |  |  | 1 |  |  |  | 1 |  |  |  |  | 1 |  |  |  |
| Andrew Gotee | 4 | 1 |  | 1 | 1 |  |  |  |  |  |  |  |  | 1 |  | 1 |  |
| Rachel Cole |  |  |  |  | 1 |  |  |  | 1 |  |  |  |  | 1 |  |  |  |
| George Booze |  | 2 |  |  |  |  |  |  | 1 | 1 |  |  |  |  |  | 1 |  |
| Adam Bramble |  |  |  | 1 |  |  |  |  |  |  |  |  |  |  |  |  |  |
| George Booz |  |  |  |  |  |  | 1 |  |  |  |  |  |  |  |  |  |  |
| John McGraw |  | 1 |  | 1 |  |  |  |  | 2 |  |  |  |  | 1 |  |  |  |
| Diannah Cole | 2 |  |  |  |  |  |  |  |  | 1 | 1 |  |  | 1 |  | 1 |  |
| Charles Paul | 1 |  |  | 1 |  |  |  |  |  |  | 1 | 1 |  |  |  |  |  |
| John Wooten |  |  |  |  | 1 |  |  |  | 3 |  |  |  |  | 1 |  |  |  |
| David Whitley | 1 |  |  |  | 1 |  |  |  | 1 |  |  |  |  | 1 |  | 1 |  |
| Bettey Bramble |  |  |  |  |  |  |  |  | 1 | 1 |  |  |  |  |  |  |  |
| Stephen Buley | (no enumeration) | | | | | | | | | | | | | | | | |
| John Edger | 1 | 1 |  | 1 |  |  |  |  | 1 | 2 |  |  | 1 |  |  |  |  |
| James Edger | 1 |  |  | 1 |  |  |  |  | 1 | 1 |  |  | 1 |  |  |  |  |
| Solomon Insley | 1 |  |  | 1 |  |  |  |  | 1 |  |  |  | 1 |  |  |  |  |
| James Greenlief |  |  |  |  | 1 |  |  |  | 1 |  |  |  | 1 |  |  |  |  |
| James Edger | 2 |  |  |  | 1 |  |  |  | 2 | 1 |  |  | 1 |  |  |  |  |
| William Edger | 1 |  |  | 1 | 1 |  |  |  | 2 | 1 |  |  | 1 |  |  |  |  |
| Mary Edger |  | 1 |  |  | 1 |  |  |  | 1 |  |  |  |  | 1 |  | 1 |  |
| John Bramble | 1 | 2 |  |  | 1 |  |  |  | 1 |  |  |  | 1 |  |  |  |  |
| Bettey Deane |  | 1 |  |  |  |  |  |  | 1 |  |  |  |  |  |  | 1 |  |
| James Booz |  |  |  | 1 | 1 |  |  |  |  |  |  |  | 1 |  |  |  |  |
| Molley Ferguson | 1 |  |  |  |  |  |  |  | 2 |  |  |  | 1 |  |  |  |  |
| Uriah Dean | (no male enumeration) | | | | | | | | | 1 | 1 | 1 | 1 |  |  | 1 |  |
| William Reed | 1 |  | 1 |  |  |  |  |  |  |  |  |  |  | 1 |  |  |  |

|  | MALES | | | | | | | FEMALES | | | | | | |  |
|---|---|---|---|---|---|---|---|---|---|---|---|---|---|---|---|
|  | -10 | 10 to 16 | 16 to 21 | 21 to 30 | 30 to 40 | 40 to 50 | 50 to 60 | 60 to 70 | -10 | 10 to 16 | 16 to 21 | 21 to 30 | 30 to 40 | 40 to 50 | 50 to 60 | 60 to 70 |
| Head of the Household | | | | | | | | | | | | | | | | | Negroes |
| John Wingate |  |  |  |  | 1 |  |  |  |  |  |  |  | 1 |  |  |
| James Wingate | 1 | 1 |  | 1 |  |  |  |  | 4 |  | 1 |  |  |  |  |
| Jabis Todd | 1 |  | 1 |  |  |  |  |  |  |  |  | 1 |  |  |  |
| John Wingate | 1 |  |  |  |  |  |  |  |  |  |  |  |  |  |  |
| Thomas Carwan | (no enumeration) | | | | | | | | | | | | | | |
| Thomas Barns | 2 | 1 |  |  |  |  |  |  | 2 |  |  |  |  |  |  |
| James Davis | 1 |  |  | 1 | 1 |  |  |  | 2 |  | 1 |  |  |  |  |
| Richard Woodling | 2 |  |  | 1 |  |  |  |  | 1 | 1 | 1 |  | 1 |  |  |
| Lewis G. Paul |  |  |  |  | 1 |  |  |  | 1 |  | 1 | 1 | 1 |  |  |
| John Tyler | 1 |  |  | 1 |  |  |  |  |  | 1 |  | 1 | 1 |  |  |
| Joseph Hall | 2 |  |  |  |  |  |  |  | 2 | 1 |  | 1 | 1 |  |  |
| Richard Wallace | 1 |  |  | 1 |  |  |  |  | 1 |  |  |  | 1 |  |  |
| Aquiloe Wotten | 1 |  |  |  |  |  |  |  | 2 |  | 1 |  |  |  |  |
| Rhode Wallace |  |  |  |  |  |  |  |  |  |  |  |  | 1 |  | 1 |
| Allen Hayard | 3 |  |  | 1 |  |  |  |  |  |  |  |  | 1 |  |  |
| Joseph Clarkinson | 2 | 1 |  | 1 | 1 | 1 |  |  |  |  | 3 | 1 |  | 1 |  |
| (Jo)hn Booth |  |  |  | 1 |  | 1 |  |  | 1 |  |  | 1 |  |  |  |

The 1776 Census of Straight's Hundred was taken by Charles Sapleport and completed by September 16, 1776. Sworn before John C. Harrison, Clerk

### TRANSQUAKIN HUNDRED

| | | | | | | | | | | | | | | | | |
|---|---|---|---|---|---|---|---|---|---|---|---|---|---|---|---|---|
| Henry Hooper |  |  |  | 1 | 1 |  |  |  |  |  |  | 2 |  | 1 |  | 22 |
| John Bromajim | 1 | 1 |  | 1 |  |  |  |  | 1 | 2 |  |  | 1 |  |  | 5 |
| General Henry Hooper |  |  | 1 | 2 |  | 1 |  |  |  | 1 | 1 |  | 2 |  | 1 | 59 |
| Thomas Pitt | 1 | 1 | 2 |  |  | 1 |  |  | 1 | 2 |  | 1 | 1 |  |  | 11 |
| Mary Burk |  |  |  |  |  |  |  |  |  |  |  |  | 1 |  | 1 |  |
| John Lamb | 1 | 1 | 1 |  | 1 |  |  |  | 2 |  | 1 |  |  |  |  | 1 |
| James Mills | 2 | 1 |  |  | 1 | 1 |  |  |  | 1 |  | 1 | 1 |  |  | 2 |
| Mary Wheelar | 3 |  |  |  |  |  |  |  | 1 |  |  |  | 1 |  |  |  |
| Nicholas Smith | 2 | 1 |  |  | 1 |  |  |  | 1 | 1 |  | 1 |  |  |  |  |
| John Sewel |  | 1 |  |  |  | 1 |  |  | 1 | 1 | 1 | 1 |  |  |  |  |
| James Delihay | 1 |  | 2 | 1 |  | 1 |  |  | 2 |  |  |  |  | 1 |  | 1 |
| Thomas Davidson | 1 |  |  |  | 1 |  |  |  | 2 |  |  |  |  | 1 |  | 5 |
| Ann Turner |  |  |  |  |  |  |  |  | 1 |  |  |  |  | 1 |  |  |
| William Price |  |  | 1 |  |  | 1 |  |  |  | 1 | 1 |  |  |  |  | 4 |
| David Harvey |  |  |  | 1 |  |  |  |  | 2 |  | 1 | 1 |  |  |  |  |
| John Dorley | 3 | 1 | 1 |  | 1 |  |  |  | 1 | 1 | 1 |  | 1 |  |  |  |
| Water Rayley | 2 | 2 |  | 1 |  |  |  |  | 1 |  |  | 2 |  |  |  | 4 |
| Frederick Chaice |  |  |  | 1 |  |  |  |  |  |  |  |  |  |  |  | 17 |
| Augustus Webb |  |  |  | 1 |  |  |  |  | 1 |  | 1 |  |  |  |  |  |
| Barthow Ennalls Sr. |  |  |  | 1 |  |  |  |  |  |  |  |  |  |  |  |  |
| William Noble | 1 | 1 |  | 1 | (Very hard to read this enumeration) | | | | | | | | | | | |
| Thomas Windows |  |  |  | 1 |  |  |  |  |  |  | 1 |  |  |  |  |  |
| John Tootle | 2 | 1 |  | 1 |  |  |  |  | 1 | 1 | 1 |  | 1 |  |  | 4 |
| Addling Hayward | 1 | 1 | 1 |  |  |  |  |  | 1 | 1 |  |  |  | 1 |  |  |
| James Giffin | 2 | 1 | 1 | 1 |  | 2 |  |  | 2 | 1 | 1 |  | 1 |  |  | 4 |
| Francis Hayward |  |  |  | 1 |  | 1 |  |  | 1 |  | 1 | 1 |  | 1 |  | 10 |
| Stephen Whittington | 2 |  |  |  | 1 |  |  |  | 1 | 1 |  |  | 1 |  |  | 5 |
| Ann Hodson |  |  | 1 | 2 | 1 |  |  |  | 1 |  |  |  |  | 1 |  | 14 |

| Head of the Household | MALES | | | | | | | FEMALES | | | | | | | Negroes |
|---|---|---|---|---|---|---|---|---|---|---|---|---|---|---|---|
| | -10 | 10 to 16 | 16 to 21 | 21 to 30 | 30 to 40 | 40 to 50 | 50 to 60 | 60 to 70 | -10 | 10 to 16 | 16 to 21 | 21 to 30 | 30 to 40 | 40 to 50 | 50 to 60 | 60 to 70 | |
| Thomas Ennalls | 1 | | 1 | | | | | | | | 1 | | | | | | 8 |
| George Dent | 2 | | 1 | | | | | | | | 1 | | | | | | |
| William Ennalls | | | | 1 | | | | | | | | 1 | | | | | 22 |
| Coll. Barthow Ennalls | | | | | | 1 | | | | | 1 | 1 | | | | | 27 |
| Henry Ennalls | | | | 1 | | | | | | | | | | | | | 17 |
| Jersey Rue | 2 | | 1 | 1 | | | | | 1 | 3 | | | | 1 | | | |
| Moses Morain | | | 1 | | | | | | | | 1 | | | | | | |
| Robert Callender | | 2 | 1 | | 1 | | | | 2 | | 1 | 1 | | | | | |
| Mary West | 2 | | 1 | | | | | | 2 | 1 | 1 | | 1 | | | | |
| James Stewart | | | | 1 | | | | | 1 | | | 1 | | | | | |
| Joseph Griffin | (Black Man) | | | | | | | | | | | | | | | | 9 |
| Stephen Vinson | 1 | | | 1 | | | | | 1 | 1 | | 1 | | | | | |
| Joseph Ennalls, Magr. | 5 | | | 1 | | | | | 2 | | 1 | | | | | | 18 |
| Daniell Paul | | | | 1 | | | | | 2 | 1 | 1 | | | 1 | | | |
| John Knott | 1 | 1 | 1 | 1 | | 1 | | | 1 | 1 | 1 | | | 1 | | | |
| John Sheppard | | | | | | 1 | | | 1 | | | | | | | | |
| Lousey Ward | 2 | 1 | 1 | 1 | | | | | 1 | 1 | 1 | | | 1 | | | |
| William Badley | 1 | 1 | 1 | 1 | | 1 | | | 3 | | 2 | 1 | | 1 | | | |
| Lewis Pike | | 2 | 1 | | 1 | | | | | | 1 | | | | | | |
| Zeabulon Cook | 2 | | | 1 | | | | | | | | | | 1 | | | |
| Mary Cook | | | | | | | | | | | | | | | 1 | | |
| Robert Clark | | | 1 | | | | | | 1 | | 1 | | | | | | |
| Thomas Killender | 1 | | | 1 | | | | | | | | | | 1 | | | |
| William Phillips | 1 | | 1 | 2 | | | | | 2 | | | 2 | | | | | |
| Benjamin Sherman | 4 | 2 | | | 1 | | | | | | 1 | 1 | | | | | |
| Edward Paul | 1 | 1 | | | 1 | | | | 1 | | 2 | 1 | 1 | | | | |
| John Webb | | 1 | | 1 | | | | | 3 | | | 1 | | | | | |
| Sarah Barnes | | | | | | | | | 1 | 1 | | 1 | | | | | |
| John Hayward | 1 | 1 | | | | 1 | | | 1 | 1 | | 1 | | | | | |
| Thomas Rogers | | 2 | | | | 1 | | | | | | 1 | | | | | |
| Richard Nuton | 2 | 2 | | 1 | 1 | | | | 5 | | | 1 | | | | | 5 |
| Luke Hevens | 2 | 2 | | | 1 | | | | 3 | 1 | | | 1 | | | | 1 |
| Thomas Hevens | 1 | | 1 | | | | | | | 1 | | | | | | | |
| Siney Sweatten | | | | | | | | | 1 | 1 | | | | | | | 1 |
| Edward Morris | 1 | 1 | | 1 | | | | | 2 | 1 | 1 | | | | | | |
| Rose Plug | (Black Women) | | | | | | | | | | | | | 1 | | | 1 |
| Jeremiah M. Callister | 2 | 1 | 1 | | | | | | | | 1 | | | | | | |
| Southy Littleton | 1 | 2 | | | 1 | | | | 3 | 4 | | | 1 | | | | 1 |
| Mark Littleton | 1 | | 1 | | | | | | | | 1 | | | | | | |
| William Littleton | 2 | 1 | | 1 | 1 | | | | 1 | 1 | 2 | 1 | | | | | |
| Daniel Sulivane Magr. | | | | 1 | 1 | | | | | | | | | 1 | | | 11 |
| Daniel Sulivane Jr. | 2 | | | 1 | | | | | 1 | | | 1 | | | | | 12 |
| Athilda M. Callister | 2 | | 1 | | | | | | 1 | | | 1 | | | | | |
| Ezekiel M. Callister | | 1 | 1 | 1 | | | | | 1 | | | | 1 | | | | |
| William Badley | | | | | 1 | | | | | 1 | | | | 1 | | | |
| Nathan Badley | 1 | | | 1 | | | | | 1 | | | 1 | | | | | |
| Elizabeth Woodards | 1 | | | 1 | | | | | | | 1 | | | 1 | | | |
| William Granger | 4 | 1 | | | 1 | | | | | | 2 | | 1 | | | | 1 |
| Luke Russum | 1 | 1 | 1 | | | 1 | | | 2 | 1 | | 1 | | | | | |

| Head of the Household | Males <10 | 10 to 16 | 16 to 21 | 21 to 30 | 30 to 40 | 40 to 50 | 50 to 60 | 60 to 70 | Females <10 | 10 to 16 | 16 to 21 | 21 to 30 | 30 to 40 | 40 to 50 | 50 to 60 | 60 to 70 | Negroes |
|---|---|---|---|---|---|---|---|---|---|---|---|---|---|---|---|---|---|
| John Scott |  |  |  | 1 |  |  |  |  | 3 | 1 | 1 |  | 1 |  |  |  |  |
| Diana Higens | 1 |  |  | 1 |  |  |  |  |  |  |  |  |  |  | 1 |  |  |
| John Wayford | 3 | 1 |  |  | 1 |  |  |  | 1 |  | 1 |  | 1 |  |  |  |  |
| Edward Granger | 1 | 1 | 1 |  | 1 |  |  |  | 3 |  |  |  | 1 |  |  |  |  |
| Eliner Cook | 1 |  |  |  |  |  |  |  |  |  | 1 |  | 1 |  |  |  |  |
| Solomon West | 4 |  | 1 |  | 1 |  |  |  |  |  | 1 |  | 1 |  |  |  |  |
| Denward Hicks | 1 | 1 |  | 1 |  | 1 |  |  | 1 | 1 |  |  |  | 1 |  |  | 27 |
| Mary Scott |  |  | 1 |  |  |  |  |  |  | 1 |  | 1 | 1 |  | 1 |  |  |
| James Brinsfield |  | 2 | 2 |  |  | 1 |  |  | 3 | 1 |  |  |  | 1 |  |  | 6 |
| Leavin Handley | 1 | 1 | 1 | 1 | 1 |  |  |  | 3 | 1 |  |  | 1 |  |  |  |  |
| John Anderton |  |  |  |  |  | 1 |  |  | 1 |  |  |  |  |  |  |  | 16 |
| John Glanding | 1 |  |  | 1 |  |  |  |  | 1 | 1 |  | 1 |  |  |  |  |  |
| James Sulivane | 2 |  |  | 2 |  |  |  |  | 3 |  |  | 1 | 1 |  |  |  | 21 |
| James Southerlin(Doctor) |  |  | 2 |  |  |  |  |  |  |  |  |  |  |  |  |  | 1 |
| Francis Smith | 2 |  |  |  |  |  |  |  | 1 |  |  | 2 | 1 |  |  |  |  |
| John Scott | 1 |  |  | 1 |  |  |  |  | 2 |  |  | 2 | 1 |  |  |  | 10 |
| Mary Morain | 1 | 2 | 2 |  |  |  |  |  | 2 | 1 |  |  |  | 1 |  |  | 1 |
| John Stevens |  | 1 |  | 1 | 1 |  |  |  | 1 |  |  | 3 |  |  |  |  | 3 |
| Nancy Shaw | 1 |  |  |  |  |  |  |  |  | 1 |  |  |  |  |  |  |  |
| George Robinson | 1 |  |  | 1 |  |  |  |  |  |  |  | 1 |  |  |  | 1 | 1 |
| Mary Adams |  |  |  |  |  |  |  |  |  | 1 | 1 |  |  |  | 1 |  |  |
| John Marshall | 2 | 1 |  | 1 |  |  |  |  | 2 |  |  | 1 | 1 |  |  |  | 13 |
| Hodson Roylins |  |  |  | 1 |  |  |  |  | 2 |  |  | 1 | 1 |  |  |  |  |
| Ester Norman | 1 | 2 | 1 |  |  |  |  |  | 1 | 1 |  |  |  | 1 |  |  |  |
| Margrit Davis |  | 3 | 1 |  |  |  |  |  |  |  | 2 | 1 |  | 1 |  |  |  |
| Bettey Adams | 1 |  |  |  |  |  |  |  | 1 | 1 |  |  |  | 1 |  |  |  |
| William Saunders | 2 | 1 |  |  | 1 |  |  |  | 1 |  |  | 2 |  |  |  |  | 6 |
| Richard Rollisten | 2 |  |  |  |  |  |  |  |  | 1 |  | 1 |  |  |  |  |  |
| Aron Bramble |  |  | 1 | 1 |  |  |  |  | 1 |  |  | 1 |  |  |  |  |  |
| Thomas Bramble | 1 |  |  | 1 |  |  |  |  |  |  |  |  |  |  |  |  |  |
| Sarah Wright |  | 2 |  |  |  |  |  |  |  |  |  | 1 |  |  | 1 |  |  |
| Mary Hardin | 2 |  |  |  |  |  |  |  |  |  |  | 1 |  |  |  |  |  |
| Ezekiel Whitchits |  |  | 1 |  |  |  |  |  |  |  |  |  |  |  |  |  | 3 |
| William Billings | 2 | 1 | 1 |  |  |  |  |  | 2 |  |  |  |  | 1 |  |  |  |
| Elizabeth Williams | 1 | 1 |  |  |  |  |  |  |  |  | 1 |  |  |  | 1 |  |  |
| John White |  |  | 1 |  |  |  |  |  |  | 1 |  |  | 1 |  |  |  | 3 |
| Thomas White |  |  |  | 1 |  |  |  |  | 1 |  |  | 1 |  |  |  |  | 6 |
| John Thompson | 3 |  |  |  | 1 |  |  |  |  |  |  |  |  |  | 1 |  |  |
| John Hubbard |  |  | 1 |  |  |  |  |  | 1 | 1 |  | 1 | 1 |  |  |  |  |
| John Hooper |  | 1 |  |  | 1 |  |  |  | 1 |  | 1 | 1 |  |  |  |  |  |
| Solomon Wheelar | 2 |  |  |  |  | 1 |  |  | 3 | 1 |  |  | 1 | 1 |  |  |  |
| Mary Layton | 1 | 1 | 1 | 1 |  |  |  |  |  |  |  |  | 1 | 1 |  |  |  |
| Phillip Williams |  |  |  | 1 |  |  |  |  | 1 |  |  | 1 |  |  |  |  |  |
| John Boudle |  |  |  | 1 | 1 |  |  |  |  |  |  | 1 |  |  | 1 |  | 6 |
| Henry Boudle | 2 |  |  |  |  |  |  |  |  |  |  |  |  |  |  |  | 2 |
| Edward Scotter |  | 1 |  |  | 1 |  |  |  | 1 |  |  |  |  | 1 |  |  |  |
| William Lecompt |  | 2 |  |  |  | 1 |  |  |  | 1 |  |  | 2 |  |  |  | 19 |
| ____ Ennalls |  |  |  |  |  |  |  |  |  | 1 |  |  | 1 |  |  |  | 16 |
| Owen Owens | 2 | 1 | 1 | 1 |  |  |  |  | 1 |  | 1 | 1 |  |  |  |  |  |

|  | MALES | | | | | | | | FEMALES | | | | | | | | |
| --- | --- | --- | --- | --- | --- | --- | --- | --- | --- | --- | --- | --- | --- | --- | --- | --- | --- |
| Head of the Household | -10 | 10 to 16 | 16 to 21 | 21 to 30 | 30 to 40 | 40 to 50 | 50 to 60 | 60 to 70 | -10 | 10 to 16 | 16 to 21 | 21 to 30 | 30 to 40 | 40 to 50 | 50 to 60 | 60 to 70 | Negroes |
| Samuel Lecompt | 1 |  | 1 |  |  |  |  |  |  |  | 1 |  |  |  |  |  |  |
| David Cavender |  | 1 |  |  | 1 | 1 |  |  | 1 | 2 |  |  |  | 1 | 1 |  |  |
| John Dawson | 1 | 1 | 1 | 1 |  |  | 1 |  |  | 1 | 1 |  | 2 |  |  |  |  |
| Thomas Cavender | 1 |  | 1 |  |  |  |  |  |  |  | 1 |  |  |  |  |  |  |
| Henry Hooper | 3 | 1 |  |  | 1 |  |  |  | 3 |  | 1 |  | 1 |  |  |  |  |
| Thomas Wheelar | 2 |  |  | 1 |  |  |  |  | 2 |  |  | 1 |  |  |  |  |  |
| Sam Rose |  | 2 |  |  |  | 1 |  |  |  | 1 | 1 |  |  | 1 |  |  |  |
| Nimrod Nuton | 1 | 1 | 1 | 1 |  |  |  |  |  |  | 2 |  |  |  |  |  |  |
| Willis Nuton | 1 | 1 |  | 1 | 1 |  |  |  | 2 |  | 1 | 1 |  |  |  |  | 5 |
| Joseph Hicks | 1 | 2 | 1 | 2 |  | 1 |  |  | 1 |  | 1 |  | 1 |  |  |  |  |
| Henry Wright | 1 | 2 |  |  | 1 |  |  |  | 1 |  | 1 |  |  |  |  |  | 3 |
| Collen Ferguson |  |  |  |  | 1 |  |  |  |  |  |  |  |  |  |  |  |  |
| Jimmimey Molix | (Black Man) | | | | | | | | | | | | | | | | 5 |
| Roger A. Hooper | 2 | 2 | 2 |  |  |  |  |  | 2 |  |  |  | 1 |  | 1 |  | 12 |
| Peatrick Linningham |  |  |  | 1 |  |  |  |  | 1 |  | 1 | 1 |  |  |  |  |  |
| James Cummins | 2 | 2 |  |  | 1 |  |  |  | 2 |  | 2 |  | 1 |  |  |  |  |
| Thomas Brodess |  |  |  | 1 |  |  |  |  | 2 |  |  | 3 |  |  |  |  | 10 |
| Mary Harrison | 1 |  | 1 |  |  |  |  |  |  |  | 1 | 1 |  |  |  |  | 1 |
| Joseph Ward | 1 |  |  | 1 |  |  |  |  | 1 |  | 1 |  |  |  |  |  |  |
| Francis Langfit | 1 |  |  | 1 |  |  |  |  | 1 |  | 1 |  |  |  |  |  |  |
| Elizabeth Heron |  | 1 | 2 | 1 | 1 |  |  |  | 2 |  | 2 |  |  |  | 2 |  | 8 |
| Mary Jones | 3 |  |  |  |  |  |  |  | 2 | 1 |  |  | 1 |  | 1 |  |  |
| Leavin McDaniel | 2 |  |  | 1 |  |  |  |  | 1 |  |  |  |  | 1 |  |  |  |
| Morgan Jones |  | 1 |  |  |  |  | 1 |  | 4 | 1 |  | 1 |  |  |  |  | 1 |
| Magor Bird | 2 |  | 1 | 1 |  |  |  |  | 3 | 1 |  | 1 |  |  |  |  | 10 |
| John Lecompt | 3 | 3 |  | 1 |  | 1 |  |  |  |  | 1 | 1 | 1 |  | 1 |  | 17 |
| Alexander McHenry |  |  |  |  | 1 |  |  |  | 1 | 1 |  |  |  | 1 |  |  |  |
| Elizabeth Godding |  |  | 2 |  |  |  |  |  | 2 |  |  |  |  |  |  |  |  |
| Francis Kees | 1 | 1 |  |  |  |  |  |  |  |  | 1 |  |  | 1 |  |  |  |
| William Tripe | 2 |  |  | 1 |  |  |  |  |  |  | 1 |  |  |  |  |  | 8 |
| John Darbey |  |  |  |  | 1 |  |  |  | 1 | 1 |  |  |  | 1 |  |  | 12 |
| George Dodson | 2 |  | 1 | 1 | 1 |  |  |  | 2 |  |  | 1 | 1 |  |  |  | 2 |
| William McDaniel | 2 |  |  | 1 | 1 |  |  |  | 2 | 2 | 1 |  |  |  |  |  |  |
| Hoopes Hodson | 2 | 1 |  |  |  | 1 |  |  | 2 | 1 |  | 1 |  |  |  |  | 6 |
| Anthony Manning | 2 |  |  |  | 1 |  |  |  |  |  |  | 1 |  |  |  |  |  |
| John Coopper | 2 |  |  |  | 1 |  |  |  |  |  |  |  | 1 |  |  |  | 12 |
| Mark Noble | 2 |  |  |  | 1 |  |  |  | 5 | 1 |  |  | 1 |  |  |  | 5 |
| John Hodson | 1 | 2 | 2 | 1 |  |  | 1 |  | 2 | 1 |  |  | 1 |  |  |  | 28 |
| Henry Hodson |  |  |  | 1 |  |  |  |  | 1 |  | 1 |  |  |  |  |  |  |
| Thomas Cocklin |  |  |  |  |  | 1 |  |  | 1 |  |  |  |  |  | 1 |  | 8 |
| Edward Smith | 1 |  | 1 |  |  |  |  |  |  |  |  | 1 |  |  |  |  |  |
| Handy Handley | 2 | 2 |  |  | 1 |  |  |  | 2 |  |  |  | 1 |  |  |  | 6 |
| John Brown | 2 |  |  |  | 1 |  |  |  | 1 |  |  |  |  |  |  |  | 1 |
| William Alexander | 1 |  |  | 1 |  | 1 |  |  | 1 |  | 1 |  |  |  |  |  |  |
| Elizabeth Monrow | 1 |  |  |  |  |  |  |  | 1 |  |  |  | 1 |  |  |  |  |
| Beazil Warron | 1 |  |  |  |  | 1 |  |  | 1 |  |  | 1 | 1 |  |  |  |  |
| Bettey Hubbart |  | 1 |  |  |  |  |  |  |  | 1 | 1 |  |  | 1 |  |  |  |
| Leavin Lecompt | 6 | 1 |  | 1 |  |  |  |  |  |  | 1 |  |  |  |  |  |  |
| James Ross | 2 | 1 |  | 1 | 1 |  |  |  | 3 | 1 |  | 1 |  |  |  |  | 1 |

| Head of the Household | MALES 10 to -10 | 16 to 16 | 21 to 21 | 30 to 30 | 40 to 40 | 50 to 50 | 60 to 60 70 | FEMALES 10 to -10 | 16 to 16 | 21 to 21 | 30 to 30 | 40 to 40 | 50 to 50 | 60 to 60 70 | Negroes |
|---|---|---|---|---|---|---|---|---|---|---|---|---|---|---|---|
| John Owens |  |  | 1 | 1 |  |  |  |  |  | 1 |  |  |  |  | 5 |
| Robert Jackson | 2 |  |  | 1 |  |  |  |  |  | 1 |  |  |  |  |  |
| William Lecompt | (Black Man) |  |  |  |  |  |  |  |  |  |  |  |  |  | 3 |
| John Cook | 3 |  |  | 1 |  |  |  |  |  | 1 | 1 |  |  |  |  |
| Charles Lecompt |  |  |  | 1 | 1 |  |  |  |  | 1 |  | 1 | 1 |  | 5 |
| Pegey Phillips |  | 1 | 1 |  |  |  |  | 1 |  |  | 1 |  |  |  |  |
| James Lecompt | 2 |  | 1 |  | 1 |  |  | 2 | 1 |  | 1 |  |  |  |  |
| Peggey Oggan | 2 |  | 1 |  |  |  |  | 1 | 1 |  | 1 |  |  |  |  |
| Thomas Basset | 1 | 1 |  |  |  |  |  | 1 |  | 1 |  |  |  |  | 2 |
| Thomas Sulivane | 1 |  | 1 |  |  |  |  | 1 |  |  | 1 |  |  |  |  |
| John Covey | 1 |  | 2 |  |  |  |  |  |  |  | 1 |  | 1 |  |  |
| John Long | 2 | 2 |  |  |  | 1 |  | 1 | 2 |  | 1 |  | 1 |  | 1 |
| Ralph Green |  | 1 |  | 1 |  |  |  | 1 |  |  | 1 |  |  |  | 13 |
| Elijah Brown |  |  | 1 |  |  |  |  | 1 |  | 1 | 1 |  |  |  |  |
| Francis Smith | 2 | 2 | 2 | 1 |  |  |  | 1 |  |  | 1 |  |  |  |  |
| Garner Bruffit | 1 |  | 1 |  |  |  |  | 1 | 1 | 1 |  |  |  |  | 1 |
| Lavin Traverse | 3 | 2 |  |  | 1 |  |  | 1 | 1 |  | 2 | 1 |  |  | 15 |
| Elizabeth Claridge | 3 | 1 |  |  |  |  |  |  |  |  |  |  | 1 |  |  |
| Robert Goldsborough, Esq. |  |  |  |  |  |  |  |  |  |  |  |  |  |  | 15 |
| Christopher Moore |  | 1 |  |  | 1 |  |  | 2 | 1 | 1 |  |  | 1 |  |  |
| Samuel McClemmey |  |  | 1 | 1 | 1 |  |  |  |  |  |  |  |  |  |  |
| John Hooper |  |  | 1 | 2 |  |  |  |  |  |  |  |  |  |  |  |
| Nehemiah Vinson |  | 2 |  | 2 |  | 1 |  | 1 | 1 | 1 |  | 1 |  |  |  |
| Summars Ward |  |  | 1 |  |  | 1 |  | 2 | 1 | 1 | 1 |  |  |  | 3 |
| John Hamiltown | 2 | 2 | 1 |  |  |  |  |  | 1 | 1 |  | 1 | 1 |  | 3 |
| John Greenwood | 1 | 2 | 1 | 1 | 1 | 1 |  | 2 | 1 |  |  | 1 |  |  | 2 |
| Col. John Dickinson | 3 | 3 | 1 |  |  | 1 |  | 1 |  | 1 |  |  | 1 |  | 40 |
| Daniel Parker | 2 |  |  | 1 |  |  |  | 1 |  |  | 1 |  |  |  | 8 |
| Edward Brodess | 2 | 1 |  | 2 |  |  |  | 1 |  |  | 2 |  |  |  | 4 |
| William Formar |  |  |  |  | 1 |  |  |  | 2 |  |  |  | 1 |  |  |
| Joseph Notherwood |  | 1 |  |  |  |  |  |  |  | 1 |  |  |  |  | 7 |
| Tabitha Brodess |  | 1 | 2 |  |  |  |  |  |  |  | 2 |  | 1 |  | 4 |
| Coll. John Ennalls |  |  |  | 1 |  |  |  |  |  |  |  |  |  |  | 38 |
| Salathal Harvey | 2 |  |  | 1 |  |  |  | 2 |  | 1 | 1 |  |  |  |  |
| Alise Burge | 1 | 2 |  |  |  |  |  |  | 1 |  | 1 |  |  |  |  |
| Capt. Hugh Eccleston |  | 2 |  |  | 1 |  |  | 2 | 1 |  | 1 | 1 |  |  | 32 |
| Isaac Cullins |  |  |  |  |  | 1 |  |  |  | 1 |  |  | 1 |  |  |
| John Denney | 1 | 1 | 1 |  |  |  |  |  | 1 | 1 |  |  |  |  |  |
| Parks Summers | 1 |  |  | 1 |  |  |  | 1 |  | 1 |  |  |  |  |  |
| John Beotpich | 1 | 1 |  | 1 |  |  |  | 2 |  | 1 | 1 | 1 |  |  | 2 |
| William Becks | 2 | 2 | 1 |  |  | 1 |  | 1 | 1 |  |  | 1 |  |  |  |
| Samuel Evans | 1 | 3 |  |  |  | 2 |  | 2 | 3 |  | 2 |  |  |  |  |
| Jonathan Beotpitch | 2 | 1 |  |  | 1 |  |  | 4 |  | 1 |  | 1 |  |  | 4 |
| George Bacon | 2 |  |  |  | 1 |  |  | 2 | 1 | 1 |  | 1 |  |  |  |
| William Saunders | 1 |  |  |  |  | 1 |  | 3 |  |  |  |  | 1 |  |  |
| Isaac Foxwell | 2 |  | 1 |  |  |  |  | 1 |  |  |  | 1 |  |  |  |
| Joseph Slight | 1 |  | 1 |  |  |  |  |  | 1 | 1 |  |  |  |  |  |
| William Lewis | 2 |  |  |  | 1 |  |  | 1 |  |  | 1 |  |  |  |  |
| Jabus Goutee | 2 |  | 1 |  |  |  |  | 3 |  |  | 2 |  |  |  |  |
| Ann Smith |  | 1 |  |  |  |  |  |  | 2 |  |  |  | 1 |  |  |

| Head of the Household | Males -10 | 10 to 16 | 16 to 21 | 21 to 30 | 30 to 40 | 40 to 50 | 50 to 60 | 60 to 70 | Females -10 | 10 to 16 | 16 to 21 | 21 to 30 | 30 to 40 | 40 to 50 | 50 to 60 | 60 to 70 | Negroes |
|---|---|---|---|---|---|---|---|---|---|---|---|---|---|---|---|---|---|
| Samuel Lawson |  | 3 |  | 1 |  | 1 |  |  |  |  |  |  |  | 1 |  |  |  |
| Mary Keene |  | 1 |  |  |  |  |  |  |  | 1 |  |  |  |  | 1 |  | 2 |
| Gustavis Copper |  |  |  | 1 |  |  |  |  |  |  |  | 1 |  |  |  |  |  |
| Isaac Partridge |  |  |  |  | 1 |  |  |  |  |  |  | 1 |  |  | 1 |  | 10 |
| Martin Driver | 1 | 1 |  |  | 1 |  |  |  | 1 |  |  |  | 1 |  |  |  |  |
| Atthow Pattison |  |  | 1 |  |  | 1 |  |  | 1 |  | 2 | 1 |  | 1 |  |  | 5 |
| Thomas F. Eccleston |  |  |  | 1 |  |  |  |  |  |  |  |  |  |  |  |  | 15 |
| John Harrison |  | 1 |  | 1 |  |  |  |  |  |  |  |  |  | 1 |  |  | 1 |
| John Hanford | 2 |  |  | 1 |  |  |  |  | 1 |  |  | 1 |  |  |  |  |  |
| William Laine | 1 | 1 | 1 | 1 |  |  |  |  | 1 |  |  | 1 |  | 1 |  |  | 1 |
| John Brierwood | 3 | 1 | 1 |  |  | 1 |  |  | 1 | 1 |  |  |  |  | 1 |  | 5 |
| Right Mills | 2 |  | 1 |  |  |  |  |  | 1 | 1 |  |  | 1 | 1 |  |  | 1 |
| William Hooper |  | 2 |  | 1 |  |  |  |  |  |  | 2 |  |  |  | 1 |  | 4 |
| Nuton Tregor | 2 |  | 1 |  | 1 |  |  |  | 2 | 1 |  |  |  | 1 |  |  | 4 |
| Leavin Willis | 1 |  | 1 |  | 1 |  |  |  | 1 |  | 1 | 1 | 1 |  |  |  | 2 |
| Leavin Woollen | 2 |  | 1 |  | 1 |  |  |  | 1 | 1 | 1 |  | 1 |  |  |  |  |
| Edward Mills | 1 |  | 1 |  |  |  |  |  |  |  |  | 1 | 1 |  |  |  |  |
| Solomon Hill | 1 |  | 1 |  |  |  |  |  | 1 |  |  | 1 |  |  |  |  | 1 |
| Thomas Keene | 2 | 1 |  | 1 |  |  |  |  | 2 |  |  | 1 |  |  |  |  |  |
| John Whitaker |  |  | 1 |  |  |  |  |  | 2 |  | 2 |  |  |  |  |  | 1 |
| Thomas Saunders |  |  |  |  |  | 1 |  |  | 1 | 1 |  |  |  | 1 |  |  |  |
| Siller Harrison |  |  |  |  |  |  |  |  | 1 |  | 1 | 1 |  |  |  |  | 2 |
| Lambreth Byron | 2 |  | 1 |  |  |  |  |  |  |  | 1 |  | 1 |  |  |  | 1 |
| Elizabeth Ennalls |  |  |  |  |  |  |  |  |  |  |  |  |  |  |  |  | 10 |
| Daniel Gossage | 3 |  |  |  | 1 |  |  |  |  |  |  |  |  |  | 1 |  |  |
| Emanuel Beckwith |  | 1 |  | 1 |  |  |  |  |  |  |  |  |  | 1 |  |  |  |
| Thomas Norman |  |  |  | 1 |  |  |  |  | 3 | 2 |  | 1 | 1 |  |  |  | 1 |
| Ann Arnett | 1 | 1 |  |  |  |  |  |  |  |  | 1 |  |  | 1 |  |  |  |
| James Arnett | 1 |  |  | 1 |  |  |  |  | 1 |  |  | 1 |  |  |  |  |  |
| Thomas Martin |  |  |  |  |  |  |  |  |  |  |  |  |  |  |  |  | 7 |
| James Porter | 1 |  |  | 1 |  |  |  |  | 1 |  |  | 1 |  |  |  |  |  |
| Thomas Muse Magr. |  |  |  |  |  |  |  |  |  |  |  |  |  |  |  |  | 10 |
| Mary Cheshire | 1 | 1 | 1 |  |  |  |  |  | 1 |  |  | 1 | 1 |  |  |  | 3 |
| Jonathan Partridge | 1 |  |  |  | 1 |  |  |  | 1 |  | 1 |  |  |  | 1 |  | 8 |
| Arthur Porter |  | 1 | 1 |  |  | 1 |  |  |  |  |  |  |  |  | 1 |  | 2 |
| Rosanna Reed |  |  | 2 | 1 |  |  |  |  |  |  |  |  |  | 1 |  | 1 |  |
| Henry Stewart | 2 |  |  |  | 1 |  |  |  | 2 |  | 1 | 1 | 1 |  |  |  | 5 |
| John Manning |  | 1 |  | 2 |  |  |  |  | 1 | 2 |  |  |  | 1 | 1 |  | 18 |
| William Griffin | 3 |  |  | 1 |  |  |  |  | 1 | 1 |  |  |  |  |  |  | 1 |
| Roger Woolford |  |  | 1 |  |  | 1 |  |  |  |  |  |  |  |  | 2 |  | 15 |
| Henry Saunders | 3 | 1 | 1 |  |  | 1 |  |  | 4 | 1 | 1 | 1 | 1 |  |  |  | 3 |
| James Parmer | 2 |  |  |  |  | 1 |  |  | 1 | 1 |  | 1 | 1 |  |  | 1 | 9 |
| Thomas Ennalls | 2 |  | 1 |  | 1 |  |  |  | 3 |  |  | 1 |  |  | 1 | 1 | 27 |
| Charles Wheelar |  |  |  |  | 1 |  |  |  | 1 | 1 |  |  |  |  |  |  |  |
| William Button | 2 | 1 | 1 |  |  |  |  |  | 3 | 1 |  | 1 | 1 |  |  |  | 8 |
| John T. Stewart | 3 |  | 1 | 1 |  |  |  |  | 2 |  | 1 | 1 |  |  |  |  | 10 |
| Thomas Stewart | 2 |  |  |  | 1 |  |  |  |  |  |  |  | 1 |  |  |  | 2 |
| John Cheshire | 1 |  | 1 |  |  |  |  |  | 1 | 2 | 1 |  |  | 1 |  |  | 3 |
| Mary Manidier |  | 1 |  |  |  |  |  |  |  | 1 | 1 |  |  | 1 |  |  | 15 |

|  | MALES | | | | | | | | FEMALES | | | | | | | |
|---|---|---|---|---|---|---|---|---|---|---|---|---|---|---|---|---|
| Head of Household | -10 | 10 to 16 | 16 to 21 | 21 to 30 | 30 to 40 | 40 to 50 | 50 to 60 | 60 to 70 | -10 | 10 to 16 | 16 to 21 | 21 to 30 | 30 to 40 | 40 to 50 | 50 to 60 | 60 to 70 | Negroes |
| Dr. James Murray |  |  |  |  |  |  |  |  |  |  |  |  |  |  |  |  | 5 |
| Segar Penningtton |  |  |  |  |  |  |  |  |  |  |  |  |  |  |  |  | 7 |
| Capt. Joseph Daffin |  |  | 1 | 1 | 1 |  |  |  |  |  |  | 1 |  | 1 |  |  | 20 |
| William Bluch |  | 1 |  |  |  | 1 |  |  |  |  |  |  |  |  |  |  |  |
| Thomas Muir | 1 |  |  | 1 | 1 |  |  |  |  | 1 |  | 1 | 1 |  |  |  | 2 |
| Jene Hale | 2 |  | 1 |  |  | 1 |  |  | 1 |  |  |  | 1 |  |  |  | 2 |
| Rev. Phillemon Hughs |  |  |  |  | 1 | 1 |  |  |  | 2 |  |  | 1 |  | 1 |  | 4 |
| Joseph Slee |  |  | 1 |  |  |  |  |  |  |  |  |  |  |  |  |  | 1 |
| Moliein Norris | 3 | 1 |  | 1 |  |  |  |  |  |  |  | 1 |  |  |  |  |  |
| Nathaniel Cox | 1 | 2 |  |  |  | 1 |  |  | 1 | 1 | 1 |  | 1 |  | 1 |  |  |
| Elizabeth Haile | 2 |  |  |  |  |  |  |  |  | 1 |  | 1 |  | 1 |  |  | 8 |
| Andrew S. Ennalls |  |  | 1 |  | 1 |  |  |  |  |  |  |  | 1 |  |  |  | 6 |
| Joseph Ennalls |  |  |  |  | 1 | 1 |  |  |  |  |  | 1 |  |  | 1 |  | 29 |
| James Mulania |  |  | 1 |  | 1 |  |  |  | 3 |  |  | 1 |  |  |  |  |  |
| John Colson | 1 |  |  | 1 |  |  |  |  |  | 1 |  | 1 |  |  |  |  |  |
| Thomas H. Airey | 1 |  |  | 1 |  |  |  |  |  | 1 |  | 1 |  |  |  |  | 28 |
| Charles Scott |  | 1 |  |  | 1 | 1 |  |  | 2 | 2 |  | 1 |  |  |  |  | 6 |
| Joseph Dawson | 1 |  | 1 | 1 |  |  |  |  | 1 |  |  |  |  |  |  |  |  |
| William Dawson | 2 | 3 | 1 |  | 1 |  |  |  | 1 | 1 |  |  | 1 | 1 |  |  |  |
| James Kees | 4 | 2 | 1 |  |  | 1 |  |  | 1 |  | 1 |  | 1 |  |  |  |  |
| John Kees | 3 | 1 |  | 1 |  |  |  |  |  | 1 |  |  | 1 |  |  |  | 1 |
| William Vincent |  |  |  | 1 |  |  |  |  | 1 |  |  | 1 |  |  |  |  |  |
| Thomas Muse, Magr. |  |  |  |  |  |  |  |  |  |  |  |  |  |  |  |  | 12 |
| John Dawson |  | 1 | 1 | 1 |  |  | 1 |  | 1 |  | 1 | 1 |  | 1 |  |  |  |
| William Wheelar |  |  |  | 1 |  |  |  |  | 2 |  | 1 | 1 |  |  |  |  |  |
| Nathan McCollister |  |  |  | 1 |  |  |  |  | 1 |  |  | 1 |  |  |  |  |  |
| Leavin Hayward | 1 | 1 |  | 1 |  |  |  |  | 1 | 1 |  | 1 |  | 1 |  |  |  |
| John Cornish |  |  |  |  |  |  |  |  |  |  |  |  |  |  |  |  | 2 |
| Dennis Connerway |  | 1 |  |  |  | 1 |  |  | 3 | 1 |  |  | 1 |  |  |  | 1 |
| John Dingle | 3 |  |  |  | 1 |  |  |  |  |  |  | 1 |  |  |  |  | 1 |
| Thomas Hanford |  |  |  | 1 |  |  |  |  |  |  |  | 1 |  |  |  |  |  |
| Edward Stephens | 3 | 2 | 1 | 1 |  | 1 |  |  |  |  |  | 1 |  |  | 1 |  | 9 |
| Loten West | 2 |  |  |  | 1 |  |  |  | 1 |  |  |  | 1 |  |  |  |  |
| John Nixon |  |  | 1 |  | 1 |  |  |  |  |  |  |  |  |  |  |  |  |
| John Blair |  |  |  | 1 |  |  |  |  |  |  |  |  |  |  |  |  |  |
| Mary Evans |  |  |  |  |  |  |  |  |  |  |  |  |  | 1 |  |  |  |

The 1776 Census of Transquakin Hundred was taken by Samuel Hooper and completed by September 9, 1776. Sworn before John C. Harrison, Clerk

1776 Census of FREDERICK COUNTY, MARYLAND

ELIZABETH HUNDRED

Taken by John Miller, and completed by August 9, 1776. Sworn before James Beall, Jr.

Males From the Age of 16 to 50

| Name | Age | Name | Age | Name | Age |
|---|---|---|---|---|---|
| Rudolph Bley | 30 | Jacob Ott | 27 | William Brown | 17 |
| Martin Steck | 23 | Peter Bell | 40 | James Leyor | 20 |
| Ernst Dietz | 28 | Adam Dile | 37 | Jones Emry | 34 |
| Francis Wagoner | 25 | John Barkes | 39 | Jacob Katz | 43 |
| Michael Fesler | 35 | George Woltz | 33 | Jacob Belshoober | 27 |
| Jacob Whymer | 49 | John Konn | 25 | George Rinehart | 31 |
| Jacob Wolsleger | 27 | Adam Smith | 25 | John Leidy | 44 |
| Frederick Rohrer | 34 | Peter Woltz | 30 | Jacob Nicolous | 24 |
| John Krumbach | 40 | Herman Creily | 28 | John Leidy | 28 |
| David Hellen | 40 | Francis Creily | 24 | Stephen McClasby | 37 |
| Michael Kline | 50 | Andrew Backus | 26 | William Muffet | 44 |
| Jacob Hoobes | 50 | William Conrad | 27 | John Odear | 50 |
| William Hieser | 44 | Eistations Young | 50 | Thomas Simmons | 29 |
| John Stineseiver | 33 | John Reap | 27 | Henry Shryock | 39 |
| Andrew Filler | 27 | Isaac Gneadig | 36 | Michael Fackler | 36 |
| John Unsill | 32 | Simon Householder | 31 | Frederick Steidinger | 50 |
| George Zinn | 27 | Jost Weyand | 27 | Noah Hart | 30 |
| Jacob Bardon | 37 | John Fackler | 47 | Frederick Highskill | 24 |
| Jacob Fisher | 46 | Henry Weikle | 27 | Peter Hoefligh | 34 |
| Nicholas Hagan | 23 | Philip Oster | 32 | Michael Domer | 30 |
| John Oster | 26 | George Arnold | 31 | John Skryock | 28 |
| Edward Braun | 39 | Andrew Miller | 45 | Moses Chaplin | 22 |
| Melker Belshoober | 37 | Peter Wagoner | 35 | William Pullin | 25 |
| Henry Quere | 38 | Peter Haut | 48 | Christopher Alder | 29 |
| Joseph George | 50 | Daniel Callaghan | 24 | Peter Hoze | 28 |
| Henry Dudweiler | 30 | George Shoaner | 25 | Jacob Hoze | 34 |
| Jonathan Henry | 31 | George Squiers | 21 | Charles Heterick | 26 |
| William Scott | 33 | Leonhard Nave | 17 | Adam Wise | 24 |
| John Herry | 35 | George Beverly | 20 | Christopher Trapp | 40 |
| Baltzer Goll | 50 | Martin Peyfer | 24 | John Wraken | 24 |
| Michael Ott | 28 | William Coner | 23 | Samuel Paten | 20 |
| William Messy | 17 | James Furney | 18 | John Hoefligh | 25 |
| Daniel M. Cardon | 24 | Thomas Leyfine | 20 | John Woodcock | 36 |
| Nathaniel Morgan | 28 | John Lee | 20 | Philip Riefenagh | 25 |
| Phillip Badolph | 18 | Jacob Shryock | 30 | Mathew Horne | 25 |
| Joseph Gelsin | 20 | Jacob Hoddel | 27 | Alexander Megare | 20 |
| David Morgin | 23 | John Michael | 20 | Frederick Alder | 35 |
| Thomas Foot | 22 | Jacob Hoober | 20? | Michael Walter | 26 |
| John Reab | 29 | James Dunken | 18 | John Korepening | 26 |
| George Booke | 19 | William Welsh | 19 | Michael Yegley | 36 |
| David Herry | 25 | John Marrain | 29 | Conrad Shitz | 26 |
| Martin Herry | 20 | Gotlieb Willerd | 33 | Joseph Hansman | 25 |
| Jacob Herry | 19 | Peter Feved | 20 | James Clark | 35 |
| Mathias Need | 50 | Samuel Young | 28 | Leonhard Shryock | 37 |
| Benjamin Campbell | 27 | Philip Greegbaum | 17 | Christian Mantle | 49 |

| Name | Age | Name | Age | Name | Age |
|---|---|---|---|---|---|
| Agtious Fleeger | 36 | Thomas Clasby | 30 | Augustine Liphard | 42 |
| Michael Deibelbeis | 28 | Joseph Peifer | 24 | George Hutson | 30 |
| Dewalt Gellhoober | 30 | Michael Ekenbergh | 40 | William Shenafield | 40 |
| George Young | 35 | Robart Gettry | 49 | John Thomsan | 28 |
| Francis Burgess | 35 | John Gettry | 20 | Samuel Finley | 47 |
| Moritz Bouer | 49 | John Sciles | 35 | Jacob Deibley | 42 |
| William Bishop | 23 | George Friend | 24 | Joseph Sprigg | 40 |
| George Ableider | 30 | David Friend | 22 | Thomas Belt | 34 |
| Abraham Bouer | 33 | Philip Friend | 21 | John Lincoler | 25 |
| Barney Reily | 22 | Ludwig Reitenaur | 26 | Thomas Sprigg | 27 |
| George Dile | 27 | Joseph Hanna | 30 | Brian McConnal | 30 |
| Martin Where | 39 | Henry ___ man | 28 | Martin Robinson | 28 |
| Thomas Rinehard | 33 | John Steiner | 20 | Michael Cary | 29 |
| Thomas George | 31 | Henry Blume | 35 | James Cullin | 30 |
| Felix Meyer | 30 | John Meyer | 20 | James McKay | 30 |
| John Klaber | 38 | Jacob Meyer | 18 | Timothy McKay | 40 |
| Paul Ward | 23 | Martin Snyder | 43 | Martin Bauman | 32 |
| Philip Harnish | 21 | Nicolaus Ellis | 19 | Samuel Dugles | 23 |
| Henry Baumward | 22 | John Kunes | 26 | John Dugles | 18 |
| George Good | 30 | Peter Rench | 20 | Robert Dugles | 26 |
| William Lewis | 20 | John Rench | 19 | Christian Koenigh | 46 |
| John Swan | 29 | John Mowen | 24 | William Martin | 40 |
| Konn ___ | 18 | George Charles | 24 | Daniel Gleabsalter | 42 |
| Peter Grose | 29 | Lawrence Breyner | 18 | John Setis | 31 |
| Benjamin Moll | 25 | George Dunn | 23 | Henry Smith | 23 |
| Joseph Downey | 21 | Henry Moll | 34 | Jost Biddle | 17 |
| William Downey | 22 | Ruedy Rufe | 34 | John Scot | 50 |
| Michael Beard | 22 | Stephen Mowen | 25 | David Scott | 17 |
| Peter Stuky | 42 | Andrew Rench | 48 | Peter Simon | 50 |
| James Wassin | 21 | George Booghman | 22 | Peter Beaker | 38 |
| Francis M.yer | 21 | Isaac Newswanger | 24 | Frederick Eyle | 23 |
| Jacob Rohrer | 32 | George Green | 32 | Andrew Maggey | 28 |
| Herman Klaber | 42 | Ludwig Young | 47 | Andrew Witman | 26 |
| Christian Rohrer | 49 | Samuel Baghtel | 45 | Frederick Hoze | 24 |
| John Braum | 33 | Samuel Baghtel | 22 | Alberdus Hiffner | 49 |
| Jost Kline | 49 | Isaac Baeghtle | 22 | John Hiffner | 21 |
| John Stull | 43 | Martin Funk | 22 | Jacob Hiffner | 19 |
| Daniel Stull | 21 | Conrad Brendlinger | 48 | Jacob Sneyder | 30 |
| Feodorus Felmet | 20 | Baltzer Shoomaker | 40 | George Hitler | 49 |
| William Corkrey | 22 | Henry Funck | 24 | Martin Jacob | 46 |
| Frederick Craft | 33 | John Funck | 26 | James Dawney | 22 |
| Peter Giden | 50 | Peter Sailor | 23 | Jacob Smith | 29 |
| James Nox | 40 | John Sailor | 21 | Michael Boyer | 29 |
| John Seiman | 37 | George Nave | 21 | Henry Klaber | 26 |
| Paul Christman | 38 | Philip Dusiner | 30 | Peter Shees | 21 |
| Mathias Reitenaur | 20 | John Henry Snyder | 47 | Christian Grove | 28 |
| Philip Renner | 28 | Michael Where | 26 | Abraham Daruse | 35 |
| Imanuel Smith | 21 | George Stuard | 31 | Henry Fore | 50 |
| George Smith | 38 | William Garment | 31 | Michael Fore | 18 |
| Henry Manigher | 27 | Henry Hinkle | 23 | Christian Leyder | 40 |
| H nry Miller | 33 | Thomas Gross | 39 | Christian Metz | 24 |
| Peter Prakunier | 45 | William Beard | 44 | Christian Bentz | 36 |
| George Draocel | 41 | Samuel Dawney | 23 | Leonard Sheafer | 25 |
| Michael Haushalter | 20 | John Dilles | 44 | Christian Sitze | 21 |
| Jacob Reitenaur | 37 | William Dilles | 17 | John Sitze | 23 |
| Christian Foghler | 19 | Simon Foghler | 44 | Adam Leiser | 17 |

| Name | Age | Name | Age | Name | Age |
|---|---|---|---|---|---|
| Henry Kowe | 27 | Henry Sneyder | 44 | Abraham Leyder | 35 |
| Dewalt Kowe | 22 | Philip Reimal | 50 | Jacob Leydor | 27 |
| Henry Brote | 33 | George Reimal | 17 | Andrew Fuller | 28 |
| Baltzer Lanabach | 49 | Jacob Ritter | 50 | Ludwig Mowen | 20 |
| Fred. Nicodemus | 44 | Elias Ritter | 20 | Ludwig Hart | 30 |
| Conrad Nicodemus | 20 | | | Robard Gray | 26 |

Females From the Age of 16 to 50

| Name | Age | Name | Age | Name | Age |
|---|---|---|---|---|---|
| Barbara Bley | 22 | Margaretha Meglin | 19 | Mary Caldwell | 17 |
| Catherina Steck | 23 | Lidia Shookard | 18 | Elisabeth Mantle | 18 |
| Catharine Dietz | 24 | Margaretha Gellin | 20 | Margaret Mowen | 18 |
| Sharlote Wagoner | 21 | Catharina Soin | 19 | Ann Hoefligh | 25 |
| Catharine Fesler | 28 | Christiana Miller | 21 | Martha Sneydor | 20 |
| Mary Salome | 46 | Catharina Fackler | 19 | Catherina Davis | 30 |
| Susanna Sauder | 50 | Catharina L. Need | 44 | Elisabeth Silkerd | 22 |
| Catharina Wolsleger | 26 | Mary Link | 25 | Magdalene Mettler | 48 |
| Catharine Rohrer | 30 | Mary Campbell | 18 | Susanna Leidy | 28 |
| July Crumback | 47 | Catharina Ott | 20 | Mary Gare | 31 |
| Susanna Hellin | 36 | Catharina Kogh | 28 | Catharine Wenner | 23 |
| Christiena Hoober | 46 | Elizabeth Bell | 35 | Mary Hall | 31 |
| Ann Heiser | 32 | Mary Dile | 35 | Julianna Hooder | 18 |
| Margaretha Stineseiver | 31 | Margaretha Barkes | 32 | Eve Reigel | 48 |
| Magdalane Filler | 19 | Jane Long | 31 | Margareth Emery | 22 |
| Magdalan Unsel | 27 | Charlote Woltz | 25 | Catharina Katz | 27 |
| Mary Zinn | 26 | Susanna Kann | 27 | Mary Belshoober | 26 |
| Margaretha Bardon | 30 | Mary Smith | 21 | Barbara Rinehard | 36 |
| Elisabeth Fisher | 47 | Mary Woltz | 22 | Mary Sneyder | 43 |
| Elisabeth Haggy | 19 | Catherina Creily | 27 | Eve Nicolous | 20 |
| Elisabeth Oster | 25 | Elizabeth Blackburn | 33 | Ann Maffet | 24 |
| Eliz. Beltshoover | 34 | Charlote Bakes | 27 | Sarah O'Dear | 26 |
| Catharina Shumkin | 36 | Catharine Conrad | 20 | Ann Simms | 20 |
| Mary Dudweiler | 24 | Margaretha Young | 42 | Cathrin Shryock | 29 |
| Mary Michel | 46 | Elisabeth Robinson | 20 | Sarah Johnson | 43 |
| Dorothea Berry | 27 | Elisabeth Gneadig | 28 | Helfena Fackler | 32 |
| Ann Scott | 28 | Elisabeth Householder | 24 | Rachel Hart | 27 |
| Fronica Miller | 30 | Margaretha Weyand | 26 | Catharine Highskil | 19 |
| Elizabeth Goll | 46 | Mary Miller | 44 | Ann Hoefligh | 37 |
| Margaretha Ott | 23 | Eve Fackler | 39 | Ann Domer | 21 |
| Mary Monger | 27 | Susana Weikle | 20 | Ann Shryock | 28 |
| Christianna Sneyder | 35 | Magdalena Bowman | 30 | Mary Chaplen | 20 |
| Catharina Heflybauer | 46 | Catharina Oster | 34 | Mary Pullin | 31 |
| Margaretha Weyer | 46 | Catharina Arnold | 26 | Susanna Alter | 25 |
| Catharina Burger | 18 | Mary Miller | 26 | Salmey Hoze | 23 |
| Mary Knepsin | 17 | Margaretha Wagoner | 35 | Elisabeth Donelley | 38 |
| Susanna Fisher | 20 | Elisabeth Herman | 24 | Magdalena Hoze | 31 |
| Ann Magin | 20 | Catharina Creily | 24 | Elisabeth Sitzler | 43 |
| Magdalena Gies | 20 | Elisabeth Wagoner | 22 | Susanna Heterick | 22 |
| Christiana Sauder | 22 | Catharina Crime | 18 | Elisabeth Wise | 26 |
| Barbara Need | 17 | Mary Young | 27? | Eve Wise | 42 |
| Mary Ebrey | 40 | Elisabeth Moll | 28 | Barbara Trapp | 36 |
| | | Elisabeth Ruhe | 19 | Margaret Alter | 23 |
| | | Ann Chaplin | 29 | Mary Tillhard | 46 |

| Name | Age | Name | Age | Name | Age |
|---|---|---|---|---|---|
| Rosina Reitenauer | 24 | Susanna Hix | 30 | Amilia Sprigg | 22 |
| Catharina Walter | 23 | Eve Steitzman | 33 | Elisabeth Lauman | 26 |
| Mary Horepening | 19 | Cathrin Blume | 34 | Rachel Dugles | 47 |
| Catharina Yegly | 34 | Elisabeth Myer | 49 | Elisabeth Koenig | 46 |
| Margaret Shitz | 22 | Margret Myer | 21 | Rosina Martin | 40 |
| Margaretha Hiensman | 33 | Mary Sneyder | 34 | Catherina Klebsadler | 36 |
| Jane Clark | 35 | Margret Roofe | 43 | Elisabeth Smith | 26 |
| Margaretha Shryock | 25 | Ann White | 19 | Mary Scot | 47 |
| Ann Doose | 43 | Margret Rench | 43 | Mary Jess | 21 |
| Barbery Mantle | 28 | Rosina Smith | 28 | Catharina Simon | 26 |
| Catharina Haeger | 25 | July Boyer | 20 | Christiana Beaker | 32 |
| Margaretha Ibelbies | 26 | Susanna Dunn | 17 | Elisabeth Hittler | 22 |
| Mary Gellhoober | 29 | Ester Wise | 40 | Jane Maggal | 27 |
| Mary Baward | 46 | Ann Evely | 30 | Barbara Hittler | 19 |
| Margaret Young | 22 | Elisabeth Mull | 24 | Elisabeth Reeb | 22 |
| Elisabeth Bourgess | 30 | Margret Roofer | 20 | Catherin Hiffner | 43 |
| Ann Bauer | 17 | Mary Mowen | 20 | Catherin Hitler | 45 |
| Margaret Bishop | 47 | Elisabeth Rench | 38 | Barbara Jacob | 48 |
| Margaret Bishop | 17 | Margret Darton | 22 | Mary Jacob | 18 |
| Catharine Boogh | 50 | Mary Green | 21 | Rosina Dawney | 18 |
| Eve Bauer | 31 | Magdalina Young | 38 | Ann Smith | 23 |
| Fronica Dile | 25 | Magdalina Young | 20 | Margret Boyer | 27 |
| Elisabeth Where | 27 | Margret Young | 19 | Christiana Klaber | 50 |
| Eve Rinehard | 28 | Ann Beaghtle | 41 | Catrin Klaber | 20 |
| Christiana Rohrer | 28 | Magdalana Beaghtle | 18 | Elizabeth Klaber | 17 |
| Cathrin Klaber | 28 | Mary Brendlinger | 42 | Frances Klaber | 17 |
| Fronica Rohrer | 35 | Rosina Brendlinger | 18 | Margret Reab | 42 |
| Catharina Braun | 28 | Christianna Shoomaker | 40 | Elisabeth Reab Sees | 43 |
| Mary Kling | 48 | Ann Funck | 23 | Susanna Shees | 19 |
| Mary Stull | 30 | Barbara Funck | 23 | Cathrin Grove | 25 |
| Martha Stull | 19 | Elisabeth Messer | 19 | Elisabeth Druse | 26 |
| Susanna Stull | 17 | Barbara Sailor | 21 | Cathrin Fore | 42 |
| Elisabeth Craft | 25 | Magdalina Sailor | 27 | Elisabeth Leyder | 34 |
| June Nox | 38 | Magdalina Nave | 24 | Cathrin Metz | 19 |
| Ann Seiman | 27 | Ann Dusinger | 23 | Magdalena Bentz | 30 |
| Catharina Haut | 19 | Susanna Sneyder | 33 | Margret Sheafer | 24 |
| Ann Bowman | 39 | Ann Where | 28 | Hannah Sitze | 48 |
| Magdalena Christman | 32 | Eve Smith | 18 | Barbara Sitze | 23 |
| Magd. Reitenaur | 17 | Ann Stuard | 34 | Cathrin Leiser | 38 |
| Magdalena Smith | 36 | Rebecca Garment | 37 | Mary Kowe | 23 |
| Eliz. Maninger | 26? | Ann Hinkle | 19 | Elisabeth Kowe | 17 |
| Catharina Miller | 20 | Sharlote Gross | 36 | Elisabeth Brote | 25 |
| Margret Prakunie | 42 | Ester Beard | 18 | Elisabeth Lanebach | 34 |
| Margretha Prakunie | 17 | Elisabeth Dawney | 22 | Christianna Sneyder | 32 |
| Elizabeth Drascel | 26 | Margret Dilles | 43 | Cathrin Reimel | 44 |
| Margret Housholder | 19 | Catharine Dilles | 19 | Mary Reimel | 23 |
| Barbara Reitenauer | 22 | Elisabeth Foghler | 46 | Elisabeth Reimal | 20 |
| Hannah Gare | 18 | Dorethea Lekron | 42 | Judith Ritter | 44 |
| Dorathea Hoffman | 50 | Elisabeth Roush | 40 | Ann Ritter | 22 |
| Elisabeth Peifer | 20 | Elisabeth Roush | 17 | Cathrin Ritter | 17 |
| Catherin Ekenborgh | 34 | Catharina Liphard | 46 | Cathrin Leyder | 35 |
| Ester Gutry | 46 | Jane Hutsen | 24 | July Leyder | 24 |
| Ann Gutry | 21 | Ann Shenafeild | ? | Ester Fuller | 19 |
| Pheeb Gutry | 18 | Susanne Thamson | 28 | Catrin Mowon | 18 |
| Elisabeth Sciles | 35 | Ann Deibely | 40 | Margret Heard | 18 |
| Elisabeth Friend | 50 | Hanna Sprigg | 40 | | |
| Dorethe Friend | 18 | Eliz. Lawson Belt | 22 | | |

## MALES AGE 50 and OVER

| Name | Age | Name | Age | Name | Age |
|---|---|---|---|---|---|
| Eberhard Michael | 69 | Adam Crime | 51 | Joseph Rench | 52 |
| Felix Sauder | 56 | Patrick McArdell | 60 | John Feigely | 55 |
| Christian Crytzer | 65 | Thomas McArdell | 61 | Abraham Nave | 56 |
| Martin Herry | 56 | William Sisler | 66 | Jacob Chips | 56 |
| Henry Reitenauer | 62 | George Wise | 53 | Michael Waker | 73 |
| Andrew Link | 55 | Godfry Sillhard | 52 | Christian Where | 56 |
| Jacob Greaber | 58 | John Billmore | 52 | Nicholous Raush | 53 |
| Thames Long | 52 | John Boyer | 62 | Adam Thamson | 67 |
| John Shooman | 51 | Christian Doose | 55 | Lawrence Keller | 65 |
| Lawrence Shitz | 69 | Jacob Bishop | 52 | William Duklis | 56 |
| Andrew Miller | 53 | Christian Bandure | 55 | Daniel Kehn | 56 |
| Salomon Miller | 64 | William Beaker | 66 | Joseph Eber | 60 |
| Mathias Sailor | 56 | Nicolous Reitenauer | 64 | Henry Klaber | 58 |
| John Herman | 55 | George Smith | ? | Michael Reab | 53 |
| Simon Bauman | 51 | Henry Stertzman | 55 | Peter Shees | 52 |
| John Robinson | 56 | George Hoffman | 70 | Wendle Sitze | 56 |
| Adam Reigel | 67 | George Householder | 52 | Mathias Leiser | 51 |
| Larance Althard | 66 | Philip Friend | 58 | Henry Kowe | 60 |
| Jacob Metler | 60 | John Urwan | 56 | Frederick Fuller | 62 |
| Jacob Bauman | 73 | Leonhard Fleeger | 60 | Daniel Mowen | 55 |
| | | Simon Myer | 52 | | |

## FEMALES AGE 50 and OVER

| Name | Age | Name | Age | Name | Age |
|---|---|---|---|---|---|
| Mary Michael | 55 | Margaret Leidy | 56 | Margret Miller | 70 |
| Eve Reitenauer | 62 | Magdalen Steidinger | 53 | Magdalana Simon | 80 |
| Elisabeth Creily | 60 | Elisabeth Billmore | 54 | Margaretha Urrvine | 55 |
| Mary Windon | 65 | Mary Bauer | 51 | Christianna Nave | 52 |
| Catharina Shitz | 65 | Catharin Letherman | 52 | Margret Chips | 55 |
| Barbara Miller | 54 | Magdalena Beeker | 66 | Elisabeth Where | 51 |
| Magdalena Sailor | 56 | Elisabeth Giden | 53 | Susanna Beard | 60 |
| Barbara Haut | 52 | Mary Sheid | 52 | Elisabeth Weshbach | 76 |
| Magdalena Rinehard | 71 | Magdalena Reitenauer | 55 | Margret Kehn | 55 |
| Margaret Pyfer | 52 | Christian Smith | 62 | Catharina Nicodemus | 53 |
| Catharin Althard | 54 | Margarethe Stertzman | 86 | Cathrin Sneyder | 88 |
| Elisabeth Bauman | 58 | Margretha Householder | 52 | Ann Fuller | 57 |
| Mary Crime | 66 | Elisabeth Ekenbergh | 67 | Catharina Mowen | 54 |
| | | Rachel Feigely | 55 | | |

## MALES AGE 16 and UNDER

| Name | Age | Name | Age | Name | Age |
|---|---|---|---|---|---|
| John Rohrer | 5 | Fredrick Craft | 7 | David Stertzman | 8 |
| Jacob Rohrer | 3 | Henry Giden | 5 | Peter Prakunier | 11 |
| Henry Klaber | 10 | James Nox | 3 | David Prakunier | 9 |
| John Klaber | 3 | John Seiman | 6 | Henry Prakunier | 4 |
| Christian Rohrer | 11 | Valentine Seiman | 1 | Jacob Prakunier | 4 |
| John Rohrer | 9 | Jonathan Heked | 15 | Peter Draxel | 11 |
| Samuel Rohrer | 2 | William Christman | 6 | Abraham Draxel | 7 |
| George Braun | 1 | Jacob Smith | 7 | Daniel Draxel | 6mos. |
| Jacob Gidigh | 12 | John Smith | 5 | George Householder | 9 |
| John Kline | 11 | George Smith | 3 | John Householder | 6 |
| William Kline | 8 | Adam Stertzman | 14 | George Miller | 5mos. |
| Henry Furnear | 11 | Peter Stertzman | 11 | Peter Reitenauer | 7 |

| Name | Age | Name | Age | Name | Age |
|---|---|---|---|---|---|
| Joseph Reitenauer | 2 | Henry Nave | 12 | George Jacob | 14 |
| George Pfifer | 5mos. | Henry Sneyder | 10 | Henry Jacob | 12 |
| John Ekenbergh | 3 | John Sneyder | 9 | John Smith | under 1 |
| Jacob Ekenbergh | 2 | Arnold Sneyder | 4 | Henry Boyer | 3 |
| James Guthry | 14 | Valentine Sneyder | 3 | John Boyer | 2 |
| Richard Guthry | 9 | Christian Where | 2mos | Herman Klaber | 9 |
| Robert Guthry | 6 | Abeija Garment | 3 | Ludwig Klaber | 7 |
| Jacob Sciles | 12 | Jeremia Gross | 11 | Peter Reab | 15 |
| John Sciles | 6 | Humphrey Gross | 9 | John Reab | 6 |
| William Sciles | 3 | William Gross | 7 | John Grove | 4 |
| Christopher Friend | 12 | William Beard | 14 | Abraham Grove | 4 mos. |
| Peter Feigely | 15 | John Dilles | 1 | Abraham Daruse | 5 |
| Andrew Hix | 10 | Henry Foghler | 13 | John Daruse | 1 |
| William Hix | 8 | Sabastian Raush | 14 | Jacob Fore | 15 |
| Joseph Hix | 6 | George Raush | 7 | Henry Fore | 10 |
| Timothy Hix | 4 | John Raush | 4 | Felix Fore | 7 |
| Martin Stertzman | 7 | Henry Liphard | 15 | Abraham Leyder | 15 |
| Henry Stertzman | 5 | Isaac Hutson | 8 | John Leyder | 10 |
| Christian Meyer | 14 | Charles Hutson | 6 | John Bley | 5 |
| Abraham Meyer | 11 | Jacob Shenafield | 12 | John Dietz | 5 wks. |
| Henry Meyer | 6 | John Shenafield | 10 | Michael Fisler | 1 |
| Jacob Sneyder | 6 | Henry Shenafield | 8 | Peter Kline | 7 |
| Henry Sneyder | 5 | William Shenafield | 4 | John Binlie | 14 |
| Peter Sneyder | 4 | Adam Thamson | 5 | Frederick Rohrer | 9 |
| Levy Sneyder | 2 | John Thamson | 1 | Jacob Rohrer | 6 |
| John Rench | 15 | George Deibley | 7 | John Rohrer | 3 |
| Peter Rench | 12 | Frederick Deibley | 2 | George Rohrer | 2 mos. |
| Joseph Rench | 8 | Philip Sprigg | 15 | John Grumbach | 13 |
| David Rench | 5 | Casber Sprigg | 15 | Conrad Grumbach | 9 |
| Jacob Rench | 14 | Joseph Sprigg | 11 | George Hellen | 15 |
| John Dunn | 1 | John Bauman | 2 | Thomas Hellen | ? |
| Jacob Wise | 13 | Samuel Duglis | 8 | Peter Hellen | ? |
| Adam Wise | 4 | Joseph Duglis | 12 | Alexander Hellen | 1 |
| Samuel Wise | 2 | Robert Dugles | 3 | Henry Hoober | 10 |
| Christian Wise | 1mos. | Jost Koenig | 12 | Christopher Hoober | 6 |
| Henry Moll | 1 | Mathias Koenig | 10 | Adam Hoober | 3 |
| John Roof | 2mos. | Peter Konig | 6 | William Hoober | 3 wks. |
| Leonhard Mowen | 1 | James Martin | 10 | William Heiser | 9 |
| Michael Rench | 13 | Samuel Martin | 6 | Jacob Haiser | 6 |
| Daniel Rench | 7 | John Wine | 14 | John Fiteneiger | 15 |
| Jacob Young | 15 | Robert Macal | 3 | Henry Citig | 12 |
| Isaac Young | 13 | Errhard Smith | 16 | Henry Filler | 8 |
| Ludwig Young | 11 | James Scot | 15 | Henry Unsel | 5 |
| Martin Beaghtle | 11 | John Scot | 7 | John Unsel | 2 |
| Jacob Beaghtle | 6 | Milker Scot | 3 | Alexander Seller | 15 |
| George Brendlinger | ? | John Simon | 3 | Jacob Zinn | 3 |
| Andrew Brendlinger | 6 | Peter Simon | 1 | George Zinn | 2 |
| Michael Shoomaker | 13 | John Beaker | 2 | John Bardon | 5 |
| Jacob Shoomaker | 10 | William Welsh | 12 | John Fisher | 12 |
| John Shoomaker | 7 | Valentin Hiffner | 15 | David Fisher | 4 |
| Martin Funk | 6mos. | Frederick Hiffner | 8 | Henry Fisher | 1 |
| Henry Funk | 3 | Peter Hiffner | 4 | Henry Hagin | 4 mos. |
| John Funk | 2 | Conrad Hiffner | 2 | John Oster | 2 |
| Michael Nave | 14 | George Hitler | 11 | George Mantel | 15 |

| Name | Age | Name | Age | Name | Age |
|---|---|---|---|---|---|
| Jacob Belshoober | 6 | Jacob Weickle | 1 | Philip Silkerd | 9 |
| John Belshoober | 2 | John Bauman | 9 | Frederick Sillhard | 4 |
| Henry Belshoober | 6mos. | Frederick Arnold | 5 | Christian Yegley | 6 |
| Henry Dudweiler | 7 | John Arnold | 4 | John Yegley | 3 |
| John Herry | 16 | Daniel Arnold | 2 | Christopher Yegley | 7 |
| Andrew Herry | 9 | George Miller | 3 | Henry Shitz | ½ |
| Peter Dile | 15 | Valentine Wagoner | 7 | John Hinsman | 2 |
| Samuel Scot | 1 | Conrad Wagoner | 8mos. | Samuel Clark | 8 |
| Jacob Coll | 5 | Jacob Heaflybauer | 12 | John Clark | 4 |
| Jacob Ott | 4 | George Heaflybauer | 11 | Henry Shryock | 10 |
| Michael Ott | 1 | Michael Crime | 14 | John Shryock | 5 |
| Philip Baumward | 12 | Jacob Sneydor | 9 | Nicolaus Mantel | 7 |
| Jacob Need | 2 | John Sneydor | 5 | Christian Mantel | 1mos. |
| Frederick Killer | 9 | Henry Sneydor | 3 | Michael Deibelbies | 5 |
| Jacob Ott | 1 | Jacob Sneydor | 3mos. | John Deibelbies | 3 |
| Peter Kooke | 3 | Jacob Nicolous | 5mos. | Christopher Gallhover | 5 |
| Frederick Bell | 7 | Jacob Hoze | 12 | Henry Gellhover | 5mos. |
| Peter Bell | 1 | Isaac McArdell | 10 | Peter Baward | 7 |
| Samuel Ritcharson | 15 | William McArdell | 8 | John Young | 1 |
| Henry Dile | 14 | Benjamin Odear | 9 | Jacob Bishop | 15 |
| John Dile | 10 | James Rarrone | 6 | George Bishop | 12 |
| Doruse Dile | 8 | Jacob Shryock | 10 | Jacob Tile | 8mos. |
| George Dile | 4 | Henry Shryock | 7 | Peter Where | 5 |
| Andrew Barkes | 3 | George Shryock | 1½ | Henry Where | 2 |
| John Barkes | 1 | David Furney | 16 | George Rinehard | 6 |
| John Long | 8 | Samuel Sprigg | 16 | Benjamin Elke | 9 |
| Jacob Shooman | 4 | John Fackler | 4 | Jacob Lekron | 13 |
| John Kann | 5mos. | Jacob Fackler | 2 | Simon Lekron | 10 |
| Jacob Woltz | 4 | Thomas Barry | 15 | Christian Metze | 3mos. |
| George Woltz | 2 | Daniel Bittier | 15 | Christopher Bentz | 6 |
| John Creily | 1 | George Wentel | 15 | George Bentz | 4 |
| Leonhard Baward | 15 | Lawrence Wishler | 12 | John Bentz | 7mos. |
| George William | 16 | (Elke Squire) | | John Sheafer | 5 |
| Daniel Need | 16 | George Wise | 16 | Andrew Sheafer | 3 |
| Sebastian Bauer | 15 | George Giedig | 14 | Henry Sitze | 16 |
| Hugh Hagen | 15 | John Wise | 15 | Peter Sitze | 12 |
| John Blackburn | 15 | Henry Sauder | 12 | George Sitze | 5 |
| Thames Shooman | 15 | Frederick Sweier | 16 | William Leiser | 14 |
| Jacob Bauman | 12 | Charles White | 1 | George Leiser | 12 |
| Ritchard Kelly | 15 | John Highskill | 1 | Peter Leiser | 6 |
| Sebastian Mettler | 15 | Peter Hoefligh | 11 | Henry Leiser | 3mos. |
| Henry Mettler | 14 | John Hoefligh | 3mos. | Henry Kowe | 5mos. |
| Augustin Meyer | 15 | Michael Domer | 4 | Henry Breat | 3 |
| Samuel Leidy | 1 | Frederick Domer | 3mos. | Jacob Laneback | 2 |
| William Bakes | 5 | John Shryock | 3mos. | Andrew Nicodemus | 16 |
| James Smith | 12 | Adam Beck | 8 | John Sneyder | 5 |
| Henry Gneadig | 8 | Peter Hoze | 1 | Frederick Sneyder | 2 |
| John Gneadig | 3 | Frederick Hoze | 9 | Christian Sneyder | 3mos. |
| James Montgomry | 4 | Henry Hoze | 5 | Elias Reimal | 15 |
| William Montgomry | 2 | Peter Hoze | 2 | John Reimal | 13 |
| Jacob Weyand | 3 | Henry Sisler | 3 | Philip Reimal | 7 |
| Daniel Sneyder | 1 | Charles Hederick | 1mos. | Jacob Reimal | 3mos. |
| Henry Miller | 10 | Ludwig Wise | 9 | Andrew Maggry | 3 |
| George Fackler | 15 | Jacob Trapp | 6 | Tobias Ritter | 11 |
| Peter Fackler | 5 | Henry Trapp | 4 | Jacob Ritter | 5 |

| Name | Age | Name | Age | Name | Age |
|---|---|---|---|---|---|
| Andrew Leyder | 6 | Baltzer Mowen | 15 | Daniel Mowen | 11 |
| Jacob Leyder | 4 | George Mowen | 13 | Peter Mowen | 8 |
| John Leyder | 2mos. | | | Jacob Hart | 6mos. |

## FEMALES AGE 16 AND UNDER

| Name | Age | Name | Age | Name | Age |
|---|---|---|---|---|---|
| Mary Stull | 2 | Catherin Rench | 16 | Sophia Dilles | 7 |
| Madilta Stull | 4mos. | Ester Rench | 10 | Dorethea Dilles | 5 |
| Sarah Seiman | 4 | Catharina Rench | 12 | Margret Lekron | 5? |
| Elisabeth Brughin | 16 | Elisabeth Rench | 10 | Dorethea Lekron | 2 |
| Elisabeth Beeker | 4 | Mary Wise | 10 | Catharine Roush | 15 |
| Margaretha Meguire | 6 | Elisabeth Wise | 8 | Susanna Roush | 14 |
| Elisabeth Christman | 1 | Catharin Wise | 6 | Magdalena Roush | 7 |
| Cathrin Reitenauer | 15 | Margaret Evely | 2 | Margret Roush | 2 |
| Rosina Reitenauer | 11 | Elisabeth Mull | 4 | Elisabeth Liphard | 13 |
| Elisabeth Smith | 2 | Catherin Mull | 3 | Sarah Hutson | 1 |
| Salome Smith | 1 | Susanna Rench | 10 | Jane Dimbleton | 16 |
| Magdalane Smith | 6mos. | Elisabeth Rench | 2 | Margaret Shenafield | 7 |
| Susanna Kern | 4 | Ann Green | 2 | Susanna Shenafield | 5 |
| Susanna Prakunier | 15 | Margret Young | 8 | Catherina Shenafield | 2 |
| Elisabeth Prakunier | 13 | Ester Beaghtle | 16 | Hanna Thomson | 3 |
| Barbara Prakunier | 6 | Susanna Beaghtle | 14 | Margret Deibley | 12 |
| Magdalena Draxeixel | 14 | Ann Beaghtle | 12 | Catherina Deibley | 9 |
| Catharina Draxser | 2 | Elisabeth Beaghtle | ? | Lettica Sprigg | 14 |
| Elisabeth Householder | 15 | Barbara Beaghtle | 5 | Corbin Sprigg | 9 |
| Cathrin Householder | 11 | Sarah Brendlinger | 15 | Ann Sprigg | 10 |
| Barbara Householder | 9 | Christianna Brendlinger | 13 | Hannah Sprigg | 6 |
| Susanna Reitenauer | 10 | Elisabeth Brendlinger | 5 | Isabella Frasier | 9 |
| Dorothy Reitenauer | 8 | Catherin Shoomaker | 4 | Elisabeth Frasier | 7 |
| Mary Reitenauer | 8mos. | Susanna Shoomaker | 3 | Catherina Lauman | 4 |
| Christianna Hoffman | 15 | Elisabeth Wise | 12 | Elisabeth Lauman | 1mos. |
| Margret Ekenbergh | 5 | Elisabeth Funck | 3mos. | Martha Dugles | 16 |
| Mary Gutry | 16 | Elisabeth Snyedor | 13 | Rachel Dugles | 10 |
| Sarah Gutry | 11 | Susanna Sailor | 15 | Mary Dugles | 5 |
| Sarah Jane Gutry | 1 | Cathaina Urrvine | 9 | Catharin Koenig | 15 |
| Rachel Sciles | 10 | Margret Nave | 15 | Mary Koenig | 6? |
| Cathrin Sciles | 1 | Sophia Nave | 8 | Elisabeth Koenig | 4 |
| Catharina Friend | 16 | Cathrin Dusinger | 6mos. | Magdalena Koenig | 2 |
| Elisabeth Friend | 10 | Barbara Sneydor | 6 | Catharina Smith | 8 |
| Dorothy Feigely | 9 | Susanna Sneydor | 2 | Mary Scot | 12 |
| Christiana Feigely | 7 | Susanna Where | 11 | Martha Scott | 8 |
| Eve Reitenauer | 3 | Christiana Where | 8 | Susanna Beaker | 7 |
| Elisabeth Reitenauer | 2 | Elisabeth Where | 2 | Elisabeth Beaker | 3 |
| Eliz. Magdalena Reitenauer | 2 | Mary Garment | 6 | Margret Hiffner | 13 |
| Rosina Reitenauer | 1mos. | Rebecca Garment | 1 | Elisabeth Hiffner | 10 |
| Mary Hix | 2 | Ester Gross | 11 | Mary Hiffner | 6 |
| Susanna Hix | 4mos. | Elisabeth Gross | 9? | Catherin Hiffner | 4mos. |
| Margret Stertzman | 3 | Elsy Gross | 8 | Mary Snydor | 16 |
| July Stertzman | 2 | Susanna Gross | 6 | Margret Hittler | 7 |
| Barbara Myer | 15 | Ruth Beard | 16 | Eve Hittler | 3 |
| Christianna Sneyder | 7 | Mary Dilles | 13 | Cathrin Jacob | 9 |
| Elisabeth Sneyder | 4 | Elisabeth Dilles | 11 | Mary Reeber | 13 |
| Mary Sneyder | 1 | Magdalena Dilles | 9 | Mary Reap | 14 |
| | | | | Eve Reap | 3 |
| | | | | Catharin Shees | 14 |

| Name | Age | Name | Age | Name | Age |
|---|---|---|---|---|---|
| Elisabeth Shees | 12 | Elisabeth Bell | 5 | Jane Odear | 4 |
| Magdalena Shees | 2 | Margaretha Bell | 3 | Catharina Althard | 13 |
| Cathrin Daruse | 3 | Margaretha Dile | 6 | Margaretha Metler | 12 |
| Elisabeth Fore | 11 | Elisabeth Robinson | 10mos. | Lorey Caldwell | 11 |
| Susanna Fore | 9 | Mary Gneadig | 5 | Jane Caldwell | 8 |
| Cathrin Fore | 3 | Susana Gneadig | 1 | Catharine Shryock | 14 |
| Susanna Leyder | 12 | Margaretha Sneyder | 13 | Mary Smith | 13 |
| Elisabeth Leyder | 7? | Elisabeth Sneyder | 9 | Julianna Steidinger | 15 |
| Magdalene Leyder | 5 | Mary Sneyder | 5 | Magdalana Where | 16 |
| Mary Leyder | 2 | Elisabeth Hausholder | 2 | Margretha Clark | 6 |
| Cathrin Bentz | 8 | Elisabeth Weyand | 1 | Jane Clark | 1 |
| Margret Sheafer | 6mos. | Margaretha Miller | 15 | Catherina Sneydor | 13 |
| Cathrin Seitz | 14 | Mary Miller | 12 | Elisabeth Pullin | 9 |
| Hannah Seitz | 10 | Elisabeth Seller | 11 | Elisabeth Davis | 8 |
| Margret Leiser | 5 | Magdalena Fackler | 14 | Magdalane Hoze | 14 |
| Cathrin Leiser | 7 | Margaretha Fackler | 11 | Juliana Hoze | 13 |
| Christianna Leiser | 4 | Barbara Fackler | 8 | Susanna Hoze | 10 |
| Susanna Leiser | 3 | Hellina Fackler | 6mos.? | Mary Mantle | 16 |
| Elisabeth Bread | 1 | Susanna Bouman | 11 | Susanna Wise | 13 |
| Christiana Bley | 1 | Catharina Gessinger | 7 | Elisabeth Wise | 11 |
| Mary Steck | 2 | Elisabeth Miller | 7 | Catharin Fackler | 10 |
| Sophia Fesler | 8 | Eve Miller | 6 | Elisabeth Fackler | 8 |
| Mary Fesler | 4 | Elisabeth Wagoner | 10 | Susanna Fackler | 6 |
| Sophia Sander | 14 | Juley Need | 10 | Catharina Hoefligh | 5 |
| Elisabeth Sander | 12 | Sharlote Need | 8 | Susanna Shryock | 5 |
| Barbara Rohrer | 8 | Elisabeth Link | 1 | Ann Shryock | 3 |
| Eve Sneydor | 12 | Margarethe Campbell | under 1 | Elisabeth Shryock | 2 |
| Ann Hellin | 13 | Elisabeth Kogh | | Catharina Alter | 3 |
| Jane Hellin | 12 | Elisabeth Barkes | 5 | Mary Alter | 1 |
| Susanne Hellin | 8 | Margareth Kogh | 4 | Elisabeth Hoze | 4 |
| Dorothea Hoober | 15 | Elisabeth Long | 10 | Magdaline Young | 10 |
| Christiana Hoober | 13 | Margaretha Long | 3 | Ann Sisler | 5 |
| Catharina Heiser | 11 | Elisabeth Woltz | 6 | Catharina Sisler | 6mos. |
| Elisabeth Heiser | under 1 | Mary Woltz | 2 | Elisabeth Heterick | 1 |
| Elisabeth Stineseiver | 3 | Dorathea Shooman | 10 | Cathrin Wise | 3 |
| Catharine Stineseiver | 2 | Magdalane Shooman | 7 | Elisabeth Wise | 2 |
| Mary Stineseiver | 10wks. | Magdalane Smith | 8mos. | Christiana Wise | 7 |
| Margareth Kilin | 15 | Susanna Blackburn | 12 | Mary Wise | 4 |
| Elisabeth Unsel | 3 | Mary Becks | 1 | Elisabeth Trapp | 8 |
| Elisabeth Zinn | 1 | Cathaina Herman | 3 | Susanna Alter | 5 |
| Catharina Bardon | 1 | Mary Herman | 1 | Elizabeth Alter | 2 |
| Barbara Fisher | 15 | Margaretha Haut | 14 | Elisabeth Walter | 1mos. |
| Magdalena Fisher | 8 | Magdalina Creily | 1 | Catharina Yegley | 9 |
| Elisabeth Oster | 7 | Margartha Reight | 1 | Elisabeth Shitz | 4 |
| Catharine Oster | 5 | Magdalena Emry | 2 | Cathrin Shitz | 6mos. |
| Mary Oster | 1 | Elisabeth Emry | 3mos. | Catharina Heinsman | 4 |
| Catharina Belshoober | 4 | Elisabeth Katz | 2 | Margret Pope | 6 |
| Mary Herry | 3 | Catharina Katz | 6mos. | Cathrin Shryock | 3 |
| Sarah Scot | 6 | Ann Gray | 1 | Mary Shryock | 1 |
| Ann Scot | 4 | Catharina Sneyder | 8 | Christiana Mantle | 9 |
| Catherine Miller | 5 | Elisabeth Sneyder | 5 | Cathrin Deibelbies | 3mos. |
| Elisabeth Goll | 1 | Elisabeth Muffet | 2 | Fanny Burgess | 7 |
| Sophia Silhard | 12 | Margaretha Muffet | 6mos. | Elisabeth Burgess | 2 |
| Juley Bell | 9 | Ann Odear | 7 | Mary Ann Burgess | 5mos. |
| | | Jane Barkes | 4 | | |

| Name | Age | Name | Age | Name | Age |
|---|---|---|---|---|---|
| Rebecca Rogers | 7 | Mary Rohrer | 5 | Cathrin Sneider | 11 |
| Magdaline Hoze | 6 | Ann Rohrer | 4 | Christianna Sneyder | 7 |
| Catharina Bower | 12 | Elisabeth Rohrer | 2 | Mary Sneyder | 4 |
| Margaret Bower | 10 | Magdalena Braun | 7 | Elisabeth Sneyder | 3 |
| Magdalana Bower | 9 | Cathrin Braun | 4 | Margret Ritter | 14 |
| Susanna Bower | 8 | Mary Kline | ? | Elisabeth Ritter | 3 |
| Mary Stineseiver | 5 | Magdalena Kline | 10 | Barbara Ritter | 4mos. |
| Elisabeth Dile | 3 | Elisabeth Kline | 6 | Susanna Leyder | 12 |
| Catharina Where | 7 | Cathrin Kline | 4 | Judith Leyder | 10 |
| Catharina RineHard | 8 | Susanna Kline | 1 | Cathrin Leyder | 8 |
| Ann Rinenard | 1 | Litha Stull | 11 | Elisabeth Leyder | 7 |
| Ann Rohrer | 7 | Prudence Ross | 7 | Julyanna Leyder | 6 |
| Cathrin Rohrer | 5 | Mary Ross | 5 | Eve Leyder | 4 |
| Elisabeth Rohrer | under-1 | Mary Lannabach | 13 | Elisabeth Leyder | 7 |
| Cathrin Klaber | 6 | Catharina Lannabach | 9 | Mary Mowen | 1 |
| Mary Klaber | 1 | Susanna Lannabach | 7 | Magdalena Mowen | 4 |
| | | Elisabeth Lannabach | 4 | | |

In 1814 the name of Elizabeth Town was changed to Hagerstown and this is now in Washington County, Maryland.

## LOWER POTOMACK HUNDRED

Taken by Levin Magruder and completed by August 22, 1776.   Sworn before Robert Peters.

| Name | Age | Name | Age | Name | Age |
|---|---|---|---|---|---|
| Robert Anderson | 65 | Richard Blacklock | 26 | Samuel Bucey | 20 |
| John Austin | 37 | Richard Blacklock Jr. | 3 | Thomas Blockley | 50 |
| William Aubrey | 40 | Moses Beasley | 60 | Nehemiah Blockley | 3 |
| Joseph Atkins | 40 | Isaac Brook | 17 | Monjoy Baley | 21 |
| Edward Adams | 33 | Zepheniah Burch | 26 | Philip Bryan | 23 |
| Alexander Adams | 30 | John Barber | 60 | David Bloyce | 24 |
| John Adams | 1 | Barney Barber | 7 | William Bloyce | 1 |
| John Ahare | 13 | George Beall Jr. | 46 | John Broadie | 55 |
| Thomas Austin | 15 | Alexander Beall | 8 | William Baley | 30 |
| Zechariah | 13 | Erasmus Beall | 14 | Samuel Baley | 2 |
| James Austin | 11 | Hezekiah Beall | 10 | William Belt | ? |
| John Kindrick Austin | 6 | Thomas Brook Beall | 8 | William Colyar | 44 |
| Hezekiah Austin | 4 | Col. George Beall | 81 | William Colyar Jr. | 17 |
| Amos Austin | 1 | Josiah Beall | 18 | John Colyar | 11 |
| Alexander Austin | 19 | Thom.Beall of Saml. | 36 | James Colyar | 6 |
| Joseph Benton | 32 | John Brook | 7 | Thomas Clagett | 63 |
| Benjamin Benton | 16 | Josiah Beall | 6 | Nathan Clagett | 20 |
| Mordecai Benton | 10? | Edward Baley | 23 | John Clagett | 32 |
| Nathan Benton | 12 | Bashual Badfoot | 22 | Thomas Clagett | 5 |
| Erasmus Benton | 10 | James Brown | 25 | Ninian Clagett | 2 |
| Hezekiah Benton | 8 | William Brown | 20 | Arthur Carnes | 19 |
| Leonard Belt | 45 | Gregory Bonnifield | 50 | Rich.Keene Clagett | 30 |
| James Blackmore | 33 | Henry Bonnifield | 10 | Christopher Cocendorer | 24 |
| Lawrence Owen | 8 | Arnold Bonnifield | 8 | Michael Cocendofer | 25 |
| Samuel Blackmore | 4 | William Bonnifield | 6 | John Cocendofer | 3 |
| James Blackmore | 2 | William Brodie | 30 | Michael Cocendofer | 2 |
| Prime Barnes | 18 | Joshua Bucey | 65 | William Carnes | 25 |
| Henry Beall | 28 | John Eucey | 25 | John Cheshire | 23 |

| Name | Age | Name | Age | Name | Age |
|---|---|---|---|---|---|
| Harmon Clark | 47 | Joseph Glaze | 64 | Henry Hardy | 10 |
| Leonard Clark | 21 | William Glaze | 23 | David Hennes | 49 |
| Thomas Cowan | 24 | Benjamin Gittings | 40 | John Hennes | 17 |
| Arthur Conwell | 25 | Kinsey Gittings | 7 | Benjamin Hennes | 15 |
| George Clark | 21 | Joshua Gragg | 42 | Henry Hennes | 14 |
| Lancelot Crown | 26 | George Gringul | 32 | Giles Hill | 52 |
| Josiah Crown | 2 | Jeremiah Gittings | 30 | John Hill | 1 |
| Thomas Clark | 30 | Colmore Gittings | 14 | Jacob Hedley | 25 |
| Benedict Clark | 23 | Erasmus Gittings | 1 | Charles Hickey | 28 |
| James Collings | 33 | Joseph Gill | 49 | Andrew Heugh | 49 |
| John Collings | 7 | John Gill | 14 | John Heugh | 11 |
| James Collings Jr. | 5 | Joseph Gill Jr. | 13 | Andrew Heugh Jr. | 6 |
| Nathan Collings | 22 | William Gill | 8 | John Hurdle | 9 |
| Thomas Collings | 13 | Thomas Gill | 6 | William Hurdle | 5 |
| John Collings | 60 | Samuel Gill | 1 | Leonard Hurdle | 3 |
| Joshua Collings | 17 | Walter Smith | | John Jackson | 20 |
| Zechariah Collings | 10 | Greenfield | 45 | James Jackson | 17 |
| John Chapple | 30 | Charles Greenfield | 15 | William Jackson | 11 |
| William Chapple | 2 | Thomas Greenfield | 13 | John Johnston | 35 |
| Vincent Caster | 67 | Walter Greenfield Jr. | 9 | Joseph Johnston | 9 |
| William Caster | 16 | Thomas Graves | 47 | William Johnston | 11 |
| Thomas Caster | 10 | Peregrine Graves | 26 | John Johnston | 2 |
| John Clagett | 63 | John Graves | 16 | Charles C.D. Jones | 64 |
| John Clagett Jr. | 22 | Humphrey Graves | 13 | Henry Jones | 27 |
| Walter Clagett | 12 | Joshua Graves | 12 | Willie Janes | 1 |
| Zadock Clagett | 8 | George Graves | 9 | John Courts Jones | 21 |
| Henry Chapple | 60 | Thomas Gilham | 42 | Charles Courts Jones | 13 |
| Thomas Chapple | 21 | Jacob Gilham | 13 | Charles R.C. Jones | 65 |
| George Chapple | 16 | Benjamin Gilham | 5 | Henry Jeanes | 23 |
| Thomas Duly | 36 | Thomas Gilham Jr. | 3 | Thomas Johns | 39 |
| Thomas Duly Jr. | 1 | John Gilham | 1 | Richard Johns | 1 |
| Francis Duis | 33 | Joseph Godfrey | 19 | Stephen Karr | 22 |
| Michael Downing | 17 | Kinsey Hance | 24 | Stophel Keizer | 30 |
| Samuel Duckett | 25 | Benjamin Harris | 34 | Jacob Keizer | 8 |
| John Day | 8 | John Cramphin Harris | 3 | John Keizer | 7 |
| John Douglass | 10 | John Higdon | 60 | Stophel Keizer Jr. | 1 |
| Robert Douglass | 8 | John Higdon Jr. | 20 | Matthew Kennett | 25 |
| Benjamin Earley | 43 | Joseph Higdon | 17 | John Keizer | 37 |
| William Ellson | 21 | Peter Higdon | 11 | Jacob Keizer | 15 |
| Samuel Evans | 51 | Edward Hughes | 25 | John Keizer Jr. | 1 |
| Zechariah Evans | 17 | John Henman | 23 | Samuel King | 23 |
| John Evans | 16 | William Hurley | 16 | John Lewis | 4 |
| James Evans | 14 | John Hawkins | 38 | Thomas Lingoe | 16 |
| George Evans | 12 | Thomas Hawkins | 7 | John Lingoe | 11 |
| Samuel Evans | 9 | Alexander Hurley | 7 | Thomas Lewis | 34 |
| Thomas Flint | 45 | George Harris | 27 | Benedict Woodward | |
| Robert Fulton | 55 | Thomas Hackett | 28 | Lewis | 4 |
| James Fulton | 11 | William Harp | 47 | Thomas Lewis Jr. | 2 |
| George Frederick | 44 | William Harp | 17 | William Lewis | 20 |
| George Frederick Jr. | 6 | Josiah Harp | 14 | Wm. Fardoe Lewis | 20 |
| Nicholas Frederick | 2 | Erasmus Harp | 11 | James Long | 45 |
| Elisha Fowler | 42 | Samuel Harp | 6 | Thomas Long | 17 |
| Elisha Fowler Jr. | 8 | Philip Harp | 21 | John Long | 4 |
| Thomas Fowler | 6 | Richard Hurdle | 35 | Charles Long | 1 |

| Name | Age | Name | Age | Name | Age |
|---|---|---|---|---|---|
| James Langton | 43 | Matthew Maddox | 26 | Robert Robertson | 34 |
| John Langton | 17 | William Masters | 25 | Zechariah Robertson | 14 |
| James Langton Jr. | 11 | John Masters | 1 | Daniel Robertson | 8 |
| Thomas Langton | 9 | Zechariah Mockby | 24 | Samuel Robertson | 2 |
| William Langton | 4 | Zephaniah Mockby | 19 | Nathan Robertson | 1 |
| Aaron Lanham | 45 | John Mockby | 3 | William Rowan | 22 |
| Walter Lanham | 5 | Dennis Mockby | 1 | Nathan Robertson | 24 |
| Charles Low | 25 | Jacob Mills | 25 | Robert Robertson | 4 |
| Sam Wade Magruder | 48 | Hezekiah Magruder | 47 | Middleton Robertson | 2 |
| Levin Magruder | 17 | Daniel Magruder | 12 | Alexander Ross | 25 |
| Charles Magruder | 15 | George Magruder | 10 | Samuel Sole | 25 |
| Brooke Magruder | 12 | Ninian Magruder | 25 | William Scoffield | 40 |
| George Magruder | 10 | Nathaniel Magruder | | William Scoffield | 1 |
| Patrick Magruder | 8 | of Ninian | 54 | Patrick Stephens | 25 |
| Thomas Magruder | 5 | Enoch Magruder | 17 | William Steel | 33 |
| James Mulkehy | 25 | Nathaniel Magruder Jr | 15 | Richard Steel | 8 |
| Nath. Magruder of Alex. | 50 | Theodore Middleton | 17 | William Steel | 4 |
| Walter Magruder | 16 | James Nicholls | 50 | John Steel | 2 |
| Aquila Magruder | 2 | Thomas Nicholls | 9 | James Shearlock | 31 |
| John McCormack | 24 | James Nicholls Jr. | 7 | Thomas Sandsbery | 28 |
| James McCormack | 2 | John Nicholls | 4 | Middleton Sandsbery | 2 |
| Sam Bruce Magruder | 30 | John Nicholls | 26 | Solomon Sandsbery | 1 |
| James Magruder | 8 | Thomas Nicholls | 23 | John Sargo | 18 |
| Ninian Magruder | 4 | Henry Nicholls | 7 | Bryan Steuart | 27 |
| Samuel Magruder | 2 | John Nicholls | 4 | Jonathan Sparrow | 30 |
| Zechariah Magruder | 65 | Baruch Odle | 21 | Solomon Sparrow | 10 |
| Wm. Beall Magruder | 39 | Nicholas Pierce | 40 | William Sparrow | 4 |
| Richard Magruder | 26 | William Poland | 20 | Jonthan West | |
| Josiah Magruder | 24 | William R.C. Parker | 45 | Sparrow | 2 |
| Normond Bruce Magruder | 22 | David Parker | 11 | Rich. Lewis Sparrow | 1 |
| Nathaniel Magruder | 20 | William Parker Jr. | 7 | Benj. Battey Sparrow | 23 |
| Stephen Mahall | 37 | John Rutherford | 23 | Stephen Smith | 43 |
| Elias Magruder | 50 | John Ramington | 25 | Matthew Smith | 26 |
| Samuel Magruder 3rd | 69 | James Ramington | 1 | James Shehone | 55 |
| John Magruder | 67 | Robert Ridgway | 60 | Richard Shehone | 6 |
| Archibald Magruder | 25 | Isaac Ridgway | 24 | Joseph Shehone | 1 |
| Ezekiel Magruder | 19 | Jonathan Ridgway | 27 | Nathaniel Slicer | 62 |
| Thos. Hughes McCrown | 20 | Joseph Ridgway | 22 | James Slicer | 25 |
| Edward Magruder | 33 | Thomas Riggs | 9 | Nathaniel Slicer Jr | 2 |
| Ninian Magruder | 6 | George Reed | 23 | John Sutton | 29 |
| John Magruder | 1 | Walter Riley | 24 | Robert Sutton | 27 |
| Andrew Moore | 20 | James Ray | 52 | Thomas Smith | 26 |
| Adam Mires | 19 | Robert Riggs | 14 | William Summers | 25 |
| Barney Maffatt | 30 | James Riggs | 35 | Thomas Simmonds | 20 |
| William Maffatt | 3 | Basil Riggs | 2 | David Smith | 40 |
| Zechariah Maccubbin | 25 | Zechariah Robertson | 11 | John Spyvey | 35 |
| Thomas Maccubbin | 28 | James Robertson | 13 | Jonathan Spyvey | 5 |
| Zachariah Maccubbin Jr. | 7 | William Roberts | 1 | John Spyvey | 1 |
| Samuel Maccattee | 22 | Hugh Riley | 50 | William Spyvey | 2 |
| Charles Maccattee | 16 | James Riley | 13 | Zadock Soper | 25 |
| Col. John Murdock | 42 | George Campden Riley | 8 | John Smith | 50 |
| John McDonald | 30 | Amos Riley | 6 | Nicholas Smith | 1 |
| John McDonale | 30 | Isaac Riley | 2 | Charles Smith | 13 |
| William McDonald | 50 | Thomas Ray | 55 | James Sung | 15 |
| Thomas MacDonald | 3 | Aaron Russel | 17 | Hezekiah Speaks | 19 |

| Name | Age | Name | Age | Name | Age |
|---|---|---|---|---|---|
| William Styles | 41 | Benjamin Walker | 13 | Martha Bonnifield | 16 |
| John Styles | 13 | Jonathan Walker | 4 | Dorcas Bonnifield | 3 |
| Thomas Styles | 11 | George Walker | 2 | Eleanor Bucey | 60 |
| William Styles Jr. | 7 | _____ Walker | 15 | Mary Blockley | 33 |
| Thomas Sullivan | 23 | Thomas Woodward | 30 | Elizabeth Blockley | 14 |
| William Summers | 25 | James Wood | 32 | Mary Blockley | 6 |
| Joshua Shoemaker | 23 | Nathaniel Wallace | 22 | Mary Bloyce | 20 |
| Jacob Shoemaker | 3 | William Wallace | 18 | Sarah Colyar | 43 |
| Thomas Shoemaker | 1 | James Wallace | 39 | Keziah Colyar | 20 |
| William ____ (servant) | 40 | John Wallace | 5 | Sarah Colyar | 15 |
| William Talbot | 35 | William Wallace | 40 | Elizabeth Colyar | 13 |
| Edward Talbot | 11 | Alexander Wallace | 14 | Lucy Colyar | 4 |
| Nathaniel Talbot | 10 | William Wallace | 12 | Ann Colyar | 2 |
| Enock Talbot | 7 | James Wallace | 6 | Jeane Cramphin | 66 |
| Daniel Talbot | 4 | Charles Wallace | 3 | Ann Clagett | 63 |
| William Talbot Jr. | 1 | Robert Wallace | 1 | Mary Clagett | 27 |
| William Taylor | 14 | John Williams | 48 | Mary Clagett | 8 |
| Benjamin Taylor | 13 | James William | 2 | Martha Clagett | 24 |
| Edward Tucker | 56 | Michael Wiser | 17 | Sarah Claggett | 5 |
| Alexander Tucker | 21 | Abraham Wilson | 1 | Elizabeth Clagett | 4 |
| James Topping | 62 | James Young | 25 | Hannah Cocendofer | 23 |
| William Thomas | 24 | Peter Young | 17 | Mary Cocendofer | 1 |
| Walter Tucker | 34 | Abraham Young | 25 | Aray Carnes | 18 |
| William Tucker | 10 | | | Judea Canady | 20 |
| Rezin Tucker | 8 | Elizabeth Adams | 26 | Ann Canady | 1 |
| Osborn Tucker | 6 | Mary Adams | 2 | Sarah Cheshire | 21 |
| Walter Tucker | 4 | Charity Austin | 44 | Mary Clark | 38 |
| Nathaniel Tucker | 2 | Hezekiah Austin | 18 | Elizabeth Clark | 2 |
| Benjamin Tucker | 1 | Amelia Austin | 8 | Elizabeth Clark | 29 |
| Benjamin Tucker | 22 | Mary Austin | 80 | Hannah Clark | 32 |
| Joseph Tucker | 25 | Elizabeth Adkins | 40 | Grace Clark | 12 |
| John Tucker | 4 | Mary Ann | 12 | Rebecca Clark | 24 |
| David Thompson | 25 | Elizabeth Benton | 48 | Mary Clark | 2 |
| Hezekiah Tucker | 25 | Elizabeth Benton | 6 | Mary Crown | 20 |
| Joseph Townsend | 24 | Rebecca Belt | 47 | Elizabeth Crown | 1 |
| William Turner | 22 | Rachel Blackmore | 28 | Jemima Collings | 25 |
| Richard Talbott | 31 | Elizabeth Blackmore | 6 | Cassandra Collings | 11 |
| George Ummell | 30 | Mary Blacklock | 20 | Elizabeth Collings | 4 |
| John Humphreys | 20 | Elizabeth Blacklock | 1 | Mary Collings | 2 |
| Herbert Wallace | 50 | Elizabeth Beasley | 65 | Elizabeth Collings | 50 |
| Zepheniah Wallace | 25 | Elizabeth Batts | 75 | Rachel Collings | 24 |
| James Wallace | 24 | Elizabeth Barber | 39 | Virlinda Chapple | 20 |
| Herbert Alex Wallace | 20 | Mary Barber | 16 | Sarah Chapple | 1 |
| William Wallace | 15 | Dorothy Barber | 11 | Elizabeth Caster | 52 |
| Nathaniel Wallace | 15 | Ann Beall | 42 | Margaret Caster | 13 |
| John Wallace | 8 | Elizabeth Beall | 12 | Mary Caster | 8 |
| William Wilcoxon | 43 | Anne Beall | 5 | Sarah Clagett | 52 |
| John Wilcoxon | 20 | Violinda Beall | 36 | Sarah Clagett | 24 |
| Josiah Wilcoxon | 18 | Eleanor Beall | 10 | Ann Clagett | 10 |
| Amos Wilcoxon | 2 | Lucy Beall | 9 | Uphane Chapple | 55 |
| Jesse Wilcoxon | 38 | Ann Beall | 5 | Rebecca Chapple | 19 |
| Thomas Wilcoxon | 3 | Elizabeth Beall | 4 | Margaret Duley | 20 |
| Jesse Wilcoxon | 1 | Sarah Bonnifield | 48 | Mary Dunley | 20 |
| John Woodward | 68 | Elizabeth Bonnifield | 20 | Ann Duckett | 22 |
| Benedict Woodward | 22 | Sarah Bonnifield | 13 | Katharine Day | 71 |

| Name | Age | Name | Age | Name | Age |
|---|---|---|---|---|---|
| Sarah Day | 40 | Chloe Graves | 23 | Sarah Johnston | 11 |
| Mary Day | 16 | Elizabeth Graves | 17 | Eleanor Johnston | 9 |
| Ann Douglass | 29 | Cassandria Graves | 7 | Ann Johnston | 1 |
| Margaret Evans | 23 | Lucy Grimes | 35 | Esther Johnston | 30 |
| Sarah Early | 43 | Mary Gilham | 38 | Ann Johnston | 13 |
| Rachel Earley | 15 | Elizabeth | 14 | Charity Jones | 33 |
| Elizabeth Earley | 12 | Margaret Gilham | 11 | Eleanor Jones | 13 |
| Johannah Elder | 57 | Mary Gilham | 7 | Malintha Jones | 10 |
| Sarah Elder | 16 | Jeane Harris | 30 | Elizabeth Jones | 8 |
| Hannah Elder | 13 | Jeane Harris | 5 | Keziah Jones | 6 |
| Eleanor Elder | 27 | Rachel Harris | 7 | Elizabeth Jones | 49 |
| Amelia Elder | 7 | Sarah Harris | 1 | Mary Ann Jones | 23 |
| Tressia Elder | 5 | Mary Higdon | 50 | Sarah Jones | 19 |
| Hadassy Elder | 3 | Susanna Higdon | 23 | Henrietta Jones | 16 |
| Ann Evans | 50 | Mary Higdon | 14 | Eleanor Coats Jones | 15 |
| Hannah Evans | 11 | Katharine Higdon | 8 | Susanna Courts Jones | 8 |
| Ann Evans | 10 | Amelia Hughes | 24 | Elizabeth(Servant) | 51 |
| Margaret Evans | 7 | Elizabeth L.Hawkins | 30 | Mary Jones | 68 |
| Mary Evans | 6 | Katharine Harris | 23 | Mary Jeanes | 21 |
| Ruth Evans | 5 | Sarah Harris | 1 | Sarah Johns | 25 |
| Rachel Evans | 4 | Priscilla Harp | 48 | Mary Johns | 3 |
| Eleanor Evans | 3 | Esther Harp | 19 | Margaret Keizer | 30 |
| Margaret Perrol | 20 | Ann Harp | 10 | Rebecca Keizer | 33 |
| Mary Fulton | 48 | Sarah Harp | 1 | Elizabeth Keizer | 11 |
| Uney Frederick | 35 | Eleanor Hardy | 8 | Susanna Keizer | 8 |
| Elizabeth Frederick | 12 | Sarah Hennes | 40 | Ann Keizer | 4 |
| Mary Frederick | 8 | Sarah Hennes | 12 | Mary King | 19 |
| Margaret Frederick | 4 | Elizabeth Hennes | 6 | Rachel Lingoe | 14 |
| Molley Frederick | 10 | Katharine Hennes | 2 | Mary Lewis | 20 |
| Mary Fowler | 42 | Sophia Hill | 24 | Lucy Lee | 50 |
| Mary Fowler | 16 | Ann House | 75 | Ruth Lee | 17 |
| Rachel Fowler | 14 | Sarah Hugh | 45 | Elizabeth Lee | 16 |
| Rebecca Fowler | 3 | Elizabeth Heugh | 21 | Lucy Lee | 12 |
| Ruth Glaze | 60 | Sarah Heugh | 19 | Ann Long | 45 |
| Dorcas Glaze | 20 | Ann Heugh | 17 | Mary Long | 9 |
| Ann Gittings | 36 | Margaret Heugh | 15 | Elizabeth Langton | 44 |
| Amelia Gittings | 13 | Jeane Heugh | 12 | Ann Langton | 15 |
| Virlinda Gittings | 11 | Mary Heugh | 8 | Elizabeth Langton | 13 |
| Elizabeth Gittings | 2 | Harriot Heugh | 2 | Eleanor Langton | 10 |
| Sarah Gittings | 3 | Susanna Hurdle | 30 | Elizabeth Lanham | 25 |
| Jeane Gittings | 34 | Ann Hurdle | 7 | Eleanor Lanham | 4 |
| Virlinda Gittings | 15 | Priscilla Hurdle | 2 | Elizabeth Lanham | 2 |
| Cavia Gittings | 12 | Ann Hedley | 30 | Lucy Magruder | 38 |
| Liley Gittings | 9 | Henrietta James | 16 | Elizabeth Magruder | 20 |
| Cassandra Gittings | 7 | Mary Jackson | 45 | Ann Magruder | 19 |
| Jeane Gittings | 5 | Mary Jackson | 16 | Sarah Magruder | 13 |
| Hannah Gregg | 26 | Susanna Jackson | 15 | Lucy Magruder | 6 |
| Ann Gill | 49 | Ann Jackson | 12 | Mary Magruder | 1 |
| Sarah Gill | 10 | Ann Johnston | 16 | Elizabeth Magruder | 38 |
| Katharine Garrott | 4 | Sarah Johnston | 26 | Elizabeth Magruder | 6 |
| Keziah Greenfield | 24 | Precious Johnston | 7 | Lethe Magruder | 4 |
| Eleanor Greenfield | 19 | Virlinda Johnston | 2 | Eve McCormack | 19 |
| Sarah Greenfield | 1 | Ann Johnston | 36 | Rebecca Magruder | 40 |
| Jeane Graves | 65 | Elizabeth Johnston | 13 | Margaret Magruder | 65 |

| Name | | Name | | Name | |
|---|---|---|---|---|---|
| Jeane Magruder | 58 | Mary Russel | 26 | Redy Smith | 5 |
| Mary Magruder | 28 | Sarah Reed | 22 | Sarah Smith | 20 |
| Priscilla Magruder | 4 | Priscilla Reed | 2 | Mary Steel | 8 |
| Susanna Maffatt | 22 | Elizabeth Reed | 1 | Priscilla Steel | 5 |
| Rachel Maffatt | 1 | Mary Ray | 72 | Susanna Steel | 3 |
| Martha Maccubbin | 28 | Ann Ray | 18 | Mary Speaks | 18 |
| Mary Maccubbin | 1 | Mary Riggs | 27 | Elizabeth Speaks | 41 |
| Hellen Maccubbin | 25 | Maxemelia Riggs | 7 | Virlinda Styles | 33 |
| Ann Maccattee | 55 | Mary Riggs | 4 | Sarah Styles | 2 |
| Mary Maccatee | 22 | Virlinda Robinson | 32 | Montha Summers | 23 |
| Elizabeth Maccatee | 24 | Sarah Riggs | 50 | Mary Shoemaker | 21 |
| Lucy Maccatee | 18 | Sarah Riley | 39 | Elizabeth Thomas | 34 |
| Ann McDonald | 26 | Sarah Riley | 18 | Elizabeth Tucker | 56 |
| Sarah McDonald | 4 | Eleanor Riley | 15 | Eleanor Tucker | 14 |
| Mary McDonald | 1 | Esther Riley | 13 | Margaret Topping | 62 |
| Katharine Murphey | 29 | Martha Riley | 4 | Jude Topping | 24 |
| Elizabeth McDonald | 30 | Jemima Ray | 22 | Susanna Taylor | 69 |
| Henrietta Martus | 22 | Mary Ray | 56 | Susanna Tucker | 26 |
| Rachel Maddox | 23 | Rachel Robinson | 36 | Elizabeth Tucker | 28 |
| Dorcas Maddox | 2 | Mary Robinson | 12 | Susanna Tucker | 2 |
| Barsheba Masters | 23 | Susanna Robinson | 4 | Elizabeth Tucker | 1 |
| Margaret Masters | 50 | Elizabeth Robinson | 23 | Elizabeth Tucker | 31 |
| Ann Mockby | 24 | Eleanor Robinson | 1 | Mary Tucker | 35 |
| Joice Mockby | 9 | Eleanor Schoffield | 25 | Ann Truman | 24 |
| Alethea McGinnis | 26 | Elizabeth Steel | 33 | Elizabeth Ummell | 25 |
| Susanna McGinnis | 5 | Sarah Steel | 6 | Ann Weston | 13 |
| Susanna Magruder | 40 | Martha Steel | 1 | Eleanor Wallace | 50 |
| Ann Magruder | 15 | Jeane Shearlock | 37 | Mary Wallace | 21 |
| Mary Magruder | 55 | Elizabeth Sansberry | 35 | Elizabeth Wallace | 17 |
| Ann Magruder | 21 | Elizabeth Sparrow | 30 | Anne Wallace | 12 |
| Mary Magruder | 51 | Tidings Sparrow | 6 | Rebecca Wilcoxon | 44 |
| Ann Magruder | 21 | Dinah Sparrow | 8 | Elizabeth Wilcoxon | 17 |
| Amelia Magruder | 12 | Elizabeth Sparrow | 20 | Rachel Wilcoxon | 14 |
| Katharine McCoy | 13 | Luranah Sparrow | 3 | Ann Wilcoxon | 12 |
| Ann Needham | 34 | Mary Sparrow | 1 | Sarah Wilcoxon | 1 |
| Sarah Needham | 14 | Eleanor Shehone | 16 | Elizabeth Wilcoxon | 25 |
| Charity Nichols | 30 | Luranah Shehone | 35 | Ruth Wilcoxon | 4 |
| Susanna Nichols | 1 | Luranah Shehone | 14 | Mary Woodward | 66 |
| Elizabeth Nichols | 26 | Ann Shehone | 12 | Vineay Walker | 48 |
| Mary Ann Nichols | 1 | Lucy Shehone | 9 | Elizabeth Walker | 11 |
| Ann Nichols | 48 | Thomason Shehone | 3 | Susanna Walker | 8 |
| Ursula Offutt | 16 | Mary Slicer | 21 | Martha Woodward | 23 |
| Elizabeth Purliven | 30 | Sarah Slicer | 1 | Chloe Wood | 37 |
| Mary Parker | 42 | Sarah Smith | 40 | Sarah Wood | 9 |
| Elizabeth Parker | 18 | Elizabeth Smith | 11 | Charlotte Wood | 5 |
| Ann Parker | 16 | Barsheba Spyvey | 25 | Ann Wood | 2 |
| Margaret Parker | 9 | Ann Spyvey | 4 | Frances Wallace | 50 |
| Sarah Parker | 5 | Ann Soaper | 26 | Martha Wallace | 30 |
| Amelia Parker | 3 | Mary Soaper | 5 | Margaret Wallace | 27 |
| Martha Parker | 1 | Rachel Soaper | 2 | Mary Wallace | 25 |
| Margaret Pritchett | 63 | Esther Soaper | 1 | Barbara Wallace | 20 |
| Sarah Ridgway | 50 | Sarah Smith | 48 | Eleanor Wallace | 29 |
| Jemima Ridgway | 16 | Ann Smith | 9 | Eleanor Wallace | 4 |
| Sarah Ridgway | 18 | Rebecca Smith | 11 | Susanna Wallace | 35 |

| Sarah Wilson | 22 | Elizabeth Whittle | 48 | Rachel Weldon | 3 |
| --- | --- | --- | --- | --- | --- |
| Jeane Wager | 7 | Elizabeth Williams | 22 | Eleanor Young | 40 |
| Jeane Wade | 23 | Mary Williams | 5 | | |

A LIST OF THE GEORGE TOWN HUNDRED, FREDERICK COUNTY, AUGUST 22, 1776

| | | | | | |
| --- | --- | --- | --- | --- | --- |
| John Asbeld | 22 | Michael Donboch | 13 | John Mounce | 36 |
| Thomas Branen | 46 | Caltron Donboch | 8 | John Mounce Jr. | 4 |
| George Branen | 15 | John Daley | 26 | Jacob Mounce | 2 |
| Thomas Branen | 15 | Charles Dave | 22 | Michael Mungle | 25 |
| Jeremiah Branen | 13 | William Dixon | 23 | Frederick Mirey | 13 |
| John Branen | 10 | Simon Dixon | 1 | William McFercen | 10 |
| Jesse Branen | 5 | Caleb Earp | 22 | William Monger | 22 |
| Samuel Branen | 2 | John Faulks | 45 | Antoney Murphey | 28 |
| James Bisbind | 53 | William Farbairn | 30 | Alexander McFadden | 25 |
| John Beall | 48 | Anthony Gussaler | 40 | James Morry | 27 |
| S. Sebert Beall | 14 | John Gussaler | 9 | Jacob Milley | 18 |
| William Baker | 27 | George Gussaler | 2 | Thomas Messor | 7 |
| Sam. Henson Baker | 3 | Philip Graver | 27 | Kidd Marques | 32 |
| Philip Thom. Baker | 1 | Jacob Graver | 1 | James Marques | 6 |
| Joseph Belt | 60 | Daniel Garrin | 17 | William Marques | 4 |
| William Belt | 21 | Samuel Hatt | 58 | Nicholls Paul | 38 |
| Thomas Barber | 25 | Jacob Hess | 36 | Peter Paul | 9 |
| Thomas Been | 18 | John House | 63 | Jacob Paul | 8 |
| Volendine Borrough | 33 | Thomas Jingrims | 23 | John Pringle | 28 |
| Volendine Borough Jr. | 8 | John Kiphart | 38 | Charles Putty | 8 |
| Loyd Beall Blackmore | 11 | John Kiphart Jr. | 12 | Thomas Purdy | 14 |
| Daniel Bulgar | 17 | Jacob Kiphart | 9 | Benj. Nolley Pearce | 48 |
| Simon Borough | 36 | George Kiphart | 5 | John Pasley | 36 |
| John Borough | 6 | Phillip Kiphart | 4 | John Petor | 20 |
| Simon Borough Jr. | 4 | Leonard Kiphart | 1 | Robert Petor | 50 |
| Volendine | 2 | Nicholas Kirtze | 16 | Robert Petor Jr. | 19 |
| Thomas Brooks | 30 | Theodoris Kraus | 39 | Thomas Petor | 8 |
| Joseph Brooks | 12 | Peter Kraus | 5 | Alexander Petor | 7 |
| George Brooks | 12 | John Kraus | 2 | Robert Petor | 3 |
| Thomas Brooks | 2 | Jacob Kraus | 1 | Jacob Risoner | 26 |
| Jos. Tompson Bonser | 13 | John Kennerson | 38 | Thomas Rigdon | 29 |
| John Tompson Bonser | 12 | Frederick Kizer | 50 | Henry Right | 21 |
| James Tompson Bonser | 7 | Frederick Kizer Jr. | 9 | John Edw. Rigdon | 4 |
| Thomas Barrett | 33 | John Kizer | 3 | John Ravenscroft | 42 |
| Benjamin Becraft Jr. | 35 | Peter Kurtze | 26 | Daniel Rowen | 22 |
| John Cammel | 17 | William Lanham | 23 | Arthur Roberts | 28 |
| William Carter | 24 | James Lingan | 22 | Zachariah Roberson | 15 |
| Frederick Cokendofer | 22 | Joseph Lingan | 1 | Valentine Runhel | 56 |
| Michael Casner | 17 | Jeremiah Leech | 27 | Daniel Runhel | 20 |
| Gollings Cammel | 30 | Thomas McKenery | 30 | Valentine Runhel Jr | 15 |
| Henry Clevley | 40 | John McKenery | 4 | John Runhel | 9 |
| Daniel Chue | 22 | James McKenery | 2 | John Randle | 39 |
| Thomas Conley | 16 | James Manen | 35 | Thomas Richardson | 35 |
| Paul Conner | 43 | Robert Moses | 35 | Wm. Stewardweall | 25 |
| John Conner | 6 | William Murphey | 27 | John Smith | 2 |
| Hezekiah Collings | 7 | Thomas Summers | 25 | Andrew Schoolfield | 14 |
| Frederick Donboch | 50 | Issachar Schoolfield | 10 | Joseph Schoolfield | 15 |

| Name | Age | Name | Age | Name | Age |
|---|---|---|---|---|---|
| Maland Schoolfield | 6 | Eles Bisbend | 60 | Margaret House | 50 |
| John Schoolfield | 55 | Ann Bores | 13 | Margaret Harmon | 66 |
| Walter Smith | 32 | Mary Beall | 36 | Susanna Hatt | 50 |
| Walter Smith Jr. | 3 | Ruth Beall | 13 | Barbary Hess | 29 |
| Patrick Smith | 2 | Mary Beall | 21 | Lucy Jinnings | 19 |
| Clement Smith | 18 | Susanna F. Baley | 25 | Mary Johnston | 16 |
| William Sloven | 16 | Mary P. Bayley | 6 | Elizabeth Jinkins | 26 |
| Joseph Sisor | 8 | Mary Brigg | 50 | Susanna Kiphart | 34 |
| Butler Stonestreet | 19 | Elizabeth Brotan | 19 | Elizabeth Kiphart | 13 |
| John Siles | 50 | Ann Baley | 20 | Katherine Kiphart | 8 |
| John Siles Jr. | 6 | Mildred Baker | 30 | Dorothy Kraus | 30 |
| Jacob Siles | 4 | Esther Belt | 53 | Susanna Kraus | 11 |
| George Siles | 4 | Ann Belt | 25 | Katherine Kraus | 8 |
| Major Sweeny | 32 | Ann Barber | 18 | Elizabeth Kizer | 40 |
| Henry Threlkield | 60 | Margaret Borough | 26 | Elizabeth Kizer | 16 |
| John Threlkild | 17 | Sarah Borough | 5 | Katharine Kizer | 14 |
| Thomas Tucker | 59 | Margaret Borough | 2 | Susanna Kiser | 12 |
| John Tucker | 13 | Elizabeth Borough | 1 | Margaret Kiser | 11 |
| David Tucker | 5 | Elizabeth Borough | 1 | Christine Kizer | 7 |
| Jacob Trissoler | 32 | Mary Brooks | 26 | Margaret Kagan | 22 |
| George Trissoler | 4 | Amelia Brooks | 9 | Christene Linnenbery | 30 |
| John Trissoler | 2 | Christian Bonser | 44 | Rusener Linnenbery | 14 |
| Jacob Trissoler Jr. | 1 | Elizabeth Bramley | 20 | Elizabeth Linnenbery | 10 |
| Richard Tomson | 38 | Mary Barrett | 25 | Mary Linnenbery | 4 |
| Richard Taylor | 15 | Ann Barrett | 1 | Martha Lewis | 50 |
| Jacob Upright | 54 | Ann Cammel | 21 | Mary McKenery | 26 |
| Even Vessel | 25 | Martha Cammel | 14 | Margaret McKenery | 1 |
| John Wise | 36 | Eleanor Conner | 25 | Margaret Moses | 25 |
| John Wise Jr. | 6 | Christian Casner | 22 | Sarah McCloud | 8 |
| Abraham Winard | 4 | Harriott Colbrock | 21 | Elizabeth Mounce | 30 |
| George Winbargle | 30 | Margaret Corner | 31 | Katharine Mounce | 8 |
| John Winbargle | 6 | Susanna Corner | 10 | Elizabeth Mounce | 1 |
| Jacob Winbargle | 4 | Margaret Corner | 7 | Evey Messay | 8 |
| John Waggoner | 22 | Febe Corner | 5 | ___ Mungle | 22 |
| Adam Wickel | 15 | Elizabeth Corner | 2 | Elizabeth Murphey | 26 |
| John Wingle | 5 | Mary Corner | 1 | Rebecca Murphey | 1 |
| William Wilson | 20 | Ann Cammell | 19 | Alse Messor | 25 |
| Lazurus Wingal | 27 | Mary Clarion | 3 | Eleanor Marques | 30 |
| Lazuress Wingal Jr. | 7 | Cassandra Chew | 47 | Mary Marques | 2 |
| Joseph Yates | 26 | Elizabeth Donboch | 48 | Lucy Orme | 53 |
| Tobias Youst | 21 | Elizabeth Donboch | 18 | Ruth Orme | 15 |
| Phillip Youst | 14 | Mary Donboch | 6 | Eleanor Orme | 15 |
| John Youst | 33 | Drusilla Donboch | 2 | Elizabeth Paul | 26 |
| John Youst Jr. | 5 | Sarah Duncastle | 20 | Margaret Paul | 10 |
| Thomas Young | 33 | Elizabeth Daley | 27 | Elizabeth Paul | 4 |
| George Young | 28 | Ann Dixon | 20 | Ann Pearce | 3 |
| Thomas Young Jr. | 1 | Marthe Ellett | 41 | Elizabeth Petor | 33 |
| Willaim Young | 15 | Katharine Gussaler | 28 | Elizabeth Petor | 6 |
| Casbery Youst | 64 | Rebecca Gussaler | 10 | Margaret Petor | 1 |
| | | Elizabeth Gussaler | 5 | Elizabeth Risoner | 20 |
| Elizabeth Adley | 30 | Katherine Gussaler | 4 | Mary Risoner | 2 |
| Rechel Anderson | 20 | Mary Gussaler | 1 | Eleanor Risoner | 14 |
| Mary Anderson | 45 | Katherine Graver | 28 | Mary Rigdon | 36 |
| Elizabeth Branen | 39 | Margaret Graver | 7 | Sarah Runhel | 54 |
| Mary Branen | 17 | Elizabeth Graver | 3 | Mary Runhel | 13 |

| | | | | | | |
|---|---|---|---|---|---|---|
| Katharine Runhel | 11 | Mary Tucker | 52 | Katharine White | 39 |
| Sophiah Ready | 11 | Mary Tucker | 10 | Margaret Winbargle | 30 |
| Mary Strannum | 20 | Mary Trissoler | 23 | Susanna Winbargle | 1 |
| Mary Smith | 30 | Elizabeth Trissoler | 7 | Elizabeth Wingal | 28 |
| Rachel Scholfield | 46 | Margaret Taylor | 67 | Elizabeth Wingal | 1 |
| Ann Scholfield | 18 | Katharine Upright | 32 | Eleanor Youst | 58 |
| Esther Smith | 31 | Eleanor Vessel | 15 | Susanna Youst | 17 |
| Elizabeth Smith | 1 | Elizabeth Wise | 30 | Rebecca Youst | 27 |
| Ann Siles | 30 | Katharine Wise | 4 | Katharine Youst | 7 |
| Susanna Siles | 1 | Elizabeth Wise | 1 | Elizabeth Youst | 2 |
| Margaret Smith | 31 | Elizabeth Winard | 21 | Mary Youst | 4 |
| Ann (servant) | 24 | Elizabeth Winard | 1 | Sarah Young | 15 |
| Mary Threlkild | 58 | Elizabeth Wiseam | 17 | | |

NORTH WEST HUNDRED. Taken by ROBERT BEALL OF JAMES
Completed by August 10, 1776

| | | | | | | |
|---|---|---|---|---|---|---|
| Trundle, Thomas | 65 | Lee, Elizabeth | 13 | King, Edward | 36 |
| Johanah | 43 | Dan | 11 | Rebeckah | 34 |
| Johannah J. | 5 | Emelia | 9 | Elizabeth | 13 |
| Rachol | 3 | | | Sarah | 12 |
| Mila | 1 | Ferrel, Joseph | 60 | Mary | 9 |
| Darkus Kor | 14 | | | Charity | 7 |
| 13 Negroes | | Thrasher, William | 45 | Benjamin | 4 |
| | | Margret | 35 | Edward Jr. | 2 |
| Housle, Robert | 56 | Mary | 17 | Rebeckah | 5mos. |
| Sarah | 43 | Elizabeth | 13 | | |
| Elizabeth | 23 | John Jr. | 11 | Madding, Joseph | 48 |
| Mary | 17 | Sarah | 8 | Mary | 43 |
| Robert Jr. | 15 | Thomas | 5wks. | Ann | 21 |
| Jonathan | 11 | William | 3 | James | 20 |
| Sarah | 9 | | | Joseph | 17 |
| Proscoolah | 7 | Goodrick, Benjamin | 30 | Benjamin | 15 |
| Lucy | 5 | Rachel | 25 | Thomas | 14 |
| Samuel | 3 | Elender | 8 | Sarah | 11 |
| Malmaduke | 6mos. | Elizabeth | 6 | Elizabeth | 9 |
| Leviah | 4mos. | Benj. Jonson | 4 | Margra | 8 |
| | | John | 2 | Rebeckah | 6 |
| Wood, Thoma | 58 | 1 Negro | | Hezekiah | 4 |
| Rache | 15 | | | Catharine | 2 |
| | | Jennens, John | 56 | John | 24 |
| Tracy, William | 53 | Sarah | 35 | Margrett | 21 |
| Elenor | 53 | Elizabeth | 14 | | |
| Philip | 19 | Ann | 11 | Collens, John | 34 |
| Elnor | 17 | Sarah | 9 | Sarah | 30 |
| James | 10 | John Jr. | 7 | Mary | 9 |
| | | Mary | 5 | John Jr. | 6 |
| Marchle, James | 50 | Rachel | 2 | Elizabeth | 2 |
| Mary | 34 | Margaret | 2wks. | | |
| Greetree, Benjamin | 14 | | | Maddox, Thomas | 38 |
| | | Higdon, Thomas | 25 | Jannet | 28 |
| Lee, John | 45 | Rachel | 30 | Elizabeth | 4 |
| Elizabeth | 52 | John | 3 | John Mad | 2 |
| Daniel | 18 | Margaret | 1 | Jacob Wood | 4mos. |
| James | 15 | 1 Negro | | Wilson, Sarah | 9 |
| | | | | 6 Negroes | |

71

| | | | | | | |
|---|---|---|---|---|---|---|
| Gentle, Elizabeth | 23 | Harrison, Priscilla | 23 | Gittings, Henry | 46 |
| Darkey | 2mos. | | | Elizabeth | 14 |
| | | Crown, Joseph | 66 | William | 10 |
| Holmod, Anthony | 52 | Elizabeth | 50 | Fletcher, Sarah | 43 |
| Susanah | 42 | Catharin | 17 | Gordon, Joseph | 23 |
| Jane | 16 | Sarah | 15 | | |
| John | 14 | Arter | 12 | Lowe, William | 30 |
| Sarah | 12 | Thomas | 7 | Sarah | 18 |
| Antony Jr. | 10 | Whitnell, Soloman | 50 | | |
| George | 8 | Evens, Mary | 18 | Speaks, William | 60 |
| Loveday | 2 | | | Mary | 55 |
| 7 Negroes | | Young, John | 54 | | |
| | | Jane | 35 | Hufman, Martain | 41 |
| Taylor, William | 52 | Mary | 14 | Barbara | 35 |
| Elizabeth | 49 | Jane | 11 | John | 14 |
| Gentle, Rebecka | 4 | Elenor | 5 | Elizabeth | 12 |
| | | John Jr. | 1 | Joseph | 10 |
| Gimlish, Frances | 42 | | | Hannah | 8 |
| Mary | 39 | Goodman, Humphry | 40 | Mary | 4 |
| Charlot | 12 | Kesiah | 32 | | |
| Mary | 9 | Ann | 15 | Day, Lenerd | 40 |
| Ariat | 7 | Jeramiah | 13 | Tobitha | 36 |
| Michel | 5 | Patsey | 11 | Samuel | 14 |
| Macket | 2mos. | Betsy | 9 | Susanah | 11 |
| | | Tomma | 7 | Ezekel | 9 |
| Ozburn, William | 53 | Kesiah | 6 | Sarah | 7 |
| Mary | 37 | Samuel | 4 | Bazel | 5 |
| Elander | 18 | Rebeckah | 2 | Tobitha | 2 |
| Archabald | 15 | Charlot | 8mos. | | |
| Charlot | 14 | Carthew, Edmond | 20 | Lambeth, Samuel | 33 |
| Ann | 12 | (servant) | | Mary | 35 |
| Issac | 9 | Conn, Mary | 21 | Ann | 3 |
| Lenard | 7 | | | John | 2 |
| Potter | 4 | Wilson, Henry | 51 | Lucy | 2mos. |
| Toppon, William | 15 | Folander | 47 | | |
| Evens Joh | 19 | Zadock | 19 | Higgens, Joseph | 30 |
| | | Lucy | 16 | Martha | 26 |
| Hill, John | 36 | Thomas | 13 | Ann | 6 |
| Kesiah | 34 | Mary | 11 | Elizabeth | 4 |
| Sarah | 13 | Elender | 7 | Elender | 4mos. |
| Joseph | 11 | Lanclot | 9 | Hennes, Mary | 18 |
| Jonathan | 9 | Henry | 5 | | |
| | | Folandor | 3 | Stallons, Griffon | 27 |
| White, Mary | 45 | 1 Negro | | Elizabeth | 17 |
| James | 16 | | | Susanah | 2mos. |
| Samuel | 14 | Trundle, John | 27 | | |
| Jach | 12 | Ruth | 22 | Stallons, Jacob | 25 |
| Elsia | 10 | David | 3 | Margaratt | 20 |
| Mary | 8 | John Lewos | 8mos. | Susanah | 1 |
| Robert Beall | 6 | 2 Negroes | | Cash, Calan | 15 |
| 1 Negro | | | | Wilson, James | 13 |
| | | Madding, John | 84 | | |
| Peirce, Margratt | 55 | Sarah | 68 | Cumphen, James | 70 |
| Catharin | 26 | 1 Negro | | Bearlander | 22 |
| John Baptis | 22 | | | William | 4 |
| 8 Negroes | | | | | |

| Name | Age | Name | Age | Name | Age |
|---|---|---|---|---|---|
| Harres, Ezekel | 36 | Barratt, Ninian | 25 | Whallen, Michel | 60 |
| Maggon, Philip | 26 | Mary | 24 | Bridgett | 50 |
| William, Ann | 60 | Isac | 1 | Mathew | 20 |
| Daniel | 20 | Richard | 12 | Margrett | 18 |
| Elizabeth | 21 | | | Mark | 15 |
| Cooke, William | 45 | Moore, Benjamin | 23 | Thomas | 9 |
| Sharrad, John | 8 | Sarah | 21 | Martin | 6 |
| | | Elizabeth | 1 | Mary | 2 |
| Beall, Richard | 54 | Lee, John | 21 | Dulany, Bridgett | 21 |
| Elenor | 47 | Dickson, Sarah | 11 | | |
| Priscilla | 22 | | | Roe, Robert | 21 |
| Margaret | 19 | Becraft, Petter | 35 | | |
| Elizabeth | 13 | Mary | 25 | Wood, Robert | 35 |
| Wilobe | 11 | Jonathan Nixon | 6mos. | Elizabeth | 34 |
| | | Day, Elizabeth | 11 | Ama | 5 |
| Beall, Samuel Sr. | 70 | 8 Negroes | | Zadock | 3 |
| Jane | 61 | Becraft, Benjamin | 67 | Mary | 67 |
| Jemima | 32 | Deborah | 57 | Jay, Sarah | 22 |
| Margret | 22 | | | Grindle, Eliza. | 33 |
| Joseph Belt | 22 | Whitehead, Timothy | 67 | (servant) | |
| Alexander Robert | 19 | New, Mary | 40 | 6 Negroes | |
| Dickson, Susanah | 16 | Jones, Abraham | 22 | | |
| 4 Negroes | | 12 Negroes | | Cash, Caleb | 41 |
| | | | | Elenor | 48 |
| Beall, Rich.of Saml. | 38 | Abington, John | 40 | Ruth | 19 |
| Sarah | 38 | Lucy | 18 | Mary | 14 |
| Saml. Brook | 14 | Bob | 15 | Dawson | 11 |
| Thos. Brook | 13 | Elizabeth | 13 | Rachel | 6 |
| Mary | 11 | John Jr. | 11 | Plommer, Sarah | 18 |
| Robert Brook | 7 | Henry | 9 | | |
| Walter Brook | 5 | Mackeay, Wm.(servant) | 30 | Wilson, Verlander | 80 |
| Asa Brook | 2 | Agga | 6 | Zachariah | 45 |
| 17 Negroes | | 5 Negroes | | | |
| | | | | Plommer, Jane | 50 |
| Beall, Clement | 42 | Mackette, James | 43 | Mary | 20 |
| Priscilla | 35 | Mary | 39 | Rebeckah | 16 |
| Perry | 9 | Mary | 16 | Kesiah | 15 |
| Elizabeth | 3 | Joseph | 14 | Elizabeth | 12 |
| Normand | 1 | Elisha | 12 | Robeson, Elizabeth | 13 |
| Cassandra | 7 | Agness | 10 | | |
| 7 Negroes | | Ignatious | 8 | Mitchel, Moredeca | 50 |
| | | Cloa | 4 | Sarah | 51 |
| Ward, Andrew | 48 | Loweser | 2 | Lucy | 18 |
| Rachel | 32 | | | Bathsheba | 15 |
| Ann | 7 | Tyson, Ann | 60 | Notly | 13 |
| Mary | 4 | Mary | 29 | Barbara | 12 |
| Tracy | 1 | Beall, Mary | 9 | Lankford, Jas.Frosman-40 | |
| | | Alarina | 6 | MacDonald, Edw.Olson-4 | |
| Alby, Joseph | 30 | 1 Negro | | | |
| Cassandra | 24 | | | Tucker, William Jr. | 29 |
| Joseph Jr. | 4 | Begarley, Henry | 30 | Margary | 25 |
| Ann | 2 | Elizabeth | 26 | Levi | 2 |
| | | Hezekiah | 3 | unnamed son | 1mos. |
| | | Ann | 1 | | |
| | | Wood, John(servant) | 17 | | |

| | | | | | | | |
|---|---|---|---|---|---|---|---|
| Tucker, William | 63 | Lashlee, Thomas | 23 | | Honnos, Cavea | 24 | |
| Elizabeth | 49 | Elizabeth | 27 | | | | |
| Henry | 17 | | | | Beall, Robert of James | 54 | |
| Sarah | 15 | Harris, Zadock | 26 | | Brigges, Rich.-servant | 22 | |
| Jemima | 14 | Sarah | 27 | | Mackgyer Andw. servant | 18 | |
| Sebina | 12 | Ann | 2 | | 1 Negro | | |
| Alen | 7 | Elizabeth | 7mos. | | | | |
| | | 2 Negroes | | | Summers, Hezekiah | 26 | |
| Stallons, Joseph | 60 | | | | Rebacka | 32 | |
| Elizabeth | 53 | Larrow, Michel | 23 | | William Dent | 3 | |
| Thomas | 19 | Jane | 23 | | Benjamin | 1 | |
| | | | | | Glaz, Charity | 53 | |
| 6 Negroes | | Clark, Henry | 42 | | Elenor | 23 | |
| | | Nancy | 42 | | | | |
| Tannehill, William | 55 | Seven | 14 | | Harwood, Samuel | 29 | |
| Sarah | 59 | Walter | 12 | | Mary Eliza. | 24 | |
| Rebeckah | 25 | Hennerietta | 11 | | Elizabeth Ann | 3 | |
| Anne | 18 | Henry Jr. | 9 | | Thomas Noble | 2 | |
| Wm. Harres | 16 | Baless | 8 | | Mary Ann | 2mos. | |
| 4 Negroes | | Nancy | 7 | | 20 Negroes | | |
| | | Lesson | 5 | | | | |
| Nixson, Jonathan | 19 | Thomson | 5 | | Beall, Zachariah | 33 | |
| Herod (servant Boy) | 18 | Justson | 3 | | Rebeckah | 23 | |
| | | Johnson | 1 | | Orasha | 2 | |
| Bloys, Davis | 26 | 13 Negroes | | | unnamed girl | 2mos. | |
| Mary | 25 | | | | 1 Negro | | |
| William Jr. | 2 | Larrew, Frances | 23 | | | | |
| | | Martha | 31 | | Doxse, Elenor | 20 | |
| Bloys, William Sr. | 63 | Abraham | 10 | | Martha | 2 | |
| Sarah | 50 | Elizabeth | 8 | | | | |
| Elizabeth | 24 | James | 6 | | Woodard, Frances | 63 | |
| Mary | 22 | George | 3 | | Weneford | 55 | |
| Rebeckah | 17 | John | 6mos. | | Frances | 19 | |
| Charles | 15 | Colbo, John(servant) | 21 | | Hezekiah | 16 | |
| Ann | 14 | | | | Zachariah | 13 | |
| Sarah | 13 | Harris, Aaron | 30 | | Sarah | 11 | |
| Mordeca | 12 | Mary | 26 | | Weneford | 6 | |
| Zachah | 10 | Elizabeth | 6 | | | | |
| Jonathan | 8 | Sarah | 9 | | Stallons, Elizabeth | 27 | |
| Zadock | 5 | Walter | 3 | | Patsa | 4 | |
| Robeson James | 1 | Thomas | 3mos. | | William | 1 | |
| | | Camblo, Danl-servant | 20 | | | | |
| Cicil, Sabrot | 53 | Knight, John(servant) | 30 | | Stallons, Isaac | 66 | |
| Mary | 46 | 4 Negroes | | | Ezable | 53 | |
| Samuel | 23 | | | | Sarah | 17 | |
| Elinor | 20 | Frances, Joseph | 34 | | 8 Negroes | | |
| John | 18 | Elizabeth | 28 | | Tucker, Martha | 32 | |
| James | 15 | Lucy | 7 | | Catharine | 11 | |
| William | 13 | Elizabeth | 6 | | Susanna | 10 | |
| Mary | 11 | Jacob | 4 | | 1 Negro | | |
| Jemima | 9 | Hessa | 2 | | | | |
| Thomas | 4 | unnamed son | 4mos. | | Mackmaness, Thomas | 30 | |
| Anne | 1 | Elemont, Elizabeth | 32 | | Ann | 22 | |
| Hall, Rebeckah | 6 | | | | Thomas | 3 | |
| 1 Negro | | Clark, William | 26 | | | | |

74

| | | | | | | | |
|---|---|---|---|---|---|---|---|
| Dixon, James | 6 | | Carroll, Daniel Jr. | 23 | | 11 Negroes | |
| Sarah | 40 | | Elizabeth | 23 | | Roe, Robert (Overseer) | |
| Carroll, Mrs. Ellr. | 67 | | Servants: | | | | |
| Mary | 34 | | Vaun, Betty | 45 | | Watson, John | 42 |
| Elizabeth | 31 | | Buckley, John | 40 | | Sarah | 38 |
| John | 40 | | Gilligan, John | 30 | | John Wright | 5½ |
| 46 Negroes | | | Purley, Ned | 10 | | Sally | 2½ |
| | | | 5 Negroes | | | Abington, Elizabeth | 13 |
| Nickolls, Thomas | 47 | | | | | Murdock, Martha | 25 |
| Casandra | 39 | | Barrett Elizabeth | 53 | | Servants: | |
| Ann | 75 | | Ann | 20 | | Dixon, Richard | 45 |
| William | 17 | | John | 19 | | McCoy, Janet | 17 |
| Daniel | 13 | | Isaac | 11 | | (Hired for 1 year) | |
| Thomas Jr. | 11 | | | | | McGirtt, James | 45 |
| Samuel | 6 | | May, Ann | 21 | | Bannerman Betsey | 54 |
| Isaiah | 4 | | | | | 8 Negroes | |
| Benjamin | 2 | | Carroll, Daniel | 46 | | | |
| Rebeckah | 15 | | Servants: | | | Summers, Dent | |
| Elizabeth | 9 | | Condon, John | 25 | | (9 in the family | |
| 22 Negroes | | | John | 45 | | but he refused to | |
| 1 Female Servant | | | Kelly, Tom | 16 | | make a return) | |
| | | | Kenney | 24 | | | |
| | | | Bush | 23 | | White, Bazil-8 in family | |
| | | | | | | refused to make return | |

**SUGAR LAND HUNDRED TAKEN BY SAMUEL BALCKMORE SEPTEMBER 2, 1776**

| | | | | | | | |
|---|---|---|---|---|---|---|---|
| Speight, Robert | 37 | | Mackall, Benjamin | 41 | | Dowden, John | 35 |
| William | 12 | | John | 1 | | John B. | 5 |
| ___son | 8 | | Mary | 31 | | Thomas P. | 3 |
| Robert | 6 | | Elizabeth | 11 | | Michael A. | 1 |
| Elisabeth | 38 | | Mary | 8 | | Jean | 25 |
| Ann | 4 | | Darke | 6 | | 1 Negro | |
| Mary | 2 | | Rebaca | 4 | | | |
| | | | Kelley, Mary | 29 | | Dowden, Mary | 70 |
| Hickman, Solomon | 40 | | Davis, John | 8 | | Warde, Elizabeth | 19 |
| Joshua | 14 | | 3 Negroes | | | 3 Negroes | |
| Jesse | 9 | | | | | | |
| Geats, James | 34 | | Dyson, Barton | 25 | | Ellis, Solomon | 32 |
| Ruth Taylor | 23 | | William | 5mos. | | Charles | 4 |
| an infant | | | Anna | 25 | | Solomon | 2 |
| Carter, Pegey | 21 | | Martha | 2 | | James | 12 |
| 2 Negroes | | | Dignum, Lucy | 18 | | Margaret | 32 |
| | | | | | | Verlinder | 12 |
| Hickman, Ellenor | 32 | | Williams, Elisha | 41 | | Martha | 10 |
| Nansey | 11 | | Hazel | 18 | | Ann | 8 |
| Sarey | 3 | | John | 14 | | Gibson, John | 18 |
| Henry | 12 | | Thomas | 12 | | 1 Negro | |
| Elisha | 5 | | Jarred | 10 | | | |
| Barlow, Zachariah | 26 | | Elisha | 6 | | Tomlinson, Heugh | 24 |
| Collings, John | 24 | | Ann | 40 | | John | 2 |
| Thompson, Mary | 17 | | Mary | 16 | | Mary | 20 |
| 1 Negro | | | Martha | 3 | | Kelley, Frederick | 19 |
| | | | Ford, Jean | 28 | | | |
| Sebon, John | 26 | | | | | | |

| Name | Age | | Name | Age | | Name | Age |
|---|---|---|---|---|---|---|---|
| Jacobs, Jeremiah | 58 | | Wood, John | 47 | | O'Neal, John | 57 |
| Zachariah | 23 | | James | 19 | | Peter | 22 |
| Edward | 16 | | John Jr. | 5 | | Barton | 16 |
| John | 12 | | Walter | 3 | | Joseph | 10 |
| Rachel | 56 | | Thomas | 9mos. | | Margaret | 49 |
| Rebeca | 20 | | Anna | 43 | | Margaret | 18 |
| Ruth | 13 | | Mary | 13 | | Phebe | 16 |
| 4 Negroes | | | Charity | 10 | | Janet | 14 |
| | | | Elizabeth | 8 | | Mary | 10 |
| Willson, Hannah | 22 | | Ginkinks, Edward | 20 | | | |
| John | 1 | | | | | Willson, Mathew | 35 |
| | | | Warren, George | 54 | | Henry | 7 |
| Clearwaters, Silvester | 64 | | Johan | 24 | | Benjamin | 5 |
| Lettes | 62 | | George | 21 | | Rachel | 26 |
| Elisabeth | 25 | | Mary | 35 | | Rachel | 3 |
| | | | Alley | 16 | | | |
| Hoskinson, Heugh | 21 | | Mary | 8 | | Wood, Zephonioh | 32 |
| Charles | 18 | | Mary | 64 | | Eli | 4 |
| Josiah | 12 | | | | | | |
| Charles | 7mos. | | Warren, Thomas | 26 | | Lucas, Mary | 43 |
| Margaret | 19 | | Charles | 3 | | Nansy | 10 |
| | | | Elisabeth | 25 | | Charles | 23 |
| Stimpson, Capt.Solomon | 40 | | Mary | 5 | | William | 19 |
| Dorkus | 35 | | Sary | 2 | | 5 Negroes | |
| 6 Negroes | | | | | | | |
| | | | Johnson, Isaac | 24 | | Gatten, Benjamin | 42 |
| Rian, William | 25 | | Horasha | 2 | | Benjamin | 1mos. |
| Joshua | 1 | | Elisabeth | 20 | | John | 10 |
| Jamima | 18 | | Mary | 6mos. | | Elisabeth | 33 |
| | | | Yeates, John Sr. | 25 | | Phillinder | 15 |
| Worker, William | 21 | | | | | Medly, George | 13 |
| John | 12 | | Whitaker, Alexander | 30 | | Prusten, Edward | 40 |
| Agnes | 85 | | Hester | 25 | | Niles, George | 30 |
| Margaret | 38 | | Eliza.Magruder | 2 | | 8 Negroes | |
| | | | Price, Thomas | 23 | | | |
| Ellis, Samuel | 55 | | Gilks, Mary | 21 | | Else & Blackburn's Quarter | |
| Samuel Jr. | 10 | | 6 Negroes | | | 8 Negroes | |
| Mary | 52 | | | | | | |
| Cassandra | 17 | | Soper, James | 44 | | Dowell, Peter | 57 |
| Anna | 14 | | Thomas | 7 | | Peter | 27 |
| Suger, William | 18 | | Alvan | 5 | | John | 25 |
| | | | John | 3 | | William | 15 |
| Ellis, Zaphaniah | 21 | | Mereen | 1 | | John of John | 1 |
| Thomas | 2 | | James | 7 | | Elisabeth | 59 |
| Hannah | 20 | | Ann | 26 | | Mary | 1 |
| | | | 9 Negroes | | | Mary | 27 |
| Colliar, William | 31 | | | | | 6 Negroes | |
| James | 6 | | Riggs, Thomas | 31 | | | |
| William | 4 | | Azariah | 22 | | Tomlinson, Wm. | 26 |
| John | 1 | | John | 7 | | Hester | 18 |
| Jean | 25 | | Ophea | 6 | | Martha | 1 |
| Rachel | 58 | | Rachel | 25 | | Casey, James | 22 |
| | | | Nansey | 4 | | Riggs, Elisabeth | 14 |
| Henley, James | 40 | | Ruth | 1 | | Phelps, Margaret | 9 |

| | | | | | |
|---|---|---|---|---|---|
| Smallwood, Derecter | 24 | Belt, Higinson | 31 | Pool, John | 43 |
| | | Alley | 20 | John | 7 |
| Palmer, Tobitha | 40 | Elisabeth | 1 | Eary | 28 |
| Jariat | 3 | Harris, James | 18 | Elisabeth | 6 |
| | | 5 Negroes | | Ann | 4 |
| Hopkins, Ann | 28 | | | Tary | 1 |
| Lear | 4 | Wood, Stephen | 25 | Riggs, John | 12 |
| | | Bennet | 1 | Crellin, James | 15 |
| Allison Hendery | 56 | Preasha | 23 | | |
| Silvester | 22 | Anna | 3 | Blackmore, William | 31 |
| Hendery | 18 | Elisabeth | 12 | Dawson | 4 |
| Ellenner | 91 | | | Sary | 28 |
| Elisabeth | 48 | Fletchall, John | 49 | Sary | 4mos. |
| Ellenner | 24 | Thomas | 16 | Servants: | |
| Maryan | 14 | John | 6 | Burch, Holford | 48 |
| 8 Negroes | | Elisabeth | 45 | Dixon, James | 30 |
| | | Ann | 19 | Brubly, Joseph | 26 |
| Samders, Charles | 45 | Elisabeth | 14 | Frasher, Andrew | 23 |
| Edward | 3 | Cintha | 12 | Bowers Jean | 9 |
| John | 1 | Warters, James | 30 | 3 Negroes | |
| Hennaratter | 23 | Grimes, Ann | 28 | | |
| 7 Negroes | | Fox, Ann | 25 | Perry, Charles' Quarter | |
| | | (3 Servants) | | 1 servant | |
| Adams, Ann | 56 | 12 Negroes | | 1 negro | |
| Maryan | 16 | | | | |
| Cassandra | 12 | Coarts, Charles | 62 | Perry, James' Quarter | |
| Jesse | 18 | James | 23 | 3 Negroes | |
| Rullan, Rachel | 10 | Notley | 21 | | |
| | | 3 Negroes | | Pollixfin, John Willis-36 | |
| Hardy, John | 46 | | | John W. | 9 |
| George | 15 | Pool, Joseph | 38 | James W. | 2 |
| Ashford | 9 | Joseph | 10 | Matthew W. | 5mos. |
| Hennary | 4 | Benjamin | 4 | Mary W. | 31 |
| Anna | 43 | Mary | 28 | Ellennas W. | 14 |
| Mary | 18 | Mary | 6 | Elisabeth W. | 13 |
| Anna | 13 | Rachel | 2 | Victory W. | 11 |
| Darcus | 6 | Mccolley, Sary | 14 | Jemeny W. | 7 |
| Martha | 2 | Felphs, Sary | 11 | Ann W. | 4 |
| 1 Negro | | | | Willett, Griffeth | 26 |
| | | Mackall, Mary | 65 | Henson, Samuel | 12 |
| Atchinson, John | 26 | Darbay, Asa | 2 | | |
| Efrom | 2 | 5 Negroes | | Brown, James | 52 |
| Lody | 19 | | | | |
| Ruth | 18 | | | | |

### FREDERICK COUNTY HUNDRED. NOW INCLUDED IN MONTGOMERY COUNTY

| | | | | | |
|---|---|---|---|---|---|
| Dowden, Thomas | 31 | Davis, Bexly | 22 | Watson, Samuel | 48 |
| Jonnas | 5 | Poly Carp | 8 | Elkanah | 20 |
| Archabald | 6mos. | Joseph | 3 | Sary G. | 11 |
| John St. | 17 | Elizabeth | 31 | Sary | 49 |
| Sary | 25 | Maryan | 6 | Lucy | 15 |
| Martha | 7 | Elizabeth | 1 | Rebecca | 8 |
| Richard | 3 | | | Elizabeth | 4 |
| Jones, Mary St. | 23 | | | Dyer, Jonathan | 21 |

| Name | Age | | Name | Age | | Name | Age |
|---|---|---|---|---|---|---|---|
| Hickman, Arthur | 63 | | Gentle, Stephen | 66 | | Briggs, William | 36 |
| Margaret | 11 | | George | 23 | | Catron | 6 |
| illegible | 35 | | Stephen | 21 | | Mary | 4 |
| Mary | 63 | | John | 15 | | Ann | 1 |
| 8 Negroes | | | William | 10 | | | |
| | | | Samuel | 8 | | Ashen, Ellender | 39 |
| Meginias, Neal | 30 | | Sary | 52 | | Samuel | 16 |
| Thomas | 2mos. | | Mary | 23 | | William | 12 |
| Catarin | 22 | | Ellender | 17 | | John | 14 |
| Mary | 5 | | Dianna | 13 | | James | 8 |
| Alleyfar | 2 | | John | 4mos. | | | |
| Brandon, Abraham St. | 22 | | | | | Rigney Terance | 30 |
| 1 negro | | | Owen, John | 70 | | Lusey | 25 |
| | | | Thomas | 17 | | Ann | 2 |
| Hickman, William | 30 | | Elizabeth | 68 | | 3 Negroes | |
| Rossel | 2 | | Riggs, Charles | 5 | | | |
| Jean | 25 | | Ann | 33 | | Walter, David | 35 |
| Betty | 1 | | Mary | 8 | | Stephen | 4 |
| 1 Negro | | | Colliar, Elizabeth | 24 | | Ann | 26 |
| | | | 2 Negroes | | | Sary | 2 |
| Jackson, Bennett | 48 | | | | | Thomas, Notley | 21 |
| Jafaras | 15 | | Dowel, Phillip | 24 | | Marten, John | 21 |
| John | 18 | | Bachelder | 4 | | Brannen, Lawrence | 21 |
| Sary | 54 | | Prissiller | 22 | | Marten, Samuel | 10 |
| Ellenner | 16 | | Elisabeth | 3 | | Mearet, Margaret | 18 |
| | | | Allay | 1 | | Green, Sary | 5 |
| Warker, Thomas | 39 | | | | | | |
| William | 9 | | Robinson, James | 49 | | Arnold, Joseph | 33 |
| Cassandra | 28 | | Charles | 12 | | Ellenner | 35 |
| Virlinder | 5 | | John | 7 | | | |
| | | | Susey | 36 | | Case, Israel | 27 |
| Lovlis, Benjamin | 49 | | Ann | 16 | | John | 4 |
| Eleanah | 21 | | Mary | 14 | | Margaret | 22 |
| Barton | 19 | | Elisabeth | 10 | | Lowrey, John | 20 |
| Zadock | 16 | | Charity | 4 | | | |
| Reson | 12 | | Sary | 2 | | Dyson, Philip | 30 |
| Benjamin | 2 | | Ale, Robert | 14 | | Mash | 20 |
| Sary | 41 | | | | | Rebeca | 1 |
| Sary | 6 | | Robinson, John | 33 | | Smith, Johanah | 6 |
| | | | William | 9 | | | |
| Willson, Mary | 23 | | Carlos | 7 | | McDaniel, William | 47 |
| George | 30 | | Jaen | 31 | | William Jr. | 23 |
| William | 8 | | Elizabeth | 1 | | Hennary | 19 |
| Michel | 6 | | Tolbert, George | 16 | | Daniel | 6 |
| George | 4 | | Basil | 22 | | Ann | 47 |
| Lidia | 26 | | Mary | 44 | | Linder | 16 |
| Elisabeth | 1 | | Rockford, Edward | 28 | | Mary | 13 |
| Hools, Joseph | 37 | | | | | Ann | 3 |
| Shaw, Benjamin | 13 | | Talbert, Ellenner | 14 | | Elisabeth | 23 |
| Hibbey, John | 8 | | Ann | 9 | | Poplin, Elisabeth | 29 |
| Robey, Elizabeth | 56 | | Notley | 19 | | Hoskinson, Mary | 16 |
| Shaw, Dorraty | 20 | | Lewis | 12 | | 1 Negro | |
| | | | Leven | 6 | | | |
| Sinclear, Dunkin | 26 | | Reson | 3 | | Currenton, John | 42 |
| Mary | 18 | | | | | Hopkins, Ann | 25 |

| Name | Age | | Name | Age | | Name | Age |
|---|---|---|---|---|---|---|---|
| Fyffe, James Sr. | 63 | | Smith, Nathan | 41 | | Dyson, Matdox | 32 |
| James Jr. | 23 | | Ali | 19 | | Bennett | 8 |
| Jonathan | 21 | | Archabald | 16 | | Aquila | 6 |
| John | 16 | | Leander | 14 | | John | 3 |
| Sary | 56 | | Benjamin | 9 | | Jean | 40 |
| Elisabeth | 18 | | Nathan | 4 | | Mary | 1 |
| Abija | 30 | | Rebeca | 44 | | Mary | 56 |
| James | 8 | | Preshey | 12 | | Swann, Thomas | 15 |
| Daniel | 8mos. | | Drusiller | 10 | | Ann | 10 |
| Ellenner | 25 | | Roda | 3 | | Clark, Nester | 38 |
| Elisabeth | 5 | | Sweatman, Susannah | 23 | | 1 Negro | |
| Sary | 3 | | Randell, Elisabeth | 50 | | | |
| 10 Negroes | | | | | | Dyson, Zaphaniah | 26 |
| | | | Purdom, John | 37 | | Thomas | 18mos. |
| Fyffe, Joseph | 25 | | Walter | 11 | | Dorraty | 19 |
| Samuel | 5 | | Joshua | 9 | | | |
| William | 3 | | Kesiah | 36 | | Veares, Capt. Wm. | 41 |
| Drusiller | 25 | | Kesiah | 4 | | Lien | 17 |
| Sary | 1 | | Henna | 7 | | William | 15 |
| Burk, John | 30 | | | | | John | 13 |
| 7 Negroes | | | Love, Leonard | 30 | | Edward | 12 |
| | | | Thomas | 27 | | Heszakiah | 8 |
| Neall, Dr. Charles | 71 | | Levy | 1 | | Solomon | 6 |
| Ralph | 36 | | Elisabeth | 35 | | Levy | 4 |
| 13 Negroes | | | Ann | 8 | | Mary | 36 |
| | | | Sary | 5 | | Levy | 7 |
| Henry, Daniel | 21 | | Elisabeth | 3 | | unnamed infant | |
| Elizabeth | 19 | | | | | Woodfield, Mariar | 19 |
| Lanner, Thomas | 23 | | Veares, Nehemiah | 43 | | 1 Negro | |
| Longenston, Daniel | 46 | | Daniel | 20 | | | |
| 2 servants | | | Brice | 12 | | Purdey, Richard | 45 |
| | | | Elisha | 10 | | Catron | 33 |
| Cleckett, Ninian | 26 | | Basil | 3 | | Ann | 13 |
| | | | Luranar | 39 | | Richard | 1 |
| Windham, George | 16 | | Sary | 17 | | | |
| Elizabeth | 52 | | Elisabeth | 15 | | Darnold, John | 40 |
| Robert | 9 | | Ann | 13 | | Cornelas | 14 |
| 1 Negro | | | Ellender | 11 | | William | 12 |
| | | | Cassandra | 2 | | Hennary | 10 |
| Heard, Bennet | 25 | | | | | Thomas | 7 |
| | | | Case, Jean | 58 | | Ezekil | 5 |
| Swann, Zephaniah | 36 | | Elizabeth | 22 | | Rubin | 1 |
| Jesse | 1mos. | | More, Mary | 24 | | Marion | 31 |
| Mary | 25 | | Martha | 4mos. | | Rebeca | 8 |
| Orpha | 5 | | Nathon | 27 | | Prissillar | 2 |
| Anna | 2 | | Samuel | 25 | | 1 Negro | |
| Short, Richard | 22 | | 1 Negro | | | | |
| McCanna, Patrick, St. | 18 | | | | | Nisbet, Charles | 55 |
| Barker, Elisabeth | 18 | | Dyson, Samuel | 33 | | Barnett | 17 |
| | | | John | 11 | | Ann | 22 |
| Cole, Barnett | 26 | | Lydia | 31 | | Ellenner | 20 |
| Tunons ? | 3 | | Mary | 9 | | Catron | 15 |
| William | 1 | | Sary | 5 | | Mary | 13 |
| Susannah | 19 | | Darkes | 2 | | Lydea | 9 |
| | | | Walters, William | 15 | | Metawe, Betsey | 19 |

| | | | | | | |
|---|---|---|---|---|---|---|
| McCray, Zaphaniah | 30 | Harbin, James | 50 | Locker, Patrick | 40 |
| | | Joshuah | 21 | Jesse | 10 |
| Allnutt, Jesse | 63 | Jarratt | 15 | John | 7 |
| William | 20 | Elias | 13 | Elisabeth | 4 |
| John | 15 | Ellenner | 47 | Ellenner | 2 |
| Joseph | 13 | Mary | 7 | | |
| Talbart | 7 | Darkes | 5 | Steall, William | 67 |
| Daniel | 6mos. | Norman, Phillip | 76 | James | 26 |
| Jean | 40 | Larnan, Ann | 18 | John | 21 |
| Mary | 19 | Case, Hester | 20 | Samuel | 19 |
| Susanna | 17 | | | Joseph | 3 |
| Rebeca | 11 | Tucker, Jonathan | 38 | William | 1 |
| 2 Negroes | | Leonard | 12 | Elisabeth | 48 |
| | | Edward | 10 | Mary | 28 |
| Allnutt, James | 25 | James | 4 | Mary | 14 |
| Virlinder | 20 | Mary | 30 | Elisabeth | 7 |
| Sary | 1 | Darkis | 8 | Margaret | 4 |
| 1 Negro | | Miltrue | 6 | | |
| | | Sary | 1 | Ferguson, John | 53 |
| Allnutt, Lawrence | 26 | Truman, Richard | 28 | Daniel | 19 |
| Ellender | 25 | Sutten, William | 41 | Elias | 16 |
| Ellender | 3 | 2 Negroes | | Reson | 14 |
| Mary | 1 | | | Mordecai | 12 |
| 1 Negro | | Ward, Benjamin | 22 | Ellenner | 55 |
| | | 5 Negroes | | John | 26 |
| Allnutt, Jesse | 31 | | | Mary | 24 |
| Ann | 25 | Lewis, Samuel | 35 | Elisabeth | 4 |
| Sary | 1 | John | 3 | Ellenner | 2 |
| Mary Ruth | 19 | Mary | 26 | | |
| 1 Negro | | Margaret | 8 | Whalen, Daniel | 30 |
| | | Ann | 6 | Rebeca | 20 |
| Jones, Thomas | 25 | Susanna | 2 | 5 Negroes | |
| Thomas | 2 | | | | |
| Mary | 22 | Ellett, March | 50 | Downden, Michel | 39 |
| Susanna | 3 | Benjamin | 20 | Ward, Matten | 17 |
| | | Joseph | 18 | Beard, William | 7 |
| Burler, Andrew | 33 | Mark | 15 | Beall, Edward | 13 |
| Susanna | 23 | Richard | 6 | William | 10 |
| Ellennder | 5 | John | 4 | Dowden, Elisabeth | 40 |
| Elisabeth | 1 | Kissiar | 35 | Robinson, Mary | 20 |
| | | Elisabeth | 13 | 1 Negro | |
| Lewis Elisabeth | 61 | Ann | 8 | | |
| Ellennder | 15 | Kassa | 7mos. | Williams, James | 23 |
| George | 23 | Tiffendale, Mary | 25 | | |
| Abraham | 2 | 1 Negro | | Davis, William | 30 |
| Mary | 19 | | | | |
| Denton, James | 29 | Dennair, William | 40 | Byrn, Charles | 29 |
| | | Mary | 39 | | |
| Messicopp, Christopher | 24 | | | Beegding, Hennary | 27 |
| George | 19 | McDaniel, Elisha | 21 | | |
| John | 3 | Mary | 15 | Hutts, Andrew | 36 |
| Margaret | 33 | 9 Negroes | | | |
| Mary | 1 | | | Cartwright, Samuel | 42 |
| Kiltey, Frances | 17 | Holland, Joel | 27 | | |
| Howel, Joseph | 33 | Lydia | 26 | Walter, Levy | 27 |

| Name | Value | Name | Value | Name | Value |
|---|---|---|---|---|---|
| Woodyard, Jesse | 25 | Taylor, John | 24 | Gillom, John | 23 |
| Stalons, William | 19 | Gentle, George | 23 | Hopkins, Leven | 35 |
|  |  |  |  | Stephen | 4 |
| Hennary, John | 27 | Miles, John | 37 | 1 Negro |  |
|  |  | Nicholas | 10 |  |  |
| Lucas, Charles | 29 | James | 4 | Jewell, William | 35 |
| Lindoes | 18 | Mary | 42 | Bassel | 11 |
| Richard | 2 | Elisabeth | 6 | William | 2 |
| Susanna | 26 | Baker, Bartain | 21 | Ann Tabitha | 38 |
| Nancy | 4 |  |  | Rebecah | 15 |
| Jamima | 3 | Lewis, Richard | 27 | Amay | 7 |
| Mary | 3mos. | Hyrom | 3 | Betty | 5 |
| Orne, Michel | 9 | Ann | 21 | 1 Negro |  |
| Young, John | 33 | Blackmore, Samuel | 40 | Hickman, William | 21 |
| William | 7 | James | 12 | Stephen | 14 |
| Benjamin | 3 | Samuel Jr. | 5 | Richard | 12 |
| Kessiah | 29 | William | 2 | Jeane | 18 |
| Nancy | 7mos. | Abriller | 35 | Ann | 16 |
| 4 Negroes |  | Ellenner | 17 | 5 Negroes |  |
|  |  | Mary | 16 |  |  |
| Lucas, Thomas | 25 | Elisabeth | 14 | Arnold, William | 35 |
| Kissiah | 26 | Ann | 10 | John | 6 |
| Woodyard, John | 20 | Amma | 8 | Ann | 26 |
| 3 Negroes |  | unnamed child | 1mos. | Elisabeth | 11 |
|  |  | Heughes, John | 34 | Mary | 8 |
| Hoskinson, George | 25 | Hennahon, Patrick | 19 | Anna | 3 |
|  |  | Lockton, Michel | 18 | unnamed child | 2mos. |
| Locker, Joseph | 43 | 5 Negroes |  | Robertson, Andrew |  |
| Shaderick | 18 |  |  | Green | 22 |
| Joseph Jr. | 14 | Allison, Charles | 25 |  |  |
| Lusey | 47 |  |  | Beeding, Joseph | 25 |
| Virlinder | 17 | Swearinger, Van | 29 |  |  |
| Marick, John | 16 | Leonard | 7 | Beeding, Edward | 35 |
| Tolbart, Ellenner | 30 | Samuel | 5 | Jacob | 8 |
| Rebeca | 8 | Clemmey | 2 | John | 5 |
| 1 Negro |  | Lacy | 34 | Solomon | 2 |
|  |  | Mary | 7 | Tabitha | 25 |
| Johnson, Bartholomew | 35 | Hortley, John(servant) | 29 | Gillum, Thomas | 23 |
| Joseph | 6 | Ford, Ralph(servant) | 23 |  |  |
| John | 4 |  |  | Thompson, William | 37 |
| Lisbell | 35 | Byrn, Matthias | 33 | John | 15 |
| Rebeca | 9 | Patrick | 1 | William | 8 |
| Lisbell | 2 | Martha Ann | 22 | Joseph | 1 |
|  |  | Mary | 50 | Susanah | 37 |
| Lintrage, Samuel | 27 | Catharine | 22 | Susanah | 6 |
|  |  | Clementena | 18 | Nancy | 3 |
| Hyser, Martain | 25 | Mary | 15 | Perryman, Richard | 45 |
|  |  | Verlinder | 13 | Ellgin, Mary | 12 |
| Hardey, Zadock | 20 | Curtin, John | 17 |  |  |
| Mary | 29 | 2 Negroes |  | Chilton, Mark | 22 |
| 1 Negro |  |  |  |  |  |
|  |  | Henwood, Ann | 26 | Draper, William | 22 |
| Fedrick, Grace | 30 | Azariah | 2 |  |  |
| Milkey | 10 |  |  | Thomas, Martin | 25 |
|  |  | 81 |  |  |  |

| Name | Age | Name | Age | Name | Age |
|---|---|---|---|---|---|
| Woodgerd, William | 32 | Carsey, Daniel | 24 | Barlow, John | 31 |
| John | 6 | Ann | 23 | Zachariah | 3 |
| Jisse | 3 | Elisabeth | 14 | Ann | 21 |
| William | 1 | Ealce | 8 | Zachariah | 66 |
| Dennis | 21 | Sary | 5 | Mary | 78 |
| Elisabeth | 23 | unnamed child 1wk. | | Susanna | 29 |
| Jene | 4 | Eales | 49 | Elisabeth | 21 |
| Jerry | 26 | Ferguson, Basil | 21 | Martain, Virlinder | 7 |
| Campbell, Eneas Sr. | 46 | Beckwith, Mary | 1 | Davis, Efrom | 41 |
| Eneas Jr. | 18 | Ann | 29 | Jaramiah | 4 |
| Magrate | 45 | William | 6 | Darkis | 35 |
| Hester | 17 | | | Anna | 8 |
| Lidia | 15 | Jones, Joseph | 40 | Mary | 6 |
| Ann | 8 | | | Nansey | 3 |
| Ketty White | 4mos. | Osborn, Ann | 42 | | |
| Connor, Cattrine | 20 | Mary | 12 | Dickson, John | 52 |
| Linn, Barbra | 23 | David | 14 | William | 19 |
| 13 Negroes | | Benjamin | 21 | John | 17 |
| | | Wallace, Mathew | 45 | Zachariah | 3 |
| Hickman, Gilbert | 7 | | | Hannah | 44 |
| Lidia | 10 | Walter, Clement | 32 | Mary | 14 |
| | | Rebeca | 32 | Ruth | 8 |
| Tall, Arthur | 28 | Sary | 2 | Ellenner | 6 |
| Benjamin | 4 | Elisabeth | 6mos. | Susanna | 1 |
| Pentacast | 3 | Hardesty, Hennary | 10 | | |
| Maryann | 33 | Miller, Thomas | 15 | Elgin, Christopher | 63 |
| Melarve, John | 25 | Stallons, Margaret | 13 | Jesse | 8 |
| Osben, Hannah | 19 | Green, Mary | 10 | John | 6 |
| | | | | William | 1 |
| Fealds, Joseph | 33 | McIntoush, Alex. | 47 | Mary | 34 |
| Thompson, John | 13 | Alexander | 11 | Ann | 14 |
| Fowler, Ann | 28 | William | 9 | Mary | 13 |
| Elisabeth | 10 | Lowre | 7 | Anabella | 10 |
| Hennaritter | 8 | Macke | 5 | Cloe | 3 |
| Fealds, Mathew | 41 | Benjamin | 3 | | |
| | | Ann | 40 | Duglace, William | 37 |
| Fealds, James | 35 | Ellender | 12 | Samuel | 13 |
| William | 5 | 6 Negroes | | George | 8 |
| Joseph | 3mos. | | | William | 6 |
| Martha | 23 | Johnjones, John | 20 | Sue | 10 |
| Sary | 3 | 7 Negroes | | | |
| | | | | Haris, John | 23 |
| Landard, Johnana | 27 | Evens, William | 52 | Robert | 2 |
| | | Mary | 41 | Vinaford | 32 |
| Flether, Abraham | 51 | Essex, Elisabeth | 13 | 3 Negroes | |
| George | 25 | | | | |
| John | 13 | Davis, Joseph | 25 | Chilton, Mary | 37 |
| Elias | 3 | | | Jewell, Jonathan | 14 |
| Prisilla | 47 | Farguson, Nathaniel | 22 | Elisha | 12 |
| Hannah | 34 | Peggey | 21 | George | 10 |
| Sary | 24 | Prissilla | 1 | David | 5 |
| Betty | 20 | | | Smallwood | 1 |
| Pressella | 16 | Hickman, Prisilla | 48 | Mary | 3 |
| Rachel | 6mos. | | | 6 Negroes | |

| Walter, George | 88 | Walter, John | 43 | Green, John | 50 |
| Thomas | 5 | John | 11 | Thomas | 23 |
| Mary | 37 | Daniel | 5 | Isaac | 21 |
| Elisabeth | 15 | Sary | 39 | William | 10 |
| Sary | 13 | Crips, Mary | 21 | Jamima | 45 |
| Rebeca | 11 | 4 Negroes | | Dianna | 15 |
| Mary | 8 | | | Martha | 13 |
| Osoorn, Thomas | 13 | Rigeaway, Wm. | 30 | | |
| 5 Negroes | | John | 1 | Franklin, Joseph | 46 |
| | | Sary | 31 | William | 19 |
| Crips, Edward | 25 | Elisabeth | 5 | Barker | 15 |
| | | Hathaliah | 3 | Zaphaniah | 9 |
| Jones, Lewis | 37 | 1 Negro | | Maryan | 46 |
| James | 10 | | | Ann | 12 |
| Jeane | 28 | Gatten, James | 38 | Benedicter | 5 |
| Elisabeth | 7 | Azariah | 14 | Driver, Edward | 20 |
| Backster, Gabriel | 30 | Elisha | 7 | | |
| 14 Negroes | | Mary | 35 | Hurnman, Jacob | 30 |
| | | Rebeca | 10 | Thomas | 4 |
| Jewel Arnay | 64 | Elisabeth | 3 | William | 12 |
| John | 3 | 1 Negro | | Samuel | 10 |
| Elisabeth | 6 | | | John | 3 |
| Sary | 1 | Botts, Aron | 68 | Alexander | 1 |
| Backster, Betty | 27 | Margaret | 58 | Ann | 30 |
| 3 Negroes | | Susannah | 23 | | |
| | | Francis | 18 | Taylor, John | 28 |
| Hall, Sillar | 30 | | | Delitha | 20 |
| Margaret | 12 | Hunter, Joshua | 26 | Ann | 1 |
| Ann | 10 | Sary | 28 | Hickman, Elihu | 15 |
| Mary | 5 | Martha | 3 | Mary | 14 |
| Susan | 4 | Mary | 1 | Joshuah | 12 |
| Elisabeth | 2mos. | Otten, John | 28 | 10 Negroes | |
| Basil | 7 | 12 Negroes | | | |
| | | | | Wilkerson, Wm. | 27 |
| Howman, Benjamin | 36 | Bright, Fannah | 22 | | |
| Isaac | 10 | Margaret | 3 | Chitton, Thomas | 24 |
| Stayson | 6 | | | Saffiah | 20 |
| Jesse | 5 | Allison, John | 36 | Barlow, Bettey | 5 |
| Martha | 21 | John | 2 | | |
| Elisabeth | 3 | Hennary-infant | | Cartwright, Thomas | 50 |
| | | Mathew | 30 | John | 7 |
| Maxley, John | 31 | Osiller | 8 | Barbary | 30 |
| John | 1 | Rachel | 5 | Beard, Jean | 18 |
| Ann | 25 | | | Richards, John | 23 |
| Susanna | 8 | Chilton, James | 36 | Lawder, Mary | 17 |
| Elisabeth | 4 | John | 7 | 5 Negroes | |
| Ann | 48 | Jesse | 4 | | |
| Daniel | 17 | James | 1 | Rigg, Benjamin | 45 |
| Sillavin, Philip | 30 | Ann | 28 | Charles | 11 |
| 6 Negroes | | Sary | 8 | Benjamin | 4 |
| | | Hall, Richard | 18 | Rebeca | 13 |
| Fagin, John | 25 | Collop, George | 20 | Ann | 8 |
| | | 5 Negroes | | Hennaritta | 2 |
| Howley, William | 22 | | | | |
| | | Jones, Daniel | 45 | Sible, James | 25 |

83

| | |
|---|---|
| Davis, William | 22 |
| Cassandra | 16 |
| Samuel | 24 |
| Hennary | 3 |
| Levisa | 35 |
| Ann | 1 |
| 3 Negroes & 1 Servant | |
| | |
| Williams, Andrew | 36 |
| William | 6 |
| | |
| Allen, Archabald | 35 |
| Elisabeth | 34 |
| Elisabeth | 5 |
| Woodgard, Ann | 22 |
| 6 Negroes | |
| | |
| Harwood, John | 32 |
| Casaway W. | 3 |
| John H. (infant) | |
| Mary | 23 |
| 12 Negroes | |
| | |
| Green, Phillip | 22 |
| Ann | 26 |
| Mary | 1 |
| Yates, Mary | 66 |
| Newton, Mary | 38 |
| James | 7 |
| 1 Negro | |
| | |
| Lazenby, Robert | 26 |
| Thomas | 21 |
| Joshua | 1 |
| Margery | 25 |
| McCarty, Flurrance | 21 |
| | |
| Elles, John | 24 |
| John Jr. | 3 |
| Mary | 21 |
| Prisila | 52 |
| Zachariah | 43 |
| Shadrack | 21 |
| Christopher | 12 |
| Zachariah Jr. | 1 |
| Ann | 43 |
| Elisabeth | 17 |
| Rule | 15 |
| William | 17 |
| Ann | 8 |
| Charity | 6 |
| 3 Negroes | |
| | |
| Veatch, Thomas | 40 |
| Elijah | 14 |
| Hensenk | 12 |

| | |
|---|---|
| Veatch, John T. | 10 |
| Thomas | 4 |
| Lurana | 31 |
| Barshaba | 8 |
| Mary | 1mos. |
| Phillips, Jesse | 12 |
| Amos | 7 |
| Howard, Thomas | 3 |
| Sary | 2 |
| Conner, Mary-servant | 22 |
| Mahannah, Elener " | 20 |
| Margaret | 1 |
| Conner, Richard | 3 |
| Frances | 4mos. |
| 6 Negroes | |
| | |
| Luckett, John | 25 |
| Phillip H. | 10mos. |
| Moley Ann | 21 |
| McDaniel John | 24 |
| Wats, James | 14 |
| Fitchgarrel, Margaret | 25 |
| Barbary, Ann | 15 |
| 5 Negroes | |
| | |
| Burn, Adam | 40 |
| William | 14 |
| Sary | 12 |
| 7 Negroes | |
| | |
| McCullugh, James | 26 |
| | |
| Mires, Conrod | 38 |
| John | 11 |
| Margaret | 45 |
| Mary | 10 |
| Lestenbarro, Henry | 16 |
| Solomon, John | 30 |
| | |
| Harding, Walter | 22 |
| Elias | 4mos. |
| Mary | 26 |
| Anna | 1 |
| 6 Negroes | |
| | |
| Green, Benedict | 34 |
| Francis | 4 |
| Margaret | 35 |
| Cloe | 7 |
| Jean | 6mos. |
| David | 20 |
| | |
| Fennamoe, Wm. | 65 |
| | |
| Henson, Patrick | 30 |

| | |
|---|---|
| Davis, Ann | 62 |
| Susanna | 40 |
| Ann | 36 |
| Cresey | 29 |
| Aza | 38 |
| Moses | 8 |
| Azariah | 2 |
| Rohdom | 2mos |
| | |
| Nobbs, John | 64 |
| Hennary | 26 |
| Elisabeth | 58 |
| Nansey | 17 |
| | |
| Hardey, Fielder | 40 |
| Sary | 17 |
| Rebeca | 12 |
| Fielder | 10 |
| Mary | 9 |
| Elisabeth | 7 |
| Barbary | 3 |
| Elias | 15 |
| Kenzey | 14 |
| Samuel | 5 |
| Self, John | 16 |
| | |
| Williams, John | 48 |
| John Jr. | 17 |
| Rezen | 11 |
| Thomas | 9 |
| Jesse | 6 |
| Daniel | 4 |
| Sary | 44 |
| Ellenner | 15 |
| Prissilla | 12 |
| Cassandra | 6 |
| Sary | 2 |
| Lalar, Hennary | 24 |
| McComb, John | 21 |
| | |
| Jones, Phillip | 24 |
| Elisabeth | 24 |
| Susanna | 1 |
| Joseph | 23 |
| Elisabeth | 22 |
| Sary | 2 |
| Margaret | 18mos. |
| 10 Negroes | |
| | |
| Wallase, William | 52 |
| Susanna | 57 |
| Rilay, Dansis | 10 |
| Fanning, Thomas | 37 |
| Bowan, John | 29 |
| | |
| Power, Nicholas | 32 |

| | | | | | | |
|---|---|---|---|---|---|---|
| Draper, John | 62 | Breeding, Thomas | 37 | Willson, Josiah | 45 |
| Ellener | 40 | William | 9 | Absolom | 14 |
| Elisabeth | 14 | James | 7 | Thomas | 7 |
| Ann | 4 | Thomas Jr. | 5 | James | 1 |
| | | Mary | 34 | Jamima | 35 |
| Edelin, Thomas | 26 | Susanna | 3 | Nansey | 13 |
| Bartholomew | 28 | Elisabeth | 3 | Rebecah | 4 |
| Monica | 24 | | | | |
| Ann | 1 | Biggs, Samuel | 46 | Warner, Samuel | 57 |
| 3 Negroes | | Hammator | 47 | Hennary | 3 |
| | | McGlocklanen, Mary | 30 | Drusila | 16 |
| Luckett, Capt. Wm. | 65 | 8 Negroes | | Mary | 10 |
| Charity | 59 | | | Haes, William | 25 |
| Virlinder | 29 | Dyson, Basil | 27 | 2 Negroes | |
| Susanna | 18 | George | 3 | | |
| Leven | 13 | Jamima | 27 | Shabord, Samuel | 31 |
| Walch, Mary-servant | 34 | Margaret | 1 | Samuel Jr. | 8 |
| 22 Negroes | | Taylor,Griffin(serv. | 28 | Benony | 5 |
| | | | | Middleton | 3 |
| Beggerly, Charles | 25 | Belt, Carlton | 32 | Sary | 25 |
| Isaac | 5 | Watson | 7 | Rachel | 7 |
| Samuel | 3 | Carlton | 2mos. | Sary | 1mos. |
| Ann | 22 | Mary | 32 | Fealds,Geo.servant | 32 |
| | | Molley | 2 | | |
| Warker, James | 39 | Neall, Thomas | 34 | Seares, James | 78 |
| William | 5 | | | Elisabeth | 70 |
| Archabald | 1 | Baker, John | 31 | Hickman, Sary | 13 |
| Elisabeth | 8 | Adams, Thomas | 33 | 3 Negroes | |
| | | Head, William | 26 | | |
| Hocker, Wm. Sr. | 55 | Chiliten, William | 24 | Seares, Wm. Jr. | 48 |
| William | 24 | Riley, Patrick | 24 | James | 16 |
| Susanna | 60 | Evens,Sary-servant | 26 | William | 14 |
| Margaret | 21 | 6 Negroes | | Israel | 12 |
| Dianner | 19 | | | John | 10 |
| Elisabeth | 15 | Tully, James | 33 | Elias | 7 |
| Swann, Heza | 7 | John | 3 | Joshua | 6 |
| 1 Negro | | Ann | 33 | Elisabeth | 36 |
| | | Ellenner | 8 | Prissilla | 13 |
| Duglace, Samuel | 33 | Mary | 5 | Anna | 1 |
| Heza | 11 | Elisabeth | 1 | Mary - an infant | |
| John | 8 | | | | |
| Charles | 4 | Peddicoat, Nicholas | 26 | Veatch, Richard | 34 |
| Rebeca | 27 | Morrow, John | 24 | Sary | 37 |
| Elisabeth | 6 | Roach Richard | 22 | Rebeca | 11 |
| Mary | 2 | Kirck, William | 13 | Matha | 2 |
| Ann | 9mos. | | | Russell, Thomas | 18 |
| Hoskison, Ruth | 16 | Willson, William | 43 | 1 negro | |
| | | Heza | 12 | | |
| Veatch, Ninian Jr. | 51 | Elisabeth | 33 | Willson, Wodsworth | 51 |
| Nin | 21 | Sary | 10 | James | 16 |
| John | 19 | Elisabeth | 8 | Leven | 3 |
| James | 18 | Mary | 6 | Ellenner | 49 |
| Solomon | 15 | Margaret | 4 | Francis | 24 |
| Elisabeth | 46 | Priscilla | 2 | Mary | 14 |
| Jamima | 13 | 4 Negroes | | Ellenner | 9 |
| 1 Negro | | | | | |

| | | | | | | | |
|---|---|---|---|---|---|---|---|
| Veatch, Grase | 60 | Gatten, James | 38 | Leatch, Catron | 34 | | |
| Silas | 45 | John | 15 | Mary | 11 | | |
| William | 20 | Richard | 14 | John | 12 | | |
| Silas | 9 | Thomas | 12 | James | 3 | | |
| Lander | 7 | James | 5 | Ragen, Andrew | 8 | | |
| Jean | 45 | Zachariah | 2 | | | | |
| Kessiah | 16 | Elisabeth | 41 | Ogden, Heugh | 54 | | |
| Susanna | 14 | Susanna | 16 | D vid | 14 | | |
| 4 Negroes | | Elisabeth | 10 | Heugh | 12 | | |
| | | Anna | 8 | Charles | 8 | | |
| Shekelworth, Phillip | 28 | Virlinder | 6 | Mary | 48 | | |
| Luranah | 24 | 5 Negroes | | Dorraty | 17 | | |
| | | | | Ann | 11 | | |
| | | | | Ruth | 5 | | |

It is thought by the compiler that the above unnamed Hundred is actually a part of Sugar Land Hundred. This is now part of Montgomery County, Maryland. Other Montgomery County Hundreds were Lower Potomack, Northwest, and Georgetown.

Additions to Frederick County, inadvertently omitted

| Lower Potomack Hundred: | | North West Hundred: | | George Town Hundred: | |
|---|---|---|---|---|---|
| Magruder, Rebecca | 30 | Williams, John | 35 | Gittings, Levy | 1 |
| Charlotte | 6 | Mary | 32 | Lingan, Nicholas | 17 |
| Sarah | 56 | Nancy | 12 | Linenbery, Nichoals | 48 |
| Elizabeth | 18 | Elizabeth | 10 | Linenberry, Benj. | 6 |
| Mahil, Eleanor | 33 | Charles | 8 | Linenberry, John | 1 |
| | | Basol | 3 | Lange, Peter | 22 |
| Wallace, Mary | 16 | William | 1 | Borough, Margaret | 32 |
| Eleanor | 10 | | | | |
| Ann | 8 | Lashlee, William | 30 | North West Hundred: | |
| Susanna | 4 | Margry | 25 | Lashlee, John | 40 |
| with the family of | | Robert | 6 | Rachel Lee | 46 |
| Frances Wallace | | Rebackah | 5 | Mary | 9 |
| | | Aaron | 3 | Arnold | 6 |
| | | Moses | 5 mos. | John, Jr. | 3 |
| | | | | 2 negroes | |

## 1776 CENSUS OF BROAD CREEK HUNDRED, HARFORD COUNTY, MARYLAND

| | | | | | | |
|---|---|---|---|---|---|---|
| Armond, William | 32 | Barnard, Mark | 30 | Foster Betsey | | |
| Elizabeth | 28 | Jane | 26 | Peggey | 6 | |
| Thomas | 8 | James | 6 | John | | |
| Hanna | 6 | Thomas | 4 | Fedelious | | |
| William | 4 | Samuel | 2 | Keatty | | |
| Isaac | 2 | Mark | 1mos. | | | |
| | | | | Gordon, John | 3_ | |
| Anderson, George | 40 | Beard, John | 19 | Rebecca | 33 | |
| Jane | 49 | | | Henry | 13 | |
| Mary | 13 | Cunningham, John Isaac Thomas | | Mary | 10 | |
| Jenny | 7 | | 28 | John | 8 | |
| | | | | Sarah | 4 | |
| Allison, Wm. Lame | 1 | Crooks, Henry | 28 | Rebecca | 2 | |
| | | Jane | 23 | | | |
| Bodkin, Robert | 40 | William | 5 | Glen, Mary | 60 | |
| Margrett | 36 | Andrew | 3 | Robert | 18 | |
| Rachell | 16 | Margrett | 6mos. | Joseph | 16 | |
| John | 15 | Elizabeth Kerby | 26 | | | |
| William | 14 | | | Guppey, Henry | 45 | |
| Thomas | 12 | Daubt, Roger | 40 | Margrett | 40 | |
| Robert | 10 | Margrett | 26 | John | 12 | |
| Charles | 9 | Sanuel | 4 | Jane | 10 | |
| James | 8 | ? | 2 | Henry | 7 | |
| Richard | 6 | Robert | 6 | Mary | 3 | |
| Margrett | 6 | | | Margrett | 3mos. | |
| Molly | 5 | Duncan, William | 28 | 3 negroes | | |
| Nancey | 4 | wife | 34 | | | |
| Janey | 2 | Thomas | 1 | Gordon, James | 31 | |
| Sally | 1 | | | Jane | 30 | |
| | | Downing, Francis | 40 | John | 10 | |
| Brice, James | 25 | Susanna | 37 | Agnis | 6 | |
| Alice | 20 | William | 23 | Margrett | 4 | |
| Barnett | 1 | Rebecca | 18 | Elizabeth | 2 | |
| Owen Corker | 20 | John | 6mos. | Mary | 1mos. | |
| Mary Perry | 20 | John | 15 | Aurthur Gilles | 13 | |
| Thomas Perry | 1 | Samuel | 13 | | | |
| | | Molley | 12 | Howlett Andrew | 50 | |
| Barclay, John | 30 | Puck | 10 | Margrett | 49 | |
| Elizabeth | 20 | Frances | 5 | Mary | 19 | |
| 3 negroes | | Ruth | 2 | Elizabeth | 17 | |
| | | 8 negroes | | Ann | 15 | |
| Bennington, Henry | 51 | | | John | 10 | |
| Mary | 20 | Ekin, Samuel | 48 | 1 servant | | |
| (Han)iah | 21 | Nelly | 36 | | | |
| ? | 15 | Jusch | 13 | Henry, Samuel | 58 | |
| Priscilla | 12 | Jane Cud ? | 30 | Mary | 55 | |
| Henry | 10 | Delieca ? | 6mos. | Robert | 23 | |
| Tom | 6 | | | Elizabeth | 19 | |
| Kessia | 4 | Foster, Phidelis | 4_ | John | 15 | |
| Nancey McDaniel | 4 | Keatty | 3_ | Isaac | 13 | |
| Mary Hagerty | 23 | Rebecca | 15? | | | |

| Name | Age | Name | Age | Name | Age |
|---|---|---|---|---|---|
| Hood, Andrew | 40 | McNabb, James | 35 | Rummage, George | 61 |
| Margrett | 38 | Alice | 30 | Mary | 30 |
| Jennett | 8 | Jim | 10 | Geor | 14 |
| Robert | 4 | Alice | 8 | Tom | 15 |
| James | 1½ | Keatty | 6 | | |
| | | Elizabeth | 4 | Robinson, Walter | 40 |
| Howlet, James | 22 | Rachell | 2 | | |
| Margrett | 18 | | | Reese, William | 59 |
| | | Mafford, James | 4 | Ann | 55 |
| Hubard, Ruth(mulato) | 54 | | | Mary | 30 |
| Belt | 13 | Morrison, Ann | 42 | Nancey | 19 |
| Joe | 10 | Ann | 10 | Hanna | 17 |
| Hanna | 6 | John | 13 | Nelly | 16 |
| | | Mary | 3 | Margrett | 14 |
| Hamilton, Jonathan | 35 | Morger Joseph | 19 | Alexander | 12 |
| Betsey | 30 | | | William | 8 |
| Polly | 10 | McKisson, John | 32 | Jese | 6mos. |
| Robin | 8 | Jane | 30 | | |
| Reggy | 6 | James | 8 | Sweeny, David | 28 |
| Alexander | 4 | | 6 | Mary | 30 |
| Sally | 2 | Aurthur | 4 | Sarah | 9½ |
| Betsey | 2 | Sally | 14 | Henrietta | 8½ |
| John | 1 | | | Richard | 6 |
| | | McClam, James | 45 | Olive | 2 |
| Johnson, Thomas, Jr. | 26 | Mary | 40 | Mary-servant | 25 |
| | | Betsey | 19 | Dinia | 6mos. |
| Jones, Aquila | 27 | | | 1 negro | |
| | | McGeomery, John | 37 | | |
| James, Jefferry(negro) | 31 | McGomery, Wm. | 37 | Scharbraugh, Euclid | 62 |
| Martha | 20 | Karr, Rachell | 18 | Mary | 51 |
| James | 3 | John | 6mos. | Thomas | 20 |
| Nancey | ½yr. | | | Rebecca | 19 |
| | | Penix, John | 35 | Sally | 16 |
| Johnson, Thomas | 50 | Sarah | 33 | Sammy | 14 |
| Mary | 40 | Sarah Poage | 70 | Hanna | 15 |
| James | 15 | Keatty | 6 | Jemmy | 10 |
| Isaac | 13 | Sarah | 4 | | |
| Thomas | 10 | James | 3 | Shores, Richard | 23 |
| Mary | 8 | Susanna | 6mos. | Elizabeth | 19 |
| Elizabeth | 6 | | | Mary | 6mos. |
| Sarah | 4 | Rigbies J. | 40 | | |
| | | | | Sims, Robert | 45 |
| Knight, Hanna | 36 | Parks, James | 63 | Alice | 26 |
| Sally | 17 | Jane | 52 | Betsey | 10 |
| Thomas | 14 | Martha | 15 | Rol | 8 |
| Cassandra | 12 | James | 12 | Jane | 6 |
| Aquillia | 7 | | | William | 4 |
| Michael | 8 | Robinson, William | 35 | Margrett | 3 |
| James | 6 | Mary | 30 | Frances | 6mos. |
| Abraham | 2 | Jane | 6 | | |
| | | Mary | 4 | Sims, Ralph | 36 |
| Litten, John | 58 | James | 2 | Ann Boyle | 30 |
| Mary | 44 | | | Mary | 6 |
| Mary | 13 | Rumage, David | 22 | Ann | 4 |
| Hannah | 10 | Martha | 18 | | |
| John Lee | 11 | | | Sims, James | 60 |

| | | | | | | |
|---|---|---|---|---|---|---|
| Spain, Beaver | 72 | Tarbert, James | 26 | Wilson, James(blind) | 50 | |
| Elizabeth | 45 | Mary | 20 | Isable | 48 | |
| Nelly | 19 | Janey | 1 | 2 mulatoes | | |
| Hana | 16 | | | | | |
| William | 13 | Wilson, John Glade | 57 | Wilson, Archable | 48 | |
| Jacob | 10 | Jane | 50 | Margrett | 30 | |
| | | Jane | 17 | Jane | 6 | |
| Taylor, William | 23 | Betsey | 14 | Mary | 3 | |
| Ruth | 20 | Robert | 12 | Agnis | 2 | |
| | | John | 21 | | | |
| Thomas, John | 30 | | | Whyle, Nathaniel | 40 | |
| Mary | 47 | Winman, John | 60 | Kathrine | 38 | |
| Nancey | 3½ | | | John | 18 | |
| Rachell | 1½ | West, John | 39 | James | 15 | |
| Martha | 17 | Susanna | 34 | Philip | 13 | |
| ——— | 13 | John | 13 | Mary | 10 | |
| ——— | — | James | 11 | Sarah | 8 | |
| | | William | 10 | Jane | 4 | |
| Thomas, Isaac | 23 | Margrett | 6 | Gillisson, John | 40 | |
| | | Lidia | 4 | Jane | 30 & 16 | |
| | | Susanna | 3mos. | John | 5 | |
| | | Sarah | 3mos. | Mary | 3 | |
| | | | | Noble | ? | |

## 1776 CENSUS OF BUSH RIVER LOWER HUNDRED, HARFORD COUNTY

Taken by Joseph Renshaw and completed by August 15, 1776 in Md.

| | | | | | |
|---|---|---|---|---|---|
| John Latimore | 35 | Barnard Preston | 22 | Mary Rhoads | 50 |
| Mary Dermott | 55 | Elizabeth | 17 | Thomas | 19 |
| John | 22 | Sarah | 3wks. | Magdeline | 15 |
| James | 14 | 1 negro | | Martha | 13 |
| Caterine | 18 | | | Hannah | 8 |
| | | James Scott | | Mary | 6 |
| William Bay | 20 | of Aquila | 19 | | |
| Jennet Sr. | 53 | Wm. Butler-servant | 19 | Thomas Thompson | 30 |
| Hugh | 18 | 1 servant & 5 negro | | Sarah | 30 |
| Alexander | 12 | | | Andrew | 7 |
| Jennet Jr. | 18 | Thomas Thurston | 40 | Elizabeth | 5 |
| Elizabeth | 16 | Milky | 30 | Ann | 4 |
| Sarah | 16 | William | 12 | Martha | 8mos |
| | | Barnet | 6 | Mary | 3 |
| Alexander Frew | 67 | Unity | 9 | John Thomas-servant | 49 |
| Rose | 67 | Ann | 7 | | |
| James | 23 | Martha | 2 | Isaac Whitaker | 42? |
| Rose Simpson | 30 | | | Elizabeth | 35 |
| Margaret Simpson | 5 | Aquila Scott | | John Sweynard | 15 |
| | | of Aquila | 25 | Joshua | 14 |
| Job Spencer | 26 | Mary | 22 | Samuel | 12 |
| | | James | 5 | Elizabeth Jr. | 10 |
| Nathaniel West | 36 | Clemmency | 3 | Benjamin | 6 |
| Hannah | 40 | Elizabeth | 1 | Martha | 2 |
| Jacob Johnson | 16 | 3 negroes | | Esau Turk-servant | 27 |
| Phebe West | 9 | | | Edmond Evans-servant | 40 |
| Jonathan West | 4 | Alexander Hughston | 24 | 5 negroes | |
| Ruth West | 2 | | | | |

| Name | Age | | Name | Age | | Name | Age |
|---|---|---|---|---|---|---|---|
| Richard Robinson | 32 | | Lemuel Howard | 40 | | Joshua Durham | 43 |
| Ann | 29 | | Martha | 34 | | Sarah | 43 |
| William | 5 | | Ruth | 14 | | John | 21 |
| Thomas | 3 | | Elizabeth | 12 | | Elizabeth | 19 |
| Elizabeth | 1day | | Ann | 8 | | Daniel | 16 |
| Richard Burris-servant | 35 | | Martha Jr. | 6 | | Benjamin | 14 |
| 3 negroes | | | Sarah | 4 | | Alizanah | 11 |
| | | | Susannah | 4 | | Cleminey | 7 |
| James Scott | 48 | | Aquila | 10 | | Pricilla | 5 |
| Margaret | 37 | | Dorsey | 2 | | Hannah | 3 |
| Alexander | 17 | | 10 negroes | | | Richard Jewel-servant-20 | |
| Elizabeth | 14 | | | | | | |
| John | 10 | | Benjamin Howard | 44 | | Robert Trimble | 27 |
| Ozbel | 6 | | Mary | 29 | | Ann | 27 |
| Sarah | 5 | | Benjamin Jr. | 15 | | Robert Jr. | 3 |
| Mary | 2 | | John Dutton | 14 | | William | 2 |
| Bartholomew Savage-ser | 30 | | Lemuel | 7 | | Esther | 4mos. |
| Mary Bryon-servant | 26 | | Fannah | 18 | | Jude Sillery-servant | 30 |
| | | | Elizabeth | 8 | | | |
| John Fulton | 50 | | Mary | 4 | | John Taylor | 62 |
| Hannah | 42 | | Sarah | 2 | | Sarah | 59 |
| Casandra | 19 | | Mary Dutton | 54 | | Mary | 20 |
| William | 17 | | 12 negroes | | | Elizabeth | 18 |
| Alexander | 15 | | | | | Ann | 15 |
| Letitia | 13 | | William Smithson | 32 | | Frederick | 12 |
| Pricilla | 8 | | Elizabeth | 27 | | Delea | 11 |
| Susannah | 6 | | Servants: | | | Ann | 7 |
| James | 11 | | Christopher Semour-22 | | | Daniel | 7mos. |
| Rachel | 4 | | Laughron Cooney | 23 | | | |
| | | | 6 negroes | | | Thomas Whitting | 33 |
| Henry Wilson Sr. | 55 | | | | | Sarah | 33 |
| Pricilla | 62 | | Thomas Smithson | 63 | | Ann | 6 |
| Casandra | 13 | | Mary | 53 | | Elizabeth | 3 |
| 13 negroes | | | Nathaniel | 21 | | Hannah | 5 mos. |
| | | | Arch | 11 | | | |
| Henry Wilson Jr. | 29 | | Mary Jr. | 18 | | Elizabeth Mager | 64 |
| Margaret | 27 | | Margaret | 16 | | Thomas | 23 |
| Henry | 4 | | Casandra | 13 | | Rachel | 22 |
| William | 2 | | 4 negroes | | | Abigal Williams | 15 |
| Samuel | 1 | | | | | | |
| 6 negroes | | | Edward Hamilton | 37 | | John Pain | 33 |
| John Wakeland-servant | 25 | | Margaret | 35 | | Elizabeth | 47 |
| | | | Edward Jr. | 5 | | Pricilla | 10 |
| Doctor Tate | 55 | | | | | Elizabeth Jr. | 9 |
| Ann | 58 | | Buckler Bond | 30 | | John Jr. | 6 |
| | | | Charity | 32 | | | |
| Mary Dooley | 20 | | Martha | 3 | | Isiah Rately | 23 |
| | | | Sarah | 1 | | Giles Hodges-servant-25 | |
| Thomas Barnes | 50 | | Sarah Fox-servant | 30 | | | |
| Mary | 25 | | Jesse Hicks | 3 | | Richard Norris | 56 |
| Joshua | 5 | | Rebeccah Fox | 6mos. | | Jane | 31 |
| Thomas Jr. | 2 | | 3 negroes | | | Mary | 10 |
| | | | | | | Hannah | 6 |
| James Deal | 27 | | John Lang | 58 | | Margaret | 5 |
| Mary | 24 | | | | | Jane Jr. | 3wks. |
| William | 1 | | | | | | |

| | | | | | | | |
|---|---|---|---|---|---|---|---|
| Jacob Bull | 46 | Samuel Wilmott | 28 | | John Weaks | 31 | |
| Renis | 44 | Ann | 28 | | Mary | 37 | |
| Jacob Jr. | 10 | Samuel Davis | 4 | | Zachariah | 10 | |
| William | 15 | | | | Elizabeth | 8 | |
| Bennett | 7 | Vincent Gouldsmith | 25 | | Ruth | 6 | |
| Jerrett | 5mos. | Rosannah | 20 | | Rachel | 4 | |
| Mary | 13 | | | | Mary Jr. | 2 | |
| Eli | 5 | Charles Coleman | 52 | | Ann | 2mos. | |
| Renis Jr. | 11 | Rose | 44 | | | | |
| Jesse | 9 | Margaret | 13 | | Sarah Patee(Potee?) | 60 | |
| Esther | 3 | Charles Jr. | 7 | | Peter | 21 | |
| 5 negroes | | Rose Jr. | 5 | | Elizabeth | 24 | |
| | | John | 3 | | Sarah | 1 | |
| Edward Bull | 22 | | | | John Howling Hughs | 6 | |
| Sarah | 20 | Aquila Standiford | 35 | | John Hague | 43 | |
| Jacob | 1 | Sarah | 32 | | 3 negroes | | |
| Geo.O.Kell-servant | 23 | Hannah | 18 | | | | |
| Mary Rigdon | 20 | Milkey | 8 | | William Anderson | 29 | |
| | | Nathan | 7 | | Mary | 29 | |
| Ann Bond | 56 | George | 5 | | Robert | 5 | |
| Ann Jr. | 24 | Sarah Jr. | 3 | | Elizabeth | 4 | |
| Elizabeth | 16 | Mary | 1 | | William Jr. | 2 | |
| James | 19 | Thomas James-serv. | 22 | | John | 5mos. | |
| 15 negroes | | 8 negroes | | | Daniel Calihon-serv. | 26 | |
| William Cuthbert | 36 | Mary Driskin | 18 | | John Lewis | 36 | |
| | | Ann | 3mos. | | Sarah | 34 | |
| William Bond | 30 | | | | Mary | 8 | |
| Sarah | 30 | Benjamin Sedgwick | 25 | | Walter | 4 | |
| Doctor Finley Bond | 29 | Sarah | 30 | | Rebecca | 5mos. | |
| John Taylor | 45 | | | | | | |
| Amelia Bond | 12 | Sarah Bothe | 27 | | James Jervis | 36 | |
| Mich.McKenn-servant | 30 | David | 9 | | Esther | 78 | |
| 2 negroes | | Rachel | 3 | | Elizabeth | 33 | |
| | | | | | William | 16 | |
| Saran Norris | 79 | John Wadlow | 25 | | Joseph | 4 | |
| Sarah | 51 | Ruth | 20 | | Thomas | 2 | |
| Sarah | 18 | Moses | 5 | | Mary | 6mos. | |
| Benedict | 10 | Francis | 6mos. | | | | |
| 5 negroes | | | | | William Smith | 27 | |
| | | Andrew Shell | 76 | | Rachel | 26 | |
| John Norris of John | 27 | Mary | 78 | | Isabel | 5 | |
| Susannah | 51 | | | | Theophilus | 2 | |
| Alexander | 17 | Benjamin Bradford | | | | | |
| Susarah Jr. | 22 | Norris | 30 | | Ann Wright | 46 | |
| Sarah | 20 | Elizabeth | 28 | | Christopher Clements | -22 | |
| Andrew Jackling-serv. | | Martha | 6 | | Thomas Wright | 13 | |
| | | Sarah | 2 | | Dennis Downs-serv. | 37 | |
| Patrick Cunting | 52 | unnamed son | 9wks. | | | | |
| Elizabeth | 48 | Thomas | 21 | | Daniel Scott of Aquila | -29 | |
| Mary | 17 | John Andrews-serv. | 21 | | 1 negro | | |
| Thomas | 14 | 1 negro | | | Servants: | | |
| Patrick | 23 | | | | Patrick Wagon | 30 | |
| | | Christopher Kent | 36 | | Mary Armstrong | 34 | |
| James Steal | 22 | Rosannah | 60 | | Peter Ratican | 14 | |

| | | | | | | |
|---|---|---|---|---|---|---|
| Edward Tredway | 26 | William Jones | 53 | Ann Scott | 50 |
| | | Elizabeth | 43 | Aquila | 20 |
| Patrick McKinsey | 30 | Gilbert | 23 | Martha | 17 |
| Mary | 24 | Elizabeth Jr. | 20 | Ann Jr. | 14 |
| Elenor | 1 | Magdeline | 20 | 6 negroes | |
| | | William Jr. | 17 | | |
| Mary King | 25 | Jacob | 14 | Samuel Greenlea | 24 |
| | | Isaac | 12 | Rachel | 23 |
| Jane Nugen | 60 | Casandra | 11 | Susannah Gilbert | 18 |
| Ann | 30 | Stephen | 8 | 18 negroes | |
| Sarah | 7 | Benjamin | 6 | | |
| Elizabeth | 5 | Curvil | 1 | William Paris | 49 |
| Rebeccah | 3 | John May-servant | 27 | Sabinah | 36 |
| Hannah Thurston | 13 | Christopher Long- | 23 | Elizabeth | 18 |
| | | servant | | Rachel | 15 |
| John Buckley | 28 | 1 negro | | Susanah | 12 |
| | | | | Kisiah | 12 |
| Timothy Neave | 59 | John McComas | 33 | William Jr. | 10 |
| Sarah | 50 | Mary | 25 | Mary | 7 |
| Mary | 21 | Aquila | 2 | Sabinah Jr. | 5 |
| John | 10 | Thomas Boovey-serv. | 29 | Moses | 3 |
| William | 7 | 2 Negroes | | Rebeccah | 6mos. |
| Thomas Prendergast | 71 | William Brown | 50 | John Shinton | 54 |
| Electhea | 23 | Sarah | 25 | Sarah | 56 |
| Rich. Fitzgerald-serv. | 14 | Ann | 5wks. | Elizabeth | 20 |
| | | | | Ann | 15 |
| Francis Billingslea | 39 | James Monday | 35 | William | 1 |
| Arsena | 28 | | | | |
| Samuel | 11 | Joseph Penshaw | 53 | Jane Davis | 24 |
| Sarah | 9 | Elizabeth | 53 | Isaac | 2 |
| William | 7 | Casandra | 28 | | |
| Walter | 5 | Jane | 26 | Thomas Waters | 46 |
| Francis | 3 | Joseph Jr. | 25 | Rebeccah | 34 |
| Sias | 8mos. | Elizabeth Jr. | 23 | John | 13 |
| Joseph Connoly-serv. | 35 | Thomas | 21 | Martha | 11 |
| 4 negroes | | Philip | 18 | Sarah | 10 |
| | | Samuel | 15 | Bazel | 6 |
| James Holmes | 48 | Susanah | 14 | Elizabeth | 5 |
| Mary | 30 | 9 negroes | | Fenritte | 4 |
| James | 9 | | | Ann | 4mos. |
| Thomas Sheredine-serv. | 25 | Daniel Thomson | 36 | | |
| John Tilbrook-serv. | 22 | Mary | 39 | William Rotherick | 55 |
| William Jewel | 13 | John | 15 | Mary | 40 |
| Ann Griffith | 20 | Ann | 13 | Elizabeth | 3 |
| Margaret McGown | 22 | Mary Jr. | 11 | | |
| | | Thomas | 8 | William Hanna | 27 |
| William Bennington | 50 | Sarah | 6 | Deliverence | 20 |
| Jonathan Cole-serv. | 26 | Margaret | 3 | | |
| Stephen Scarlet-serv. | 25 | Alexander | 1 | James Matthews | 40 |
| Mary Smith-serv. | 19 | Elizabeth | 1 | John Scarf | 30 |
| 1 negro | | 1 negro | | John Tenssil-serv. | 38 |
| | | | | 4 negroes | |
| Jacob Norris | 23 | John Teasewell | 34 | | |

| | | | | | |
|---|---|---|---|---|---|
| Daniel Dugless | 36 | George Burns | 28 | James Cadigin | 6 |
| Sarah | 26 | Ann | 14 | Sarah Cadigin | 4 |
| Bennet | 4 | | | Rachel Nower | 4 |
| Lindy | 1 | Alexander Ewing | 45 | | |
| | | Jane | 40 | Margaret Gordin | 72 |
| Elizabeth Thomson | 29 | Joseph | 18 | William | 39 |
| Thomas | 5 | James | 11 | Hannah | 37 |
| Mary | 3 | John | 10 | Elizabeth | 15 |
| Caterine | 3wks. | Jane Jr. | 5 | Margaret | 11 |
| Elinor Edleton | 23 | | | Philip | 5 |
| | | James Carol Jr. | 30 | | |
| Samuel Durham | 48 | Mary | 19 | Daniel Norris | 46 |
| Ann | 38 | William | 8mos. | Sarah | 49 |
| Mary | 20 | Richard Harvey-serv. | 25 | Elizabeth Beavor | 20 |
| Susanah | 17 | 1 negro | | Richard Broth | 52 |
| Elinor | 15 | | | 1 negro | |
| Samuel Jr. | 11 | Jacob Bond Jr. | 26 | | |
| Thomas | 8 | Elizabeth | 24 | Joseph Rose | 25 |
| Aquila | 6 | Ann Dutton | 12 | Constant | 24 |
| Loyd | 5 | Sarah Wheeler | 5 | Rebeccah | 3 |
| Lee | 2 | William Ross | 21 | Aquila | 6mos. |
| Mary McGanley-serv. | 20 | James Wheeler | 19 | Joshua Day | 15 |
| 8 negroes | | 9 negroes | | Samuel Ingram | 19 |
| | | | | | |
| Robert Collins | 65 | Elenor Ross | 47 | Thomas Saunders | 35 |
| Jimimah | 60 | Mary | 18 | Joseph | 31 |
| Joseph Bates-serv. | 21 | Casandrew | 16 | William | 25 |
| 3 negroes | | Sarah | 12 | Elizabeth | 20 |
| | | Elenor Ross jr. | 7 | Elizabeth Grinley | 20 |
| Jacob Bond | 51 | 1 negro | | Will Geo. Whitlow | 4 |
| Elizabeth | 28 | | | | |
| John | 23 | John McComas | 45 | Capt. Wm. Bradford | 40 |
| Pricilla | 17 | Salinah | 35 | Sarah | 30 |
| Dennis | 16 | Hannah | 12 | Martha | 12 |
| Ralph | 13 | Elizabeth | 4 | Elizabeth | 10 |
| Martha | 10 | Wm. Joshua | 2 | Mary | 8 |
| Charlote | 9 | Elias Smith-serv. | 15 | Sarah Jr. | 6 |
| John Sadler-servant | 26 | Deborick Smith | 2 | George | 4 |
| 20 negroes | | 5 negroes | | Samuel | 2 |
| | | | | John Johnson-serv. | 20 |
| John Hays | 30 | Robert Mitchel | 40 | Wm. Williamson | 14 |
| 5 negroes | | Elizabeth | 28 | 1 negro | |
| | | Sarah | 6 | | |
| Joseph Morrison | 50 | William | 2 | Robert Price | 30 |
| Mary | 29 | John | 2wks. | Hannah | 25 |
| Martha | 1 | Peter Overstocks | 80 | James | 9mos. |
| | | | | | |
| Thomas Bond Sr. | 73 | James Nower | 46 | Caterine England | 35 |
| Elizabeth | 71 | Phebe | 45 | | |
| Martha | 29 | Mary Cadigin | 22 | Edward McComas | 24 |
| Charles Goodman | 40 | Casandra Jackson | 15 | Mary | 20 |
| Stephen Onion | 15 | Samuel Jackson | 13 | Aquila | 3 |
| Thomas Onion | 14 | Jesse Nower | 11 | Alexander | 1 |
| Christian Poland | 60 | Alexander Nower | 9 | | |
| 8 negroes | | Ann Nower | 6 | Patrick Campbell | 35 |

| | | | | | | | |
|---|---|---|---|---|---|---|---|
| Robert Waters | 27 | William Wilson Jr. | 26 | James Saunders | 52 |
| Mary | 25 | 14 negroes | | Mary | 28 |
| Deborah | 6mos. | | | Charlotte | 7 |
| Mary Elebin | 60 | Robert Callender | 65 | Casandra | 4 |
| | | Jane | 25 | Benedict | 2 |
| Elinor Durham | 73 | Robert Jr. | 15 | | |
| James | 40 | William | 12 | Elijah Joyce | 30 |
| Mordicai | 38 | Ann | 7 | | |
| Aquila | 30 | Thomas | 1 | John Sturgis | 55 |
| Hannah | 27 | | | | |
| 10 negroes | | James McComas | 40 | Elizabeth Carrol | 60 |
| | | Elizabeth | 30 | Rachel Kiteley | 20 |
| John Green | 50 | William | 14 | 8 Negroes | |
| Ann | 50 | James | 12 | | |
| Henry | 19 | Josiah | 10 | James Mather | 53 |
| John Jr. | 15 | Martha | 6 | Jemimah | 57 |
| Joshua | 14 | Elizabeth | 4 | Michael | 25 |
| Ann Jr. | 5 | Susannah | 2 | Thomas | 23 |
| Elizabeth Weekly | 15 | Nathaniel | 2mos. | Mary | 20 |
| 4 negroes | | 8 negroes | | Jeremiah | |
| | | | | Darby Devur | 40 |
| Robert Rogers | 4 | Martha McComas | 60 | senLucy Morgan | 25 |
| Ruth | 4 | Hannah | 30 | | |
| Ruth Jr. | 1? | 8 negroes | | Solomon McComas | 45 |
| Sarah | 11 | | | Ann | 40 |
| Belinda | 8 | John Maddox | 31 | William | 19 |
| Robert Jr. | 5 | Catrine | 25 | Aron | 16 |
| Daniel Reardin | 3 | Martha | 2 | Mary | 14 |
| Elizabeth Williams | 24 | Charlotte | 6mos. | Hannah | 12 |
| | | | | 1 negro | |

### 1776 CENSUS OF DEER CREEK LOWER HUNDRED, HARFORD COUNTY
### Taken by William Fisher Jr.

| | | | | | |
|---|---|---|---|---|---|
| Armstrong, Robert | 55 | Bruce, John | 53 | Cromwell, Joseph | 30 |
| Sarah | 54 | Ann | 32 | Susannah | 18 |
| David | 21 | Robert | 10mos. | Vinisha | 54 |
| Mary | 19 | Morgan, Hugh | 11 | 4 negroes | |
| | | Sarah | 9 | | |
| Armstrong, Robert Jr. | 23 | Echsah | 7 | Cook, Robert | 43 |
| Mary | 19 | Druzillah | 5 | Sarah | 36 |
| David | 2 | Rich, John-servant | 25 | Daniel | 53 |
| | | | | John | 14 |
| Ammons, Thomas | 26 | Barns, Job | 52 | Grace | 11 |
| Margaret | 28 | Mary | 45 | Cassandria | 9 |
| Mary | 3 | Job | 23 | James | 6 |
| Ann | 1 | Rachael | 21 | Sarah | 3 |
| | | Ezekiel | 17 | Easter | 6mos. |
| Arnold, William | 29 | Mary | 14 | Bowdy, John | 13 |
| Sarah | 39 | Fannah | 11 | | |
| Ephraim | 5 | Ruth | 6 | Collens, Sarah | 39 |
| Sarah | 3 | Sarah | 3 | Tolston, Mary | 21 |
| Elizabeth | 1mos. | 2 negroes | | Sarah | 1 |
| Brown, James | 22 | Camp, George | 45 | Colston, Casandria | 11 |

| | | | | | | | |
|---|---|---|---|---|---|---|---|
| Cumberland Forge | | Dallam, Winston | 27 | Gallion, Joseph | 44 | | |
| 12 negro workman | | Magrett | 26 | Sarah | 45 | | |
| | | Francis | 4 | John | 19 | | |
| Cotsgrave, John | 32 | Elizabeth | 2 | Gregory | 22 | | |
| Watkins, William | 3 | Coale, William | 21 | William | 16 | | |
| | | McMath, Matthew | 17 | Alexander | 13 | | |
| Coale, Skipwith | 38 | 2 negroes | | James | 10 | | |
| Sarah | 38 | | | Elizabeth | 7 | | |
| Margrett | 60 | Dallam, Richard | 42 | Joseph | 5 | | |
| Margrett | 1 | Frances | 65 | | | | |
| Wallis, Samuel | 11 | 3 negroes | | Gover, Elizabeth | 50 | | |
| 13 negroes | | | | Cassandria | 33 | | |
| | | Dallam, John | 32 | Prissilla | 28 | | |
| Coale, William Sr. | 66 | Samuel | 5 | Gittings | 17 | | |
| Sarah | 61 | Frances | 3 | 14 negroes | | | |
| Sarah | 30 | Margret | 1 | | | | |
| Ann | 26 | 2 negroes | | Gover, Samuel | 21 | | |
| Skipwith | 22 | | | 1 negro | | | |
| 9 negroes | | Ely, Thomas Jr. | 24 | | | | |
| | | Hannah | 17 | Hawkins, Richard | 27 | | |
| Coale, Philip | 40 | | | Lurana | 29 | | |
| Ann | 36 | Ely, Hugh | 22 | John | 2 | | |
| Cassandria | 9 | Sarah | 18 | 1 negro | | | |
| Frances | 7 | Joseph | 16 | | | | |
| Sarah | 5 | Scott, Sarah | 7 | Hall, Christopher | 27 | | |
| Richard | 3 | | | | | | |
| Ann | 1 | Ely, Thomas Sr. | 61 | Heaton, John | 33 | | |
| Sate, Elizabeth | 17 | Malin | 21 | Rebecca | 33 | | |
| 2 negroes | | William | 18 | Margrett | 11 | | |
| | | Ruth | 27 | Sarah | 9 | | |
| Crawford, Mordecai | 40 | Rachael | 25 | Thomas | 7 | | |
| Susannah | 39 | Chapman, William | 4 | John | 4 | | |
| James | 17 | | | James | 1 | | |
| Hannah | 15 | Ellis, Ellis | 36 | | | | |
| Mordecai | 10 | | | Husband, William | 48 | | |
| John | 5 | Fisher, James | 40 | Elizabeth | 46 | | |
| Ruth | 3 | Mary | 36 | James | 13 | | |
| 5 negroes | | Elizabeth | 15 | Meleson | 12 | | |
| | | Thomas | 13 | Mary | 7 | | |
| Chew, Thomas | 23 | Isabella | 10 | Hannah | 5 | | |
| Yates, Sarah | 49 | Sarah | 8 | Susannah | 2 | | |
| Susannah | 25 | Mary | 6 | William | 6wks. | | |
| Sarah | 19 | William | 3 | | | | |
| 9 negroes | | James | 1 | Hill, William | 56 | | |
| | | Linch, John | 19 | Shem | 15 | | |
| Coale, William Jr. | 33 | West, Thomas | 18 | | | | |
| Elizabeth | 28 | 3 negroes | | Hill, James | 45 | | |
| Isaac | 12 | | | Sarah | 27 | | |
| Susannah | 3mos. | Fisher, William Sr. | 66 | Mary | 6 | | |
| Connaly, Jane | 17 | Sarah | 61 | Martha | 4 | | |
| Webster, James | 15 | John | 11 | James | 2 | | |
| Lemmons, Marshal | 15 | 9 negroes | | | | | |
| Coale, Samuel | 23 | | | Hendley, Joseph | 70 | | |
| 2 negroes | | Griffith, Evan | 33 | | | | |

| | | | | | | | |
|---|---|---|---|---|---|---|---|
| Harris, Margrett | 41 | Hopkins, William | 58 | Jones, Ruben | 25 | | |
| Ann | 21 | Rachael | 56 | Mary | 27 | | |
| Elizabeth | 15 | Susannah | 27 | Joseph | 10mos. | | |
| George | 10 | William Jr. | 25 | | | | |
| William | 9 | John | 23 | Jones, Joseph | 91 | | |
| Benjamin | 7 | Leven | 21 | Patience | 81 | | |
| Sarah | 5 | Hannah | 18 | Rachael | 41 | | |
| Thomas | 9mos. | Charles | 15 | | | | |
| 8 negroes | | Samuel | 12 | Johnston, Armstrong | 25 | | |
| | | Thompson, Andrew | 18 | | | | |
| Hopkins, Joseph Sr. | 70 | 16 negroes | | Lilley, William | 45 | | |
| Ann | 65 | | | Linch, William | 21 | | |
| Joseph Jr. | 34 | Harris, Daniel | 31 | | | | |
| Elizabeth | 34 | | | Laughlin, William | 38 | | |
| Ann | 7 | Johns, Skipwith | 28 | Rachael | 34 | | |
| John | 5 | Hannah | 23 | Sarah | 11 | | |
| Joseph | 4 | McClure, Ann | | Mary | 6 | | |
| Elizabeth | 1½ | (hired girl) | 26 | Elizabeth | 4 | | |
| 16 negroes | | 7 Negroes | | William | 2 | | |
| | | | | | | | |
| Hawkins, John | 60 | Jolley, John | 42 | Love, James | 51 | | |
| Samuel | 22 | Elizabeth | 38 | Margarett | 44 | | |
| Johns, Hosea | 7 | Edward | 17 | Thomas | 13 | | |
| Tribble, John | 79 | Sarah | 15 | | | | |
| 8 negroes | | Ann | 13 | Lee, James Sr. | 72 | | |
| | | Cassandria | 11 | Elizabeth | 66 | | |
| Hawkins, Thomas | 31 | William | 8 | Vancleave, Elizabeth | 9 | | |
| Sarah | 29 | John | 6 | Mary | 8 | | |
| Hargrove, Ruth | 53 | Elizabeth | 2½ | 24 negroes | | | |
| Absalom | 11 | Apprentices: | | | | | |
| Richard | 6 | Smith, John | 16 | Morgan, William | 32 | | |
| Lydia | 3 | Chew, Richard | 20 | Cassandria | 32 | | |
| Elizabeth | 1 | Conry, Margaret-serv. | 17 | Elizabeth | 3 | | |
| Davis, Rachael | 23 | 9 negroes | | Sarah | 1½ | | |
| | | | | Cassandria | 1 | | |
| Hopkins, Samuel | 30 | James, Robert | 35 | 10 negroes | | | |
| Mary | 30 | Sarah | 26 | | | | |
| Elizabeth | 6 | John | 9 | Morgan, Lydia | 46 | | |
| Ephraim Gover | 5 | Thomas | 7 | Mary | 31 | | |
| Phillip | 3 | William | 5 | Ruth | 18 | | |
| Samuel | 1 | Robert | 3 | Robert | 15 | | |
| 3 negroes | | Mary | 4mos. | Sarah | 12 | | |
| | | | | Margret | 7 | | |
| Husband, Elizabeth | 31 | Jay, Stephen | 43 | | | | |
| Rachel | 11 | Hannah | 40 | McWilliams, Christian- | 46 | | |
| Mary | 9 | Elizabeth | 13 | Elizabeth | 14 | | |
| Susanna | 7 | Hannah | 12 | McKenny, Joseph | 22 | | |
| Elizabetn | 4 | Samuel | 7 | | | | |
| Ensinger, Susannah | | Joseph | 5 | Morgan, John | 36 | | |
| Maria-serv. | 23 | Thomas | 2 | Mary | 28 | | |
| 5 Negroes | | Martha | 1mos. | Rachael | 10 | | |
| -- | | Humphreys, Richard | | Thomas | 8 | | |
| Hopkins, Gerrard | 33 | servant | 40 | Joel | 6 | | |
| Sarah | 29 | Lamford, James " | 35 | William | 4 | | |
| Wallis, John Hopkins | 8mos. | 18 negroes | | Elizabeth | 2 | | |
| 5 negroes | | | | John | 3mos. | | |

| | | | | | |
|---|---|---|---|---|---|
| Murray, Alexander | 49 | Patrick, John | 34 | Ann | 12 |
| Jane | 50 | Elizabeth | 29 | Mary | 6 |
| Mary | 18 | Margret | 9 | Massey, Isaac | 19 |
| John | 15 | John | 7 | 11 negroes | |
| Elizabeth | 14 | Ann | 5 | | |
| Archibald | 12 | Hugh | 3 | Stapleton, Joshua | 29 |
| Sarah | 10 | Elizabeth | 1½ | Susannah | 26 |
| | | Mary | 1½ | David | 4 |
| Macklemurray John | 59 | Little, Nathan | 17 | Edward | 1 |
| Patrick | 27 | Amos, John | 17 | Lydia | 2mos. |
| Margaret | 25 | Stephenson, John | 25 | | |
| Starrat | 2 | Stuart, Jane | 20 | Shaw, Armintha | 23 |
| Charity | 5mos. | Rees, Margrett | 20 | Ann | 5 |
| Hawkins, John | 8 | 3 negroes | | | |
| | | | | Smith, Martha | 40 |
| McBrayerta, Michael | 27 | Rigbie, Nathan | 54 | Ann | 22 |
| | | Sarah | 45 | Ralph | 20 |
| McCullough, Thomas | 60 | Sheridine, Nathan | 4 | Sarah | 15 |
| Jane | 53 | Giles, Nathaniel children: | | Martha | 13 |
| Williams, William | 8 | Hannah | 14 | Andrew | 11 |
| | | Sarah | 9 | 1 negro | |
| McCann, Arthur | 21 | Elizabeth | 7 | Smith, Ruth | 8 |
| | | Carolina | 4 | Wells, Susannah | 23 |
| Henny, Easter | 69 | Low, Deborah | 43 | | |
| Mary | 25 | Wood, Elizabeth | | Wells, Richard Jr. | 20 |
| | | (hired girl) | 20 | | |
| Miller, Mary | 41 | Servants to Skip.Johns | | Wells, Richard Sr. | 89 |
| John | 20 | Evans, Henry | 35 | Cassandra | 31 |
| Martha | 16 | Jarrod, Henry | 35 | Daws, Elisha | 20 |
| Hannah | 14 | 2 negroes | | 4 negroes | |
| Miller, Joseph | 31 | Rees, Soloman | 64 | Wells, Richard Jr. | 60 |
| | | Mary | 62 | Jane | 50 |
| Nowland, Mary | 25 | | | Elizabeth | 26 |
| | | Rees, John | 23 | Drusillah | 17 |
| Norton, Stephen | 26 | Hector | 30 | Samuel | 14 |
| Sophia | 20 | | | Mary | 11 |
| Lambden, Thomas | 12 | Rodgers, Samuel | 34 | 7 negroes | |
| | | Susannah | 25 | | |
| Nott, William | 33 | William | 14 | Ward, Edward | 67 |
| Jane | 28 | | | Cassandria | 49 |
| Mary | 6 | Rodgers, Mary | 26 | Richard | 21 |
| Sarah | 4 | | | Avis | 14 |
| William | 2 | Rodgers, Elizabeth | 32 | Margret | 9 |
| | | Cessandra | 4 | Hubbard, Geo.servant | 20 |
| Proctor, Richard | 23 | | | 3 negroes | |
| | | Rodgers, Joseph | 28 | | |
| Peacock, John | 58 | Rachael | 16 | Warner, Joseph | 48 |
| Mary | 39 | | | Ruth | 46 |
| Mary | 8 | Rigbie, James | 55 | James Jr. | 21 |
| Cassandria | 5 | Sarah | 42 | Hizekiah | 15 |
| Jenkins, John | 13 | James Jr. | 19 | Aseph | 19 |
| 12 negroes | | Susannah | 23 | Mordecai | 12 |
| | | | | Silas | 10 |

| | | |
|---|---|---|
| Warner, Cuthbert | 23 | |
| Wiggons, Joseph | 30 | |
| Sarah | 28 | |
| Tarace | 7 | |
| Bezleel | 5 | |
| Hannah | 3 | |
| Cuthbert | 1 | |
| Warner, Crosdale | 47 | |
| Mary | 42 | |
| Mary Jr. | 15 | |
| Aaron | 13 | |
| Amos | 11 | |
| Crosdale | 9 | |
| Sarah | 7 | |
| Agnes Crosdel | 4 | |
| Asa | 2 | |
| Wallis, Grace | 54 | |
| Phanney | 27 | |
| 10 negroes | | |
| Wilson, Benjamin | 33 | |
| Elizabeth | 27 | |
| John | 4 | |
| Sarah | 3 | |
| Margret | 2 | |
| Mary | 1mos. | |
| Wilson, John | 80 | |
| Knight Elizabeth (hired girl) | 21 | |
| 7 negroes | | |
| Worthington, John | 42 | |
| Prissilla | 27 | |
| Sarah | 6 | |
| Prissilla | 4 | |
| Henry | 3 | |
| John | 2 | |
| 14 negroes | | |
| Worthington, Samuel | 21 | |
| 6 negroes | | |
| Worthington, Charles | 40 |
| Mary | 32 |
| Sarah | 11 |
| Joseph | 9 |
| Charles | 4 |
| Ann | 2 |
| Margret | 1wk. |
| 9 negroes | |
| Wallis, Thomas | 24 |
| Wilson, Joseph | 74 |
| Hannah | 70 |
| Martha | 33 |
| Mary | 30 |
| Sarah | 28 |
| 7 negroes | |
| Wilson, Samuel | 40 |
| 1 negro | |
| Wilson, Joseph Jr. | 41 |
| 1 negro | |

## 1776 CENSUS OF HARFORD LOWER HUNDRED, HARFORD COUNTY
### Taken by William Hollis, August 30, 1776

| | | |
|---|---|---|
| Osborn, James Jr. | 31 | |
| Osborne, Benjamin | 20 | |
| Semelia | 20 | |
| Susannah | 6mos. | |
| Cord, Aquila | 12 | |
| 12 negroes | | |
| Thomas, John | 49 | |
| Martha | 36 | |
| John Jr. | 9 | |
| Joseph | 7 | |
| Elizabeth | 5 | |
| William | 3 | |
| Hollis, Amos | 40 | |
| Martha | 30 | |
| Amos Jr. | 11 | |
| Abirila | 13 | |
| William | 8 | |
| James | 5 | |
| Benjamin | 3 | |
| Cathrin | 11mos. | |
| 3 negroes | | |
| Osborn, William Sr. | 53 | |
| 5 negroes | | |
| Rhodes, George | 35 | |
| Chauncey, George Sr. | 68 | |
| Benjamin | 17 | |
| Margret | 59 | |
| Greenfield, Jacob | 13 | |
| Greenfield, Mary | 9 | |
| 15 negroes | | |
| Little, George | 35 | |
| Cathrin | 44 | |
| Ann | 11 | |
| Prewit, James | 2 | |
| 12 negroes | | |
| Diction, Morris | 43 | |
| Drusilla | 43 | |
| Susan | 18 | |
| Sarah | 16 | |
| John | 8 | |
| Hannah | 6 | |
| Frances | 3 | |
| Reason, James | 18 | |
| Mires, John | 39 | |
| Hannah | 24 | |
| James | 3 | |
| Leamah | 1 | |
| Beck, Caleb | 47 |
| Hannah | 35 |
| Ann | 14 |
| Hannah | 10 |
| Joshua | 8 |
| Bethsheba | 5 |
| Sophia | 3 |
| James | 1 |
| Jewry, Richard | 34 |
| 1 negro | |
| Drew, James | 22 |
| Sarah | 25 |
| Phillip | 5mos. |
| Bennet, Joshua(orphan) | 4 |
| 1 negro | |
| Drew, Anthony Sr. | 50 |
| Henry | 18 |
| Mary | 17 |
| Sarah | 15 |
| Anthony Jr. | 13 |
| Reason, John | 14 |
| 15 negroes | |
| Farrell, Thomas | 35 |
| Phillips, Samuel | 60 |

| | | | | | | | |
|---|---|---|---|---|---|---|---|
| Drew, George | 25 | Cormoway, Mickael | 33 | Brown, Thomas | 32 |
| Letitisha | 25 | Elizabeth | 19 | Mary | 26 |
| Ann | 4 | | | Jacob | 6 |
| Anthony | 2 | Brown, John | 26 | Elizabeth | 3 |
| Rebecca | 9mos. | Ann | 23 | Mary | 1 |
| Pettlehiser, Lewis | 20 | Lowman, Elizabeth | 52 | Gonins, George | 40 |
| | | Crown, Henry | 45 | Jones, Robert | 27 |
| Kenard, Michael | 30 | | | Thomas, Marget | 26 |
| Hannah | 20 | Jackson, Thomas | 33 | Thomas, John | 1 |
| Ann | 10 | Sarah | 18 | Suttone, Thomas | 22 |
| George | 7 | Beb, John | 27 | 6 negroes | |
| Mary | 6 | Ogg, Stocke | 5 | | |
| Michael | 4 | Cordelia | 6mos. | Stephenson, Jonas | 25 |
| James | 3 | 1 negro | | Rebeca | 15 |
| Folkner, Ann | 43 | | | Mary | 2 |
| Folkner, Robert | 22 | Forwood, Jacob | 39 | Kady, John | 20 |
| Curry, Brian | 27 | Faithful | 33 | 2 negroes | |
| 3 negroes | | Constance | 10 | | |
| | | Gean | 4 | Garrettson, Garrett | 22 |
| Hanson, John Sr. | 55 | Steel, Elizabeth | 23 | Alley | 20 |
| Keziah | 53 | Warner, Ludwick | 37 | Benjamin | 15 |
| John Jr. | 30 | Celly, Volintine | 27 | 2 negroes | |
| Hollis | 28 | Celly, Mary | 27 | | |
| Elizabeth | 18 | Fitsimons, Patrick | 13 | Suttone, Samuel | 37 |
| Phillips, Samuel | 12 | 5 negroes | | Sarah | 40 |
| Phillips, Martha | 10 | | | Mary | 15 |
| 6 negroes | | Lanagin, James | 35 | Marget | 13 |
| | | Chauncey, Cathrin | 24 | Elizabeth | 11 |
| Osborne, William Jr. | 30 | Chauncey, Elizabeth | 5 | Hannah | 9 |
| Mary | 26 | Chauncey, Margret | 3 | Sarah | 7 |
| Cordelia | 8 | Chauncey, Susan | 3 | Robert | 7 |
| Abariler | 6 | Chauncey, Mary | 1 | Ann | 4 |
| Cyrus | 4 | | | Azel, Martha | 15 |
| Cord, John | 11 | Williams, Mary | 42 | Eagle, James | 30 |
| Canfield, Ann | 14 | 5 negroes | | Herrings, Thomas | 25 |
| 4 negroes | | | | Reed, Elizabeth | 90 |
| | | Evans, Benjamin | 34 | | |
| Osborn, James Sr. | 64 | Deaver, Thomas | 21 | Ducon, Francis | 42 |
| Gean | 55 | | | Mary | 45 |
| Martha | 18 | Wadkins, John | 42 | Brooks, Thomas | 3 |
| 4 negroes | | Purify | 41 | | |
| | | John | 14 | Fisher, Amelia | 52 |
| Buckley, John | 53 | William | 13 | William | 14 |
| Sarah | 37 | Amos | 9 | Thomas | 12 |
| James | 11 | Ann | 2 | Asil | 9 |
| William | 3 | Hoy, Roger | 58 | Johnson, Mary | 32 |
| | | | | Johnson, Samuel | 5 |
| Marcum, William | 45 | Hughs, John Hall | 34 | Johnson, Amelian | 3 |
| | | Ann Hall | 22 | Whitacre, John | 23 |
| Blackstone, Thomas | 29 | Everitt Hall | 6 | Whitacre, Hezekiah | 21 |
| Elizabeth | 28 | John H. | 4 | Whitacre, Isaac | 18 |
| James | 8 | Scott H. | 2 | McGown, Ann | 11 |
| Thomas | 6 | James H. | 3mos. | | |
| John | 4 | 3 negroes | | Adams, John | 38 |
| Elizabeth | 2 | | | | |

| | | | | | | | |
|---|---|---|---|---|---|---|---|
| Brown, Robert | 36 | | Macky, George | 30 | | Diemer, John | 30 |
| Elizabeth | 23 | | Vanhorn, Peter | 15 | | Johanna | 30 |
| John | 2 | | | | | Rachel | 11 |
| Sarah | 1 | | Hall, Edward | 28 | | Magee, Sarah | 38 |
| Abirilah | 8mos. | | 9 negroes | | | Magee, Sarah Jr. | 12 |
| 2 negroes | | | | | | 13 negroes | |
| | | | Hall, John "Cry" | 57 | | | |
| Megay, Robert | 48 | | Barthia | 52 | | Armstrong, John | 47 |
| Sarah | 38 | | Avarile | 20 | | Ezebel | 42 |
| George | 17 | | Crasilla | 18 | | William | 12 |
| John | 14 | | Mary | 16 | | John | 8 |
| Robert Jr. | 12 | | Eliza | 13 | | Robert | 5 |
| William | 10 | | McGlogian, Patrick | 49 | | Ezebel | 8days |
| Hugh | 8 | | Davis, Mary(Hired) | 59 | | Williams, Elizebeth | 3 |
| James | 6 | | Timons, Lawrance | 45 | | Gawley, William | 23 |
| Alee | 4 | | Scovin, Francis | 40 | | | |
| Richards, John | 34 | | 26 negroes | | | Giles, Jacob at Bush Mills | |
| Sheridine, Mary | 30 | | | | | Wilkinson, John | 46 |
| Curry, Vionah | 18 | | Punteny, Joseph | 48 | | Hyfield, Charles | 25 |
| | | | Sarah | 40 | | Robins, John | 22 |
| Oliver, James | 60 | | Aquila | 17 | | Williams, Thomas | 20 |
| Cathrin | 60 | | Ann | 15 | | Reese, Sary | 27 |
| James Jr. | 19 | | Prisela | 12 | | | |
| Garland, Cathrin | 14 | | George H. | 9 | | Bennet, Peter | 51 |
| Brown, Sarah | 2 | | Nelson | 6 | | Mary | 27 |
| | | | Samuel | 4 | | Abram | 22 |
| Burns, Mathew | 60 | | James | 2 | | Leaven | 16 |
| Mary | 41 | | John | 2mos. | | Sarah | 14 |
| Nevel, Ruth | 10 | | 3 negroes | | | Peter | 12 |
| Nevel, John | 7 | | | | | Aquila | 7 |
| | | | Giles, James | 26 | | Benjamin | 2 |
| Bennet, Benjamin | 50 | | Ann | 32 | | John | 11mos. |
| Gean | 40 | | Johanna | 5 | | Allham, Daniel | 25 |
| Benjamin Jr. | 13 | | Susanna | 1 | | 1 negro | |
| Vensieler, Alener | 13 | | Jacob W. | 2mos. | | | |
| | | | Fell, William | 15 | | Garrettson, Freeborn | 23 |
| Hanson, Benjamin | 53 | | Cooper William | 35 | | Richard | 18 |
| Mary | 21 | | Caine Edward | 25 | | Mahon, Thomas(hired) | 25 |
| Abbrilah | 13 | | Duke, Thomas | 25 | | 3 negroes | |
| Elizabeth | 11 | | Henry, Andrew | 15 | | | |
| Luke | 9 | | Coulson, Mary | 21 | | Eden, William | 31 |
| Sarah | 5 | | 15 negroes | | | Sarah | 26 |
| Tredway, Elizabeth | 11 | | | | | Jeremiah | 8 |
| Pitt, Frances | 23 | | Henderson, Sarah | 39 | | Elizabeth | 6 |
| 10 negroes | | | George | 2 | | Benjamin | 3 |
| | | | Chauncey, John | 26 | | Mary | 10mos. |
| Munroe, William | 34 | | Nelson, John | 18 | | Codonia, Peter | 15 |
| Mary | 32 | | Nelson, Aquila | 10 | | Boayer, Elizabeth | — |
| John | 13 | | Nelson Pesilla | 7 | | | |
| Elizabeth | 7 | | 6 negroes | | | West, William | 39 |
| Thomas | 5 | | | | | Susanna | 39 |
| William F. | 1mos. | | McComas, Benjamin | 33 | | George William | 6 |
| 1 negro | | | Alexander | 30 | | Marget | 4 |
| | | | Mary | 25 | | Sibyl | 2 |
| Carty, Marget | 45 | | Clark, Patrick | 11 | | negroes living at the Glebe & with Wm. West - 17 | |

| | | | | | | | |
|---|---|---|---|---|---|---|---|
| Diemer, Rachael | 50 | Gallion, Rachael | 34 | Reding, William | 39 |
| | | Prisilla | 17 | Ann | 38 |
| Ball, Aquila Sr. | 49 | Sarah | 15 | Milcah | 8 |
| Sophia | 44 | Abariller | 12 | John | 3 |
| William | 19 | Phebe | 10 | William | 8mos. |
| Charlotta | 18 | Martha | 7 | Burchfield, Hannah | 20 |
| Mary | 16 | George | 5 | Prisilla | 16 |
| John | 14 | Mary | 3 | Adam | 13 |
| Edward | 12 | Rachael | 1 | Frances | 11 |
| Sophia | 11 | | | Dunn, Thomas | 24 |
| Martha | 8 | Garland, Henry | 66 | Brown, James | 26 |
| Benedict | 5 | 1 negro | | | |
| Parker, John | 21 | | | Linch, Daniel | 35 |
| Asker, Jane | 22 | Moubrey, Mary | 29 | Mary | 24 |
| McLaughlin, James | 15 | James | 7 | | |
| 45 negroes | | Robert | 5 | Young, William | 37 |
| | | Mary | 1 | Agness | 28 |
| Copeland, George | 26 | | | Agness Jr. | 2 |
| Frances | 22 | Gallion, Phebe | 63 | Jones, Mary | 18 |
| Mary | 2 | Nathan | 27 | 5 negroes | |
| Calliban, Mical | 24 | Christian | 27 | | |
| 5 negroes | | Martha | 23 | Young, George | 24 |
| | | Sarah | 3 | | |
| Copeland, John | 22 | 11 negroes | | Hollis, William | 50 |
| 6 negroes | | | | Sarah | 48 |
| | | Chauncey, George | 38 | William Jr. | 27 |
| Phillips, James | 35 | Mary | 29 | Clark | 16 |
| Martha | 32 | Sarah | 10 | 8 negroes | |
| James | 5 | Martha | 4 | | |
| Elizabeth P. | 3 | William | 1 | Diction, Peter | 54 |
| John P. | 1 | 14 negroes | | Marget | 42 |
| 28 negroes | | | | Johannah | 15 |
| | | Ore, Mary | 19 | William | 9 |
| Phillips, Susannah | 23 | Rebecca | 14 | Sarah | 5mos. |
| 10 negroes | | | | Cambell, Ann | 8 |
| | | Ruff, John | 27 | | |
| Edwards, Joseph | 29 | Sarah | 25 | Perry, John (Schoolmaster) |
| Finna, Alender | 20 | Dansichlor, Eliza. | 33 | refused to give information |
| Handley, James | 25 | Christian, John | 21 | | |
| | | 9 negroes | | | |

**1776 CENSUS OF SPESUTIA LOWER HUNDRED, HARFORD CO., MARYLAND**
**Taken by Ashberry Cord and completed by August 19, 1776. Sworn before Amos Garrett**

| | | | | | |
|---|---|---|---|---|---|
| Taylor, Stephen | 28? | Frisby, Thom.Peregrine-29 | Sutton, Reubin | 33 |
| Rachel | 26 | Mary | 25 | Rebecca | 25 |
| James | 3mos. | Hariot | 2 | Reubin Jr. | 12 |
| | | Murphey, Thomas | 15 | Mary | 6 |
| Draper, John | 62 | 9 negroes | | Elizabeth | 5 |
| | | | | Solomon | 4 |
| Kelley, James | 25 | Townsell, Hester | 31 | Samuel | 2 |
| Sarah | 23 | Charity | 13 | | |
| Mary | 6mos. | William | 11 | Deaver, John | 27 |
| | | Cassandra | 10mos. | James | 25 |
| Querrer, Oniah | 26? | | | | |

| Name | Age | Name | Age | Name | Age |
|---|---|---|---|---|---|
| Marsh, Lloyd | 27 | Ayres, Thomas | 38 | Combest, Martha | 32 |
| Mary | 27 | Betheah | 23 | Jacob | 27 |
| Catherine | 5 | Elizabeth | 6 | Charity | 15 |
| Hannah | 2 | Milbie | 3 | Susanna | 14 |
| | | Abraham | 1½ | Mary | 7 |
| Fawsett, Jonathan | 31 | Todd, George | 17 | Israel Jr. | 1 |
| Frances | 24 | Kimble, Giles | 26 | Israel | 32 |
| Elizabeth | 3 | | | Susanna | 27 |
| 17 negroes | | Brown, James | 25 | Aquila | 11 |
| | | Mary | 29 | | |
| Brucebanks, Edward | 22 | Thomas | 11 | Wrain, William Jr. | 23 |
| Jane | 31 | 1 negro | | Ann | 18 |
| Ann | 7 | | | 1 negro | |
| Francis | 6mos. | Murphy, Timothy | 22 | | |
| William | 17 | Mary | 31 | Collins, Moses | 48 |
| | | John | 19 | Patience | 48 |
| McCartee, Hannah | 50 | Sarah | 10 | Jacob | 22 |
| Sarah | 16 | Frances | 20 | Patience Jr. | 15 |
| Bendon, Joseph | 45 | Yokely, Mary | 31 | Mary | 11 |
| | | John | 14 | Susanna | 8 |
| Deaver, Micajah | 29 | Elizabeth | 3 | Cassandra | 2 |
| Sarah | 21 | | | Moses | 7 |
| Martha | 5 | Taylor, James | 66 | | |
| Hannah | 1mos. | Sarah | 54 | Combest, Utice | 26 |
| | | Asia | 22 | Elizabeth | 25 |
| Kimble, John | 23 | Laania | 15 | Thomas | 7 |
| Susanna | 18 | Jesse | 14 | John | 5 |
| | | Mashman, Susanna | 23 | Mary | 4 |
| Gordon, Joseph | 50 | 5 negroes | | Elizabeth Jr. | 5mos. |
| James | 16 | | | Mary | 74 |
| Eleanor | 15 | Cord, Amos | 37 | | |
| Reardon, Osias | 36 | Susanna | 32 | Griffith, Jones | 26 |
| Mary | 25 | Hannah | 12 | Patience | 24 |
| John | 1 | Greenberry | 10 | Rice | 16 |
| | | Aquila | 8 | William | 1 |
| Garrettson, John | 24 | Sarah | 5 | Thorn, Catherine | 60 |
| Martha | 21 | Amas, Jr. | 1½ | Alice | 17 |
| Connar, Jane | 49 | Hamby, William | 16 | Maddocks, Elizabeth | 20 |
| 6 negroes | | Mathews, Ann | 15 | | |
| | | | | Duzan, John | 27 |
| Lee, John | 33 | Horner, Thomas | 20 | Rachael | 27 |
| Ann | 22 | | | William | 5 |
| | | Lovell, Peter | 33 | Elizabeth | 3 |
| Kimble, Stephen | 38 | Elizabeth | 30 | John | 1 |
| Margaret | 39 | Elizabeth Jr. | 6 | Abraham | 13 |
| George | 15 | John | 4 | | |
| Josias | 14 | Mary | 2 | Duzan, Peter | 52 |
| William James | 12 | Frances | 6mos. | Elizabeth | 16 |
| Stephen Jr. | 9 | | | Peter Jr. | 11 |
| James | 7 | Cruit, Cassandra | 30 | Ezekiah | 9 |
| Francis | 4 | John | 8 | Ezekial | 6 |
| Eleanor | 1 | Nathan | 1 | Nathaniel | 5 |
| | | Evans, Elizabeth | 1 | | |
| Shaw, James | 31 | | | Hosier, John | 10 |
| Jane | 28 | Evans, William | 34 | Murphey, Hannah | 28 |

| Name | Age | | Name | Age | | Name | Age |
|---|---|---|---|---|---|---|---|
| Delany, Isaac | 44 | | Beaty, Archibald | 30 | | Babe, Patrick | 33 |
| Ann | 33 | | Jane | 25 | | Ann | 33 |
| Joshua | 9 | | William | 4 | | Mary | 5 |
| Elizabeth | 7 | | Hannah | 2 | | Sarah Hall | 3 |
| Mary | 7 | | Jane Jr. | 4mos. | | | |
| John | 5 | | Pritchard, Thomas | 30 | | McSwain, Isaac | 20 |
| Sarah | 1 | | Jones, June | 17 | | | |
| | | | Newbon, Thomas | 14 | | Holland, Francis | 30 |
| White, Jonathan | 27 | | 1 negro | | | Hannah | 25 |
| Margaret | 20 | | | | | Francis Utia | 5 |
| Eleanor | 18 | | Fie, Baltus | 41 | | John | 3 |
| Dinney, Oliver | 16 | | Mary | 21 | | Atkinson, Ann | 21 |
| | | | John | 13 | | Obrien, Roger | 30 |
| Gallion, Elizabeth | 40 | | | 10 | | 8 negroes | |
| Martha | 15 | | Jones, Joseph | 23 | | | |
| Rachael | 12 | | Collins, John | 32 | | Campbell, Daniel | 38 |
| Mary | 13 | | Fitzgarrell, James | 24 | | Catherine | 50 |
| James | 10 | | | | | Jeremiah | 23 |
| Henrietter | 7 | | Wiggins, James | 36 | | Cassey, Mary | 20 |
| Elizabeth Jr. | 6 | | Mary | 33 | | | |
| William | 3 | | Cassandra | 2 | | Kimble, Josias | 33 |
| Presbury, Hannah | 15 | | Groves, George | 10 | | | |
| Cromwell, James | 20 | | Eleanor | 15 | | Taylor, James Jr. | 42 |
| Trueborn ___ | 25 | | | | | Hannah | 40 |
| Truelove, Ann | 37 | | Collins, Ann | 80 | | Cordelia | 15 |
| Mary | 8 | | Boudy, Hannah | 30 | | Mary | 14 |
| Chambers, William | 7 | | Ruth | 16 | | Ashberry | 8 |
| 2 negroes | | | Sophia | 1 | | Charlotte | 5 |
| | | | Young, Sarah | 4 | | Hannah, Jr. | 3 |
| Hearn, James | 29 | | Margaret | 4 | | 1 negro | |
| Hannah | 30 | | | | | | |
| Mary | 1mos. | | Morris, Richard | 64 | | Kimble, Josias | 33 |
| Body ___ | 2 | | Jane | 30 | | | |
| | | | Giles | 8 | | Collins, Elizabeth | 38 |
| Garrettson, Susanna | 53 | | Susanna | 4 | | Mary | 10 |
| Elizabeth | 15 | | Ufam | 2½ | | Ann | 8 |
| Sarah | 13 | | | | | Elisha | 2 |
| Garrett | 10 | | Collins, William | 50 | | | |
| League, Aquila | 35 | | Elizabeth | 15 | | Gordon, James | 53 |
| 4 negroes | | | Francis | 13 | | Catherine | 51 |
| | | | William Jr. | 11 | | Alexander | 25 |
| Stewart, James | 30 | | Edward | 7 | | Mary | 22 |
| Elizabeth | 29 | | Hannah | 4 | | | |
| Mary | 6 | | | | | Atkinson, Mary | 60 |
| Susanna | 4 | | Taylor, Abraham | 26 | | Elizabeth | 18 |
| Elizabeth Jr. | 6mos. | | Martha | 28 | | Frances | 14 |
| 7 negroes | | | Aquila | 1 | | Greenberry | 10 |
| White, Charles | 30 | | Carty, Susanna | 25 | | Beck, John | 35 |
| Mary | 34 | | William | 4 | | Ann | 26 |
| John | 5 | | Hannah | 2 | | Martha | 6 |
| William | 4 | | Ann | 7mos. | | Caleb | 3 |
| Isaac | 2 | | | | | Daniel | 6mos. |
| | | | Mocberry, William | 21 | | Peters, William | 35 |
| Toulson, Elizabeth | 30 | | Frances | 18 | | | |

| | | | | | | |
|---|---|---|---|---|---|---|
| Lancaster, Thomas | 50 | Howell, Ann | 31 | Ford ____ | 15 |
| Catherine | 52 | John | 6 | Sarah, Jr. | 13 |
| Susanna | 16 | Mary | 7 | George Jr. | 11 |
| | | Elizabeth | 4 | Joshua | 8 |
| Jenkins, Samuel | 26 | William | 6mos. | William | 4 |
| Martha | 23 | Abraham | 12 | Warham, Rachael | 25 |
| Mary | 1mos. | | | John | 4 |
| Kimble, Rowland | 19 | Reason, Richard | 40 | Fitzpatrick, Michael | 30 |
| | | | | Plunket, Michael | 28 |
| Chandley, William | 23 | Everest, Joseph | 32 | 38 negroes | |
| Frances | 17 | Margret | 28 | | |
| 1 negro | | Charles | 9 | Garrett, Amos | 53 |
| | | Joseph Jr. | 7 | Francis | 48 |
| Lary, Laurance | 26 | Eleanor | 5 | Milcah | 19 |
| Tush, Rachael | 40 | Elizabeth | 1 | Francis Jr. | 13 |
| | | Mary | 3 | Hanson, John | 17 |
| Milbourn, Sarah | 45 | Lydia | 1 | Elder, Mary | 35 |
| Mary | 14 | Armstrong, Susanna | 32 | West, Bethiah | 19 |
| 1 negro | | 4 negroes | | Conally, Sarah | 45 |
| | | | | Cannon, Sarah | 26 |
| Cruit, Francis | 34 | Walker, John | 39 | Newland, Thomas | 70 |
| | | Jane | 39 | Mand, Daniel | 65 |
| Clark, John | 26 | John Jr. | 5 | | |
| | | Margaret | 2 | Flanagin, Elizabeth | 19 |
| Kimble, James | 49 | | | Greenfield, Thomas | 12 |
| Francis | 20 | Swain, Gabriel | 30 | Swain, Nathan | 32 |
| Sarah | 2 | Bethiah | 20 | Cassandra | 8 |
| Pike, Aquila | 12 | Elizabeth | 3 | Collins, Catherine | 20 |
| Rebecca | 13 | Nathan, Jr. | 1¼ | Tracey, Usher | 28 |
| 15 negroes | | Greenfield, Eliza. | 9 | Dennison, James | 30 |
| | | | | 36 negroes | |
| Everest, Thomas | 52 | Berry, Elizabeth | 24 | | |
| Margaret | 42 | Sarah | 2 | Penrose, Isaac | 28 |
| Benjamin | 26 | Ann Elizabeth | 4mos. | Cassandra | 25 |
| John | 21 | Corbet, Margaret | 18 | Herriot | 2mos. |
| Cassandra | 18 | | | | |
| Elizabeth | 15 | Combest, Jacob | 32 | Woodward, Thomas | 28 |
| Thomas Jr. | 12 | Sarah | 22 | Ann | 25 |
| Richard | 10 | Cassandra | 5 | William | 6 |
| James | 8 | Mary | 3 | Mary | 4 |
| Joseph | 6 | Francis | 8mos. | | |
| Thompson, Nathan | 35 | | | Dorsey, Greenberry | 46 |
| Callahan, Mary | 20 | Warfield, Henry | 27 | Frisby | 17 |
| 2 negroes | | Mary | 26 | Sophia | 28 |
| | | Gallion, John | 7 | Mary | 19 |
| Fields, Joseph | 36 | Martha | 4 | Benedict | 15 |
| Sarah | 25 | 5 negroes | | Sally Frisby | 13 |
| Elizabeth | 5 | | | Frances | 10 |
| William | 2 | Ford, George | 68 | John Belt | 4 |
| Susanna | 8mos. | Sarah | 46 | Milcah | 3 |
| | | Joseph | 30 | Eassard | 1 |
| Pierce, Richard | 28 | Benjamin | 27 | Hughes, Nathan | 15 |
| Rachael | 20 | Mary | 22 | 9 negroes | |
| Ann | 2 | Marabel | 20 | | |
| | | Alexander | 18 | Johnson, Archibald | 22 |

| | | | | | | |
|---|---|---|---|---|---|---|
| Wood, John | 40 | Ward, Edward | 40 | Williamson, George | 44 | |
| Sarah | 44 | Mary | 38 | Ann | 42 | |
| Rebecca | 16 | Samuel | 14 | George Jr. | 8 | |
| Mary | 14 | John | 12 | | | |
| Susanna | 12 | Talbott | 10 | Garrettson, Garrett | 29 | |
| Joshua | 13 | Mary Jr. | 7 | Mary | 18 | |
| Murphey, Timothy | 13 | Elizabeth | 5 | James | 14 | |
| Himes, Nathaniel | 13 | Sarah | 2 | Bennett | 12 | |
| Webster, Hannah | 8 | Edward Jr. | 6mos. | Green, William | 25 | |
| Hoshorn, Elizabeth | 45 | 3 negroes | | 4 negroes | | |
| Rooke, Michael | 25 | | | | | |
| 2 negroes | | Hall, Hannah | 64 | Hall, Cordelia | 56 | |
| | | Webster, Mary | 38 | William | 26 | |
| Durbin, Daniel | 34 | 54 negroes | | Sarah | 17 | |
| Mary | 33 | | | Parker | 11 | |
| Cassandra | 9 | Dallam, Josias Wm. | 28 | Rebecca | 1 | |
| Sarah | 5 | Sarah | 26 | Green, Peter | 58 | |
| Rebecca | 5 | Elizabeth Smith | 2 | Spencer, Margaret | 20 | |
| John | 7mos. | Ruff, Ann | 25 | 31 negroes | | |
| Mary Jr. | 7 | Budd, Sarah | 14 | | | |
| Banning, James | 23 | Webster, Elizabeth | 14 | China, Richard | 37 | |
| Forrell, James | 14 | Smith, John | 20 | Thomas | 35 | |
| Doalman, Thomas | 8 | Cox, Charles | 32 | Ellis, Eleanor | 14 | |
| 9 negroes | | Catter, Edward | 26 | | | |
| | | McBride, Alexander | 15 | Nutterwell, Daniel | 30 | |
| Mathews, John | 62 | Donn, John | 26 | | | |
| Milcah | 52 | 19 negroes | | Owens, Mary | 30 | |
| Roger | 23 | | | Charles | 3 | |
| John Jr. | 19 | Murphey, William | 25 | Sarah | 6mos. | |
| Bennet | 15 | Susanna | 27 | | | |
| Milcah Jr. | 17 | Joseph | 14 | Murphey, Peter | 30 | |
| Neomy | 13 | Simon, John | 24 | | | |
| Francis | 11 | Hailey, William | 48 | Johnson, Archibald | 64 | |
| Isiah | 9 | | | Frances | 55 | |
| Carvel | 7 | Truelock, Isaac | 29 | Mary | 19 | |
| Hart, Jane | 23 | Elizabeth | 20 | Ann | 17 | |
| 16 negroes | | Sarbot | 12 | Adam | 14 | |
| | | Moses | 31 | Thomas | 12 | |
| Redman, James | 32 | Dorsey, Mary | 25 | Josias | 6 | |
| Margaret | 17 | 4 negroes | | | | |
| | | | | Brucebanks, Edward | 27 | |
| Griffith, Samuel | 39 | Mathews, Leven | 40 | Susanna | 36 | |
| Funettah | 30 | Mary | 34 | Isabella | 20 | |
| Mary | 9 | Leven Jr. | 8 | Bennett John | 11 | |
| Martha | 5 | Ann | 3 | | | |
| Frances | 3 | Elizabeth | 3mos. | Evans, Evan | 30 | |
| Sarah | 1 | 12 negroes | | | | |
| Garrettson, Francis | 19 | | | Taylor, Robert | 25 | |
| Major, John | 30 | Osborne, Cyrus | 26 | Isabella | 22 | |
| Dosha | 7 | Susanna | 18 | Sarah | 5 | |
| Jane | 40 | Ann | 6mos. | James | 3 | |
| 27 negroes | | 3 negroes | | Joseph | 1 | |
| | | | | | | |
| Roberts, Elizabeth | 30 | Norris, Lester | 25 | Aquilla Hall's Quarter | | |
| Sarah | 6 | 1 negro | | 10 negroes | | |

| | | |
|---|---|---|
| McClean, Patrick | 29 | |
| Mary | 33 | |
| Catherine | 3 | |
| Cord, Mary | 70 | |
| Ashberry | 35 | |
| 5 negroes | | |
| Daugherty, George | 48 | |
| Margaret | 30 | |
| Mary Ann | 3 | |
| John | 3mos. | |
| Samuel | 17 | |
| Brown, Martha | 3 | |
| 1 negro | | |
| Garrettson, Richard | 55 | |
| Freeborn | 18 | |
| Aquila | 14 | |
| Elizabeth | 12 | |
| Nohel, Catherine | 18 | |
| 7 negroes | | |
| Johnson, William | 36 | |
| Martha | 35 | |
| Aquila | 4 | |
| Prissilla | 1 | |
| Cowen, John | 24 | |
| Sarah | 25 | |
| Mary | 4 | |
| Mark | 1mos. | |
| John Jr. | 2 | |
| Riddall, John | 46 | |
| Eleanor | 33 | |
| Mary | 12 | |
| Sarah | 8 | |
| John | 3 | |
| Robert | 7mos. | |
| Blackbourn, William | 46 | |
| Loney, Moses | 27 | |
| Frances | 20 | |
| Amos | 2 | |
| William | 8mos. | |
| Burch, Benjamin | 7 | |
| John | 12 | |
| Gray, Robert | 15 | |
| Spratt, Sarah | 23 | |
| McMurphey, Archibald | 46 | |
| Fitzgarrell, Thomas | 60 | |
| Mary | 49 | |
| Baily, Nehemiah | 28 | |

| | | |
|---|---|---|
| Johnson, Joseph | 26 | |
| Sophia | 29 | |
| Samuel | 1 | |
| Garland, Francis | 33 | |
| Brucebanks, Abraham | 57 | |
| Mary | 43 | |
| Blanch | 20 | |
| Jane | 14 | |
| Jackson | 12 | |
| Bennett | 10 | |
| Ann | 7 | |
| Abraham | 2 | |

Jacob Forward's Quarter
| | |
|---|---|
| Jeffery, William | 28 |
| Lunan, Ormand | 39 |
| Fitzsimmonds Patr. | 17 |
| 2 negroes | |
| Kimble, Samuel | 50 |
| Sarah | 32 |
| James | 23 |
| Jamima | 16 |
| Susanna | 9 |
| Zachariah | 3 |
| Monroe, John | 19 |
| 5 negroes | |
| Vansickleton, Henry | 31 |
| Elizabeth | 26 |
| Catherine | 8 |
| Francis | 1 |
| Churnman, John | 35 |
| Dorbey, Mitchell | 17 |
| Conn, Mary | 20 |
| 2 negroes | |

Thomas Hall's Quarter
5 negroes

J. H. Hughes Quarter
2 negroes

| | |
|---|---|
| Hall, Dr. I. Carvel | 29 |
| Brannan Caleb | 28 |
| Ashley, Thomas | 21 |
| 14 negroes | |
| Hanson, Samuel | 22 |
| Mary | 23 |

Jacob Giles Quarter

| | | |
|---|---|---|
| McCrackin James | 36 | |
| Mary | 18 | |
| Nonlon, Thomas | 26 | |
| Haunce, Mary | 11 | |
| Vansickleton, Eliza. | 4 | |
| 1 negro | | |
| Barnes, Nehemiah | 2 | |
| Rachael | 26 | |
| Hitchcock, Hannah | 16 | |
| Dooley, Samuel | 27 | |
| 4 negroes | | |
| Browning, Thomas | 32 | |
| Mary | 31 | |
| ——— | 13 | |
| George | 11 | |
| Milcah | 7 | |
| Mary | 5 | |
| Martha | 1 | |
| William | 9 | |
| Cowley, Thomas | 25 | |
| Sarah | 22 | |
| Elizabeth | 7mos. | |

Luke Griffith's Quarter
| | |
|---|---|
| Castledine, John | 37 |
| Mary | 45 |
| Sarah | 11 |
| Alice | 7 |
| John Jr. | 3 |
| 4 negroes | |
| Bradey, Norren | 25 |
| Michael | 1 |
| Daugherty, William | — |
| Murphey, William | 23 |
| Sarah | 50 |
| Joab | 20 |
| Bloodworth, Timothy | 67 |
| Rebecca | 40 |
| Christie, Gabriel | 19 |
| Webster, John Lee | 41 |
| Elizabeth | 33 |
| John | 1 |
| Skinner, Mary | 25 |
| 64 negroes | |

| | | |
|---|---|---|
| Worker, George | 25 | |
| Jane | 23 | |
| Rachel | 3 | |
| Ruth | 1 | |
| Connicken, Jane | 24 | |
| | | |
| Brown, John | 50 | |
| Elizabeth | 16 | |
| Martha | 13 | |
| Sarah | 21 | |
| Sarah Jr. | 6 | |
| Amelia | 11 | |
| 14 negroes | | |
| | | |
| Carlile, John | 29 | |
| Dally, Jeremiah | 26 | |
| | | |
| Paca, Aquila Jr. | 23 | |
| 8 negroes | | |
| | | |
| Hill, William | 36 | |
| Ann | 22 | |
| Moses | 3 | |
| 1 negro | | |
| | | |
| Stokes, Robert | 19 | |
| 10 negroes | | |
| | | |
| Fowler, Samuel | 36 | |
| Frances | 23 | |
| Mary | 10 | |
| Samuel Jr. | 8 | |
| Rachael | 6 | |
| Martha | 2 | |
| Dawson, Sarah | 13 | |
| | | |
| Rev.W. West's Quarter | | |
| 9 negroes | | |
| | | |
| Brown, Sarah Sr. | 69 | |
| Bradford, Elizabeth | 40 | |
| Arnett, Isabella | 35 | |
| William | 2 | |
| Brown, Elizabeth | 6 | |
| 11 negroes | | |
| | | |
| Brown, Sarah Jr. | 33 | |
| Thomas | 12 | |
| Amelia | 9 | |
| 4 negroes | | |
| | | |
| Bennett, Jacob | 56 | |

| | | |
|---|---|---|
| Willson, Hugh | 25 | |
| Margaret | 27 | |
| Rachael | 1½ | |
| | | |
| Oliver, James Sr. | 60 | |
| | | |
| Garrettson, Martha | 26 | |
| Martha | 7 | |
| Mary Goldsborough | 6 | |
| Elizabeth | 4 | |
| Frances | 7mos. | |
| Lauder, Ann | 20 | |
| | | |
| Sutton, Oliver | 56 | |
| Tabitha | 37 | |
| Mary | 16 | |
| Jonathan | 14 | |
| William | 11 | |
| Rachael | 9 | |
| James | 7 | |
| Oliver Jr. | 5 | |
| Susanna | 4 | |
| Jacob | 6mos. | |
| Huntly, Robert | 1 | |
| 3 negroes | | |
| | | |
| Ford, James | 22 | |
| Blanch | 23 | |
| Mary | 1mos.? | |
| | | |
| Fowler, Peregrine | 32 | |
| Mary | 52 | |
| Mary Jr. | 14 | |
| William | 11 | |
| McCartee, Wm. | 10 | |
| | | |
| Deacon, William | 30 | |
| Bartlett, Jack | 14 | |
| 4 negroes | | |
| | | |
| Loney, William | 24 | |
| Mary | 60 | |
| Carlile, Margaret | 28 | |
| Coleman, Michael | 24 | |
| Fent, Peter | 35 | |
| Wright, John | 23 | |
| Dalley, Mary | 20 | |
| Dalley, John | 7mos. | |
| 6 negroes | | |
| | | |
| Duzan, Alexander | 25 | |

| | | |
|---|---|---|
| Ford, Thomas | 20 | |
| Hannah | 23 | |
| Elizabeth | 24 | |
| Elizabeth Jr. | 1 | |
| Noble, Mark | 15 | |
| Cartie, Samuel | 11 | |
| | | |
| Grace, Aaron | 42 | |
| Ann | 31 | |
| Rebecca | 14 | |
| John | 9 | |
| Peter | 6 | |
| Aaron Jr. | 4 | |
| Ann Jr. | 1 | |
| | | |
| Williams, Daniel | 27 | |
| | 19 | |
| | | |
| Gath, Thomas | 43 | |
| Elizabeth | 30 | |
| Martha | 12 | |
| Hannah | 10 | |
| Elizabeth Jr. | 3 | |
| Mary | 6mos. | |
| 41 negroes | | |
| | | |
| Talley, Edward Carvel | 23 | |
| Cordelia | 19 | |
| Martha | 7mos. | |
| Sheaver, William | 25 | |
| Plowman, Edward | 30 | |
| Corker, Patrick | 50 | |
| 7 negroes | | |
| | | |
| Hall, Edw. Benedict | 32 | |
| 13 negroes | | |
| | | |
| Risteau, Susanna | 52 | |
| Smith, William Jr. | 28 | |
| Susanna | 28 | |
| Jacob | 5 | |
| Topping, Elizabeth | 30 | |
| Paca, William | 3 | |
| 15 negroes | | |
| | | |
| Collins, John | 31 | |
| Isabeela | 19 | |
| John Patton | 3 | |
| Frances | 9 | |
| | | |
| Oliver, Esther | 23 | |
| Susanna | 21 | |

## 1776 CENSUS OF SUSQUEHANNAH HUNDRED, HARFORD COUNTY, MD.
### Taken by Charles Gilbert

| | | | | | | | |
|---|---|---|---|---|---|---|---|
| Small, Robert | 30 | Horton, William | 33 | Macantraus, Hugh | 24 |
| Elizabeth | 21 | Elisabeth | 32 | Feeby | 31 |
| John | 9mos. | William | 14 | Mary | 3mos. |
| Beacor, George | 15 | Mary | 12 | | |
| Hare, Patience | 11 | James | 10 | Hall, Josias | 24 |
| | | Sarah | 8 | Mecarty, Owing | 22 |
| Small, John | 27 | Elisabeth | 5 | 3 negroes | |
| | | Ruth | 1 | | |
| Wilson, Andrew | 46 | 2 negroes | | Choislin, Thomas | 41 |
| Lidiea | 36 | | | Young, Thomas | 40 |
| James | 10 | Cummins, Paul | 35 | Chisholm, Thomas | 11 |
| Cathron | 8 | Hannah | 27 | Chisholm, John | 7 |
| Benjamin | 4 | Samuel | 9 | | |
| Andrew | 2 | James | 3 | Hampton, John | 85 |
| Hallett, John | 25 | | | Ann | 84 |
| Prigg, Mary | 25 | Barns, Joseph | 45 | | |
| Brown, George | 14 | | | Mitchel, John | 31 |
| | | Horner, James | 29 | Mary | 34 |
| Hare, Sarah (Widow) | 39 | Mary | 28 | Gaberil | 19 |
| Mary | 17 | Elisabeth | 7 | Elisabeth | 6 |
| Sarah | 6 | Thomas | 6 | Rachel | 4 |
| Daniel | 3 | Casandrew | 4 | Fredrick | 1 |
| | | Mary Gilbert | 1 | Purkins, Ritchard | 16 |
| Rigdon, Charles | 27 | Baker, Jenny Mary | 11 | Taylor, Ritchard | 12 |
| Molton, Mathew | 15 | 2 negroes | | | |
| Sulliven, Nathaniel | 13 | | | Cortny, Thomas | 32 |
| | | Clarke, Elizabeth | 18 | Sarah | 27 |
| Donovan William | 23 | | | Jonas | 10 |
| Rachel | 19 | Culver, Benjamin | 24 | John | 8 |
| Anos | 6mos. | 1 negro | | Hollas | 6 |
| | | Culver, Ann | 62 | Semelia | 5 |
| Durbin, Avariller | 25 | 1 negro | | Sarah | 3 |
| Delila | 2 | Suillovon, John | 27 | Thomas | 2mos. |
| | | Margret | 18 | Brown, James | 13 |
| Judd, Daniel | 40 | Coolley, John | 21 | 1 negro | |
| Hanah | 39 | Rigdon, Sarah | 62 | | |
| William | 17 | Sarah | 23 | Knight, Jonathan | 56 |
| Daniel | 11 | Pritchart, Mary | 12 | Ellender | 46 |
| Joshua | 9 | | | Holliday, Mary | 12 |
| Rachel | 8 | Bedelhall, John | 27 | | |
| Ann | 6 | 5 negroes | | West, Thomas | 45 |
| Elisabeth | 3 | | | Ann | 39 |
| James | 3mos. | Michael, Belsher | 48 | Elisabeth | 17 |
| | | Ann | 28 | James | 14 |
| Thomson, Edward | 45 | John | 14 | Thomas | 12 |
| Jamine | 30 | James | 13 | Samuel | 6 |
| Martha | 10 | Bennet | 8 | Sarah | 6 |
| Mallon | 6 | Jacob | 6 | Mary | 3 |
| Mary | 3 | Susannah | 4 | Isaac | 1 |
| William | 1 | Daniel | 2 | | |
| Sullavin, James | 17 | William | 8mos. | Wright, Charles | 30 |
| | | Horten, John | 23 | Blackford, Thomas | 66 |
| Johns, Richard | 43 | 4 negroes | | | |

| Name | Age | Name | Age | Name | Age |
|---|---|---|---|---|---|
| Perry, William | 81 | Steal, John | 24 | Hamby, Sarah | 35 |
| William | 26 | Casandra | 23 | Fanney | 33 |
| Ely, Hannah | 27 | Elisabeth | 1 | Delah | 7 |
| Macarty, Jacob | 22 | | | James | 1 |
| Bendal, Joseph | 38 | Gallion, James | 47 | William | 1 |
| Mecarty, Mary | 8 | Ruth | 45 | William | 4 |
| Mecarty, Elisabeth | 5 | Thomas | 18 | Welch, William | 24 |
| Meginis, Mary | 2 | Gilbert | 14 | Cord, Roger | 20 |
| | | Betty | 13 | Glovver, Mary | 26 |
| Fort, Peter | 30 | Cumfort | 10 | | |
| Mary | 26 | Rachal | 3 | Boyls, Thomas | 40 |
| Nancy | 5 | | | Mary | 34 |
| Frances | 3 | Gilbert, Michael | 31 | Ebeth | 9 |
| Dority | 1 | Sarah | 22 | Jane | 7 |
| Oure, John | 20 | Thomas | 1 | Mathew | 3 |
| Hurley, Judy | 15 | | | Thomas | 9mos. |
| Barns, Zachariah | 11 | Coal, Jane | 56 | Cowin, Isabella | 15 |
| Tayler, Warter | 19 | Elisabeth | 18 | Smith, Henery | 13 |
| | | Thomas | 14 | Roner, John | 12 |
| Steal, Joseph | 25 | Ezecal | 10 | | |
| Elisabeth | 23 | Carrel, John | 27 | Cox, William | 58 |
| Elisabeth | 50 | | | Mary | 53 |
| Rebeca | 5 | Coal, James | 25 | Mary Banes | 20 |
| John | 3 | Sofiah | 24 | Israel | 13 |
| Abraham | 2 | John | 6 | Rachel | 11 |
| Joseph | 1mos. | James | 4 | 7 negroes | |
| | | Samilia | 4mos. | | |
| Periman, John | 43 | Phillips, James | 13 | Evett, William | 40 |
| Martha | 38 | | | Margret | 26 |
| Isaac | 16 | Coal, Ephram | 22 | Muckelrath, Sarah | 24 |
| John | 11 | Sophia | 19 | Mackfail, Martha | 26 |
| Mary | 9 | Johnson, Samuel | 17 | Slator, Thomas | 18 |
| Martha | 5 | | | Glain, Margret | 6 |
| Elisabeth | 3 | Pearson, Abel | 43 | | |
| Prise, Mary | 27 | Mary | 35 | Giles, Jacob, Jr. | 23 |
| Prise, William | 6 | Elisabeth | 14 | Ame | 21 |
| Durben, Thomas | 18 | Samuel | 10 | Guist, Amilia | 21 |
| | | Abel | 7 | Alisabeth | 2 |
| Antel, John | 59 | Joseph | 5 | Tinlan, Mary | 40 |
| Blanch | 44 | | | Lovvel, John | 22 |
| Ann | 15 | Orsburn, John | 36 | Reease, Robart | 20 |
| John | 13 | Ann | 37 | 11 negroes | |
| Hannah | 11 | Sarah | 15 | | |
| Sarah | 9 | Elisabeth | 12 | At Rockrun | |
| Thomas | 6 | Amous | 10 | Smith, William | — |
| West, Susanah | 18 | John | 8 | Giles, Jacob Jr. | |
| | | Bennet | 6 | Hampton, David | 25 |
| Gilbert, Thomas | 74 | Aquila | 4 | 10 negroes | |
| Mary | 57 | Josias | 1 | | |
| James | 19 | | | Forrage, Crister | 50 |
| Fanny | 16 | Deaver, David | 29 | Page, Mary | 49 |
| Martha | 11 | Mary | 33 | | |
| Hamby, Samuel | 10 | Rebeccah | 6 | Virthworth, William | 43 |
| Mecarty, Sarah | 6 | Ann | 4 | Sarah | 46 |
| Mecarty, Levy | 4 | James | 1 | Sarah | 8 |
| | | | | 2 negroes | |

| | | | | | | |
|---|---|---|---|---|---|---|
| Mackfiel, Daniel | 32 | Taylor, Jane | 40 | Boman, Henry | 40 |
| Jane | 20 | Hannah | 17 | Ellener | 41 |
| Ann | 2 | Mary | 15 | John | 16 |
| John | 8mos. | Alryhan | 13 | David | 14 |
| | | Evret, William Jr. | 4 | Henery | 12 |
| Mecurdy, Archa | 52 | | | Mary | 10 |
| Ellender | 35 | Johns, Nathaniel | 41 | Margret | 9 |
| Margret | 6 | Elisabeth | 33 | Affnea | 7 |
| Lemmon, Elisabeth | 63 | Ann | 13 | Elles | 4 |
| | | Ruth | 12 | Christian | 2 |
| Marshel, John | 30 | Frances | 10 | | |
| Feby | 26 | Cassandrew | 8 | Smith, Jabish | 66 |
| Henery | 2 | Elisabeth | 3 | Mary | 62 |
| Cammeron, John | 14 | William | 1 | Luis | 5 |
| | | Touchstone, Mary | 18 | | |
| Shea, William | 51 | 8 negroes | | Chesney, Richard | 24 |
| Elisabeth | 32 | | | Mary | 24 |
| Thomas | 11 | Edwards, James | 34 | William | 3mos. |
| David | 9 | Margret | 30 | | |
| Elisabeth | 4 | Thomas | 6 | Rumsey, John | 33 |
| Sarah | 4 | Mary | 5 | Martha | 38 |
| Isabel | 2 | Joseph | 2 | Harritt | 4 |
| | | | | Mary | 2 |
| Fitchgarel, Margret | 23 | Brown, Elisabeth | 46 | 14 negroes | |
| Mary | 1mos. | Cowan, Elisabeth | 16 | | |
| | | Cowing, Ann | 8 | Scantlin, John | 23 |
| Phillips, James | 37 | Brannon, Mary | 4 | Rachel | 23 |
| Bethia | 29 | | | James | 1 |
| Sarah | 10 | Howel, Samuel | 22 | | |
| James | 4 | All, Margret | 22 | Haukins, Robart | 59 |
| | | Hannah | 1 | Lidia | 56 |
| Barns, Bethia | 71 | Howard, John | 18 | Richard | 23 |
| Closson, Peter | 16 | 4 negroes | | Elisabeth | 11mos. |
| Brown, Sarah | 17 | | | Averiller | 25 |
| Hapstone, Mary | 7 | Giles, Jacob | 73 | Nancy | 3 |
| 7 negroes | | Johannah | 53 | Robert | 2 |
| | | Wartes, Johannah Giles-9 | | 5 negroes | |
| Porter, John | 63 | Scot, Sukey | 38 | | |
| Ellender | 14 | Smith, Winston | 4 | Haukins, William | 27 |
| Sarah | 23 | Littleton, Ann | 30 | Sarah | 25 |
| Agnis | 10 | Cannabal, Michael | 27 | Joseph | 5 |
| Margret | 5 | Husterfield, Charles | 27 | Margret | 4 |
| Deavour, Mary | 33 | 18 negroes | | Elisabeth | 2 |
| | | | | Musgrove, Frances | 30 |
| Thompson, Mary | 46 | Gilbert, Michael | 70 | 1 negro | |
| John | 25 | Mary | 60 | | |
| David | 23 | Samuel | 23 | Vanhorn, Eseacall | 26 |
| Jery | 18 | Mary | 20 | Sary | 21 |
| James | 16 | Presbury, Elisabeth | 13 | Jessay | 6mos. |
| Elisabeth | 13 | 9 negroes | | Smith, Cathron | 44 |
| Chappell, Mary | 8 | | | | |
| James | 7 | Wamigim, Thomas | 50 | Knight, Sarah | 55 |
| Bowlear, Peter | 21 | Ann | 48 | Mary | 22 |
| | | | | Hadaway, Richard | 40 |
| | | | | Sarah | 26 |

| | | | | | | |
|---|---|---|---|---|---|---|
| Litten, Samuel | 39 | Lampper, John | 33 | Bayles, Samuel | 40 |
| Ann | 35 | Margret | 37 | Elisabeth | 26 |
| Clemency | 17 | Soffiah | 60 | Samuel | 18 |
| Sarah | 15 | William | 21 | Elis | 16 |
| Alisabeth | 13 | Charity | 18 | John | 13 |
| Mary | 11 | Death, James | 56 | Feaby | 11 |
| Susannah | 9 | Death, Geo. Simes | 14 | Mary | 9 |
| Samuel | 7 | 5 negroes | | Mehetabet | 6 |
| Ruth | 5 | | | Sarah | 3 |
| Ann | 2 | Farmer, John | 34 | | |
| Fulk, Mary | 17 | | | Silvers, Mellison | 41 |
| Craford, John | 72 | Snodgrass, William | 36 | William | 21 |
| 1 negro | | Cathroan | 36 | Mary | 16 |
| | | Robert | 13 | Margret | 14 |
| Deven, Hugh | 22 | Margret | 14 | Ammons | 12 |
| Mary | 27 | James | 11 | David | 7 |
| Hugh | 1 | Mary | 8 | Sarah | 6 |
| | | | | Rachel | 5 |
| Husband, Joseph | 39 | Wings, Arther O. | 25 | James | 3 |
| (Hursband?) | | | | | |
| Mary | 34 | Curswell, William | 62 | Silvers, Benjamin | 24 |
| Josua | 11 | Esabeellah | 50 | Affey | 26 |
| Mary | 9 | Robert | 22 | John | 10 |
| Sarah | 7 | Mary | 19 | Gashim | 4mos. |
| Hannah | 5 | James | 59 | Smith, Sarah | 11 |
| Ann | 2 | Robert | 33 | | |
| Joseph | 4mos. | Mary | 74 | Bayles, Benjamin | 42 |
| Puesly, Lidia | 18 | 9 negroes | | Debbrow | 40 |
| Root, Mary | 25 | | | Feby | 19 |
| Aldmand, Sarah | 18 | Slone, John | 58 | Robert | 17 |
| Slond, Sarah | 16 | Mary | 37 | Hannah | 15 |
| 1 negro | | Saras | 13 | Serah | 12 |
| | | Elisabeth | 10 | Samuel | 8 |
| Root, Daniel | 57 | Hennery | 6 | Benjamin | 2 |
| Ann | 56 | | | Debrow | 6mos. |
| Daniel | 26 | Ramsey, William | 53 | Augustus | 46 |
| Jean | 21 | Mary | 40 | Hoges, John | 26 |
| John | 19 | Andrew | 22 | | |
| James | 15 | Alisabeth | 17 | Forgerson, Andrew | 33 |
| Margret | 13 | Jane | 14 | Abigill | 35 |
| Richard | 11 | James | 11 | David | 12 |
| | | William | 7 | Annah | 10 |
| Pervail, Gidian | 29 | Thomas | 3 | Samuel Smith | 6 |
| Mary | 18 | 2 negroes | | Elisabeth | 4 |
| Margret | 8mos. | | | Andrew | 2 |
| Gover, Robert | 15 | Murfey, James | 38 | Benjamin | 6mos. |
| Harres, James | 12 | Elisabeth | 37 | | |
| John | 15 | Rosannah | 80 | Clowes, George | 36 |
| Scotten, Lucey | 20 | Frances | 12 | Elisabeth | 36 |
| 3 negroes | | John | 6 | Cathron | 5 |
| | | Rosannah | 3 | Gorg | 3 |
| Smith, Patrick | 62 | Alea | 1 | John | 9mos. |
| Elisabeth | 60 | | | | |
| Gorge | 15 | Wartus, Godfrey | 37 | Umbel, Isaac | 36 |
| Elisabeth | 15 | 4 negroes | | Cathran | 24 |
| | | | | Mary | 3 |

| | | | | | | | |
|---|---|---|---|---|---|---|---|
| Swarth, Samuel | 37 | Crusan, John | 48 | Donnovan, Daniel | 58 |
| Catherine | 38 | Elisabeth | 33 | Hanah | 43 |
| Gorge | 14 | Michael | 11 | Daniel | 25 |
| Mary | 13 | John | 9 | Jacob | 21 |
| Samuel | 11 | Mary | 6 | Thomas | 21 |
| Sarah | 9 | Garret | 3mos. | John | 16 |
| Peter | 7 | 1 negro | | Elisabeth | 14 |
| Christian | 4 | | | Joseph | 9 |
| David | 3 | Wood, George | 37 | Martha | 7 |
| Isaac | 3mos. | | | Ephram | 5 |
| | | Culver, Robert | 29 | | |
| Steaverson, John | 28 | Johannah | 31 | Arnold, William | 50 |
| | | Mary | 2 | Cumfort | 56 |
| Brown, Freeborn | 32 | Benjamin | 1 | Brown, Mary | 8 |
| Crummel, Neger Oliver | 21 | Trass, Hugh Mackan | 24 | Brown, Jacob | 4 |
| 4 other negroes | | 2 negroes | | Croscil | 22 |
| Steal, Abraham | 25 | Marten, William | 29 | Arnold, Ephram | 24 |
| Sarah | 25 | | | Marah | 40 |
| Josua | 3 | Harthorn, John | 52 | William | 3 |
| Casandra | 3mos. | Margret | 37 | Taylor, Elisabeth | 15 |
| | | Jane | 15 | Mitchel, James | 22 |
| Jimmison, John | 35 | Robert | 13 | Preston, Elisabeth | 71 |
| Mary | 33 | Agnis | 10 | Watkins, Elisabeth | 16 |
| Marthie | 76 | Margery | 9 | Roberson, Sarah | 11 |
| Ellexander | 37 | Margrit | 7 | | |
| Marthie | 4 | Mary | 5 | Barns, William | 41 |
| Sarah | 2 | John | 3 | Margret | 41 |
| William | 6 | Marthy | 1 | John | 16 |
| Long, Ellender | 21 | | | William | 14 |
| Lee, James | 25 | Mecan, Patrick | 26 | Sarah | 13 |
| | | Elisabeth | 27 | Ford | 9 |
| Smith Thomas | 55 | John | 4 | Rachel | 6 |
| Hannah | 46 | Charles | 2 | Elisabeth | 3 |
| Hugh | 22 | Daniel | 1 | Cotten, John | 50 |
| Elisabeth | 16 | | | Butler, Margret | 16 |
| James | 14 | Bayles, Nathaniel | 28 | 1 negro | |
| Samuel | 11 | Sarah | 26 | | |
| Mary | 9 | Ann | 3 | Armstrong, Josua | 44 |
| William | 9 | Samuel | 1 | Margret | 37 |
| Hannah | 8 | Sutten, Edward | 17 | Sollaman | 18 |
| Nathaniel | 4 | 1 negro | | Mary | 16 |
| 1 negro | | | | Ford | 13 |
| | | Bayles, James | 22 | Margret | 9 |
| Vandigrift, George | 30 | | | Joseph | 7 |
| Mary | 22 | Bots, George | 45 | Hannah | 4 |
| Elisabeth | 5mos. | Margret | 37 | Alishea | 2 |
| | | Mary | 17 | | |
| Crues, Nicollous | 80 | Charity | 15 | Rogers, John | 47 |
| Mary | 80 | John | 14 | | |
| Purkins, John | 51 | George | 13 | Barnes, James | 45 |
| Orusan, Mary | 12 | Ruth | 11 | Benjamin | 18 |
| | | Rachel | 6 | Sarah | 16 |
| Clarke, John | 26 | Sarah | 5 | Annah | 10 |
| | | Elizabeth | 2 | Elisabeth | 4 |
| Wood, Josua | 24 | Isaac | 6mos. | | |

| | | | | | | |
|---|---|---|---|---|---|---|
| Bruer, James | 40 | Barns, Elisabeth | 45 | Standly, William | 69 | |
| Elisabeth | 40 | Ruth | 16 | Margret | 58 | |
| Jacob | 20 | Margret | 14 | | | |
| Elisabeth | 12 | Williams, John | 32 | Meake, Andrew | 28 | |
| John | 11 | Elisabeth | 21 | Martha | 27 | |
| Marah | 8 | 2 negroes | | Esther | 5 | |
| Sarah | 4 | | | John | 2 | |
| James | 2 | Kirns, Margret | 30 | Martha | 2 | |
| William | 4mos. | Elisabeth | 11 | Adam | 1mos. | |
| | | Matthew | 7 | Crage, John | 30 | |
| Mitchel, Kent | 33 | Mary | 3 | | | |
| Hannah | 33 | | | West, Enoch | 56 | |
| Shadick | 10 | Power, William | 56 | Elisabeth | 43 | |
| Elisabeth | 8 | Elisabeth | 50 | Enoch | 10 | |
| Mary | 5 | Boner, Nathan | 25 | William | 7 | |
| Thomas | 3 | Cathran | 15 | | | |
| Sarah | 1 | John | 13 | Williams, James | 26 | |
| Rachel | 27 | David | 10 | Margret | 22 | |
| Asel | 6mos. | | | William | 3 | |
| | | Doleman, Sarah | 35 | Susannah | 2 | |
| Cantler, William | 38 | | | Mary | 13 | |
| Mary | 33 | Wood, James | 43 | | | |
| Casander | 10 | Elisabeth | 40 | Williams, William | 52 | |
| William | 5 | Posaurus | 15 | Sarah | 43 | |
| Elisabeth | 3 | John | 13 | Barnet | 19 | |
| Ellabeller | 5mos. | Elisabeth | 11 | Martha | 15 | |
| | | Susana | 9 | Frances | 13 | |
| Mitchel, James | 24 | | | Margret | 12 | |
| Martha | 24 | Larance, John | 30 | Ephrame | 9 | |
| Martha | 4 | Margret | 30 | Eseakel | 7 | |
| Kent | 2 | Alexander | 8 | Sarah | 5 | |
| William | 28 | John | 1 | John | 3 | |
| 1 negro | | | | | | |
| | | Welch, Thomas | 32 | Coon, John | | |
| Barns, Ruth | 47 | Hannah | 26 | Wood, Tochua | 25 | |
| Ford | 13 | Ruth | 6 | | | |
| Hosea | 11 | | | Porter, William | 41 | |
| Asyl | 9 | Griffeth, John | 50 | Elisabeth | 37 | |
| Beck, Elisabeth | 26 | Averilla(Griffin) | 34 | | | |
| 1 negro | | Hannah | 14 | Roberson, Ellender | 37 | |
| | | Elisabeth | 12 | Eseakel | 5 | |
| Barns, Bennet | 23 | Fanney | 9 | Molten, Ann | 16 | |
| Hestor | 22 | Mary | 8 | | | |
| Durben, Thomas | 16 | James | 4 | Rees, John | 48 | |
| | | William | 2 | Cathron | 50 | |
| Mitchel, William | 28 | 1 negro | | Margret | 21 | |
| Clemmency | 27 | | | Joseph | 20 | |
| Barker | 7 | Mitchel, Edward | 50 | John | 16 | |
| Shurlotter | 4 | Rachel | 37 | James | 13 | |
| Elisabeth | 3 | Aquilla | 7 | Abraham | 10 | |
| 1 negro | | Ann | 3 | William | 6 | |
| | | Rachel | 1 | | | |
| Roles, Joseph | 29 | 3 negroes | | Wilson, William | 36 | |
| Mary | 20 | | | 27 negroes | | |
| Matthew | 1 | Thoritan, Elisabeth | 22 | | | |

| | | | | | | |
|---|---|---|---|---|---|---|
| Miller, Margret | 45 | Wilson, Rachel | 26 | Marten, Edward | 26 | |
| Samuel | 21 | 7 negroes | | Mary | 17 | |
| Agnis | 19 | | | Margret | 1 | |
| Thomisdike? | 12 | Wilson, William | 36 | | | |
| Sarah | 10 | Ruth | 23 | Mils, Robert | 71 | |
| Mary | 4 | Mary | 3 | Susannah | 62 | |
| | | Sarah | 7mos. | John | 23 | |
| Anderson, Daniel | 45 | 5 negroes | | Lookket, John | 31 | |
| Sarah | 39 | | | Grant, James | 29 | |
| Mary | 18 | Mecendlis, William | 25 | Donohue, Margret | 18 | |
| Sarah | 15 | Elisabeth | 25 | Grooms, Mary | 13 | |
| Margret | 13 | Sarah | 6 | | | |
| Charles | 5 | John | 4 | Daverson, John | 37 | |
| Prissiller | 2 | Ester | 1mos. | Sarah | 31 | |
| 6 negroes | | Homes, Ann | 22 | Agnis | 3 | |
| | | 6 negroes | | Daniel | 4 | |
| Mackfaddin, Joseph | 41 | | | Elisabeth | 9mos. | |
| | | Logue, William | 60 | 1 negro | | |
| Cox, William Jr. | 25 | Mary | 48 | | | |
| Rachel | 25 | Cathran | 19 | Nutwell, Daniel | 35 | |
| Mary | 1 | William | 16 | Minty | 19 | |
| William | 3mos. | Mary | 14 | Bennet | 2 | |
| | | Charity | 12 | 1 negro | | |
| Bonner, John | 46 | Elisabeth | 9 | | | |
| Christan | 40 | | | Hill, John | 50 | |
| Arther | 17 | Walker, James | 36 | Margret | 40 | |
| Martha | 14 | Elender | 37 | Harmin | 19 | |
| John | 11 | Elisabeth | 10 | John | 15 | |
| Ann | 8 | Gorge | 5 | Samuel | 8 | |
| Barney | 6 | Ann | 3 | Elisabeth | 6 | |
| Charles | 4 | James | 6mos. | Aurilla | 2 | |
| | | Vanhorn, Richard | 18 | | | |
| Mitchel, Micajah | 24 | Henson, Jacob | 19 | Gover, Phillip | 57 | |
| Averrillah | 19 | Brown, Gustus | 16 | Mary | 42 | |
| Martha | 2 | 1 negro | | Sam | 11 | |
| 2 negroes | | | | Elisabeth | 9 | |
| | | Cruse, Richard | 50 | Garrat | 7 | |
| Keen, Timmothy | 37 | Elisabeth | 49 | Robert | 7 | |
| Ann | 40 | Elisabeth | 19 | Phillip | 5 | |
| Rebekah | 18 | Catharine | 19 | Hennery | 5 | |
| Aquila | 15 | Richard | 17 | Prissiller | 3 | |
| Timmothy | 10 | Paydan, Thomas | 15 | 23 negroes | | |
| John | 8 | Vandigraft, Richard | 8 | | | |
| Sarah | 5 | Stiles, Elisabeth | 1 | Wilson, John | 38 | |
| William | 3 | | | Alianna | 32 | |
| 15 negroes | | Campton, Richard | 19 | Christopher | 11 | |
| | | | | Isaac | 9 | |
| Wilson, William | 56 | Marten, Edward | 26 | John | 7 | |
| Casandra | 65 | Mary | 17 | Sarah | 5 | |
| 9 negroes | | Margret | 1 | James | 3 | |
| | | | | Margret | 1 | |
| Wilson, Samuel | 22 | Medowel, Mary | 60 | Gill, John | 74 | |
| Mary | 24 | | | Roberson, Amelia | 13 | |
| 9 negroes | | Collerage, William | 25 | 1 negro | | |

| Name | Age | Name | Age | Name | Age |
|---|---|---|---|---|---|
| Wilson, Peter | 25 | Mitchel, Kent | 52 | Knight, George | 42 |
|  |  | Molten, John | 13 | Martha | 31 |
| Cox, John | 30 | 2 negroes |  | Debrow | 15 |
| Sarah | 30 |  |  | Hannah | 11 |
| Mary | 7 | Pots, Rynard | 51 | Elisabeth | 9 |
| John | 2 | Cathran | 46 | Susannah | 5 |
| Sarah | 3mos. | Cathran | 17 | Aquiller | 2 |
| Weaver, Casper | 16 | Jacob | 14 |  |  |
| 1 negro |  | John | 10 | Mitchel, Thomas | 33 |
|  |  | Elisabeth | 2 | Ann | 32 |
| Power, Nicoles | 50 |  |  | Elisabeth | 8 |
| Grant, Ann | 22 | David, Reed | 38 | Sarah | 6 |
|  |  |  |  | Ritchard | 5 |
| Pritchard, James Jr. | 33 | Cord, Elisabeth | 55 | Barnet | 3 |
| Elisabeth | 18 | Susana | 24 | Averilla | 1 |
| John | 14 | Neomie | 14 | Taylor, Aquiller | 13 |
| Sarah | 4mos. | Jacob | 11 |  |  |
|  |  |  |  | Bayley ___ | 64 |
| Pritchard, James | 63 | Fowler, Patrick | 30 | Margret | 46 |
| Elisabeth | 58 | Elisabeth | 24 | Charles | 23 |
| Harmon | 20 | Joseph | 6 | Aquillia | 21 |
| Samuel | 15 | John | 4 | Bennidick | 17 |
| Benjamin | 13 | William | 2 | Sarah | 15 |
| Daniel Jams | 3 | David | 6mos. | Eseakel | 12 |
|  |  | Smith, Mary | 80 | Averilla | 10 |
| Pritchard, Elisabeth | 26 |  |  |  |  |
| Elisabeth | 2 | Gallion, Samuel | 30 | Stuard, Alexander | 55 |
|  |  | Sarah | 21 | Ann | 55 |
| Rees, Sollimin | 32 | Mary | 2 | William | 13 |
| Averilla | 33 |  |  | Ann | 11 |
| John | 8 | Knight, Thomas | 30 | Mary | 20 |
| George | 7 | Margret | 25 | Margret | 10 |
| Sarah | 5 | William | 6 |  |  |
| Margret | 3 | Mary | 5 | Boner, Eliza.-widow | 33 |
| Sarah | 2mos. | Elisabeth | 3 | Robert | 14 |
|  |  | Light | 2 | Marry | 10 |
| Spenser, Roland | 63 |  |  | William | 8 |
| Jane? | 63 | Barns, Gregary | 42 | Brise | 6 |
| Ritchard | 28 | Elisabeth | 38 | Margret | 4 |
| Wilcock, John | 76 | Ford | 15 | Elisabeth | 1 |
| Wilcock, John | 14 | Richard | 14 |  |  |
| Brukes, Susanah | 19 | Rachel | 13 | Chandley, James | 56 |
|  |  | Gregary | 11 | Susannah | 49 |
| Ray, Gorge | 37 | Mary | 9 |  |  |
| Cathron | 31 | Sarah | 6 | Mohan, John | 42 |
| Mary | 6 | Viariner? | 4 | Judy | 38 |
| Robert | 4 | John | 2 | Edward | 13 |
| Samuel | 1 | Averilla | 1 | John | 11 |
|  |  | 4 negroes |  | Margret | 9 |
| Gallion, James | 50 |  |  | James | 7 |
| Ruth | 57 | Mitchel, Jas.Weaver | 51 | Mary | 5 |
| Thomas | 19 | Jane | 34 | Elisabeth | 3 |
| Gibert | 16 | Elaxanders | 6 | William | 1 |
| Elisabeth | 12 | James | 3 |  |  |
| Cumfort | 9 | Sarah | 3mos. | Hughs, (Ames's widow) | 60 |
| Rachel | 4 |  |  |  |  |

| | | | | | | | |
|---|---|---|---|---|---|---|---|
| Deaver, Sahar-widow | 46 | Bots, John | 43 | Durbin, Mary | 30 | | |
| Samuel | 13 | Elisabeth | 33 | Amos | 2 | | |
| David | 10 | Sarah | 12 | Elisabeth | 8mos. | | |
| | | Ann | 10 | | | | |
| Hughs, John | 24 | Isaac | 7 | Rutter, Richard | 30 | | |
| Jane | 20 | James | 2 | Ann | 24 | | |
| James | 7mos. | 3 negroes | | Esther | 2 | | |
| 2 negroes | | | | Sarah | 1 | | |
| | | Wood, Isaac | 85 | Gipson, Robert | 15 | | |
| Bayley, Josias | 26 | Elisabeth | 70 | Whiticer, Mary | 18 | | |
| Averilla | 17 | | | | | | |
| 1 negro | | Martin, Elaxander | 40 | Durbin, Francis | 28 | | |
| | | Martha | 34 | Ann | 26 | | |
| Samuel Thomases Quarter | | Isaac | 7 | Mary | 5 | | |
| 11 negroes | | | | | | | |
| | | Fleetwood, Benjamin | | Gilbert, Martin Taylor-35 | | | |
| Hughs, Nathaniel | 26 | Hannah | 28 | Martha | 31 | | |
| | | Ann | 3 | Mary | 11 | | |
| West, Robert | 39 | Wilmonton, Joseph | 15 | Charles | 7 | | |
| Ann | 36 | | | Maren Taylor | 4 | | |
| Elisabeth | 15 | Cothlon, John | 61 | Elisabeth | 1 | | |
| Benjamin | 12 | Hannah | 50 | 1 negro | | | |
| Hannah | 10 | Mary | 18 | | | | |
| John | 8 | | | Brannon, Patrick | 62 | | |
| Mary | 7 | Roberson, Abraham | 27 | Darkes | 42 | | |
| Martha | 4 | Elisabeth | 23 | William | 16 | | |
| Michael | 3 | Sarah | 5 | Hannah | 12 | | |
| Ephram | 2 | John | 5mos. | Ellender | 11 | | |
| | | | | John | 8 | | |
| Williams, Morras | 60 | Knight, Light | 59 | Joseph | 4 | | |
| Prissilla | 50 | Rachel | 46 | Jane | 2 | | |
| Mary | 22 | William | 20 | | | | |
| Martha | 19 | Mary | 26 | Rees, Joseph | 40 | | |
| John | 15 | Rachel | 16 | Aberam | 35 | | |
| Ann | 11 | Isaac | 12 | Jane | 88 | | |
| William | 9 | Sarah | 9 | Brown, Sarah | 30 | | |
| | | Hannah | 5 | Jane | 7 | | |
| Ford, James | 35 | | | | | | |
| Olive | 20 | Goodings, Margrit | 40 | Cowen, William | 52 | | |
| Mecool, Mary | 60 | Ann | 15 | Judy | 52 | | |
| Beale, Thomas | 59 | Moses | 11 | Mary | 28 | | |
| Knight, Jane | 17 | | | Susannah | 18 | | |
| | | Hagon, Cathran | 60 | Thomas | 21 | | |
| Stump, Henary | 48 | | | Edward | 15 | | |
| Rachel | 40 | Gorrel, Issabellah | 46 | Stephen | 11 | | |
| Mary | 16 | John | 24 | Rachel | 9 | | |
| John | 22 | William | 21 | | | | |
| Henery | 15 | Joseph | 20 | White, Richard | 30 | | |
| Rubin | 10 | Thomas | 19 | Sarah | 25 | | |
| William | 8 | Esther | 15 | Margret | 3 | | |
| Elisabeth | 6 | James | 14 | Ann | 1 | | |
| Hannah | 3 | Hannah | 11 | | | | |
| Esther | 2 | 3 negroes | | Dilling, Larrance | 27 | | |
| 8 negroes | | | | Catherene | 24 | | |
| | | Greandland, Richard | 32 | | | | |
| Donohue, Danniel | 33 | Homes, Merear | 21 | Joseph, Barns | 45 | | |

| | | | | | | |
|---|---|---|---|---|---|---|
| Biars, Ephraim | 28 | Patterson, Gorge | 27 | Biards, James | 33 | |
| | | Gardener, Elexander | 26 | Casander | 24 | |
| Gilbert, Charles | 53 | 12 negroes | | Jane | 3 | |
| Elisabeth | 53 | | | Rachel | 8mos. | |
| Michael | 21 | Anderson, Charles | 42 | | | |
| Elisabeth | 18 | Mary | 42 | At Harison Thomas' Quarter | | |
| Sarah | 16 | Deniel | 19 | Harris, Joseph | 23 | |
| Hare, Robert | 17 | Grace | 18 | 20 negroes | | |
| 12 negroes | | Sarah | 16 | | | |
| | | Charles | 13 | Mohon, William | 39 | |
| Dilling, Gorge | 40 | Richard | 11 | Jane | 37 | |
| Marther | 30 | James | 9 | Ann | 13 | |
| John | 6 | William | 7 | Cathron | 11 | |
| Edward | 5 | Amous | 4 | Martha | 9 | |
| Robert | 3 | | | John | 7 | |
| Hannah | 2mos. | Perry, Thomas | 56 | William | 2 | |
| | | Margret | 32 | | | |
| Baker, Nicolis | 28 | Sarah | 11 | Hargrove, Richard | 35 | |
| Agnes | 23 | Jane | 9 | Rachel | 30 | |
| Josaway | 14 | Thomas | 6 | Ruth | 4 | |
| Hare, James | 11 | William | 4 | Cassandra | 4mos. | |
| Trame(Frame)John | 19 | Peter | 1 | Hambelton, George | 9 | |
| Stareman, Alisabeth | 11 | | | | | |
| | | Judd, William | 34 | Knight, David | 49 | |
| Harbet, Benjamin | 53 | Ann | 34 | David | 21 | |
| Grace | 58 | William | 6 | Mary | 13 | |
| Benjamin | 23 | Daniel | 4 | John | 9 | |
| | | Saran & Jane | 3 | Ezekel | 7 | |
| Hall, Rebecah | 21 | Deaver, Aquillar | 15 | Green, Elisabeth | 30 | |
| Savage, Gorge | 30 | | | | | |
| | | Gilbert, Parker | 36 | Spenser, Heanary | 50 | |
| Burten, Jane | 62 | Elisabeth | 37 | Agnes | 46 | |
| Mary | 38 | Sarah | 10 | James | 21 | |
| Giffeth, Hannah | 25 | Parker | 8 | John | 19 | |
| Culber, Levy | 3 | Gidian | 7 | Jare | 17 | |
| | | Michael | 4 | Cathron | 15 | |
| Gallion, John | 25 | Prissiller | 1 | Heanary | 12 | |
| Mary | 56 | 2 negroes | | Agnes | 10 | |
| Mathew | 34 | | | Thomas | 8 | |
| Hughs, Elie | 9 | Smith, Benjamin | 30 | William | 7 | |
| Cussans, John | 3 | Mary | 26 | Sarah | 5 | |
| | | Mary | 21 | Lenard | 4 | |
| Megill, William | 42 | Sarah | 1 | Mary | 3 | |
| Elisabeth | 26 | | | Elisabeth & Ruth | 1 | |
| John | 5 | Gilbert, Michael | 42 | Gorrel, Abraham | 50 | |
| Mary | 1 | Mary | 36 | | | |
| Ars, John | 22 | Aquiller | 18 | West, James | 40 | |
| 1 negro | | James | 16 | Ann | 33 | |
| | | Sarah | 14 | Mary | 14 | |
| Cummins, Phillip | 66 | Michael | 10 | Heanary | 11 | |
| Sarah | 54 | Mathew | 8 | Ann | 8 | |
| John | 23 | William | 5 | James | 6 | |
| Casandra | 20 | Amous | 2 | Sarah | 1 | |
| Benjamin | 19 | 4 negroes | | | | |
| Samuel | 17 | | | Pritchard, Obidiah Sr.-30 | | |
| Andrew | 13 | Durbin, Averiller | 17 | Stephen(blacks) 15-· | | |

## 1776 CENSUS OF PRINCE GEORGE COUNTY, MARYLAND

St. John's and Prince George Parishes taken by Captain Thomas Dent August 31, 1776

| | | | | | |
|---|---|---|---|---|---|
| Clagett, Thomas | 35 | Vincent, John | 25 | Smith, James | 43 |
| Horatio | 19 | Joseph | 3mos. | Sarah | 15 |
| Mary | 35 & 5 | Prudence | 30 | Elianor | 14 |
| Judson M | 7 | Mary | 3 | Rebecca | 10 |
| Thomas | 3 | Frances | 27 | Walter | 11 |
| Hector | 3mos. | 1 negro | | Shine, John | 33 |
| Boswell, David | 25 | | | Leach, Ann | 37 |
| | | Dent, Richard | 28 | Beneham, Ann | 27 |
| Dent, Thomas | 41 | Mary | 67 | Holmes, Joseph | 55 |
| Geo. Fairfax | 2 | Elizabeth | 49 | 2 negroes | |
| Geo. Washington | 2mos. | Hardey, Elizabeth | 12 | | |
| Elizabeth | 28 | Welch, Elizabeth | 16 | Holliday, James | 35 |
| Clark, John | 40 | 15 negroes | | William | 1 |
| Hardey, George | 14 | | | Elizabeth | 25 |
| Murrey, Judah | 35 | Dent, Walter | 32 | Elizabeth | 8 |
| | | Elizabeth | 35 | Mary | 7 |
| Adams, John | 36 | Cloe | 9 | | |
| Mary | 43 | Jane | 5 | Simpson, Joseph | 35 |
| | | Walter C. | 4 | Solomon | 21 |
| Cox, Abraham | 25 | Ann | 2 | Charity | 30 |
| Mary | 24 | Montgomery, Margaret | 29 | Salome | 6 |
| Jesse | 5 | 2 negroes | | Amelia | 2 |
| Zachariah | 2 | | | Tennally | 14 |
| | | Edelen, Salome | 50 | Levey | 12 |
| Chapman, John | 50 | Catherine | 22 | Thomas | 10 |
| Sarah | 42 | Margarett | 20 | George | 8 |
| Lattimore, Elizabeth | 13 | Sarah | 16 | 2 negroes | |
| | | Edward | 29 | | |
| Vermillion, James | 34 | Joseph | 19 | Casey, John | 35 |
| Rachell | 34 | Samuel | 14 | Gill, John | 30 |
| Elizabeth | 15 | James | 12 | Lillis, John | 19 |
| Eleanor | 7 | Gill, Betty | 44 | Jones, William | 15 |
| Abraham | 5 | Curtain, Catherine | 60 | Feen, Patrick | 25 |
| | | 24 negroes | | 2 negroes | |
| Martin, Thomas | 40 | | | | |
| Rozia | 37 | Turton, John | 32 | Lanham, Elias | 25 |
| Smith | 12 | Harrison | 2 | John | 4 |
| Amelia | 10 | Fielder | 6mos. | Ann | 30 |
| Susanna | 1 | Aquilla | 28 | Letty | 1 |
| 2 negroes | | Hines, Henry | 25 | | |
| | | 7 negroes | | Magruder, Enoch | 53 |
| Adams, James | 35 | | | Dennis | 18 |
| Walter | 1 | Hardey, Thomas Dent | 21 | Meek | 54 |
| Elizabeth | 5 | Ann | 22 | Elizabeth | 24 |
| Susanna | 28 | Mary | 17 | Elianor | 22 |
| Dement, George | 26 | Letty | 6 | Noble, Thomas | 14 |
| | | 4 negroes | | 26 negroes | |
| Fuller, William | 40 | | | | |
| James | 7 | Neydin, Thomas | 39 | Duvall, Benjamin | 59 |
| William | 5 | Hestor | 31 | Moreen | 12 |
| Elizabeth | 35 | Mary | 1 | Ann | 45 |

| | | | | | | |
|---|---|---|---|---|---|---|
| Duvall, Nancy | 78 | Worland, John | 56 | Simms, Edward | 38 |
| Bonifant, Mary | 12 | William | 15 | Ann | 32 |
| Galiham, Rosey | 17 | James | 13 | Buddicum, Charles | 10 |
| | | Thomas | 2 | 7 negroes | |
| Bayne, Saml. Hawkins | 28 | Walter | 1 | | |
| Thomas | 48 | Mary | 39 | Clarvoe, John Jr. | 27 |
| Elizabeth | 50 | Stacey | 27 | William | 2 |
| Ann | 24 | Elianor | 24 | Henry | 2 |
| Henrietta | 1 | Mary | 20 | Mary | 25 |
| 4 negroes | | Brady, Rebecca | 65 | 2 negroes | |
| | | Murtle, Elianor | 17 | | |
| Welling, Thomas | 25 | Murtle, Ann | 11 | Tennally, John | 27 |
| William | 6 | 2 negroes | | Joanna | 52 |
| Ann | 30 | | | Elizabeth | 30 |
| Parkins, Samuel | 13 | Locker, Phillip | 57 | Sarah | 20 |
| Rachell | 10 | Phillip | 23 | | |
| Ann | 18 | James | 22 | Tennally, William | 29 |
| 1 negro | | David | 20 | Thomas | 5 |
| | | Thomas | 16 | Thomas | 4 |
| Jones, Thomas | 32 | Isaac | 8 | Lydia | 27 |
| William | 7 | Elizabeth | 50 | Lydia | 21 |
| Thomas | 5 | Elizabeth | 17 | Tracey | 2 |
| Susanna | 30 | Amelia | 13 | | |
| Elianor | 2 | | | Nevel, John | 53 |
| Brooks, Ann | 19 | Willson, Joseph | 56 | James | 23 |
| | | Nathaniel | 23 | Richard | 13 |
| Swink, William | 34 | Jane | 53 | Joseph | 11 |
| George | 5 | Martha | 18 | Ann | 47 |
| John | 3 | Elizabeth | 14 | Ann | 16 |
| Mary | 27 | 4 negroes | | Ann M. | 1 |
| Elizabeth | 10 | | | 2 negroes | |
| Susanna | 8 | Nevel, John Jr. | 29 | | |
| Catherine | 7 | Thomas | 1 | Norton, William Jr. | 36 |
| Mary | 5mos. | Mary | 23 | Mary | 33 |
| | | Gates, Ann | 14 | Amelia | 3 |
| Hoggin, Peter | 50 | 6 negroes | | Mudd, Walter | 12 |
| John | 20 | | | John | 8 |
| Richard | 16 | Lansdale, Charles | 34 | 3 negroes | |
| Peter | 12 | Harry | 5 | | |
| William | 10 | Catherine | 40 | Wade, Zachariah | 56 |
| Soloman | 8 | Elizabeth A. | 7 | George | 34 |
| Catherine | 46 | Susanna | 1mos. | Zachariah Jr. | 28 |
| Elizabeth | 84 | Lettlemore, Richard | 44 | Ann | 50 |
| Elizabeth | 15 | Scarfe, John | 36 | Saxton, Hester | 36 |
| Rebecca | 6 | Elizabeth | 40 | Leonora | 2 |
| Catherine | 3 | Wheeler, Elizabeth | 68 | 1 negro | |
| 5 negroes | | 5 negroes | | | |
| | | | | Clarkson, Edward | 54 |
| Lanham, Elisha | 52 | Keech, John | 40 | Harry | 19 |
| Jemimah | 36 | Edward | 8 | Edward Jr. | 15 |
| Rollins, John | 13 | William | 4 | Martha | 53 |
| Bayne, Charity | 17 | Clotilda | 41 | Sarah | 23 |
| Meriah | 7 | Thompson, Thomas | 14 | Martha | 21 |
| 2 negroes | | Stuart, Elianor | 17 | 5 negroes | |
| | | 1 negro | | | |

| | | | | | |
|---|---|---|---|---|---|
| Harvey, James | 30 | Harvey, Thomas | 55 | Boswell, George | 27 |
| Thomas Jr. | 6 | Henry | 21 | Peter | 22 |
| George | 3 | Elianor | 59 | Elizabeth | 65 |
| Mary | 30 | Virlinda | 17 | Redman, Mary | 20 |
| Elizabeth | 2 | Mears, Osborn | 9 | Rebecca | 6 |
| | | 2 negroes | | | |
| Acton, Henry | 44 | | | Lowe, Michael | 35 |
| Henry Jr. | 21 | Hileary, John | 35 | Lloyd M. | 9 |
| Smallwood | 17 | Thomas | 2mos. | Henry | 7 |
| Hister | 45 | Mary | 24 | Ann | 30 |
| Ann | 9 | Eleanor | 3 | Elizabeth | 6 |
| Elizabeth | 7 | | | Barbary | 10 |
| Mary | 4 | Harris, John Jr. | 50 | Long, John | 45 |
| Farrell, Ignatius | 36 | Smallwood Phillip | 32 | John | 6mos. |
| Smallwood, Richard | 9 | Francis | 23 | Venia | 23 |
| 5 negroes | | Benjamin | 17 | Tomlin, Ann | 15 |
| | | Precilla | 30 | 5 negroes | |
| Summers, George | 54 | Martha | 20 | | |
| George Jr. | 17 | 12 negroes | | Bryan, Richard | 46 |
| Paul | 10 | | | Rachel | 33 |
| Elizabeth | 54 | Beall, James | 47 | Cox, Elisabeth | 16 |
| Ann | 22 | Samuel | 6 | Lanham, Edward | 14 |
| Verlinda | 15 | Elizabeth | 42 | Lanham, Robert Poor | 10 |
| Glasgow, Thomas Bean | 6 | Mary A. | 18 | Gilder, Ann | 6 |
| 2 negroes | | Elizabeth | 16 | 4 negroes | |
| | | Rebecca | 14 | | |
| | | Eleanor | 12 | | |
| | | Casandra | 9 | | |
| | | Sarah | 3 | | |

At this point the method of recording the members of the household changes. The male head of the household is given, followed by his age and the ages of all the other males living in the household. The same form is used for the females.

Evans, Henry 44, 30, 9
   Elizabeth 36, 17, 14, 12, 7, 5, 1
   3 negroes

Carns, Richard 39, 30, 24, 23, 17, 13, 3
   Mary 38, 15, 11, 9, 7, 1
   4 negroes

Sutton, William 27, 1
   Mary 67, 23, 3
   10 negroes

Hardey, Benedict 26
   7 negroes

Lowndes, Christopher 61, 26, 27, 24, 20
                    20, 26, 13, 11
   Elizabeth 48, 27, 18, 35, 26, 50, 3
   41 negroes

Hunt, James 41, 20, 18, 16, 13, 9
   Ruth 47
   7 negroes

Gale, Edward 26
Carnes, Margaret 50
   12 negroes

Foard, William Jr. 47, 19, 8, 6, 4, 2
   Susanna 43, 18, 16, 13, 12
   2 negroes

Ross, David 60, 22, 20, 12, servant 35
   Annania 44, 14, 10, 8, 4, servant 17
   33 negroes

Deakins, William 56, 25, 20
   Elizabeth 64, 64, 18
   13 negroes

Miller, James 33, 33, 28
Mc Donald, Jean 28, 2
    9 negroes
Hatfield, Francis 52, 70, 29
    Adams, Margaret 43
    11 negroes
Bushan, Robert 59, 19, 16, 24, 23, 12
                                5, 1
    Mary 46, 14, 9
    6 negroes
Bence, George 21, 23, 15, 13, 11
    Barbara 37, 8, 6
    3 negroes.
Beall, Joshua 57
    Amelia 28, 24
    20 negroes
Beall, GeorgeIII-30
    Ann 26, 3, 3mos.
    8 negroes
Thorn, Thomas 46, 16, 13, 10, 5, 3
    Casandra 38?, 11, 8, 7, 4, 6mos.
Lowe, William 55, 19, 10
    Elienor 53, 20, 16, 50, 14, 6
Dick, Robert 40, 19, 15, 3, 2mos.
    Mason 36, 55, 8, 7, 4, 2
    15 negroes
Beall, Andrew 55, 21, 25, 19, 2
    Margaret 54, 25, 16
    19 negroes
Conn, George 44, 14, 13
    Sarah 32, 12, 8, 6, 3
    6 negroes
Isaac, Richard 55
    Sarah 57, 25, 22, 16, 8
    5 negroes
Hilragle, Christian 25, 23
    Polsin 23
Shackells, Samuel 26
    Ann 23, 4, 1
    3 negroes
Slater, Jonathan 45, 30, 11, 9
                    male servant 24
    Ann 35, 50, 7
    24 negroes
Jenkins, Frances 29, 20
Nevel, William 27
    Margaret Nevel 5
    3 negroes
Carroll, Mary 32, 30
    Law, Patrick (overseer) 45, 12, 10,
                                    8
    negroes 11
Crown, Elisha 33, 2mos.
    Elizabeth 21
Berry, Benjamin Jr. 35, 26, 1 mos.
        male servant 40

Berry, Deborah 28, 35, 35, 18, 7, 5, 4
                        2, 8
    19 negroes
Ryan, John 63, 20
    Sarah 70, 50
    2 negroes
Rantzell, Andrew 32, 23, 7, 5, 1
    Catherine 30, 8, 4, 3
Henderson, Richard 40, 7, servant 30
    Sarah 41, 12, 10, 9, 3, 19
    14 negroes
Willson, James 66, 8
    Mary 65
    21 negroes
Wyght, Jonathan 27, 7, 4
    Sarah 28, 18, 16
    2 negroes
Halsall, John 61, 17, 15, 13, 11, 9
    Mrs. Halsall 38, 6, 3, 3
Gordon, Elizabeth 46, 18, 15
    Charles 13
Clagett, Jane 51, 23, 16
Faldo, Charles 52
Parr, Nathaniel 22
    Mandate, Hannah 50, 15
    9 negroes
Ray, John Sr. 69, 27, 18, 40, 30
    Sarah 62, 20
Boyd, Abraham 40, 16, 9, 1
    Barbara 36, 12, 11, 6, 3
    7 negroes
White, James 62, 18
    Elianor 62
    9 negroes
Turner, Edmond 52
    Catherine 57, 37, 18, 9
    6 negroes
Tucker, Benjamin Jr. 3
    Bonithan, Martha 57, 27, 21, 5
Fergusson, William 31, 15, 2
    Elizabeth 25, 7, 5, 2
    1 negro
Jenkins, Enoch 45, 16
    Mary 47, 15
    2 negroes
Boucher, John Thomas 30, 26, 25
    Mary 30
    6 negroes
Thorn, Ephraim 43, 23, 6, 2
    Elianor 46, 34
    5 negroes
Willson, John 30
Stephens, William 24
Parker, John Jr. 23, 22
    Mary 24, 26, 2, 1
    3 negroes

Burch, Oliver 28, 7, 5, 2
    Verlinda 29
    2 negroes
Parker, John 48, 15, 13, 11, 5
    Drusilla 29, 10, 4, 2, 6mos.
    3 negroes
Lucas, William 51, 14, 10
    Ann 63, 27, 1 mo.
Boulton, George 35, 23
    Catherine 23
Jones, Notley 50, 14, 12, 7, 5
    Elianor 45, 17, 2
    5 negroes
Jameston, Richard 45, 20, 4, 7mos.
    Ann S. 25, 15, 10, 2
Davies, John 30
    Jane 23
Hardin, Edward 53
    Margaret 61, 38
Duley, William 21, 1 mo.
    Ann 19
Ford, John 22
Robinson, John 30, 5
    Elizabeth 33, 3, 1
Lanham, Nathan 52, 23, 20, 18, 12, 2
    Sarah 41, 18
Campbell, James 22
    4 negroes
Free, Elianor 49, 17, 10, 7
    Charles 14, 12
    1 negro
Stonestreet, Bazell 21, 13
    Elizabeth 19, 9mos.
    3 negroes
Downing, Joseph 28, 4, 2
    Jemimah 21, 3
Aunnar, William 57
    Ann 55
Harper, William 32, 7, 4, 9mos.
    Stella 27, 8
    3 negroes
Moore, Jeremiah 27, 40, 30
    Enesent 28, 57
Whealand, Nicholas 52, 12, 8, 4
    Sarah 42, 14
Conn, Jane 40, 17, 9
    William 5, 11
Hall, Ann 20, 2
Barren, John 53, 16, 9
    Jane 38, 19, 13, 9, 7, 5, 3, 2
McBew, James 22
    Susanna 21, 4mos.
    6 negroes
Janes, Edward 65, 22, 16, 9
    Ann 50, 17, 13, 12
    1 negro

Brown, William Sr. 88, 28, 21, 18, 25
    11, 9, 4
    Ruth 49, 29, 23, 15, 13, 4mos.
Janes, William 34, 8, 6, 3
    Jane 40
    3 negroes
Tucker, Thomas 41, 18, 13, 6
    Dianna 43, 16, 15, 1
Wyght, John Sr. 63, 23, 14
    Ann 57, 21, 18
    7 negroes
Duly, Henry 45, 15, 12, 9, 2
    Mary 39, 20, 17, 5, 9mos.
    1 negro
Wise, Thomas 50, 13, 11, 7, 3, 1
    Sarah 46, 9, 6
Lanham, Shadrick 47, 17, 15, 13, 10
    Sarah 35, 19, 16, 12, 7, 4, 2
Eales, Thomas 53, 10, 7, 5, 1
    Elizabeth 35, 16, 14, 12
Beanes, Christopher Sr. 70, 49, 21,
    15, 12, 6
    Jane 37, 19, 14, 10, 4, 2
Gentle, Thomas 35, 2
    Dianna 25, 7, 4
Hill, John 58, 31, 17
    Mary 56, 21
    39 negroes
Brown, John (planter) 56, 14, 9
    Elizabeth 52, 17, 12
    1 negro
Brown, John of John 31
    Elizabeth 24, 2
    1 negro
Brown, John (shoemaker) 52, 30, 2
    Elianor 50, 16, 18
    2 negroes
Beall, Thomas 34, 7, 5, 1
    White Females 6, 2
    3 negroes
Beale, John 27
    Eleanor 20
Norton, Neamiah 41, 15, 6
    Ann 60, 40, 10, 7, 3
    7 negroes
Crafford, James 80
    Mary 70
    13 negroes
Beall, Ninian Jr. 53, 22, 19, 15, 13, 10
    Catherine 52, 11, 7, 4
    2 negroes
Simmons, Jonathan 30, 40, 4, 3
    Elizabeth 26, 1
    5 negroes
Sparks, Thomas 65, 18, 14
    Elizabeth 58, 16, 14

Beall, Richard 40, 50, 30, 12, 9, 7, 5
  Rebecca 41, 17, 15, 13, 2, 1
  8 negroes
Cook, Edward 28, 2
  Precilla 30, 4, 1 mo.
Hinton, Joseph 32, 6, 5, 3
  Mary 37, 17, 15, 12, 8
Norton, John Sr. 36, 30, 3, 7
  Elizabeth 28, 5, 4, 2
Willson, Edmond 55, 4
  Lucy 40, 16, 12, 7
Smith, Orlando 52, 16, 10, 8
  Martha 35, 17, 14, 12, 6, 4, 2
Willson, Bazell 38
  Lucy 25
  2 negroes
Harvey, John 24, 12
  Elizabeth 35, 14, 4, 2
Page, Anthoney 32, 10, 3
  Winefred 31, 8, 5
  3 negroes
Chaney, Hezekiah 34
  Elianor 27, 2
  1 negro
Able, Mary 50, 20, 12
Tucker, Thomas 64, 22, 1
  Elizabeth 62, 20
Price, Benoney 50, 16, 15, 13, 12, 8
  Mary 40, 18, 16, 7, 5
  1 negro
Price, Ignatius 22
  Ann 40
  5 negroes
Ragon, Timothy 26
  Elizabeth 16
Norton, Thomas 30
  Catherine 29, 10, 8, 6, 4, 2
Willson 40, 10, 6, 1
  Norindo 14, 12, 7, 2
  2 negroes
Chens, Richard 55
  Ann 70, 44
Taylor, Jane 50, 20, 18, 13
Grant, Sarah 40, 12, 11, 7, 4
  Richard 14, 8, 1
Trigg, Alice 45, 17, 7, 3
  Samuel 16, 13, 9, 4
Broga, Daniel 26
  Mary 35
Sparks, Mathew 61, 27, 17, 15, 11, 7
  Elianor 45, 23, 3
Beans, Jane 40
  Sanuel 14
Merick, John 40, 15, 14, 12
  Elianor 55, 20, 18, 16, 12, 8

Robinson, James 30, 5
  Ann 27, 2
Hamilton, John 31, 40, 39, 6
  Sarah 37, 4, 2
Jenkins, John 53, 21, 17, 13, 9
  Frances 42, 19, 3
  7 negroes
Crafford, Adam 54, 17, 9, 7
  Elizabeth 47, 19, 13, 11, 5, 70
  5 negroes
Suit, Mary 40, 18, 14, 10, 6
  Nathaniel 19, 15, 13, 4
  2 negroes
Gray, Gilbert 39, 16, 2
  Elizabeth 32, 7
Gordon, Josiah 30, 4, 2, 2
  Lucy 26, 20, 6
White, Abednigoe 42
  Mary 24, 4, 3
Ridgeway, Robert 35, 4, 1
  Martha 35, 8, 6, 5, 2
  1 negro
Cook, Joseph 27, 11, 4, 2
  Martha 30, 10, 9
Mullican, John Jr. 40, 20, 17, 14, 13,
                    11, 9, 1
  Sarah 40
Mullican, John 70
  Catherine 50, 26
  2 negroes
Mullican, Thomas 38, 14
  Elizabeth 50
  1 negro
Warring, Elizabeth 55, 26, 24, 22, 18
  James 21, 15
  10 negroes
Magruder, Hazwell 40, 10, 9, 6
  Charity 36, 13, 7
  1 negro
Conn, Joseph 35, 2
  Elizabeth 32, 4, 1, 3
  2 negroes
Willson, Josiah 35, 5
  Mary 28, 4, 3
  2 negroes
Ross, William 36, 22, 3
  Susanna 29, 4
Salter, Thomas 25, 1
  Margaret 20
Beall, Sarah 45, 16, 10, 6
  Jeremiah 17, 21, 70, 22, 14, 9, 7
  7 negroes
Sansbury, Isaac 44, 15, 14, 11, 7, 2
  Mary 32, 13, 8
  4 negroes

Cissell, John 55
   Susanna 20, 17, 14
   1 negro
Gordon, Thomas 57
   Drucilla 17, 7, 54, 20, 53
   3 negroes
Crafford, Bazell 30
   Margaret 35
   1 negro
Thompson, John 60
   Elianor 23
Willson, William 30,28, 1
   Elizabeth 22, 16, 3
Ciseel, Philip 40, 14, 3, 1
   Elizabeth 35, 12, 10, 7, 5
   2 negroes
Ciseel, Mary 33, 12, 2
   William 4
Brooke, William Sr. 45, 40, 7
   Mary 38, 10, 9, 8, 6, 5
Fraser, George 70, 15
   Hannah 60
Willson, David 33
   Rebecca 30, 20, 7
Willson, Elizabeth 45, 20, 18
   James 31, 30, 42, 6
   4 negroes
Heron, Mary 40, 15, 20, 9, 7
   John 16
Willson, John 32, 2
   Barbary 29, 4
Cole, Joseph 56, 22, 13, 11
   Rachell 46, 20, 18, 16, 6
Crecraft, John 48, 14, 13
   Mary 40, 20, 17, 7, 5
   1 negro
Willson, Ignatius 40, 28, 1
   Elianor 30
   1 negro
Shaw, Josiah 32, 40, 9, 7
   Mary 28, 23, 30, 16, 4
   4 negroes
Hall, Nathaniel 48, 3
   Hues, Ann 20
Beall, Ninian Sr. 80, 27, 2
   Catherine 30, 36, 4
   1 negro
Trigg, Clement 40, 14, 7, 1
   Mary 41, 17, 15, 14, 1
Cover, John 45, 6, 2
   Elizabeth 40, 16, 13, 8
Legg, Edward 28, 9, 1
   Mary 20
Robinson, John 28, 4, 2
   Keziah 28, 20

Beek, Anthoney 38, 7, 4, 1
   Elizabeth 26, 17
Robinson, Isaac 49, 17, 4
   Elizabeth 51, 23
   8 negroes
Hamilton, Thomas 62, 21, 25
   Ann 45, 20, 19, 16, 14
Webb, Thomas Sr. 70, 23, 7
   Elizabeth 65, 20, 17, 3
Hopper, John 45, 4, 2
   Sarah 40, 13, 3
Riddell, John 72
   Elizabeth 70, 17
   7 negroes
Turner, Shadrick 48, 25, 22, 15, 8
   Sarah 38, 14, 10, 20, 6, 1
   4 negroes
Graves, Solomon 38, 24, 23, 14, 10, 7, 1
   Elizabeth 30, 65, 20, 13, 6, 2
Baldin, James 55, 31, 11, 8
   Elizabeth 49, 17, 13
Hinton, Thomas 46, 15, 6, 1
   Ann 30, 12, 9, 4
Baynes, John 50
   Mary 49
   31 negroes
Baynes, Joseph Noble 25
   15 negroes
Baynes, John Jr. 24
   Mary 22, 20, 1
   22 negroes
Noble, Catherine 50
   8 negroes
Jenkins, Frances 57, 14, 14, 12
   Ann 46, 25, 10
   9 negroes
Walker, Charles 23, 1
   Jane 20
   1 negro
Jenkins, William 33
Short, James 54, 16
   Jane 60, 14
Turton, William 26, 38
   Catherine 69, 30
Clubb, Mathew 60, 24
   Mary 52, 36
Hutchison, William 54, 18
   Ann 60, 21, 3
Ogdon, Robert 26, 7
   Marlow, Dorithy 28
   5 negroes
Smallwood, Ann 41, 17, 7
German, Stephen 20, 16, 2
   Sarah 53, 76, 66, 28, 26, 22, 18, 17, 13, 10

Mitchell, Joseph 52, 26, 16, 12
  Elizabeth 48, 60, 18, 8
  5 negroes
Cassell, Henry 44, 4, 2, 9
  Mary Ann 32, 16
  9 negroes
Blacklock, Thomas 60, 20, 18
  Charity 58
  16 negroes
Hugar, William 33, 18, 7, 4
  Ann Ogdon 58, 38, 25
Cato, William 35, 23, 12, 9, 2
  Christian 30, 14, 7, 15, 4
Trammill, John 30, 12, 9, 7, 3
  Ann 30, 11
Turner, Elijah 26
  Ann 17
  11 negroes
Townshend, Samuel 61, 20, 16, 9, 8
  Ann 47, 22, 16, 11, 7, 4
  8 negroes
Webster, John 40, 10, 5
  Joanna 25, 12, 2
  2 negroes
Beall, Josia 51, 15, 13, 11, 9, 5
  1 female 25
  19 negroes
Beanes, William Jr. 27
  Sarah 26
  11 negroes
Clarkson, Thomas 61, 28, 15, 8
  Sarah 59, 30
  10 negroes
Lyles, William Jr. 26, 21, 27
  Sarah 21
  25 negroes
Digges, William 63, 30
  white females 20, 21, 22, 23
  24 negroes
Riddell, Henry 30, 23
  5 negroes
Evans, John 23, 14, 12, 10, 7
  Mary 43, 20, 16, 5
  7 negroes
Talbot, Mary 34, 16, 11, 9, 1
  her sons 13, 6
Lucas, Adam 33, 26, 8, 1
  Sarah 27, 6, 3, 25
Manning, John 40, 10, 8, 6, 5, 3
  Mary Ann 35, 75,
  15 negroes
Young, Thomas 43, 16, 14, 12, 2
  Eleanor 36, 10, 8, 6, 1, 1
  8 negroes

Bond, Samuel 29
  Clarissa 20
  25 negroes
Gantt, James 22
  Ann 16, 32
  10 negroes
Turner, William 27
  Mary 18
  3 negroes
Worland, Robey 48, 16, 6, 1
  Edey 48, 23, 21, 10
  8 negroes
Howell, Thomas 22
  Mary Ann 25, 40
  2 negroes
Davidson, John 43, 10, 8, 7, 5
  Elizabeth 31
  4 negroes
Morris, Thomas 56, 12, 11
  Elizabeth 50, 23, 20
  1 negro
Jenkins, Richard 35, 10, 2
  Henrietta 30, 12, 8, 6
Shaw, Joseph 40
  Ann 48
Mudd, Thomas 36, 4, 2
  Ann 28, 1, 1
  6 negroes
Edelen, John Sr. 62
  Jane 32, 24, 18
  10 negroes
Harris, William 30, 5, 3
  Susanna 23
Foard, William 70, 18, 16, 13
  Elizabeth 66, 40
  7 negroes
Jones, William 60, 28, 20, 16, 13
  Mary 48, 26, 18, 11, 9
  3 negroes
Jones, Philip Levin 27, 17, 12, 10, 6
  Charity 31, 7, 1
Jones, Charles 25, 13
  Mary 27, 23
  4 negroes
Turner, Benjamin 47
  Patience 38, 18
  2 negroes
Herns, Henry 55, 15, 12, 9, 8, 3
  Elizabeth 49, 24, 16, 7
  4 negroes
Longly, Edward 44, 13
  his wife 32, 11, 9, 4, 2
Marbury, Luke 31, 5
  Elizabeth 29, 3, 2
  11 negroes

Lowry, James 30, 30
Green Bazell 22
   Elianor 23, 60
   8 negroes
Downing, Henry 40
   Sarah 32, 1
   1 negro
Davies, Robert 60
   Mary 55
Edelen, Thomas 55, 16, 18, 14, 10,
                     8, 5
   Precilla 51, 20, 18
   4 negroes
Harris, Josias 20, 15, 14, 13, 6
   Edith 51, 17
   1 negro
Lee, George 40, 20
   Cleo 33, 12, 10
   50 negroes
Addison, John 34, 24
   Elizabeth 27, 10, 6
   29 negroes
Addison, Rebecca 26, 45, 5, 9, 8
   Morris, Daniel 33, 11, 6, 7, 1
   67 negroes
Jenkins, Zachariah 50, 18, 20, 14,
                  9, 6, 4, 2
   Martha 28, 14, 11, 22, 1
   6 negroes
Carr, Overton 25, 30, 30, 22, 25,
            19, 15, 7, 4, 4, 1
   Ann 30, 34, 24, 30, 2
   61 negroes
Bayne, William 47, 12, 8, 3
   Mary 43, 17, 14, 1
   12 negroes
Smith, James 52, 20, 15, 10, 5
   Mary 40, 18, 13, 26, 12, 3, 2
Marlow, John 52, 22, 19, 17
   Elianor 53, 15
Lanham, Sarah 41, 17, 6
   son 6
Beall, Patrick 41, 12, 10, 5, 2
   Elianor 41, 15, 19, 8
   20 negroes
McDowell, John 52, 8, 6, 2, 1
   Elianor 37, 3
   1 negro
Lovejoy, Alexander 45, 15, 13, 12
                  10, 9, 6
   Mary 39, 14, 8, 4
Musgrave, Benjamin 84
   Jemimah 27
Brown, Ann 60, 10 & sons 21, 16
   3 negroes

Brown, Benjamin 35, 33
Thompson, John Jr. 40, 7
   Mary 38, 13, 11, 4, 1
   1 negro
Wheat, Francis 38, 12, 12, 12, 6
   white females 70, 4
   3 negroes
Alder, Elizabeth 43, 18, 13, 1
   George 20, 15, 7
   3 negroes
Rozer, Notley (no data)
   20 negroes
Snowden, Samuel 48, 50, 40, 25, 25
                  13, 11, 2
   Elizabeth 43, 40, 18, 17, 15, 6, 4
   55 negroes
Snowden, Thomas 27, 40, 30, 30, 27
                24, 22, 2
   Mary 48, 24, 6
   69 negroes
Prather, Nathan 34, 4
   Ann 33, 8, 6, 1
   4 negroes
Hoskins, Elisha 28
Gordon, John 27
   Ann 24, 3, 1
Prather, Joseph 46, 16
   Ruth 46
   3 negroes
Hughs, Joseph 50, 10
   Phebe 43
Raughlins, James 33, 2
   Mary 30, 4
   1 negro
Hall, William 61
   Margery 44
   3 negroes
Fowler, Isaac 33, 12, 6
   Elizabeth 28, 7, 1
Fowler, Jeremiah 65, 27, 21, 17, 13, 10
   Drucilla 53, 38, 16, 7
   1 negro
Willet, William 33, 15, 13, 4, 1
   Mary 32, 12, 8
   3 negroes
Jones, Samuel 48, 24, 11, 5
   Catherine 36, 17, 13, 9, 7, 3
   11 negroes
Macnew, Bazell 28, 5, 1
   Frances 26
   1 negro
Selbey, James 29, 25
   Ruth 23, 1
Selbey, Nathan 41, 8, 5
   Agnes 28, 2

Lingan 23, 1 ) no other names given
Drucilla 20 )
Selbey, William W. 47, 31, 14, 12, 4, 2
  Elizabeth 30, 17, 9, 6
Tracey, William 26
  Elizabeth 20
Richardson, Thomas 33, 5, 3, 1
  Anne 30, 24, 9, 7
  13 negroes
Thompson, Thomas 27
  Rachel 21
Thomas, William 31, 3, 1
  Amelia 27, 15, 2
  1 negro
Lansdale, Richard 53, 28, 10, 6
  his wife 47, 25, 13
  13 negroes
Turner, John 38, 36, 34, 26, 20
            13, 14, 14, 13
  Jane 73, 40, 36, 21
  2 negroes
Wheeler, Richard 29, 15, 5, 2
  Lydia 23, 3, 1
  6 negroes
Hardesty, Robert 49, 19, 12, 9, 7, 2
  Elizabeth 48, 75, 16, 14
Selby, Joshua 35
  Sarah 35, 11
Fowler, Thomas 30, 21
  females 3, 3, 1
Crow, James 28, 23, 25, 17
  Mary 58, 32
  11 negroes
Duvall, Lewis 55, 16, 14
  Alice 53, 28, 26, 23, 20
  9 negroes
Hyat, William 57, 19, 17, 14, 12, 6
  Elizabeth 48, 13, 9
Hyat, Christopher 25
  1 negro
Hyat, William 28, 3
  Martha 28, 6, 4, 1
McDougle, John 44, 17, 16, 13, 1
  Charity 42, 15, 12, 7, 5
King, Richard 85, 30, 16, 15, 13, 4, 1
  Jane 68, 43, 22, 18, 6
Simmons, Richard 28, 15, 9, 1
  Tabitha 24, 12, 5, 4, 1
  5 negroes
Selbey, William M. 67
  Martha 63, 16
  7 negroes
Shaw, Bazell 20, 2, 1
  Susana 20, 30, 1

Savil, William 42
  Ann 46
Willson, William 28
  Margaret 28, 6, 3
  12 negroes
Prather, Zepheniah 35, 14, 8, 6
  Rachell 34, 17, 11, 4, 1
  6 negroes
Prather, William 76, 15
  Martha 69
  10 negroes
Hoskins, Josias 20
Owen, Benjamin 60, 27, 16, 11
  Anne 51
  13 negroes
Adams, Robert 30, 5
  Jane 23, 7, 2
Turner, Margaret 45, 16
Higgins, William 29
  Pricilla 27, 5, 3, 1
  2 negroes
Aldridge, Jacob 35, 7, 5, 3
  Elizabeth 27, 4
  7 negroes
Watkins, Thomas 20, 15
  Jane 42, 8, 6
  7 negroes
Simmons, Van 24, 19, 1
  Mary 21
  2 negroes
Greenwell, James 54, 15, 9
  Elizabeth 18, 12
Beall, Shadrick 31, 5, 2
  Agnes 26, 7, 1
  1 negro
Edmonston, Ninian 41, 13, 11, 9, 4, 1
  Dorety 35, 6
  1 negro
Willson, George 73, 17, 15
  Mary 59, 33, 27, 23, 14, 5
  2 negroes
Short, Isaac 36, 24, 13, 6, 4
  Mary 34, 12, 8, 4
Gales, Thomas 37, 8
  Sarah 47, 15
Hardesty, Edmond 55, 1
  Elizabeth 28
Oren, Robert 34, 16, 5, 2, 1
  Precilla 37, 6, 3
Gloyd, Daniel 40, 15, 13, 4, 1
  Joanna 37, 8, 5
Shaw, Sarah 70, 40, 2
  1 negro
Lanham, Archibald 25, 1
  Jane 27, 1

Bulger, Richard 48, 7
  Margaret 38, 13, 13
Callins, James 30, 23, 1
  Sarah 65, 20
Sansberry, William 40, 15, 12, 9,
                      7, 5, 1
  Sarah 40, 2
Thomas, William of Thomas 20, 17, 1
  Elianor 63, 18
  4 negroes
Calicoe, Ignatius 35, 6, 2, 1
  Elizabeth 35, 7, 4
  2 negroes
Cecil, James 42, 12, 8, 3, 1
  Elizabeth 15, 10, 10
  1 negro
Hoskins, George 43, 6, 4, 1
  Mary 42, 9
  2 negroes
Middleton, Belt 20
  Ruth 64, 23, 23
  6 negroes
Benjamin Belt's Quarter
  6 negroes
Jones, Joseph 45, 26, 24, 19, 17, 15
  Margaret 53, 23, 13, 6
  12 negroes
Smith, Anthoney 48, 5
  1 negro
Elson, Archibald 36, 2
  Mary 30, 5
  3 negroes
Jones, Josiah 22, 1
  Anna 27
  13 negroes
Welch Thomas 54, 24, 15, 5, 5
  Darcas 53, 28, 20, 13, 11, 4
  6 negroes
Norton, Henry 40
Cheney, Samuel 46, 15, 13, 11, 1
  Martha 34, 16, 12
Duvall, John 32, 6, 5, 3
  Sarah 24, 2, 1
  1 negro
Duvall, Benjamin 63, 24, 21
  Mary 60, 4
Duvall, Thomas 37, 14, 12, 6, 4
  Sarah 40, 16, 11, 8, 6, 2, 1
  1 negro
Hancock, William 75, 14, 1
  Melkiah 46, 15, 10
Taylor, Isaac 24, 14, 4
  Mary 22, 2, 1
  3 negroes

Langwell, Robert 25
  Elizabeth 18
Shaw Charles 27, 2, 1
  Kiziah 20
Mullican, William 42, 10, 8, 6, 1
  Mary 40, 12, 2
Walker, Joseph 54, 23, 20, 14
  Elizabeth 52, 18, 16, 13, 9
  8 negroes
Conn, James 50, 16, 3
  Ruth 32, 24, 15, 11, 5
  6 negroes
Orme, Nathan 42, 5
  Ann 29, 14, 7, 2
  4 negroes
Letman, John 27
  Jane 46, 17, 15
Breashears, Jeremiah 25, 2
  Jemima 22
Case, Charles 41
  Martha 36, 6, 1
Finch, Thomas 62
Mackentoush, John 50, 9, 7, 5
  Pricilla 34, 14, 12
Beall, John of John 42, 7, 5, 1
  Tabitha 32
  1 negro
Fergusson, James 56, 5
  Catherine 57, 28, 17, 9
Beale, Mannen 38, 8, 5
  Frances 32, 3, 1
Nichols, Asa 20, 14, 4, 2
Isaac, Jacob 30, 3, 2
  Jane 22
Jonathan Church's Quarter
  Carrol, Joseph 20, 13, 15, 12
  Keziah 41
Beall, Thomas Jr. 16, 11, 7, 4
  Precilla 33, 12
Waters, William 43, 21
  1 negro
Hall, Philip 41, 21, 15, 11, 9, 5, 3, 1
  Anna 41, 14, 12, 7
Lucas, Ignatius 45, 16, 14, 6, 1, 1
  Catherine 42, 20, 18, 13, 11, 7, 4
May, Benjamin 48, 37, 21, 7
  Elizabeth 37, 22, 1
Harris, John 97
  white female 30
Downing, James 50, 9, 7
  Sarah 54, 35, 22
  3 negroes
Redman, John 60, 18, 14
  Sarah 50, 12

Green, Elizabeth 65, 15, 12
Wade, Robert 40
5 negroes
Tills, Samuel 50 (negro)
1 female black 3
Hyton, Joseph 45, 9, 7
Ann 40,11
Maccatee, John 32
Charity 25, 6, 5
1 negro
Stephens, William 62, 18, 11
Rebecca 58, 18, 15
Green, James 37, 4
Elizabeth 30, 17, 6, 1
7 negroes
Higdon, Benjamin 52, 5, 1
Ann 49, 25, 17, 7
Beck, James 40, 12, 11, 9, 7, 5, 1
Rebecca 33?, 16, 10, 4, 1
8 negroes
Bonifield, Samuel 32, 15, 7, 3, 4
13, 11, 1
Sarah 36, 5
9 negroes
Pierce, Susanna 38, 17, 10
John 15, 8
Scott, Simon 45, 20, 15, 10, 8, 1
Mary 38, 22, 17, 10, 5
Webb, Thomas 43, 25, 19, 14, 9, 7, 4, 2
Rebecca 38, 15
Sherife, John 30, 1
Ruth 20, 2
Burque, Ezekiel 30, 75
Elizabeth 25, 60, 3, 1
Beggerly, John 39, 4
Abigail 30, 60, 11, 8, 5
Walker, Isaac 55, 18, 75, 18, 15
Elizabeth 42
4 negroes
Sherife, Thomas 40
Catherine 20, 4, 2
Edmonstone, James 31, 30
Ruth 32
5 negroes
Breashears, Ignatius 43, 11, 8, 6, 3, 1
Frances 41, 16, 14, 13
10 negroes
Jenkins, Job & R. Peters 28, 20, 40
11 negroes
Digges, William Jr. 50
Catherine 40, 21
13 negroes

Webster, William 83
Elizabeth 50
13 negroes
Webster, William Jr. 45, 16, 12, 5, 3, 1
Ann 40, 19, 14, 10
Webster, James 39, 12, 10, 8, 1
Mary Ann 35, 20, 17, 6, 4, 2
Webster, Thomas 50, 19, 14
Mary 48, 21, 17, 9, 11, 6
Campbell, James 42, 12
Elizabeth 48, 23
Emerson, John 70, 34, 13
Lucy 20, 18
1 negro
Taylor, James King 28
Elianor 18, 6mos.
Athey, Benjamin 41, 20, 15, 7, 1
Edea 40, 21, 18, 13, 10
Edwards, Margaret 70, 35, 8?
Boswell, John B. 45, 7, 6, 4
Rebecca 40, 3, 1
3 negroes
Willson, Joseph Jr. 30, 6, 3, 1
Cloe 27,
4 negroes
Downes, Ann 58, 34, 30, 13, 4, 1
white males 14, 9
Graves, Lewis 58, 25, 8
Eleanor 50
4 negroes
Wood, James 45, 12, 9
Catherine 40
Shaw, John 65, 25, 20, 1
Sarah 60, 40, 20, 4, 1
1 negro
Trahern, Neamiah 49, 7, 5, 1
Amelia 30, 9
5 negroes
Delozier, Edward 53, 90, 19, 14, 5, 9
Ann 50, 20, 11
Stonestreet, Richard 22, 14
Ann 18, 15
11 negroes
Turner, Jonathan 36, 7, 5, 4
Mary 25, 9, 1
3 negroes
Lanham, Josias 47, 21, 11
Elizabeth 30, 15, 5, 3
3 negroes
Poor, John 47, 6, 1
Elizabeth 30, 24, 6, 4
1 negro

Boarman, Joseph 44, 21, 18, 15, 10
  Mary 40
  14 negroes
Hailey, John 37, 10, 8, 4, 1
  Elizabeth 40, 14, 12, 7, 2
Dunn, John 70, 14
  Mary 52, 18
  7 negroes
Abbey, Hezekiah 38, 15, 9, 4
  Rebecca 40, 10, 2
Vermilion, Robert 51, 19, 16, 13, 10
  Elizabeth 47, 27, 24
  1 negro
Lanham, Mary 47, 18, 16, 13
  white male 11
  10 negroes
Marr, Charles 26
  Hester 26, 20, 3
Carleton, Joseph 22, 17, 35
  white females 50, 32, 5, 1
Funk, Jacob 51, 9
  Ann 49, 12
Boswell, Nicholas 30
  Rachell 18?
  1 negro
Nalley, Samuel 33, 3
  Sarah 24, 2
  1 negro
Lashley, Robert 60, 28
  Lucy 55, 19
  1 negro
Edelen, Richard Sr. 60, 22, 17, 14
    12, 4mos.
  Sarah 45, 21, 18, 10, 7, 4
  2 negroes
Tucker, Robey 23
  Hester 23
McClane, George 27, 5
  Mary 37
McClane, John 64
  Precilla 60
Sparrow, Joseph 43, 12, 10, 8
  Ann 32, 6, 5
Dougal, Thomas 56, 10
  Ann 51
Hadrick, Robert 61, 11, 4, 1
  Margaret 40, 14
Miller, Peter 43, 5
  Elizabeth 30, 10
  2 negroes
Gabriel, Anthoney 30, 25, 26, 25, 22,
(free negroes)   20, 18, 1
  females 30, 22, 23

Longdon, Abell 38, 7, 4
  Margaret 38, 14, 9, 1
Collins, William 30, 2, 1
  Ann 28, 4
Bigner, Robert 30, 40
  Margaret 28
Queen, Richard 51, 22, 20, 28, 9
  Mary 24, 18, 15
  10 negroes
Tucker, John 74, 14
  Drucilla 64, 14, 12
Robey, John 62, 23, 17, 10, 8
  Mary 55, 20, 18, 13, 10
Tucker, Benjamin 31, 23, 5
  white females 55, 18, 25, 17
Williams, Joseph 55, 7, 5, 4
  Sarah 33, 9, 7, 1
Wirt, Jasper 45, 25, 15, 10
  Catherine 47, 20, 18, 6
Queen, Walter 21, 20
  Elizabeth 18, 6, 21
  14 negroes
Reagar, John 53
  Sophia 60
Graham, Moses 35, 13
  Elizabeth 47, 7
Beggarly, George 40, 6, 2, 1
  Margaret 35, 12, 9, 7
  2 negroes
Bourn, William 21, 13, 1
  Jemimah 52, 17, 15
  4 negroes
White, Alexander 28, 2
  Hannah 27
Pearce, Thomas 50, 21, 17, 14, 7, 3, 1
  Martha 43, 16, 12, 9
  2 negroes
Bourn, David 30, 4
  Ann 30, 23
  4 negroes
Pearce, William 52, 25, 14, 9
  Rachell 52, 21, 11
  6 negroes
Mahew, William 43, 70, 27, 15
  Charity 23, 65, 11, 1
Kissick, Robert 28
  Jane 44, 10, 9
  6 negroes
Woodward, Clement 45, 18, 13, 11, 1
  Frances 40, 15, 9, 7, 5
Venables, William 26, 1
  Elizabeth 18, 1
Canady, Timothy 37
  Ann 30, 8, 4

Cossey, William 26
  Margaret 26, 14
Evans, Walter 55, 5
  Elisabeth 36, 1
  9 negroes
Reyley, Jeremiah 46, 18, 20, 14, 12,
       8, 1, 1
  Elianor 23, 40, 22, 20, 1
  6 negroes
Halley, John 37, 19, 17, 13, 5, 3
  Mary 36, 36, 16, 7, 5, 1
  1 negro
Downs, Benjamin 62, 30
  Mary 59, 24, 20, 17, 2, 1
  9 negroes
Downs, Henry 26, 3
  Winefred 24, 1
  2 negroes
Tucker, William 62
  Elianor 60, 24, 20, 17
Herbin, Edward V. 45, 21, 18, 17, 10, 4
  Lydia 50, 21, 14, 12, 21, 3, 1
  3 negroes
Coomes, Joseph 36, 5, 1
  Sarah 30, 10, 8, 6, 3
  2 negroes
Young, William 70, 30, 22
  Elianor 68, 35
  18 negroes
Field, Stephen 21
  Precilla Lucas 38, 13, 7
  6 negroes
Shirtcliff, Joseph 26, 16
  Dorothey 35, 14, 11, 9, 7, 3, 2
Scott Mrs.(Eastern Branch) 50, 26, 22,
                                22, 20
  14 negroes
Berkley, Henry 49, 9, 7, 5, 32, 3, 1, 1
  Elizabeth 34, 11, 18
Mahew, John 50, 12, 10, 9, 7, 5
  Mary 45, 35, 13, 4, 2, 1
Willcoxen, Elizabeth 51, 13, 10, 5
  Thomas 29, 25, 7
  8 negroes
Soper, Robert 66, 1
  Sarah 40, 10
  17 negroes
Hardey, Rebecca 62, 33, 21
  George 16
Soper, Alexander 39, 12, 10
  Mary 39, 18, 17, 16, 73
  1 negro
Upton, Thomas 22
  Keziah 20, 5

Hardey, John 41, 3, 6, 10
  Mary 31, 12, 4, 1
Hardey, Baptist 25, 2
  Rachel 25, 1
Dorsey, John 39, 23, 14, 12, 2
  Elizabeth 23, 7, 4
  2 negroes
Soper, John 52, 16, 14, 8, 6
  Martha 50, 20, 18, 12, 4
  5 negroes
Ray, Thomas 32, 5, 1
  Mary 31, 6, 2
Gray, Leonard 52, 18, 16, 14
  Elizabeth 56, 21, 10
Darnal, Isaac 44, 19, 14, 12, 10
  Susanna 45, 18, 13, 8, 5, 3
Fish, Robert 48, 11, 8, 6, 4, 3
  Precilla 32, 10, 1
Redden, John 39, 7
  Ruth 32, 13, 3, 2
Weaver, Jacob 32, 10, 2, 7
  Ann 32, 60, 6
Piles, Osborn 28
  Mary 20, 2
  1 negro
Warringford, Ann 56, 20, 10
  Joseph 15, 15, 7
Warringford, George 23, 1
  Ammina 24
  3 negroes
Ridgeway, Richard 36, 5
  Mary 40, 14, 16, 11
Vermillion, Giles 23, 5, 3
  Mary 27, 14
Upton, John 24, 3
  Keziah 24
Morgan, Elizabeth 67, 26
Jones, Silvester 35, 13, 5
  Sarah 29, 3, 2
Mahew, James 52, 22, 20, 12, 9, 7, 5, 2
  Elizabeth 45, 17, 4
Vermillion, Thomas 57, 22, 16, 15,
                         15, 10, 5
  Sarah 51, 13
Pope, Nathaniel 40, 17, 15, 8, 5
  Elizabeth 38, 13, 11, 3, 1
  2 negroes
Johnson, Monica 60, 24
Russell, Ann 38, 10, 1
  white male 7
Carrol, Elizabeth 49, 20
  white males 18, 12, 3
Pope, Joseph 51, 15, 13, 9, 6
  Elizabeth 45, 24, 23, 20, 3
  14 negroes

Ferrol, Daniel 57, 60, 28, 13
  Ruth 52, 28, 23, 16
Hamilton, Andrew 42, 15, 7, 3
  Ruth 36, 16, 6, 1
Beall, Roger 42, 15, 3, 2
  Ruth 34, 11, 6, 5
  1 negro
Willson, Joseph 38, 11
  Agnes 86, 12
  5 negroes
Lowe, John 52, 11, 1
  Mary 52, 17, 15
Chamberlain, Clement 30
  Mary 60, 24
Marshall, Mary 53, 15
  white males 21, 20, 17, 13
  6 negroes
Tawnihill, James 71, 32, 41, 18, 7
  white females 18, 15
Riston, Babtist 20
  Mary 30, 5
Jefferson, Luke 44, 8
  Elizabeth 43
Hamilton, Andrew 60, 14, 9, 7
  Mary 40, 10
  6 negroes
Wigfield, Mathew 41, 27, 5, 3, 1
  Elizabeth 36, 12, 10, 7
  4 negroes
Thompson, Robert 85, 19
  Agnes 54, 33, 14, 12, 3
  10 negroes
Gatton, Notley 37, 5
  Mary 32, 7, 4, 1
Kirbey, Richard 50, 22, 14, 12, 1
  Mary 55, 18
  5 negroes
Willmot, Thomas 35, 6, 3, 1
  Mary 26, 8
  1 negro
St.Clair, Robert 53, 13, 7
  Rebeccah 34
Reddin, James 46, 16, 3, 1
  Rebecca 40, 12, 10, 7
Bean, George 53, 18, 7, 4
  white females 16, 15, 13
Philips, Obeddo 36, 11
  Jane 22, 20
McDonald, Ann 50
  white males 20, 17
  3 negroes
Jones, Richard 40
  Martha 35

Masters, William Jr. 22
  Mary 29, 6, 1
  1 negro
Masters, William Sr. 53, 12, 10, 8, 6
  Tryphenia 43, 20, 15, 4, 3
  5 negroes
Brown, John 28
  Mary 30
Standage, Thomas 63, 27
  Margaret 55, 25, 22, 19, 16
  4 negroes
Claxen, Notley 45, 15, 10, 5, 2, 1
  Violetta 38, 8, 3
  4 negroes
Gatton, Azariah 26
  Elizabeth 24, 31, 5, 1, 3
  9 negroes
Norton, Ann 55, 19
  5 negroes
Norton, Robert 29, 7, 1
  Chloe 27, 5, 4, 3
Tucker, William 38, 13, 7, 2
  Rachell 33, 10
Talbot, Tobias 29
  Sarah 26, 8, 6
Hoskins, John Allen 36, 6
  Susanna 36, 13, 8, 1
Bean, Ebsworth 57, 15, 7
  Susanna 47, 23, 20, 13, 11, 9
  10 negroes
Bean, John 33
  9 negroes
Weldon, John 42, 12, 6
  Ann 50, 13, 10
  1 negro
Bean, Josias 33, 10, 8
  Ann 32, 6, 4, 1
Biggs, Henry 51, 21, 19, 14, 17, 11
  Sarah 40
Allen, John 54, 15, 12, 9
  Dorithy 40, 7, 2
Jones, Henry 39, 6
  Ann 28, 30, 8, 4, 10, 1
  6 negroes
Talbott, William 66, 23, 21, 18, 16
              12, 10, 8, 6
  Sarah 41, 23, 14, 2, 2
Boswell, Edward 52, 38, 6, 6, 1
  Elizabeth 40, 24, 8, 3
Neagle, Rachell 27, 25, 10
  white male 5
Martin, John 43, 30, 16, 12, 8, 1
  Mary 40, 30, 14, 11

Ewart, James 59, 1
  Catherine 36, 9
Craig Adam 36, 21, 6, 12
  Ann 35, 10, 5
  5 negroes
Coonet, Prudence 20, 26
Crawford Alexander 36, 8, 6, 3
  Elizabeth 40, 7, 5
  2 negroes
Crawford, Thomas 39, 12, 10, 5
  Elizabeth 39, 14, 7
  1 negro
Crawford, Bazell 33
  Mary 36
  1 negro
Drown, Thomas 35
  Gran. 35, 19
Hamilton, John G. 28, 6
  Susanna 28, 57, 23, 1
Free, Nicholas 41, 25, 13, 7, 6, 2
  Catherine 40, 12, 7, 4, 1
Frances, John 57, 50, 25
  white female 25
Miller, Philip 35
  Elizabeth 21, 17, 2
Bradford, Henry 48, 23, 27, 15
  Elianor 31, 19, 8, 6
  8 negroes
Meyly, Christian B. 40, 9, 4, 1
  Margaret 33, 12
Wieghler, Felter 22, 22
Stone, Richard 62, 36, 19, 16, 13, 12
  Susanna 36, 4
  2 negroes
Fergusson, John 51, 8
  Bershiba 37, 20, 16, 14, 11
  2 negroes
Collard, Samuel 50, 66, 7, 4
  Agnes 43, 12
  6 negroes
Searce, David 30, 10, 8, 6
  Casandra 27, 4, 2
Lanham, William 26
  Catherine 24, 18
Tawnihill, William 28, 1
  Elizabeth 25, 34
Adams, Thomas 49, 17, 11, 8
  Elizabeth 46, 22, 15, 13, 6
  5 negroes
Adams, Thomas 24
  Lucy 20
Lanham, Samuel 30, 13, 9, 1
  Charity 31, 14

Worrell, Thomas 58, 40, 11
  Elizabeth Cramphin 37, 50, 16, 44
                  16, 6, 1, 3
  1 negro
Farr, Nicholas 55, 19, 15, 12, 3
  Alice 46, 17, 13, 9, 5
Tawnihill, Jeremiah 41, 6
  Lottie 33
Church, Jonathan 31, 35, 35, 3, 1
  Sarah 42, 29, 18, 7, 10, 1
  1 negro
Sydebotham, William 38, 25, 25, 22, 22
  white female 22
  2 negroes
Stuart, John 25, 19, 1
  Sarah 23, 4, 3
Stoddert, Benjamin 24, 21
Wheeler, Francis 85, 28
  Elizabeth 55
  2 negroes
Walace, Richard 36, 2
  Ann 25, 60, 8, 6, 4, 20
Scott, Henry 49, 14, 10, 7, 4, 1
  Mary 42, 38, 17
  2 negroes
Conn, William 26
  Rachell 20, 40, 3, 2
  1 negro
McGill, Thomas 30, 3
  Rachell 30, 22
Carns, Peter 27, 27, 40, 15, 6, 3
  Henrietta 37, 11, 8, 6
  9 negroes
Datford, William 40, 24
  Sarah 25, 6, 4, 2
Beall, Richard 41, 11, 8, 6, 4, 70, 27
  Rebecca 40, 17, 15, 13, 2, 1
  8 negroes
Perry, John 41, 3
  Penelope 32, 77, 20, 15, 5, 1
  10 negroes
Perry, James 49, 25, 14, 11, 7
  Marcie 42, 20, 16, 6, 3
  8 negroes
Boswell, John 36, 11, 4
  Elizabeth 29, 7, 2
Henry, Thomas 23
  Ann 22, 1
Vinn, Robert 25, 1
  Elizabeth 21
Dickerson, William 23
  9 negroes

Shanks, Thomas 29, 1
  Susanna 20
  16 negroes
Henry, Thomas 73, 7
  Mary 31, 70, 21, 8
Henry, John 30, 6, 4, 1
  Martha 33, 25, 3
Wright, Thomas 34, 2
  Ruth 21
Cramphin, Thomas 61, 34
  Precilla 29
  25 negroes
Hallum, Catherine 30, 25, 3
  white male 7, 1
Cisell, Thomas 50, 15, 5
  Mary 50, 15
  5 negroes
Page, James 48, 8
  Frances 50, 25, 81
Purdie, Henry 30, 17, 14, 12, 10, 1
  white female 26, 8
Tilley, Robert 19
  Mary 41
  11 negroes
Roberts, Jonathan 73
  Jane 63, 19, 17
Turnball, John
  29, 26, 25, 22, 19, 3
  Sarah 20, 23, 2, 1
  1 negro
Robey, John T. 48, 16, 13, 9, 6, 21
  Margaret 36, 11
Beall, John Jr. 48, 25, 19, 11, 6, 3
  Mary 45, 22, 14, 8, 22
  10 negroes
McNew, Martha 44, 12
  James 6
Jackson, Alexander 54, 12, 14
  Deborah 47, 19, 16, 7
  11 negroes
Tilley, Thomas 48, 27, 19, 7
  Mary 47, 17, 14, 12, 10
  1 negro
Lindsey, Samuel 48, 15, 13
  Sarah 44, 12, 10
Tilley, Thomas Jr. 25, 1
  Elizabeth 25
  3 negroes
Jackson, William 26, 25
  Elizabeth 22
  7 negroes
Martin, Michael 42, 9, 7
  Mary 50, 15, 6, 4
  5 negroes

Taylor, Bennet 35, 10, 1
  Sarah 28, 14, 11, 4
  14 negroes
Pear, John 30, 8, 5, 1
  Mary 30, 36
Clagett, William 27, 1
  Harriet 17
  23 negroes
Duvall, William 29, 23, 19
  Elianor 30, 34
Dyar, Clem. 30, 1
  Anna 24
  3 negroes
Hazwell, William 46, 18, 16, 13
  Anna 40, 20
Caywood, Benjamin Sr. 64, 24, 18
                13, 15, 13
  Elianor 41, 12
Edelen, Philip 45, 13, 11, 5
  Mary 33, 9, 7, 3, 1
  2 negroes
Clagett, Richard 40, 13, 11
  Mary 26, 2
  8 negroes
Fenwick, Ignatius (no data)
  9 negroes
Lowe, John 60, 28
  Ann 65
  12 negroes
Boswell, Peter 21
  Mary 30, 5
Burch, Jonathan 68, 39, 15, 6
  Elizabeth 58, 20, 18, 3
  11 negroes
Burch, Jonathan Jr. 36, 9
  Anna 42, 12
  10 negroes
Middleton, Smith 56
  Mary 45, 15
  13 negroes
Lanham, Edward 45, 16, 11, 2
  Susanna 45, 14, 7, 4
  16 negroes
Mitchell, Notley 56
  Elizabeth 54
  12 negroes
Mudd, Francis 30, 15, 3
  Sarah 28, 5, 1
  5 negroes
Clubb, Samuel 28, 2
  Mary 26
Hawkins, George F. 35, 7
  Susanna 26, 3
  21 negroes

Shearwood, Thomas 71, 24, 18
  Ann 50, 17, 12
Price, John 33, 18
  Mary 35
Simpson, Joseph 71, 26, 13
  Sarah 71, 38, 24
Shrieves, Jeremiah 33, 6
  Ann 25, 20, 6, 8
Stonestreet, Joseph 36
  Alice 28, 1
Mahew, Samuel 26, 14, 2, 1
  Lydia 20?
Whitmore, Humphrey 60, 27, 18, 9
  Elianor 50, 22, 14
Calihorn, John 63, 28, 11, 7, 5
  Elianor 38, 25, 23, 19, 10
Howe, Thomas 46, 12
  Elizabeth 45, 8, 6
Lanham, Soloman 21
  Lucy 40, 11, 8
Nichols, Henry 51, 7
  Mary 41
Lanham, Thomas 75, 7
  Margaret 55
Jarboe, James 40, 1
  Martha 29, 1
Fry, Leonard 26, 13, 10
  Christian 46, 15, 12
Palmer, William 24
Lewis, William 26
  Sarah 19
Nighton, Keizer 33, 5
  Mary 28, 3
James, John 38, 7
  females 13, 5
Stonestreet, John 25
  Ann 19, 28, 26, 8, 4, 4
  9 negroes
Gibbs, Ann 52, 14
  John Harris Gibbs 23, 100
  4 negroes
Thorn, Benjamin 43, 6, 2
  Amelia 24, 9, 4, 1
  1 negro
Athers, Ann 70
Dawson Ann 59, 27, 13, 8, 3
  3 negroes
Fraser, D.niel 59, 16
  Elizabeth 48, 18, 13, 7
Wright, Thomas 43, 10, 3, 1
  Elizabeth 38, 9, 1
Scott, John 42, 14, 9, 3
  Mary 42, 14, 12, 11, 10, 3

Weathers, Rachel 52 (**free Black**)
  1 male black 64
Cassill, John 51, 45, 11
  Rebecca 40, 1
  2 negroes
Jones, Benjamin 40, 13, 10, 7
  Elizabeth 39, 12, 1
Voice, Mary 25
  her son 1
Pane, John 30, 8
  Mary 36, 6, 4, 2
  1 negro
Lanham, Jesse 42, 14, 10, 9
  Elizabeth 37, 17, 14, 8, 4, 2
Robinson, James 54
  Mary 53, 16, 14
Edelen, Thomas P. 37
  Susanna 35, 11
  4 negroes
Rowe, George 25
  Sarah 19, 1
Fraser, Henry 22, 1
  Verlinda 22
Jones, Edward Jr. 28, 3
  Elizabeth 30
  1 negro
Norton, William Sr. 60, 20, 16, 10, 8, 6, 1
  Elianor 38, 18, 14, 12, 4
  2 negroes
Jones, John 45, 13
  Elianor 29, 11, 1
  7 negroes
Clarkson, Thomas Jr. 28, 2, 1
  Elizabeth 37, 3
  3 negroes
Gilpin, Benjamin 39, 13
  Ann 16, 28, 10, 8, 4
Goldrope, John 52, 25
  Mary 52, 22, 12
Jones, Mary 60
  her son 14
  1 negro
Jones, Notley 27, 1
  Ann 23, 4
Wheat, John 43, 12, 9, 7, 1
  Mary 11, 5
  1 negro
Breashears, John 53, 22, 14
  Mary 57, 19
Breashears, John P. 24, 4
  Ann 24, 1

Millican, Samuel 27, 5, 2, 1
  Ruth 27, 2
Talbot, Nathaniel 56
  Ann 58
  2 negroes
Dennis, Ignatius N. 31, 1
  Lucrecia 33, 8, 4
Kinsberry, Susanna 20
Kindrick, Thomas 51, 23, 18, 12, 6
  Sarah 45, 28, 16, 6
Ridgeway, Richard 24, 4, 1
  Charity 28, 8, 6
Ridgeway, Jonathan 57, 16, 21
  Elizabeth 57
Humphrey, Henry 29, 6, 4, 2
  Elizabeth 24
  6 negroes
Jones, Susanna 26
Galeworth, John 29
  Sarah 23, 2
Humphrey, Sarah 58, 26, 24, 20
  her son 15
  6 negroes
Simpson, James 39, 12, 10, 8
  Precilla 38, 5, 3, 1
Hardey, Henry 56
  Mary 60, 23, 1
  1 negro
Adams, Richard 20, 2, 1
  Elizabeth 20
  2 negroes
Walker, William 25, 2
  Elizabeth 24, 1
Dove, Samuel 35
  Martha 26, 6, 3
Thompson, John Sr. 67, 16, 15, 10, 3
  Sarah 45, 18, 13

Walker, Henry 45, 16, 3
  Elianor 29, 60, 22, 8, 6
Barrot, Robert 53, 16, 14, 1
  Sarah 40, 80, 31
Keath, George 51, 20, 12, 6, 4
  Monica 49, 17, 15, 12, 9, 2
  5 negroes
King, John 38, 7
  Elianor 39, 12, 13, 11, 9, 5, 1
  1 negro
Lewis, Thomas 34, 9, 6, 12
  Elizabeth 35, 16, 11, 1
Stone, Joseph 37, 16, 10, 7, 6, 4, 1
  Elianor 35, 12, 11, 3

Morris, Barton 20, 1
  Mary 18, 2
  1 negro
Davies, Mary 40, 19, 16, 15
Bryan, William 63, 23, 19
  Diana 45, 33, 15, 12, 6, 4, 11
  3 negroes
Bryan, George 34, 4, 3, 1
  Anna 24
Ball, Sarah 60
Walker, Martha 30, 2
  her sons 4, 1
Grigory, Richard 32, 5, 1
  Violetta 31, 11, 8, 3
Barret, Richard 51, 24, 19, 16, 15, 9
  Ann 53, 21, 12
  2 negroes
Burgess, Martha 50, 18, 17, 9, 5
  sons 21, 1
Rollins, Elizabeth 57
  Ellis, Robert 47
McDaniel, Reubin 29, 5, 1
  Catherine 25, 7
Willson, Nathaniel 60, 19, 17, 14
  Elizabeth 53, 27, 24, 22, 11
  7 negroes
Mason, Sarah 45, 17, 13, 6
  sons 19, 4
Lusby, Samuel 50, 23, 22, 6, 4, 1
  Susanna 41, 18, 12, 9
  6 negroes
Edelen, Christopher 28, 21
  Mary 28, 3, 1
  2 negroes
Dyar, Henry 26
  Ann 21
  2 negroes
Edelen, Richard 53, 14, 7
  Mary 52, 17, 12, 10, 5, 4
  8 negroes
Day, Mathew 66, 14, 13, 11
  Ann 55, 30, 28, 26, 20, 9
Mattinly, Clement 28, 11
  Frances 44, 20, 18, 15, 9, 1, 9
Gilpin, Benjamin 60, 14
  Sarah 60, 18, 16, 10
Worland, Charles 29, 23, 1
  Winefred 20, 4
  3 negroes
Walker, John 25, 6
  Elizabeth 29, 64, 52,
Ball, Richard 40, 9, 7, 1
  Sarah 28, 12, 8, 6
  4 negroes

Reaves, John 51, 11
    Sarah 61
Wheeler, Elizabeth 67, 43, 32, 27,
    24, 12, 8
    8 negroes
Riedd, James 27
    1 negro
Stonestreet, Elianor 25, 8, 4, 2
    her son 1
    3 negroes
Dyar, Henrietta 55, 20, 20, 16, 13, 4
    her sons 23, 25, 1
    8 negroes
Edelen, Charles 49, 16, 13, 7, 5
    Catherine 47, 12, 9
    10 negroes
Simms, Darius 52, 13, 10
    Mary 30, 25, 17
Smith, Hannah 40, 22, 13, 7, 5, 1
    (free Blacks) her sons 12, 9
Jenkins, Zadock 34, 10, 7
    Precilla 34, 21, 12, 5, 1
    1 negro
Scott, Zachariah 39, 13, 9, 8, 4, 1
    Elizabeth 40, 11, 6, 2
Club, Samuel 37, 12, 7, 5
    Keziah 36, 3, 1
Grymes, George 50, 19, 13, 11, 7, 1
    Catherine 42, 16, 7, 3, 3
Talbot, Paul 51, 13, 11, 6, 1
    Martha 38, 15, 12, 8, 4
Grymes, Robert 34, 4
    Hestor 31, 12, 10, 1
Talbot, John 51
    Ann 76, 30
    12 negroes
Fisher, Abraham 55
    Elizabeth 50
    10 negroes
Stone, John 55, 8, 6, 2
    Margaret 60, 13, 4
Cheyney, Joyce 53
    Sarah 37, 6
Lanham, Azariah 45
    5 negroes
Ball, Hilleary 49, 16, 18, 14, 3, 2
    Elizabeth 39, 17, 10, 9, 7
Clarkson, Joseph 27
    5 negroes
Bryan, Thomas 25, 1
    Anna 21
Bayne, Winefred 54, 20, 18, 15
    sons 22, 12
Smallwood, Sarah 38, 13

Adams, Joseph 55
    Winefred 66, 14, 40
    10 negroes
Robinson, Stephen 51, 14, 10, 1
    Jane 37, 19, 12, 6, 3
Vermilion, Benjamin N. 28, 5
    Hester 22, 3, 1
Havis, James 39, 6, 3
    Catherine 23, 4
Simpson, John 51, 22, 12
    Sarah 48, 19, 17, 14, 11, 4
Brown, James 26, 26
Harvin, Elias 23, 23, 2, 1
    Mary 24, 25
Jones, Sarah 31, 12, 11
    her son 1
Summers, Lydia 65, 25, 12
    her son 17
Waters, Joseph 40
    Margaret 9
Willicoxen, Thomas 82, 35, 29
    Ruth 73, 36, 18, 14
    25 negroes
Haviner, Dominicar 46, 11, 11, 10, 4
    Mary 38
Hardey, Ignatius 39, 17, 10
    Elizabeth 38, 15, 14, 9, 8, 6, 2
    2 negroes
Scarce, Nathan 35, 10
    Sarah 33, 8, 6, 3
    1 negro
Cary, William 50
King, John 74
    Mary 29, 18, 16
Vermillion, Henson 24
Moore, James 40, 16, 21
    female 12
    3 negroes
Moore, Benjamin 64, 21
    female 16
Parkins, Thomas 20
    Casandria 18, 69, 11
Wheeler, Ignatius 45, 12, 8
    Elizabeth 38, 19, 16, 2
    10 negroes
Caton, Stephen 30, 5, 3, 1
    Eleanor 27, 14
    1 negro
Jenkins, Bartholomew 49, 14, 12, 10
    Mary 44, 6, 4, 2
    8 negroes
Warner, Francis 30, 6, 4, 2
    Catherine 24
    5 negroes

Lowe, Ann 60
    8 negroes
Hurley, Joseph 50, 18
    Ann 48
Athey, Owen 40, 13, 11, 5, 5, 1, 2
    Lucy 43, 22, 12, 7, 1
Hurley, Thomas 41, 13, 11, 6, 3, 1
    Jane 36, 15, 9
Hurley, Daniel 75
    white females 35, 2
Saunders, Josias 25, 5, 4
    Jemima 32, 2
Minnis, John 36, 4, 1
    Dorithy 37, 11, 7, 5
Wigfield, Joseph 40, 4
    Elizabeth 28, 6, 3, 1
Magruder, Thomas 38
    Mary 39, 4
    5 negroes
Kingsberry, Demillion 50, 16, 10
    Elizabeth 51, 14, 13, 1
Brown, Edward 35, 4, 2
    Hannah 20
    2 negroes
Soper, Leonard 34, 6, 5, 3
    Elizabeth 26, 9, 7, 1
    4 negroes
Wigfield, Thomas 33, 20, 13, 2
    Radie 34, 73
Lowe, Richard 30, 1
    Sarah 20, 2
    1 negro
Wheever, Rachell 40
    son 15
Arnold, Christopher 50, 10, 6, 3, 1
    Mary 30, 13
    2 negroes
Allen, Mrs. 56
    4 negroes
Spinkes, Francis 39, 8, 6, 2
    Sarah 34, 14, 11, 4
    1 negro
Hurly, Cornelius 46, 19, 11, 3
    Mary 46, 16, 14, 8
    2 negroes
Magruder, Edward 28
    1 negro
Grymes, Thomas 52, 14, 10, 2
    Margaret 4, 5
Clarkson, Joseph 26, 1
    3 negroes
Smith, John 53, 8
    Sarah 55
    11 negroes

Nowland, John 31
    Elianor 23, 2
Robinson, James 33
    Knight, Mary 39
Lanham, Thomas 70, 8
    Margaret 60
Masey, Thomas 50, 19, 6
    Lucy 46, 17, 15, 12
King, Edward 48, 5, 1
    Ann 30, 13, 10, 6, 3
Hall, John 35, 7
    Elizabeth 30
Hardey, Anthoney 31
    Lydia 19, 1
    3 negroes
Nichleson, Nicholas 40
    Mary 47, 13, 9, 5
Piles, Dorithy 45, 28, 21, 19, 17, 9, 5, 2
    male 15
Lowe, Nickolas 28, 10
    Sarah 23, 8, 6, 4
    8 negroes
Bryne, Josiah 31, 9, 7
    Ann 30, 5, 3, 1
Lowe, Harry 27
    Elizabeth 21, 50
    9 negroes
Waugh, James 39, 28, 9, 1
    Mary 40, 13, 11, 7
Minnis, Mary 45
Fry, Thomas 29, 6, 4, 1
    Sarah 28, 3
Strong, John 38, 5
    Ann, 25, 2, 1
Knell, Richard 51, 18, 12, 10, 8, 6, 2
    Sarah 42, 15, 4, 1
    3 negroes
Walker, John 31, 6, 4, 2
    Rachell 25
Jones, Francis 51, 18, 17, 15, 12, 3
    Ann 38, 8, 6
McDaniel, Mary 46, 19
Wade, Robert Jr. 50, 21, 15, 13, 7, 4
    Mary 45, 15, 11, 9
    11 negroes
Wade, Ann 38, 13, 10, 3
    males 8, 6
    1 negro
Lanham, Elizabeth 26, 16
    sons 6, 4, 2
Clifford, John 43, 22, 15, 12
    Monica 39, 14, 8, 2
    2 negroes

Robinson, Charles 57
    Elizabeth 49
Lowe, Henry 43, 18, 10, 8, 6, 3, 10, 1
    Ann 40, 19, 16, 14, 12, 4
Herbert, Margaret 53, 15
    sons 26, 18, 8
All, Andrew 65
    Margaret 56
Hardey, John B. 67
    Mary 63, 26, 17, 15, 12
Robinson, Peter 60, 8, 4
    wife 30, 1
Pumphries, William 49, 15, 14, 11, 7, 6
    Elizabeth 38, 20, 17, 5, 2
Pickerson, Ralph 57, 31, 22, 16, 14, 5
    Elizabeth 53, 28, 26, 24, 20, 18, 12
    10
Jarbo, James 45, 1
    Elizabeth 43, 1
Hardey, Henry G. 45, 11, 4
    Mary 32, 30, 15, 13, 6, 6
    25 negroes
Hurley, William 37, 14, 12, 11, 8, 3
    Rachell 32, 7, 5, 1
    3 negroes
Vermilion, Giles 68, 36, 25, 23
    Sarah 21, 66
Hall, George 45
    Mary 50
Johnson, Thomas 30
    Margery 27, 7, 4, 1
Tolon, Ann 43, 10
    her son 14
Stonestreet, Henry 24
    Mary 23
    14 negroes
Stephens, Thomas 30, 9
    Mary 26, 50, 4, 1
    1 negro
Stephens, William Jr. 26, 4, 3, 1
    Elizabeth 24
    1 negro
McDaniel, John 39, 7
    Mary 30, 5, 1
    3 negroes
Redman, John I.S. 30, 4, 2
    Clie 25, 6
McDaniel, Walter 21
    Jane 20, 15, 1
Hatton, Joseph 55, 32, 27, 21, 19, 15
    Mary 53, 26, 24, 22, 10
    19 negroes

Rozer, Henry 51, 19, 19, 17, 26, 30, 6
    Eleanor 48, 26, 12, 8, 3
    68 negroes
Young, Notley-white male over 16
    6 white females & 6 males 16-50
    42 negroes
Moore, Thomas 31
    Hester 26, 3
    10 negroes
Wheeler, Hezickiah 37
    14 negroes
Dyar, Thomas 32, 7, 2, 1
    Ann 28, 10, 4
Newton, Nathaniel 39, 30
    females 30, 43, 33, 30, 22
    40 negroes
Hawkins, James 42
    Elizabeth 44
    25 negroes
Beall, Elizabeth 70, 38, 27
    male 10
    14 negroes
Dyar, Susanna 75, 29
    her sons 28, 27
    3 negroes
Bowling, William L. 28, 24
    Mary 74, 26, 22
    4 negroes
Coe, Samuel 32, 18, 9, 1
    Phebe 33
Coe, Mary 50, 23, 18, 16
    sons 26, 21, 6
Simpson, Elizabeth 70, 14, 10
    Green 27
    2 negroes
Parker, Alethea T. 45
    Simpson, John 34
    16 negroes
Green, Thomas E. 29, 2
    Catherine 28, 5, 3
    3 negroes
Edelen, Christopher 53, 18, 2
    Elizabeth 42, 16, 14, 12, 9, 6
    1 negro
Winn, William 24
    Ann 21
Spalding, Henry 27, 1
    Ann 24, 4
    3 negroes
Spalding, John 24, 20
    4 negroes
King, John 25, 16, 11
    Kersey 20, 14, 9, 7

Hatton, Nathaniel 55, 56
  Mary 63
  25 negroes
Miles, Nicholas 35, 10
  Ann 28, 3
  2 negroes
Addison, Anthoney
  (list cannot be got)
Mrs. Addison's Quarter
  29 negroes
Winn, John 56, 17
  Sarah 54, 15, 14, 12, 9
  6 negroes

Winn, John Jr. 37, 9, 7, 4, 1
  Mary 30, 10, 5
Smallwood, William 54, 19
  Mary 56, 20, 14
Berry, John 24
  5 negroes
Russell, Bazell 32
Philips, Robert 45, 12, 10, 8, 6, 4
  Sarah 40, 60
  1 negro
Simpson 46, 16
  Mary 40, 18, 14, 12, 10, 8, 7

Richard Thrawls & James Prather refuse to give in a list of their families
and Anthoney Addison neglicts to do it after several applications by Thomas Dent.

The following were inadvertently omitted

Beall, Ninian 25, 20, 3
  Ann 21, 1
Beall, James of John 40, 14, 12, 4
  Ann 40, 14, 2
Bowling, John 43, 13, 6, 1
  Mary 38, 13, 11, 8, 4, 25
  16 negroes

Dawson, Thomas 41, 13, 10, 6
  Mary 38, 12, 3, 1
Day, Mathew Jr 30, 9, 4, 2
  Ann 25, 11, 6
Thompson. William 38, 17, 23, 15,
                   10, 8, 6, 5, 3
  Mary 29, 16

## 1776 CENSUS OF TOWN HUNDRED, QUEEN ANNE COUNTY, MARYLAND

Taken by Mark Benton and sworn before Turbutt Wright, September 22, 1776

| Head of the household | Male over 21 | 16 to 21 | 12 to 16 | under 12 | Females over 21 | 16 to 21 | 12 to 16 | under 12 | Blacks |
|---|---|---|---|---|---|---|---|---|---|
| John Anderson | 1 | | | 1 | 2 | | | 2 | 15 |
| Dr. James Anderson | | | | | | | | | 34 |
| Richard Arescott | 1 | 1 | 1 | | 1 | | 1 | | 2 |
| Nathan Adkey | 1 | | | 1 | 1 | | | | |
| Absalom Austin | 1 | | 2 | | | | 2 | | |
| Thomas Ashley | 1 | | | | 1 | | | | 2 |
| Thomas Burrell | 1 | | | | 1 | | | | |
| Nathaniel Boots | 1 | | | | 1 | | | 1 | |
| William Mason Brown | 1 | | 1 | | 1 | | 1 | 2 | 7 |
| Samuel Poots | 1 | | | | 1 | | | | 1 |
| Thomas Barber | 1 | | | | 1 | | | | |
| Hezekiah Betts | 2 | 2 | 1 | | 3 | | | 1 | 9 |
| Charles Blervet | 1 | | 1 | | 1 | | 1 | 3 | |
| Jeremiah Bushanall | 1 | 2 | | | 3 | 1 | | 1 | 3 |
| John Bateman | 1 | | | 1 | 1 | | | 2 | |
| John Benton | 3 | 1 | | 2 | 1 | | | 3 | 15 |
| John Brown | 2 | | | | 2 | | 1 | | 38 |
| Mary Byrn | | | 1 | 4 | 2 | 1 | 1 | | 12 |
| James Bateman (taylor) | 1 | | 2 | 1 | 1 | | | 3 | 2 |
| Jacob Boots | 1 | 1 | | | 1 | | 1 | 2 | 1 |
| Samuel Brown | 1 | | 1 | 1 | 1 | 1 | | 1 | 13 |
| Ninson Benton | 3 | | | | 2 | | | | 13 |
| Ninson Benton Jr. | 2 | | 2 | 3 | 1 | | | 2 | |
| William Benton | 1 | | | 3 | 1 | | | 1 | 3 |
| William Brown | 2 | | 1 | 4 | 1 | 2 | | | 17 |
| David Burk (schoolmaster) | no data enumerated | | | | | | | | |
| Solomon, Betts | 2 | | | | 3 | | | | |
| George Bolton | 1 | 1 | | 1 | 1 | 1 | 1 | 2 | 1 |
| Michael Bateman | 2 | | 2 | | 3 | | 1 | 1 | |
| John Bustles | 1 | | | 2 | 1 | | | 2 | |
| Thomas Butler | 1 | | 1 | 1 | | | 1 | 1 | |
| Mary Benson | | | | 2 | 2 | | | 1 | |
| Jean Bennett | | | | | 1 | | | 1 | |
| William Colvin | 1 | | 1 | | 1 | | | | |
| Isaac Corbert | 3 | | | | 1 | | | 1 | |
| William Certein | 1 | | | | | | | | 2 |
| Elizabeth Chatham | | | | | 2 | 1 | | | 9 |
| Asel Cossin | 1 | 1 | | 1 | 1 | 1 | 2 | 1 | |
| Roger Colman | 1 | 1 | 2 | 3 | 1 | | 1 | 2 | |
| Charles Cavillare | 2 | | | | | | | | 1 |
| Robert Carson | 1 | | | | 1 | | | 1 | |
| John Comegys | 2 | 1 | 1 | 2 | 3 | 1 | 1 | 4 | |
| Sarah Comegys | | | 1 | | 1 | | | 1 | 1 |
| Philemon Coppage | 1 | 1 | | 2 | 1 | | 1 | | 5 |
| Thomas Chavies | 2 | | | 3 | 1 | | | 2 | 2 |
| Sech Conner | | | | | | | | | 8 |
| William Carmichael | | | | | | | | | 14 |
| Walter, Carmichael | 3 | | | 1 | 1 | | | 1 | 24 |

141

| Head of the household | MALES over 21 | 16 to 21 | 12 to 16 | under 12 | FEMALES over 21 | 16 to 21 | 12 to 16 | under 12 | Blacks |
|---|---|---|---|---|---|---|---|---|---|
| William Coleman | 1 | 2 | 2 | 2 | 1 | | | | |
| William Carmon | 2 | | | | 2 | | 1 | | |
| John Cohee | 1 | | | 2 | 1 | | 1 | | |
| Darias Coleman | 1 | | | 1 | | 1 | | 1 | |
| Thomas Cunningham | 1 | | | 1 | 1 | 3 | | | 1 |
| John Cox | 1 | 2 | | 1 | | 1 | | | 3 |
| Thomas Coursey | | | | | | | | | 5 |
| Nathaniel Cavinder | 1 | | | | 1 | | | 2 | |
| William Comer | 1 | | | | 2 | | | | |
| Mary Carson | | | | 1 | 2 | 1 | | 2 | |
| John Davis | 2 | | 1 | | 1 | | | 1 | |
| Abner Dudley | 2 | 2 | 1 | 1 | 3 | | | | 5 |
| John Demster | 1 | | | | | 1 | | | 1 |
| James Dixon | 1 | | | 2 | 2 | | | 2 | 6 |
| ___ Demster | 1 | | | 2 | 1 | | | 3 | |
| Robert Dunkin | 1 | | | | 1 | 1 | | 2 | 1 |
| Thomas Downey Jr. | 1 | | 1 | 3 | 2 | | | | |
| Valentine Dwericks | 2 | | | 3 | 2 | | | 3 | 8 |
| William Deford | 2 | | | 1 | 2 | | | 1 | 1 |
| Thomas Dawson | 1 | | | | | 1 | | 1 | |
| William Duglass | 1 | | 1 | | 1 | | 1 | | |
| Thomas Downey Sr. | 2 | | | | 2 | | | 1 | |
| James Dailey | 1 | 1 | | 1 | 1 | | 1 | | |
| John Dailey | 1 | | | 3 | 1 | | | 2 | |
| Peter Dyer | 1 | 1 | 2 | 2 | 1 | | 1 | 1 | |
| Valentine Downey | 1 | | | | 1 | | | | |
| Patrick Downey | 1 | | | 1 | 1 | | | | |
| Captain John Dean | 2 | | | | | | | | |
| Christopher Dene | 1 | | | | 1 | | | 1 | |
| James Deford | 1 | | | | 1 | | | | |
| Tabitha Downey | | | | 3 | 1 | | | | |
| Elizabeth Deaviniah | | | | 2 | 2 | | | 3 | |
| William Deford Sr. | 1 | | | 1 | 1 | | | 2 | |
| Rachel Dempster | | 1 | 1 | 2 | 2 | | | 2 | |
| Joseph Dodo | 1 | | | 1 | 1 | 1 | | | |
| Rebeckah Elliott | 1 | | | | 1 | | | 1 | |
| Valentine Eggate | 1 | | | | 2 | | | 1 | 10 |
| Jonathan Eavins | 1 | | | 1 | 1 | 1 | | 2 | |
| James Eareckson | 1 | 1 | | 1 | 2 | 1 | | 1 | |
| Arthur Foreman Jr. | 1 | | | 3 | 3 | | | 1 | 3 |
| Daniel Ford Sr. | 1 | 3 | 2 | | 2 | | | | 7 |
| Daniel Ford Jr. | 1 | 1 | | 2 | 2 | | | | 1 |
| John Foreman Jr. | 1 | | | 2 | 1 | | | 3 | |
| Isaac Ford Sr. | 1 | | | 1 | 1 | 1 | | 1 | 2 |
| John Foreman Sr. | 2 | 1 | | 2 | 3 | | | 1 | 12 |
| Edmond Ferrell | 1 | | | 1 | 1 | 1 | | 1 | 9 |
| Arthur Foreman of Arthur | 1 | | 2 | 2 | 1 | | | 1 | |
| William Falconer | 1 | | | | 1 | 1 | | | |
| Jean Farbush | | | | 1 | 2 | | | 1 | |
| George Gestes | 1 | | | | 1 | | 1 | | |
| George Bartlett | 1 | | | 1 | 1 | | 1 | 1 | 2 |

142

| Head of the Household | MALES over 21 | 16 to 21 | 12 to 16 | under 12 | FEMALES over 21 | 16 to 21 | 12 to 16 | under 12 | Blacks |
|---|---|---|---|---|---|---|---|---|---|
| Benjamin Gould, Esq. | 1 | 1 | 1 | 2 | 1 | 1 | 1 | 1 | 5 |
| John Gafford Sr. | 4 | 1 | 1 | 1 | 1 | 3 |  | 3 | 2 |
| Matthew Graves | 2 |  |  |  | 1 |  |  | 1 |  |
| James Gooding | 3 | 1 |  | 2 | 2 | 1 | 1 | 1 | 25 |
| John Gafford Jr. | 1 |  |  | 3 | 1 |  |  | 1 |  |
| Nathan Glandin | 1 |  |  | 2 | 1 |  |  | 1 |  |
| Peter Gordin Jr. |  | 1 | 1 | 2 | 2 |  |  | 2 |  |
| Richard Gould | 3 |  |  |  | 1 |  |  | 1 | 11 |
| Sarah Gafford | 2 |  | 2 |  | 1 | 1 | 1 |  | 5 |
| Thomas Graves | 1 | 1 | 1 | 3 | 1 | 1 |  | 2 |  |
| Valentine Gafford | 1 |  |  | 4 | 2 |  |  | 2 |  |
| William Gregory | 1 |  | 2 | 6 | 1 |  |  | 1 |  |
| William Gray | 1 |  |  | 1 | 1 |  | 1 | 2 |  |
| Charles Gafford | 1 |  |  | 2 | 1 |  |  | 1 |  |
| William Greenwood | 2 |  |  |  | 1 | 1 | 1 | 1 |  |
| William Garnett | 1 |  |  |  |  |  | 1 | 1 |  |
| Stephen Games |  |  |  |  |  |  |  |  | 3 |
| Elener Graves |  |  | 1 | 1 | 2 |  |  |  |  |
| Thomas Sawyer Hopkins |  |  |  |  |  |  |  |  | 6 |
| Edward Herring | 1 |  | 1 | 3 | 1 |  |  | 2 |  |
| Thomas Hopkins | 1 |  |  |  | 1 | 1 |  | 1 |  |
| George Hastings | 1 |  | 1 |  | 1 | 2 |  | 1 | 6 |
| Charles Harris | 1 |  |  | 4 | 1 |  |  |  | 1 |
| Richard Holding | 1 | 1 |  |  | 2 |  |  | 1 | 3 |
| John Hackett | 1 |  |  | 2 | 1 |  |  | 2 | 12 |
| Richard Horsley | 1 |  |  | 2 | 1 |  |  | 2 |  |
| James Hackett | 2 | 1 | 1 |  | 1 | 2 | 1 | 3 | 16 |
| John Holding Jr. | 2 |  |  | 1 | 1 |  |  | 3 |  |
| Thomas Hunt | 1 |  |  |  | 1 |  |  | 1 |  |
| Thomas Hackett | 1 |  | 1 | 2 | 2 |  |  | 4 | 11 |
| Elizabeth Hammond |  | 1 | 1 |  | 1 | 1 |  |  |  |
| William Hollingsworth | 1 |  |  | 4 | 1 |  |  | 2 |  |
| Charles Harbitt | 1 |  |  | 1 | 1 |  |  | 1 |  |
| James Hollingsworth | 1 |  | 1 |  | 1 |  |  | 2 |  |
| Matthew Hawkins | 2 |  |  |  |  |  |  |  | 4 |
| William Hales | 1 |  |  | 1 | 1 |  |  | 2 |  |
| Jonathan Hall | 2 |  | 1 |  | 1 | 1 | 1 |  | 4 |
| Walter Hudson | 2 |  |  |  | 1 |  |  | 3 |  |
| John Hinds | 1 |  |  |  | 1 |  |  | 1 |  |
| Hance Johnson | 1 | 1 | 1 | 1 | 1 |  |  | 1 |  |
| John Johnson | 1 |  | 1 | 1 | 1 |  |  |  |  |
| George Johnson | 2 |  |  |  | 1 |  |  |  |  |
| Henry Jacobs | 1 | 1 |  |  | 1 |  |  |  |  |
| Robert Jones | 1 |  |  |  | 1 |  |  |  |  |
| Stafford Jackson | 1 |  |  | 1 | 2 |  |  |  |  |
| John Taylor Jones | 2 |  |  |  | 1 |  |  |  |  |
| Samuel Jackson | 1 | 1 | 1 | 1 | 2 |  |  |  |  |
| William Kickman | 1 |  |  | 2 | 1 |  |  | 2 | 1 |
| John Kemp | 1 |  |  |  | 1 |  |  |  |  |
| Emanuel Kent | 4 |  | 1 | 1 | 1 | 1 |  |  | 23 |
| Francis Lamdin | 1 |  |  | 2 | 1 |  |  |  |  |

| Head of the Household | MALES over 21 | 16 to 21 | 12 to 16 | under 12 | FEMALES over 21 | 16 to 21 | 12 to 16 | under 12 | Blacks |
|---|---|---|---|---|---|---|---|---|---|
| Edward Linzy | 1 | | | 3 | 1 | | 1 | 1 | |
| Oinson Lee | 1 | | | 2 | 1 | | | 2 | |
| William Lee | 1 | | 1 | 1 | 2 | | | | |
| William Lary | 1 | | 1 | 1 | 1 | | | 1 | |
| Robert Lambert | | 1 | | 1 | 1 | | | 2 | |
| Rachel Lee | 2 | | 1 | 2 | 1 | 1 | 1 | | |
| William Leek | 1 | | | 1 | 1 | | | 1 | |
| William Lang | 1 | | 1 | 1 | 1 | | | 2 | |
| John McClane | 1 | | 1 | 1 | | | | | |
| Alice McCoy | 2 | | | 2 | 2 | | | 2 | 5 |
| Alexander Maxwell | 1 | | 1 | 2 | 1 | | | | 2 |
| Henry Moreland | 1 | | | 4 | | | | | |
| Enen McSkiming | 1 | | | 1 | 1 | | 1 | 2 | |
| James McGonegill | 2 | 1 | | | 1 | | | 1 | 1 |
| Thomas Marsh | 1 | | | | | | | | 24 |
| John Mumford | 1 | | | | 1 | | | | 2 |
| Timothy Moaner | 3 | 1 | | | 1 | 1 | | | |
| William Mountseer | 1 | | | | 1 | | | 3 | |
| William Mand | 1 | | 2 | 1 | 1 | | | 2 | |
| James More | 1 | | | 1 | 1 | | | 1 | |
| Samuel McClannahan | 1 | | | 1 | 1 | | | | |
| William Milburn | 1 | | | | 1 | | | | |
| Patrick Mooney | 2 | | 1 | | 1 | 2 | | | |
| William Morse | 1 | | | 1 | 1 | | | 1 | 1 |
| Thomas Meridith | 1 | | | 2 | 1 | | | 3 | 7 |
| John Milbey | 1 | | | 1 | 1 | 1 | | 2 | 5 |
| Francis Meeds | | | | 1 | 1 | 1 | | | |
| John McGinnis | 1 | | | | | | | | |
| John Murphey | 1 | | | 1 | 1 | | | | |
| Walter Mold | 2 | | | | 2 | | | 2 | |
| Elizabeth McLannahan | | | 1 | 3 | 2 | | 2 | 1 | 1 |
| Thomas Meeds | 1 | | 1 | 2 | 1 | | | 1 | 3 |
| William Clark Massey | 1 | | | | 1 | | | 2 | 2 |
| Sarah Nabb | | | | 2 | 1 | 1 | | 1 | |
| Daniel Neronam | 2 | | 2 | 4 | 3 | | | | 1 |
| James Nevil | 1 | | 1 | 3 | 1 | | | 1 | 3 |
| John Neronam | 1 | | | 2 | 1 | | | | |
| Joseph Neronam | 1 | 1 | 1 | 1 | 1 | | 1 | 2 | |
| John Nerol | 2 | | 1 | 2 | 1 | | 1 | 2 | |
| Walter Nevil | 1 | 1 | | 1 | 2 | | | 2 | 3 |
| William Neronam | 1 | | | 2 | 2 | | 2 | 2 | |
| Joseph Nicholson Jr. | | | | | | | | | 7 |
| Sarah Nevil | | | 1 | | 1 | | 1 | 1 | |
| John Owings | 1 | | | | | 1 | | | |
| Vinson Offley | 1 | | | 2 | 1 | | | 2 | 1 |
| Benton Offley | 1 | | | 1 | 1 | | | 2 | |
| John Offley | 2 | | 1 | | | 1 | | | |
| Margaret Price | | | | 1 | 2 | | | 1 | |
| Gabriel Purse | | | | 1 | 1 | | | 2 | |
| Rizdon Plummer | 2 | | | 1 | 1 | | | | 3 |

| Head of the Household | MALES over 21 | 16 to 21 | 12 to 16 | under 12 | FEMALES over 21 | 16 to 21 | 12 to 16 | under 12 | Blacks |
|---|---|---|---|---|---|---|---|---|---|
| Rachel Preston | 1 | 3 | 2 | 1 | 3 | 1 | | 1 | 3 |
| Edward Pinder | 2 | 1 | 1 | 2 | 2 | 1 | | | 2 |
| George Primrose | 1 | 1 | | | | | 1 | | 7 |
| John Ponder | 1 | | | 2 | 2 | | | | |
| John Primrose | 1 | | 1 | 1 | 1 | | | 1 | 6 |
| Robert Peacock | 1 | | | 1 | 1 | | | 1 | |
| John Peacock | 1 | | | | 1 | | | | |
| William Price | 1 | | 1 | | 1 | | | 1 | |
| William Pryor | 1 | | | 5 | 1 | | | | 7 |
| Thomas Perrarone | 1 | | | | 1 | 1 | | 1 | |
| William Pinder | 1 | | 1 | | 1 | | | | 1 |
| Samuel Pope | 1 | | | 1 | 1 | | | 1 | |
| George Hy Perraron | 1 | | | 1 | 1 | | | 2 | 1 |
| William Ponder Jr. | 1 | | | | 1 | | | | |
| Margarett Price | | 1 | 1 | | 2 | 1 | | | |
| Sarah Pooley | 2 | | | | 1 | | | 1 | |
| James Permar | 1 | | | 1 | | 1 | | | |
| William Ponder Sr. | 1 | | | | | 1 | | | 1 |
| John Quimby | 2 | | 2 | | 1 | | | 1 | |
| William Ricords | 1 | 1 | 1 | | 1 | | 1 | | |
| John Rigby | 1 | | 1 | | 1 | | | 1 | |
| Thomas Ruth | 1 | | 2 | | 1 | | | 1 | 1 |
| Francis Reed | 1 | | 1 | 3 | 1 | 2 | | 2 | |
| David Roberts | 1 | | 1 | 1 | 1 | 1 | 1 | 1 | 4 |
| Elizabeth Rochester | 1 | | | 2 | 1 | | | | 7 |
| James Rippeth | 1 | 1 | | | 1 | | | 3 | |
| James Roberts | 2 | 1 | 1 | 2 | 1 | | 1 | 2 | 11 |
| John Ruth (Smith) | 1 | | | | 1 | | | 2 | 4 |
| James Roseberry | 2 | | 1 | 3 | 2 | 2 | | 1 | |
| John Ruth of Thomas | 2 | | | | 1 | | | | |
| Mary Rochester | | 1 | | | 2 | | | | 2 |
| Nathan Rogers | 1 | 2 | | 1 | 2 | 1 | | 4 | |
| Samuel Reed | 1 | | | 2 | 1 | | | | |
| Stephen Ralph | 1 | 2 | | | | | 1 | 2 | |
| William Reed | 2 | 1 | 1 | 1 | 2 | | | 1 | 1 |
| John Rouse | 2 | 1 | | 2 | 3 | 1 | | 2 | 1 |
| William Rochester | 1 | 1 | | 1 | 1 | | | 2 | |
| Francis Rochester Jr. | 1 | 1 | 1 | 1 | 1 | 1 | 1 | | 10 |
| John Roser | 1 | | | 2 | 2 | | | 1 | |
| Francis Rochester | 3 | 1 | | | 2 | | 1 | | 3 |
| Sarah Syllavin | | | | 1 | 1 | | | 1 | |
| William Sparks of James | 1 | | | 1 | 1 | | | 1 | |
| Solomon Sparks | 1 | | | 1 | 1 | 1 | | 1 | |
| Josiah Smith | 1 | | 1 | 2 | 1 | 1 | 1 | 3 | |
| Abner Sparks | 1 | 1 | 2 | 2 | 1 | | | | |
| Daniel Smith | 1 | | | | 1 | | | 1 | |
| Thomas Smith | 1 | | | 2 | 1 | | | 1 | |
| Edward Sparks | 2 | | 1 | 1 | 1 | 1 | 1 | 1 | |
| Francis Spry | 2 | | | | 3 | 1 | | 1 | |
| George Stephans | 1 | | 1 | 1 | 1 | | 1 | 3 | |
| Henry Smith | 2 | | 1 | | 1 | | | 1 | 1 |

| Head of the Household | MALES over 21 | 16 to 21 | 12 to 16 | under 12 | FEMALES over 21 | 16 to 21 | 12 to 16 | under 12 | Blacks |
|---|---|---|---|---|---|---|---|---|---|
| John Sutton | 2 | | | 5 | 1 | | | 1 | 5 |
| James Smith | 1 | | 1 | 1 | 2 | | 2 | | 1 |
| Joseph Sudler | 2 | | 1 | 1 | 1 | 1 | | 1 | 11 |
| John Joyner Sparks | 1 | | | | 1 | | | | |
| James Sparks (F) | 1 | | | 3 | 1 | | | 1 | |
| Caleb Sparks Sr. | 1 | 1 | 1 | 3 | 2 | | 2 | 1 | |
| John Seney Esq. | 1 | 2 | 2 | 1 | 1 | | | | |
| John Spry | 1 | | | 3 | 1 | | 1 | 1 | 11 |
| John Sparks (Long) | 3 | | | 1 | | | | | |
| John Sparks (T) | 1 | | | 4 | | | | | 6 |
| Thomas Smith (weaver) | 1 | | | | 1 | 2 | 1 | | |
| James Smith (taylor) | 1 | | | | 1 | | | | |
| Edward Scott | 2 | 1 | 1 | 2 | 2 | 1 | 1 | 1 | 2 |
| William Serrell | 1 | | | | 1 | | 1 | 3 | 3 |
| Levi Sparks | 1 | | | | 1 | | 1 | 1 | |
| Millenton Sparks | 2 | 1 | | | 2 | 1 | | | |
| Nevil Seney | 1 | | 1 | | 1 | | | 1 | |
| Nathan Sparks | 1 | | 3 | 4 | 1 | 2 | | 3 | 1 |
| James Snail | 1 | | | 1 | 1 | | | 1 | |
| Sarah Syllavin | 1 | 1 | | | 1 | | | 2 | |
| Thomas Sudler | 1 | 1 | | 1 | 2 | 1 | | | 3 |
| Thomas Seward | 2 | 1 | 1 | 1 | 1 | | | | 15 |
| Mary Sparks | 1 | | 1 | | 1 | 2 | | | |
| William Sparks of B. | 1 | | | 1 | 1 | | | 4 | |
| Hannah Smith | 3 | | | 1 | 2 | | | 1 | |
| Thomas Sparks | 1 | 1 | | 1 | 2 | | 2 | 2 | |
| Jonas Sparks | 1 | | | 5 | 1 | | 1 | 2 | |
| David Stoops | 1 | 1 | | | | 1 | | | 2 |
| Vinson Sparks | 1 | | | 2 | 1 | | | | |
| John Sudler | 3 | | | 1 | 1 | | | 3 | 9 |
| William Seney | 1 | | | 1 | 1 | | 1 | 3 | |
| Joseph Smith | 1 | | | 1 | 1 | | | | |
| Moses Sharadine | 1 | | | 1 | 1 | | 1 | 1 | |
| William Scott | 1 | | | | 1 | | | | |
| Elizabeth Seean | | | | | 1 | 1 | 1 | | |
| Julyanna Sparks | 1 | | | 3 | 1 | | 1 | 1 | |
| William Sparks of William | 1 | | | 2 | 1 | | | 2 | |
| Absalom Scott | 1 | | | 1 | 2 | 1 | 1 | 1 | |
| George Turner | 1 | | | 2 | 1 | | 1 | | |
| Thomas Edward | 1 | 1 | 1 | 1 | 1 | | 2 | 2 | |
| Edward Tilghman | | | | | | | | | 6 |
| John Tittle | 1 | 2 | 2 | | 1 | | | | |
| Samuel Thompson | 1 | | | | 2 | | 2 | | 12 |
| John Thompson | 3 | 1 | | | 2 | | 1 | 3 | 29 |
| William Thompson | 1 | | 3 | 2 | 1 | | | 3 | |
| Richard Tilghman 4th | 3 | | | | 2 | | | 1 | 25 |
| Thomas Taylor | 1 | 1 | | 1 | 1 | | | | 1 |
| Ninian Taylor | | 1 | | 1 | | 1 | | | |
| Richard Thompson | 1 | | | | 1 | | | 1 | |
| Elizabeth Taylor | 1 | 1 | | 1 | 2 | 1 | | | 3 |
| James Tippins | 1 | | | | 1 | | | 2 | 3 |

| Head of the Household | MALES over 21 | 16 to 21 | 12 to 16 | MALES under 12 | FEMALES over 21 | 16 to 21 | 12 to 16 | under 12 | Blacks |
|---|---|---|---|---|---|---|---|---|---|
| William Turner | 1 | | | 2 | 1 | | | 1 | |
| Ruth Taylor | | 1 | | | 1 | | | 1 | |
| Ezabela Voice | | | 1 | | 1 | | | | |
| Edward Wright | 1 | | 1 | 2 | 1 | | 1 | 1 | 5 |
| Benjamin Wells | 1 | | 2 | 2 | 1 | 1 | | 3 | |
| Benjamin Wiggins | 1 | 1 | | 2 | 1 | | 1 | 3 | |
| Charles Wiggins | 2 | 1 | 1 | 1 | 2 | | | | 5 |
| George Willson | 1 | | | | | 1 | | | |
| George Williamson | 2 | | | 1 | 1 | 1 | | | |
| Joseph Wickes | 2 | | 1 | 1 | 1 | | | 2 | 1 |
| John Whittington | 1 | | | 1 | 1 | | | | 6 |
| Matthew Wickes | 1 | 1 | 1 | | 2 | 1 | | | 2 |
| Thomas Williams | 1 | | | 1 | 1 | | | 3 | |
| Thomas Wilkinson (Master) | 1 | 1 | | | 1 | | | | |
| Elizabeth Wiggins | 2 | | | 1 | 2 | 1 | | | |
| Ebenezer Wiggins | 1 | | | 1 | 1 | | | 1 | |
| James Ware | 2 | | | | | 1 | | 1 | 1 |
| Simon Wickes | 2 | | 1 | 1 | 1 | 1 | | 4 | 8 |
| John Willson | 1 | | | | 1 | | | 2 | |
| John White | 1 | | | | 1 | | | 3 | |
| Eliner Wadkins | | | 1 | | 1 | | | | |
| Mary Williss | | | | | 2 | | | 2 | |
| Epheram Wieley | 1 | | | | 1 | | | 3 | |
| William Young | 3 | 1 | | | 3 | | | | 4 |
| Mary Warner | | | | | | | | | 1 |

### UPPER HUNDRED, KENT ISLAND, QUEEN ANNE COUNTY, MARYLAND
#### taken July 22, 1776

| Head of the Household | MALES over 21 | 16 to 21 | 12 to 16 | MALES under 12 | FEMALES over 21 | 16 to 21 | 12 to 16 | under 12 | Blacks |
|---|---|---|---|---|---|---|---|---|---|
| Arthur Emory (negroes) | | | | | | | | | 11 |
| Richard Sneed | 1 | | 2 | 2 | | | | 1 | |
| Tobias Wells | 1 | | | | 3 | 1 | 1 | | 17 |
| William Jeffers | 1 | | | 1 | 1 | | 1 | | |
| Jeffery Beck (negro) | | | | | | | | | 9 |
| Susanah Waters | 3 | | | | 1 | | | 1 | 6 |
| James Stevens | 1 | 1 | | 2 | 1 | | 1 | 3 | 9 |
| John Brion | 1 | | | 3 | 3 | | | 1 | |
| Asalum Toyner Jr. | 1 | 1 | | | 1 | | | 3 | |
| Asalum Toyner | 1 | | 1 | 1 | 1 | 1 | 1 | | |
| Franson Benton | 1 | | 1 | 1 | 1 | | | | |
| Lues Deochbrume | 2 | | | | 2 | | | 1 | 9 |
| Fransis Wollyhand | 1 | | 3 | 2 | 3 | | | 2 | |
| Samuel Osbond | 1 | | | 1 | 1 | | | | |
| Thomas Colliar | 1 | | | | 1 | | | 1 | |
| Phillemon Tanner | 2 | | | | 1 | | 2 | | 2 |
| William Joyner | 1 | | 1 | 1 | 2 | | | 2 | |
| Elizabeth Robson | | | 1 | | 2 | | | 1 | |
| James Goodhand | 2 | | | | 1 | | | 1 | 4 |
| Richard Chambers | 1 | 1 | 1 | | 1 | | | | 1 |
| Richard Chambers Jr. | 1 | | | | 1 | | | 3 | 3 |
| Samuel Lanch | 1 | | | | | | | | 3 |
| Rebecca Wilson | | | | | 2 | | | | 8 |

| Head of the Household | MALES over 21 | 16 to 21 | 12 to 16 | under 12 | FEMALES over 21 | 16 to 21 | 12 to 16 | under 12 | Blacks |
|---|---|---|---|---|---|---|---|---|---|
| Dobs Joyner | 2 | 1 | | | 2 | | | 1 | 1 |
| James Wright | 3 | | 1 | 3 | 3 | 1 | 1 | 2 | 2 |
| Benjamin Richardson | 1 | 1 | 1 | 2 | 3 | | | 1 | 7 |
| James Welch | 1 | | | 1 | 1 | | | 2 | |
| Thomas Ringgold | 1 | 2 | 1 | 3 | 1 | | | 2 | 17 |
| Charles Barnet | 1 | 1 | 1 | | 1 | 1 | | | |
| Edward Brown | 3 | | | 1 | 1 | | | 1 | 9 |
| Benjamin Maradeth | 1 | | | 2 | 1 | | | 1 | 1 |
| Beck Greanwhich (black) | | | | | | | | | 3 |
| Marmaduke Goodhand | 1 | 1 | | 2 | 2 | | 1 | 2 | 13 |
| Letitia Goodhand | 1 | | | | 2 | | | | 4 |
| William Mason | 2 | | 1 | | 2 | | | 1 | 1 |
| Thomas Hampton | 1 | 1 | | 1 | 1 | | | | 1 |
| Aquila Brown | 1 | | | 3 | 3 | | | 4 | 8 |
| Labin Blunt | 1 | 1 | | 3 | 1 | | 1 | 2 | |
| Sara Shney | 1 | | | | 1 | | 1 | | 3 |
| William Smyth | 2 | | | | | | | | 3 |
| Sara Rouse | | | | | 1 | | | 1 | |
| James Hutchins | 14 | | | 1 | 2 | | | | 25 |
| Charles Sinners | 1 | | | | 1 | | | | |
| Samuel Coger (black) | | | | | | | | | 9 |
| William Stevens | 2 | 1 | 1 | 2 | 2 | | | 2 | 5 |
| Emory Sudler | 2 | | | | | | | | 12 |
| William Downey | 1 | | | 2 | 1 | | | 1 | |
| Dannil Molds | 1 | | | 1 | | | | | |
| Richard Grigg | 2 | | | | 1 | | | | |
| Abner Jones | 1 | | | 2 | 1 | | | 5 | |
| Elizabeth Horn | | | 1 | | 3 | | | 1 | 4 |
| James Sinners | 1 | | | 2 | 1 | | | | |
| Thomas Price | 2 | | 2 | 1 | 2 | | | 1 | 1 |
| Moses Sneed | 1 | 1 | | 2 | 1 | | | 2 | 4 |
| John Hand | 1 | | | 1 | 1 | | | 1 | |
| Benjamin Tannar | 1 | 1 | | 1 | 1 | | | | |
| Gilbert Faulkner | 1 | | | | 1 | | | 1 | |
| Thomas Wilson (black) | | | | | | | | | 4 |
| John Flames (black) | | | | | | | | | 5 |
| Sheary Greanwhich (black) | | | | | | | | | 16 |
| Thomas Allway | 1 | | | | 1 | | | | 2 |
| Nathaniel Whefing | 1 | | 1 | 1 | | | 1 | | |
| Harry Webb | 1 | | | 1 | 1 | | | 2 | |
| William Downey | 1 | | | | | | | | |
| James Tucker | 1 | | | | 1 | | | | |
| Alexander Tolson | 1 | | 1 | 4 | 1 | 1 | 1 | | 3 |
| Francis Bright | 1 | | 1 | 1 | 1 | | 2 | | 8 |
| Gabriel Kingsbury | 2 | 2 | 1 | 1 | 1 | 1 | | 2 | 10 |
| Ann Bright | 1 | | | 1 | 1 | 1 | | | 4 |
| John Watters | 1 | | | 1 | | | | | 8 |
| Benjamin Watters | 1 | | | 2 | 1 | | 1 | 3 | 9 |
| Benjamin Richardson Jr. | 1 | | | | 1 | | | 2 | 9 |
| Richard Wilson (black) | | | | | | | | | 7 |
| Nathaniel Goodhand | 1 | | | 1 | 1 | | | 1 | 4 |

| Head of the Household | MALES 16 over 21' | 16 to 21 | 12 to 16 | under 12 | FEMALES 16 over 21 | 16 to 21 | 12 to 16 | under 12 | Blacks |
|---|---|---|---|---|---|---|---|---|---|
| Elias Macconikin | 2 | 1 | | | 2 | | 1 | | 13 |
| Benjamin Kirby | 1 | | | 3 | 1 | 1 | | 1 | 7 |
| James Wilson (black) | 1 | | | 2 | 1 | | | | 4 |
| Thomas Barnes Jr. | 2 | 1 | 1 | 1 | 1 | | | 2 | 11 |
| Thomas Barnes | 2 | | | | 1 | | | | 6 |
| Thomas Surcom | 3 | | | | 3 | | | | |
| Martin Grainger | 1 | | | 1 | 2 | | | 3 | |
| William Weaver | 1 | | 1 | 2 | 1 | 1 | | 2 | |
| John Spurry | 1 | 1 | 1 | | 1 | 1 | 1 | 1 | |
| Richard Carter | 3 | | | | 3 | | | | 12 |
| Arthur Carter | 1 | | | 1 | 1 | | 1 | 4 | 7 |
| Thomas Baxter | 1 | | | 3 | 1 | | | 2 | 2 |
| Samuel Harper | 1 | | | 3 | 1 | | | 3 | |
| John Lucas | 1 | | | 2 | 1 | | | 3 | |
| James Greanwhich (black) | | | | | | | | | 4 |
| William Macconichin | 1 | | 1 | 1 | 1 | 1 | | | 2 |
| William Baxter | 1 | | 2 | 1 | 1 | 1 | | | 11 |
| John Hoxter | 1 | 1 | | 1 | 1 | 1 | 1 | 3 | |
| Wm. Legg | 1 | | | 5 | 1 | | | | |
| John Legg | 1 | 2 | | 1 | | | | | |
| Matthew Legg | 1 | | 1 | 3 | 1 | 2 | | 2 | 13 |
| Andrew Finnix | 1 | | | | 1 | | | 1 | 1 |
| Robert Watters | 2 | | | | 1 | | | 3 | 7 |
| Greenbutt Wright | 1 | | | | | | | | 5 |
| Jacob Ringgold | 1 | | | 1 | | 1 | | | 11 |
| James Burk | 1 | | | 3 | 1 | 1 | | 1 | 3 |
| Rachael Greanwhich (black) | | | | 1 | | | | | 3 |
| Elizabeth Crick | | | | 2 | 1 | | | | |
| Ann Hoxter | | | | 1 | 2 | | | 3 | |

Upper Hundred, Queen Anne County was enumerated by Alexander Waters.

### WYE HUNDRED, QUEEN ANNE COUNTY, MD.
Taken in July 1776 by Peter Rich

| | MALES 16 over 21' | 16 to 21 | 12 to 16 | under 12 | FEMALES 16 over 21 | 16 to 21 | 12 to 16 | under 12 | Blacks |
|---|---|---|---|---|---|---|---|---|---|
| William Hemsley | 3 | | | 1 | 3 | 1 | 1 | 1 | 44 |
| Daniel Caine | 1 | | 1 | | 1 | | | | 1 |
| Richard Earle | 7 | 1 | | 3 | 4 | 1 | 2 | 3 | 23 |
| Charles Mayer | 1 | | | | 2 | 1 | | 1 | 11 |
| George Jeffers | 2 | 1 | 1 | 3 | 2 | | 1 | | 10 |
| Andrew Hennesy | 1 | | | 2 | 1 | | 1 | 2 | |
| James Williams | 1 | | | 1 | 1 | 1 | | 1 | |
| Eli Cain | 1 | | | 2 | 1 | | | | |
| Jonathan Downes | 1 | | | 1 | 1 | | | 1 | 8 |
| John Davis Jr. | 1 | 3 | | 1 | 2 | | | | |
| Peter Denny | 1 | | 1 | 3 | 1 | | | 2 | 2 |
| John Lawrence | 1 | | | | 1 | | | 1 | |
| Stephen Jarman | 1 | 1 | | | 1 | 1 | | 1 | 13 |
| Aaron Yoe | 3 | 1 | | | 1 | | 1 | 1 | 12 |
| Nathaniel Wright | 2 | | | 1 | 2 | | | 5 | 22 |
| Nehemiah Noble | 3 | | 1 | 3 | 2 | | | 2 | 11 |
| Shadrach Hooper | 1 | | | 1 | 1 | 1 | | 1 | |

| Head of the Household | MALES over 21 | 16 to 21 | 12 to 16 | under 12 | FEMALES over 21 | 16 to 21 | 12 to 16 | under 12 | Blacks |
|---|---|---|---|---|---|---|---|---|---|
| John Scholar | 1 | | | 1 | 1 | | 1 | 2 | |
| James Harris | 1 | 1 | 2 | 1 | 1 | 1 | 1 | | |
| James Dodd | 1 | | | 1 | 2 | | 1 | 1 | |
| Dennis Connaway | 1 | | | 3 | 2 | | 1 | | |
| Benjamin Cooper | 2 | | | 1 | 3 | | | 1 | 2 |
| John Starkey | 1 | | | 2 | 1 | | 2 | 4 | |
| Lemuel Warner | 1 | | | 1 | 1 | | 1 | 1 | |
| Samuel Rathell | 1 | 1 | | 3 | 1 | | 1 | 2 | |
| Elisabeth Walker | 1 | | | | 1 | | | | |
| Hynson Downes Sr. | 2 | 1 | | | 2 | 1 | | | 12 |
| James Johnson | 1 | | 1 | 1 | | | 2 | | |
| H. Downes Jr. | 1 | | | 1 | 1 | | 1 | | 1 |
| James Bartlett | 1 | 1 | 1 | 3 | 2 | | | 1 | 1 |
| Richard Emerson | 1 | | | 2 | 1 | | | 3 | |
| Phil. Pratt | 1 | | 1 | 3 | 1 | 1 | | 1 | |
| Valentine Green | 1 | 1 | | | 1 | | | 2 | 1 |
| John Hargadine | 1 | 1 | 1 | | 1 | 1 | 1 | 5 | 2 |
| Edward Smith | 2 | | | | 2 | | | | |
| Thomas Oldson | 2 | | | 3 | 1 | 1 | | | 7 |
| Thomas Trezare | 2 | 1 | 2 | 4 | 2 | 1 | 1 | 2 | |
| John Trezare | 1 | 2 | | 3 | 2 | | 2 | 3 | 2 |
| James Jones | 2 | 1 | | 3 | 1 | | 1 | 2 | 3 |
| John Dodd | 1 | | 1 | | 2 | | | 1 | 2 |
| Risden Hutchings | 3 | | | | 1 | | | | 4 |
| Rhoda Cox | 3 | 1 | 1 | 3 | 3 | 1 | | 2 | 4 |
| Vincent Emerson | 1 | | | | 1 | | | | |
| John Start | 1 | | | 1 | 1 | | | 1 | |
| John Jeffers | 1 | | | | | 1 | | 1 | |
| George Dodd | | | 1 | 2 | 1 | | 1 | 2 | |
| Thomas Bradley | 1 | | | 1 | 2 | | | 2 | |
| Thomas Bradley | 1 | | | 1 | 2 | | | 2 | |
| Edward Hargadine | 2 | 1 | 1 | 3 | 2 | 1 | | 2 | |
| John Barneclew | 2 | 1 | 2 | 3 | 2 | | | 1 | 1 |
| Andrew Barneclew | 1 | | 1 | 1 | 1 | | 1 | 1 | 2 |
| Will Evans | 1 | | | 2 | 1 | | | | 10 |
| Sutt. McCallister | 2 | | | 1 | 1 | | | | |
| Litt Croney | 1 | 1 | | 1 | 1 | | | 1 | |
| Captain Will Emory | 1 | | | 1 | 1 | 1 | | 2 | 3 |
| John Ross | 3 | | 1 | 1 | 2 | | | 1 | 1 |
| Mark Dodd | 1 | 1 | | 2 | 2 | | | 2 | |
| Richard Harris | 1 | | | | 1 | | | 1 | |
| Charles Saunders | 1 | | | 1 | 1 | | | | 1 |
| James E. St.Tee | 1 | 1 | | 1 | 2 | 1 | | 4 | |
| John Ireland | 3 | | | 4 | 3 | 1 | | 2 | 6 |
| James D. Bennet | 1 | | | 2 | 2 | 1 | | | |
| George Hanson | 5 | | | 1 | 2 | | | 2 | 1 |
| Henry Pratt Sr. | 1 | | | | 2 | | | 1 | 11 |
| Turbutt Wright | 1 | | 1 | 2 | 3 | 1 | | 1 | 24 |
| Absolom Fowler | 1 | | | 3 | 1 | | | 3 | |
| William Hackett | 2 | | 1 | 1 | 1 | | | 3 | 12 |
| Mary Mitchell | | | | 1 | 1 | | | | |
| John Vanderrer | 1 | | | | | | | | |

150

| Head of the Household | MALES OVER 21 | 16 TO 21 | 12 TO 16 | FEMALES UNDER 12 | 16 OVER 21 | 12 TO 21 | TO 16 | UNDER 12 | Blacks |
|---|---|---|---|---|---|---|---|---|---|
| Nathan Wilkinson | 1 | | | 3 | 1 | | 1 | 2 | 5 |
| (Henry Pratt's Overseer) | | | | | | | | | |
| Joseph Hubbard | 1 | | | | 1 | | | | |
| Rev. Hugh Neal | 1 | 1 | | | | | 1 | | 10 |
| Captain John Davis | 1 | 1 | | | 1 | 1 | 1 | | 9 |
| Sol. Wright | 1 | | | 1 | 1 | 1 | | | 7 |
| Marg. Higgins | | | 1 | 5 | 1 | | | 1 | 1 |
| William Alley | 1 | | 1 | 1 | 1 | 2 | | 1 | |
| Deborah Williams | | | | 2 | 1 | | 1 | 3 | 1 |
| William Kirby Jones | 1 | | | 1 | 1 | | | 1 | 5 |
| John Davis 3rd | 1 | | | 1 | 1 | | | 3 | |
| Elisabeth Davidge | | 1 | | | 1 | | 1 | | 8 |
| Thomas Davis | 1 | | | 1 | 1 | 1 | | | |
| Will Ryan | 1 | | | | 1 | | | | |
| Nathaniel Davis | 1 | | | 2 | 1 | 1 | | 1 | |
| Joseph Nicolson (negroes) | 5 | | 1 | 4 | 3 | | | 3 | 16 |
| James Costin | 2 | | 1 | 2 | 1 | | | 2 | 5 |
| John Fendall | 1 | | | 3 | 3 | | | 2 | |
| James Croney | 1 | | | 2 | 1 | | | 1 | |
| John Williams | 2 | | | 3 | 1 | | | 1 | 1 |
| William Neal | 1 | | | | 1 | | | | 1 |
| Ann Reynolds | | | | 1 | 2 | | 1 | 1 | |
| John Plummer | 2 | | | | 1 | 1 | | | |
| Henry Costin | 1 | | | 1 | 1 | | | 2 | 12 |
| Catharine Proud | | | | 1 | 1 | | | | |
| Michael Maloney | 2 | 1 | 1 | 1 | 1 | 1 | | 1 | |
| Jonathan Maloney | 1 | | | | 1 | | | 2 | |
| Levin Downes | 1 | | | 2 | 2 | | 1 | 2 | 8 |
| John Stevens | 1 | 1 | | 4 | 2 | | | | |
| James Miller | 1 | | 1 | | | 1 | | | 2 |
| B. Callaghane | 1 | | 1 | 2 | 2 | | 1 | 2 | |
| George Grimes | 1 | | | | 2 | | 1 | | |
| Charles Price | 2 | 1 | 1 | 3 | 1 | | 2 | 1 | 17 |
| Richard Clark | 1 | | | 1 | 1 | | | 1 | |
| Thomas Dodd | 1 | | | 2 | 1 | | | 1 | 14 |
| Will Rursum | 1 | | | 3 | 1 | | | | |
| Samuel Neighbories | 1 | | | 1 | 1 | 1 | 1 | 2 | 2 |
| James Benny | 1 | | | 2 | 1 | 1 | | | |
| Mary Moore | | | | 1 | 1 | | | 1 | |
| John Emerson | 1 | 1 | | 1 | 1 | 1 | 1 | 1 | 19 |
| James Tuile | 1 | | | 1 | 3 | 1 | | | 40 |
| Isaac Mason | 2 | | | 2 | 1 | | 1 | 3 | 8 |
| Jonathan Start | 1 | | | | 1 | | | 2 | 1 |
| John Chapple | 2 | | | | 2 | | | 1 | 15 |
| Phil Green | 1 | 1 | | | 1 | 1 | | | 18 |
| John Meads | 3 | | | 1 | 1 | | | 3 | 2 |
| Daniel Dolvin | 2 | 1 | 1 | | 1 | | | | 1 |
| Frances Small | | | | 1 | 1 | | | 1 | 1 |
| James Harris Jr. | 1 | | | 2 | | | | | |
| Charles Callaghane | 1 | | | 4 | 1 | 1 | | | |
| James Kelly | 1 | | | 2 | 1 | | | | |
| Thomas Emory | 1 | 2 | | 1 | 1 | 1 | 1 | | 21 |
| Peter Rich | 1 | 2 | | 2 | 2 | | | 2 | 2 |

151

1776 Census of BAY HUNDRED, TALBOT COUNTY, MARYLAND
Taken by James Earl Denny, August 1776

| Head of the Household | MALES over 50 | MALES 16 to 50 | MALES under 16 | FEMALES over 50 | FEMALES 16 to 50 | FEMALES under 16 | Blacks |
|---|---|---|---|---|---|---|---|
| James Woulds |  | 1 |  |  | 1 | 4 |  |
| Thomas Dodson |  | 1 | 4 |  | 1 | 3 |  |
| Nathaniel Grace |  | 2 | 3 |  | 1 | 1 |  |
| Perry Benson |  | 1 | 7 |  | 1 | 3 | 1 |
| Nicholas Benson |  | 1 | 1 |  | 2 | 2 | 1 |
| Daniel Chezum |  | 1 |  |  | 1 |  |  |
| James Keithley |  | 1 | 1 |  | 1 | 1 | 1 |
| Richard Harrington |  | 1 | 1 |  | 1 | 1 |  |
| Thomas Thomlinson |  | 2 |  |  | 3 | 2 |  |
| Mary Nuols |  |  |  |  | 4 |  | 3 |
| Thomas Towsend |  | 2 | 5 |  | 2 | 1 |  |
| Solomon Vinton |  | 2 | 1 |  | 2 | 1 |  |
| Thomas Love | 1 | 1 |  | 1 | 2 | 1 |  |
| Thomas Ashcraft |  | 1 | 2 |  | 1 | 3 |  |
| James Harrison |  | 1 | 2 |  | 1 | 1 |  |
| Mable Tenant |  |  | 3 | 1 | 1 |  |  |
| Mary Bromwell |  | 1 |  | 1 | 1 |  |  |
| John Blades |  | 2 | 6 | 1 | 1 |  |  |
| George Glieve |  | 2 |  |  | 1 |  | 1 |
| John Johnnings Hopkins |  | 2 | 4 |  |  | 1 | 5 |
| Joseph Royal | 1 |  | 1 |  | 1 |  |  |
| Peter Brown | 1 |  | 2 |  |  | 2 |  |
| James Howes |  | 1 | 2 | 1 | 2 | 2 |  |
| Robert Wales |  | 1 | 3 |  | 1 | 3 |  |
| John Bouff |  | 1 | 3 |  | 1 | 1 | 1 |
| Jonathan Lenard |  | 1 | 2 |  | 1 | 1 |  |
| William Hopkins |  | 1 | 2 |  | 1 | 1 |  |
| John Rolle |  | 1 | 1 |  | 1 | 1 |  |
| Daniel Richardson |  | 1 | 1 | 1 | 2 | 4 | 13 |
| William Hableton Jr. |  | 1 | 1 |  | 1 | 4 | 1 |
| Charles Vickers |  | 1 |  |  | 1 | 1 | 13 |
| Albert Applegirth |  | 1 | 5 |  | 1 | 2 |  |
| Nathaniel Ledenham |  | 2 | 1 |  | 2 | 2 |  |
| James Barrow |  | 2 |  | 2 | 2 |  |  |
| Elizabeth Greenfield |  | 2 | 4 |  | 1 | 1 | 3 |
| Joseph Porter |  | 2 | 4 |  | 1 | 1 | 2 |
| John Porter |  | 2 | 6 | 1 | 2 | 1 | 2 |
| John Hall | 1 | 1 |  | 1 | 1 | 1 |  |
| Phillimon Sherwood | 1 |  |  | 2 |  |  |  |
| Phillimon Spencer |  | 2 | 3 |  |  | 1 | 6 |
| James Caultz | 1 | 2 | 1 |  | 3 | 1 | 3 |
| James Rimmer | 1 | 2 | 2 | 1 | 1 | 1 |  |
| Jane Porter | 1 | 1 |  | 1 | 2 | 4 |  |
| Mary Cummings |  |  |  |  | 2 | 1 |  |
| Aaron Ringrose |  |  | 1 |  | 3 | 3 |  |
| Sawney Sinclare | 1 | 1 | 2 |  | 1 | 1 |  |
|  |  | 3 | 2 |  | 1 | 3 |  |

|  | MALES | | | FEMALES | | | |
|---|---|---|---|---|---|---|---|
| Head of the Household | over 50 | 16 to 50 | under 16 | over 50 | 16 to 50 | under 16 | Blacks |
| Jonathan Winters |  | 1 | 1 |  | 1 |  | 2 |
| John Horney | 1 | 2 | 3 |  | 1 | 2 |  |
| Hewes Porter |  | 1 |  |  | 1 | 2 |  |
| Wrightson Lambden |  | 1 |  |  | 1 |  | 7 |
| Joseph Spencer |  | 1 | 2 |  | 1 |  | 3 |
| Adam Edgar | 1 | 2 | 2 |  | 1 | 2 |  |
| Elizabeth Hills |  |  | 2 |  | 1 | 3 |  |
| William Davis |  | 1 | 1 |  | 3 |  | 1 |
| Charles Daffin |  | 1 |  |  | 3 |  | 26 |
| George Dawson |  | 1 |  |  |  |  | 6 |
| James Morsal | 1 |  |  |  | 3 |  | 11 |
| James Wrightson Jr. |  | 1 | 1 |  | 1 | 2 | 4 |
| John Haddaway |  | 1 | 1 |  | 1 | 1 |  |
| Thomas Cummings Jr. |  | 2 |  |  | 1 | 1 |  |
| Thomas Cummings | 1 | 2 | 1 |  | 2 | 1 |  |
| John Kersey |  | 2 | 1 |  | 2 | 2 | 11 |
| Elizabeth Cummings |  | 3 |  | 1 | 1 |  |  |
| Sussanah Haddaway |  | 1 |  |  | 2 |  |  |
| George Haddaway | 1 |  | 6 |  | 1 | 1 | 1 |
| John Porter |  | 1 | 3 |  | 2 | 2 |  |
| Benjamin Sands |  | 2 |  |  | 4 | 2 | 2 |
| Thomas Horney |  | 1 | 2 |  | 1 |  | 1 |
| William Haddaway |  | 1 |  |  | 1 |  | 3 |
| Benjamin Cooper | 1 | 1 | 3 | 1 |  | 2 |  |
| John Kemp |  | 1 | 3 |  | 1 | 2 | 3 |
| Benjamin Kemp | 1 | 1 | 2 |  | 2 | 5 | 10 |
| Magdalain Kemp | 1 | 1 | 1 | 1 | 2 |  | 9 |
| Captain Haddaway |  | 2 | 1 |  | 3 | 4 | 4 |
| Robert Lambson |  | 7 | 3 |  | 3 | 2 |  |
| John Haddaway |  | 2 | 1 |  | 1 | 2 | 7 |
| Thomas Sherwood |  | 2 |  |  | 2 |  | 12 |
| Ann Fiddaman |  |  | 1 |  | 1 | 2 | 9 |
| Joseph Hopkins |  | 4 | 4 |  | 3 | 5 | 9 |
| Moses Stains |  | 1 | 3 |  | 2 |  |  |
| Joseph Harrison | 1 | 3 | 1 | 1 | 1 |  | 13 |
| Robert Harrison |  | 1 |  |  | 1 |  | 1 |
| Elizabeth Steddam |  |  | 4 |  | 1 |  |  |
| John Shanahan |  | 2 | 3? | 1 | 1 | 2 | 5 |
| William Tuttle |  | 2 |  |  | 2 | 1 |  |
| John Mather |  | 2 | 3 |  | 2 |  | 3 |
| Richard Marshall | 1 | 1 | 1 | 2 | 1 | 1 |  |
| Thomas Kemp |  | 1 | 1 |  | 1 | 4 | 2 |
| Norwood, Ann |  |  | 1 |  | 1 | 2 |  |
| Sarah Lenard |  |  | 2 |  | 1 | 1 |  |
| Daniel Vinton | 1 | 1 |  | 1 |  |  |  |
| Phillimon Skinner |  | 3 | 2 |  | 2 | 1 | 1 |
| James Hopkins |  | 1 |  |  |  |  |  |
| Thomas Hopkins | 1 | 4 | 1 |  | 1 |  | 8 |
| Joseph Harrington | 1 | 1 |  |  | 2 |  | 6 |
| Alice Harrington |  | 1 |  | 1 | 2 |  | 6 |

| Head of the Household | Males over 50 | Males 16 to 50 | Males under 16 | Females over 50 | Females 16 to 50 | Females under 16 | Blacks |
|---|---|---|---|---|---|---|---|
| Mary Barrington |  |  | 1 | 3 |  | 1 | 1 |  |
| Daniel Hull | 1 |  |  |  | 1 | 1 |  |
| James Harrison BC | 1 |  |  |  |  |  |  |
| William Hambleton |  | 2 | 2? | 1 | 3 |  |  |
| Phillip Hambleton |  | 4 | 1 |  | 2 | 2 | 8 |
| William Barney |  | 1 | 3 |  | 2 |  | 6 |
| Impey Dawson | 1 | 1 | 2? |  | 1 | 6 |  |
| Robert Dawson |  | 1 |  |  | 2 |  | 17 |
| James Tripp |  | 1 | 2 |  | 1 | 1 | 2 |
| Phillemon Fairbanks |  | 1 |  |  | 1 |  | 13 |
| Thomas Wayman | 1 | 1 | 1 | 2 | 2 |  | 1 |
| Hugh Dawson | 1 | 2 | 1 |  | 2 | 3 | 9 |
| David Fairbanks |  | 1 | 3 |  | 1 |  | 6 |
| George Applegirth |  | 1 | 5 |  | 1 | 2 |  |
| Daniel Bridges |  | 1 | 1 |  | 1 | 1 | 1 |
| Hugh Auld |  | 2 | 1 |  | 1 | 4 |  |
| John Auld |  | 1 |  | 1 | 1 |  | 6 |
| James Sewell | 1 | 3 |  | 1 |  | 2 |  |
| James Braddsetz |  | 1 | 1 |  | 1 | 2 |  |
| David Sherwood |  | 2 | 1 |  |  |  | 2 |
| John Caulty |  | 2 |  |  |  |  | 1 |
| William Haddaway |  | 3 | 4 |  | 2 | 1 | 9 |
| George Applegirth | 1 | 2 |  | 1 | 1 |  | 8 |
| Thomas Harrison | 1 | 2 | 1 |  | 3 | 2 |  |
| Denny Carrol |  | 3 | 2 |  | 1 | 3 | 8 |
| Robert Richardson |  | 1 | 1 |  | 1 | 2 | 10 |
| James Haddaway |  | 2 | 1 |  | 1 | 2 | 10 |
| Thomas Ball |  | 1 |  |  | 1 |  |  |
| James Carrol |  | 1 |  |  | 1 | 3 | 1 |
| Robert Haddaway |  | 1 | 3 |  | 1 |  |  |
| James Wrightson |  | 1 | 3 |  | 2 | 2 |  |
| James Harrisson |  | 1 | 3 |  | 1 | 3 |  |
| William Grace |  | 1 | 2 | 1 | 1 | 3 |  |
| Peter Richardson |  | 1 | 2 |  | 3 | 3 |  |
| Daniel Auld |  | 3 | 6 |  | 2 | 2 |  |
| James Ball |  | 2 | 2 |  | 3 | 2 | 5 |
| Joseph Denny | 1 | 1 | 2 | 1 | 3 | 2 | 1 |
| Joseph Denny Jr. |  | 1 | 1 | 1 |  |  | 5 |
| Joseph Reddish | 1 |  | 2 | 1 | 1 | 2 | 1 |
| Sarah Porter |  |  | 2 | 1 | 2 |  |  |
| Mary Lawrence |  |  | 2 |  | 2 | 2 |  |
| Anna Fairbanks | 1 | 1 | 2 |  | 1 |  |  |
| Marty Sewell |  | 2 | 5 | 1 | 2 | 2 |  |
| Rebecca Fitzjerrel |  | 1 |  | 1 | 1 |  |  |
| Patrick McQuay | 1 | 1 | 1 | 1 | 3 | 1 | 5 |
| Thomas Grove |  | 2 |  |  | 2 |  |  |
| Elizabeth Fooss |  |  |  | 1 |  |  |  |
| James Barnes |  | 1 | 3 |  | 2 |  | 5 |
| Thomas Jefferson |  | 1 |  |  | 1 | 1 |  |
| William Camper |  | 2 | 2 |  | 1 | 2 | 1 |

|  | MALES | | | FEMALES | | | |
|  | over 16 | to | under | over 16 | to | under | |
| Head of the Household | 50 | 50 | 16 | 50 | 50 | 16 | Blacks |
|---|---|---|---|---|---|---|---|
| Thomas Haddaway | 1 | 2 | 1 | 1 |  | 3 |  |
| Thomas Lowry |  | 2 | 2 |  | 1 | 4 | 2 |
| John Winterbottom | 1 | 2 | 1 | 1 |  |  |  |
| Robert Winterbottom |  | 1 | 1 |  | 1 | 1 |  |
| Joseph Lowry |  | 2 | 3 |  | 1 | 4 |  |
| Robert Cardeff | 1 | 1 | 1 | 1 | 1 |  |  |
| _____ Harrison |  | 2 |  |  |  |  |  |
| Richard Gardner |  | 1 |  |  |  |  |  |
| Mary Fairbanks |  | 1 | 3 | 1 | 2 | 4 |  |
| Peter Hunt | 1 | 2 | 1 |  | 4 | 4 |  |
| John Cooper | 1 | 2 | 3 | 1 | 1 | 1 |  |
| Sarah Dawson |  | 2 |  | 1 | 1 |  | 2 |
| Margaret Dawson |  | 1 | 1 |  | 1 |  | 5 |
| Richard Linkom |  | 1 | 1 |  | 1 | 1 |  |
| William Dawson |  | 1 | 1 |  | 2 |  |  |
| Philip Auld |  | 2 | 2 |  | 1 | 3 | 1 |
| George Jefferson |  | 3 | 4 |  | 1 | 2 |  |
| Robert Jones | 1 | 1 | 3 |  | 1 | 2 |  |
| William Haddaway |  | 1 | 2 |  | 1 | 3 |  |
| Mary Larramore |  | 2 | 1 | 1 | 1 | 2 |  |
| Richard Batsey |  | 1 | 1 |  | 1 | 1 |  |
| Francis Jefferson |  |  | 3 |  | 1 | 1 |  |
| Robert Harrisson |  | 1 | 1 |  | 1 | 1 |  |
| Jenney Larramoor |  | 2 | 1 |  | 2 |  |  |
| Edward Leadnenham |  | 1 | 2 |  | 1 | 2 |  |
| Cathrine Larramoor |  |  | 1 |  | 2 | 4 |  |
| Richard Mansfield |  | 3 | 1 | 1 | 2 | 2 |  |
| Thomas Camper |  | 2 | 2 |  | 2 |  |  |
| Daniel Fairbanks |  | 3 | 2 |  | 4 | 2 |  |
| Joseph Harrisson |  | 1 | 2 |  | 1 | 3 |  |
| Jonathan Harrisson |  | 1 | 3 |  | 1 | 4 |  |
| George Colleson |  | 1 | 4 |  | 1 |  | 4 |
| James Low |  | 2 | 3 |  | 2 | 4 | 7 |
| John Reaugh ? |  | 1 |  |  | 2 |  | 1 |
| William Bridges |  | 1 | 1 | 1 | 1 | 1 |  |
| Thomas Smith |  | 1 | 5 |  | 2 |  | 4 |
| Ralph Dawson | 1 |  | 3 |  | 2 | 1 | 6 |
| John McNulty |  | 2 | 1 |  | 1 | 1 |  |
| John Ploughman |  | 2 | 5 |  | 2 | 2 |  |
| Cathrine McQuay |  | 1 |  | 1 |  |  |  |
| Nathaniel? Sherwood |  | 2 | 1 |  | 2 | 3 | 1 |
| Elizabeth Lamden |  | 1 | 2 |  | 2 | 1 | 9 |
| William Webb Haddaway | 1 | 1 |  | 1 | 1 | 2 | 9 |
| Lurinah Jones |  |  |  | 1 | 1 |  |  |
| John Leeds | 1 |  |  |  |  |  | 21 |
| Mathew Tilghman | 2 | 2 |  | 1 | 2 |  | 93 |
| Anthony Mahony | 1 | 1 |  | 1 | 2 |  |  |
| William West |  | 1 | 3 |  | 2 | 3 |  |
| William Sears |  | 1 | 1 |  | 3 | 2 | 30 |

|  | | MALES | | | FEMALES | | |
|---|---|---|---|---|---|---|---|
| Head of the Household | over 50 | 16 to 50 | under 16 | over 50 | 16 to 50 | under 16 | Blacks |
| Thomas Nash | | 1 | 2 | | 1 | 1 | |
| Charles Gossage | | 1 | 5 | | 1 | 2 | |
| John Cryer? | | 2 | | | 1 | | |
| Martin Collwell (free Mullotes) | | | 1 | | | | 2 |
| Thomas Auldery      "    "    1 | | 2 | 3 | | | 1 | |
| Rebec Cornesh       "    " | | | 1 | | | 1 | 1 |

### MILL HUNDRED, TALBOT COUNTY, MARYLAND
### Taken by Thomas Tibbels in 1776

|  | over 50 | 16 to 50 | under 16 | over 50 | 16 to 50 | under 16 | Blacks |
|---|---|---|---|---|---|---|---|
| William Levell | | 2 | 1 | | 1 | 1 | 3 |
| Thomas Spery Morgan | | 1 | 1 | | 2 | 1 | 36 |
| Sarah Snelling | | 1 | 1 | | | 1 | |
| Mary Comberford | | | 1 | | 1 | 1 | |
| William Torresh | | 1 | 1 | | 1 | 2 | 1 |
| Joseph Nobs | | 1 | 1 | | 1 | 2 | |
| John Carrel | | 1 | | | 1 | | 1 |
| Johanna Nussey | | 1 | 1 | | 1 | | |
| Daniel McCarnon | 1 | | 3 | 1 | 2 | 1 | 3 |
| Henry Low | 1 | | 7 | | 3 | 2 | 1 |
| James Jackson | | 1 | 1 | | 1 | | |
| Thomas Faulkner | | 1 | 2 | 1 | 1 | 3 | 2 |
| Abram Faulkner | 1 | | 4 | | 2 | 3 | |
| Jean Davis | | | 1 | 1 | | | |
| ____ Davis | | 1 | 4 | | 1 | | |
| ____ Worner | | 1 | 1 | | 1 | 1 | |
| ____ Greenhout | 1 | | 1 | 1 | | 1 | |
| ____ Stewart | 1 | 4 | 4 | | 2 | | 2 |
| ____ Austin | | 1 | 1 | | 2 | 1 | |
| ____ Matthews | | 2 | | | 1 | 2 | |
| ____ Chapman | | 1 | 5 | | 1 | 2 | |
| ____ Wilson (free mulatto) | | | | | | | 1 |
| Isaac Faulkner | | 2 | 5 | | 2 | 2 | |
| Elizabeth Fouthner | | | | 1 | 2 | | 4 |
| John Dixon | 1 | | 3 | | 2 | 3 | 4 |
| Elizabeth Barrett | | | 1 | | 1 | 1 | 1 |
| William Burgess | 1 | | | | 2 | | |
| Vincent Trice | | 1 | 1 | | 1 | 1 | 1 |
| John Chrisp | | 1 | 2 | | 1 | 1 | |
| Aaron Atkinson | | 4 | 3 | | 3 | 2 | 13 |
| Samuel Short | | 1 | | | 1 | 1 | 1 |
| Mrs. Henney Nichols | | 1 | 2 | | 1 | 2 | 35 |
| Mathias Woolcott | | 1 | | | 1 | 3 | |
| William Dowling | | 1 | 2 | | 1 | 1 | |
| Thomas Matthews | | 1 | 2 | | 1 | 1 | |
| William Austin | | 1 | | | 1 | 2 | |
| Ann Austin | | | 1 | 1 | | 1 | |
| Denisha Terry | | 1 | 1 | | 2 | 2 | |
| Thomas Acorn | | 1 | | | 1 | | |
| Joseph Dowling | 1 | 1 | 1 | 1 | 1 | 1 | |

| Head of the Household | MALES over 50 | MALES 16 to 50 | MALES under 16 | FEMALES over 50 | FEMALES 16 to 50 | FEMALES under 16 | Blacks |
|---|---|---|---|---|---|---|---|
| William Ferrel |  | 2 | 2 |  | 1 | 1 | 5 |
| Ann Durkins |  |  | 3 |  | 1 | 3 |  |
| Isaac Jackson | 1 |  | 2 |  | 1 | 1 |  |
| William Snelling | 1 |  | n |  | 2 |  |  |
| Richard Walker |  | 1 | 1 |  | 1 |  |  |
| John Eubanks |  | 1 |  |  | 1 | 2 |  |
| Rebeccah Eubanks |  |  |  | 1 |  | 2 |  |
| Robert Norwood 3rd |  | 3 |  |  |  | 2 |  |
| Prudence Sherwood |  |  | 2 | 1 | 2 | 2 |  |
| Susannah Humes |  |  |  |  | 1 | 2 |  |
| James Barrow | 1 | 2 | 4 |  | 3 | 1 | 4 |
| Thomas Barrow | 1 | 4 | 3 |  | 2 |  | 2 |
| William Warner | 1 |  | 1 |  | 1 | 1 | 1 |
| John Neithsmith | 1 | 1 | 2 |  |  |  | 1 |
| David Fleming |  | 1 | 3 |  | 2 | 2 |  |
| Ann Coborn |  |  |  |  | 1 | 2 |  |
| Mary Evens |  | 3 | 2 |  | 1 | 3 | 9 |
| Henry Holladay | 2 | 1 | 1 |  | 5 | 3 | 55 |
| William Bowdel |  | 2 | 3 |  | 1 | 1 | 3 |
| Edward Caslick |  | 1 | 1 | 1 |  | 1 | 1 |
| William Milwood |  | 1 |  |  | 1 | 1 |  |
| Henry Buckley |  | 1 | 2 |  | 1 | 2 | 3 |
| Adam Corner | 1 | 1 |  | 1 | 1 | 1 | 9 |
| Robert Harwood | 1 | 1 | 4 |  | 2 | 1 | 21 |
| Lambath Hopkins |  | 1 | 2 |  | 3 | 4 |  |
| John Tibbels |  | 2 | 1 |  | 1 | 3 |  |
| Archibald Smith |  | 3 | 2 |  | 1 |  |  |
| William Hambleton | 1 | 2 |  |  | 2 |  | 1 |
| Zadock Botfield |  | 1 |  |  | 2 | 1 | 1 |
| Joseph Hopkins |  | 2 | 1 |  |  |  |  |
| Dennis Hopkins |  | 1 |  |  | 2? | 2 | 2 |
| Francis Hopkins | 1 | 1 | 3 |  | 4 | 2 | 5 |
| Thomas Isgate | 1 |  | 3 |  | 1 | 1 | 3 |
| William Dixson |  | 1 | 1 |  | 2 | 2 | 1 |
| Samuel Harwood | 1 |  |  | 1 | 3 | 2 | 9 |
| Joseph Atkinson | 1 | 1 |  |  | 1 | 2 | 13 |
| Mary Harwood |  | 2 | 2 |  | 1 | 2 |  |
| Robert Harwood |  | 1 | 1 |  | 1 | 2 |  |
| Ann Harwood |  |  |  |  | 1 |  | 6 |
| Rachel Low |  |  |  |  | 1 | 4 |  |
| Christopher Hews |  | 1 | 1 |  | 1 | 2 |  |
| Elizabeth Stanton |  |  |  | 1 | 3 | 1 | 1 |
| Mary Summers |  |  | 1 | 1 | 1 | 3 |  |
| Robert Goldsborough |  | 2 | 2 |  | 2 |  | 24 |
| Robert Goldsborough | 1 | 1 |  | 1 | 2 |  | 46 |
| James Condon |  | 1 | 1 |  | 1 | 1 |  |
| John Meggs |  | 1 | 1 |  | 1 |  |  |
| Howes Goldsborough |  | 1 | 1 |  | 2 | 1 | 23 |
| William Condon | 1 | 1 |  | 1 | 1 | 1 |  |
| Thomas Neighbours | 1 | 1 | 2 |  | 2 | 2 | 1 |

|  | MALES | | | FEMALES | | | |
|---|---|---|---|---|---|---|---|
|  |  | 16 |  |  | 16 | | |
|  | over | to | under | over | to | under | |
| Head of the Household | 50 | 50 | 16 | 50 | 50 | 16 | Blacks |
| Richard Bartlet |  | 1 | 2 |  | 1 | 1 |  |
| John Bartlet |  | 2 |  |  | 3 | 1 |  |
| Thomas Harper |  | 1 | 2 |  | 4 | 1 | 13 |
| John Spry |  | 2 | 1 |  | 2 |  | 6 |
| Anthoney Lecount | 1 |  | 1 | 1 | 2 | 1 | 7 |
| Andrew Robson |  | 1 | 2 |  | 1 | 1 | 4 |
| Jonathan Rigbey |  | 1 | 1 |  | 1 |  |  |
| Elijah Stokes |  | 1 | 1 |  | 1 |  |  |
| Philmon Rigbey |  | 2 |  | 2 | 1 |  | 7 |
| William Norwood | 2 | 1 | 5 |  | 2 | 1 |  |
| Archibald McNeal | 1 |  | 3 |  | 4 | 3 |  |
| David Matthews | 1 | 1 | 2 |  | 2 | 4 |  |
| Richard Tarr | 1 | 1 | 4 |  | 1 | 1 | 1 |
| Thomas Lennard | 1 | 3 | 3 | 1 | 1 |  |  |
| John Robson |  | 3 | 5 |  | 2 | 3 | 2 |
| Foster Maynard |  | 1 | 3 |  | 1 | 1 | 2 |
| Elizabeth Kirbey |  | 1 | 6 | 1 | 1 | 2 |  |
| Mary West |  | 2 | 1 | 1 | 2 | 1 |  |
| William Ridgeway | 1 | 1 |  | 1 | 1 |  | 2 |
| John Dawson |  | 1 | 2 |  | 1 | 1 | 5 |
| Mary Denney |  | 2 | 4 | 1 | 2 | 2 | 2 |
| William Wats |  | 1 | 7 |  | 1 | 1 | 4 |
| William Norress |  | 1 | 1 |  | 1 | 1 | 4 |
| Moses Rigbey |  | 1 | 2 |  | 1 | 3 | 8 |
| John Doughoty |  | 2 | 3 |  | 2 | 2 | 5 |
| James Gelon |  | 1 | 3 |  | 1 | 2 |  |
| James Smith |  | 1 | 4 |  | 1 | 2 | 7 |
| Joseph Seymour |  | 1 | 2 |  | 1 | 1 |  |
| Henry Richardson |  | 1 | 1 |  | 2 |  |  |
| James Lemon? |  | 1 | 3 |  | 2 | 3? |  |
| John Marchel |  | 1 |  |  | 1 | 2 |  |
| Ather Marchel |  | 1 |  |  | 1 | 2 |  |
| Anney Coborn |  | 1 |  | 1 | 1 |  |  |
| Henry Colston |  | 3 | 2 | 1 | 2 | 2 | 3 |
| Elisha Smith |  | 1 |  |  | 1 | 2 |  |
| John Gossage |  | 1 | 3 |  | 2 | 4 | 1 |
| John Harriss | 1 | 1 | 2 |  | 2 | 1 | 1 |
| Joseph Marchel |  | 1 | 1 |  | 1 |  | 1 |
| Rachel Oram |  | 2 | 3 | 1 | 2 | 4 |  |
| Bennet Vallont |  | 2 | 3 |  | 3 | 2 |  |
| Nicholas Vallont |  | 1 | 1 | 1 | 1 |  |  |
| John Vallont | 1 | 2 | 1 |  | 1 | 2 |  |
| Richard Eaton |  | 3 | 1 |  | 1 | 2 |  |
| Elizabeth Nix |  |  | 1 | 1 | 1 |  |  |
| John Eaton |  | 1 | 1 | 1 | 1 | 2 | 3 |
| William Oramm |  | 1 | 1 |  | 1 | 1 | 1 |
| Henry Seymour |  | 1 | 3 |  | 1 | 3 |  |
| Mordica Skinner |  | 1 |  |  | 1 |  | 5 |
| Thomas Robson |  | 1 |  |  | 1 |  |  |
| James Grace |  | 1 | 1 |  | 1 | 3 | 2 |

| Head of the Household | MALES over 50 | MALES 16 to 50 | MALES under 16 | FEMALES over 50 | FEMALES 16 to 50 | FEMALES under 16 | Blacks |
|---|---|---|---|---|---|---|---|
| James Colslon |  | 2 | 2 |  | 2 | 1 | 2 |
| Nathaniel Grace | 2 | 1 | 1 | 1 |  |  |  |
| Mary Grace |  |  | 1 |  | 1 | 4 | 2 |
| Robert Newcom | 1 | 1 | 2 | 1 | 1 | 1 | 26 |
| Dianna Sewel |  | 5 | 1 | 1 | 1 | 1 |  |
| Adeath Barisood |  |  |  |  | 2 | 1 |  |
| Jonathan Dorter |  | 1 |  |  | 2 | 1 | 35 |
| Susannah Stokes | 1 | 1 |  |  |  | 2 |  |
| Henry Whorten | 1 |  | 1 | 1 | 1 |  |  |
| ___ Whorten |  |  | 2 |  | 1 | 3 |  |
| Rachel Harmon | 1 |  |  |  |  | 1 |  |
| William Dowel |  | 1 | 1 |  | 1 | 1 |  |
| Elizabeth Aldren |  |  |  | 2 | 2 | 1 | 10 |
| Thomas Rigby |  | 1 | 1 |  | 3 | 1 | 6 |
| Edward Norwood | 1 |  |  | 1 | 3 | 1 |  |
| John Seymour | 1 | 1 | 2 | 1 |  | 1 |  |
| Ann Edwards |  |  | 1 | 1 | 1 |  |  |
| John Colston |  | 1 | 1 |  | 1 |  | 1 |
| William Hindman |  | 3 |  | 1 |  | 3 | 39 |
| Francis Morling |  | 1 | 2 |  |  |  | 10 |
| ___ Richardson | 1 |  | 2 |  | 1 |  |  |
| ___ Hopkins |  |  |  |  | 1 | 2 |  |
| ___ Beaten |  |  |  |  | 1 |  |  |
| ___ Spencer |  |  | 1 |  | 1 | 1 |  |
| ___ Coborn |  | 1 | 3 |  | 1 | 5 |  |
| ___ Bartlett | 1 |  | 2 |  | 3 | 1 |  |
| ___ Kirbey | 1 | 1 | 2 | 1 | 1 | 1 |  |
| John ___orkston |  | 1 | 1 |  | 1 |  |  |
| Mary Kirby |  |  | 1 |  | 1 | 1 |  |
| John Dunn | 1 | 2 |  |  |  |  | 1 |
| Robert Robson | 1 | 1 | 2 |  | 1 | 4 |  |
| John Lennard | 1 | 1 | 1 | 1 | 2 | 1 |  |
| ___ Gordon |  |  |  |  |  |  |  |
| ___ard Hopkins | 1 | ? | 3 | 1 | 5 | 1 | 3 |
| ___imeah Banning |  | 2 |  |  |  |  | 10 |
| Henry Banning |  | 2 | 4 |  | 2 | 2 | 15 |
| ___ Marchel |  | 1 |  |  | 2 |  | 12 |
| James Earl Denney |  | 2 | 1 |  | 2 | 2 | 8 |
| ___ Porter |  | 1 | 1 |  | 1 | 2 | 2 |
| Isaac Dixson | 1 | 1 | 1 |  | 3 | 1 | 20 |
| ___ Chapman |  | 1 |  |  | 2 | 1 | 3 |
| Moses Allen |  | 2 | 1 |  | 3 | 2 | 21 |
| Thomas Tibbels |  | 3 | 3 |  | 2 | 1 | 6 |
| John Siddel | 1 |  | 2 |  | 1 | 2 |  |
| Thomas Brascup |  | 2 | 5 |  | 2 | 1 |  |
| Joseph Floyd | 1 |  | 1 |  | 1 |  |  |
| Adam Eubanks |  | 1 | 1 |  | 1 | 1 |  |
| William Thomas |  | 2 |  |  | 3 | 4 | 14 |
| Ann Cardeff |  |  |  |  | 2 |  |  |
| Alexander Irvine |  | 2 |  |  | 2 | 4 |  |
| James Dawson |  | 1 | 1 |  | 1 | 2 | 6 |

TUCKAHOE HUNDRED, TALBOT COUNTY, MARYLAND
Taken by James Wrenst August 1776

The records of this Hundred as with Mill Hundred are in very poor condition.

| Head of the Household | MALES over 50 | MALES 16 to 50 | MALES under 16 | FEMALES over 50 | FEMALES 16 to 50 | FEMALES under 16 | Blacks |
|---|---|---|---|---|---|---|---|
| John Gibson | 1 | 3 | | | 2 | 3 | 30 |
| Francis Baker | | 4 | 2 | 1 | 3 | 1 | 9 |
| Daniel Nicholson | | 1 | 1 | | 1 | 1 | |
| Wollman Gibson 3rd | | 2 | | | 2 | | 10 |
| William Jackson | | 1? | | | 1 | 1 | 1 |
| John Clayland | | 1 | 1 | | 2 | 1 | 6 |
| John Collener | | 1 | | | | | |
| John Shepard | | 1 | 2 | | 1 | | |
| William Middleton | | 3 | 1 | | 1 | | 11 |
| Christopher Hartt | | 1 | | 1 | 1 | 4 | |
| William Porter | | 1 | 2 | | 1 | 3 | 8 |
| Edward Lloyd | | 6 | | | 4 | 3 | 15 |
| Charles Ford | | 1 | 1 | | 2 | 2 | |
| George Hall | | 1 | | | 3 | | |
| William Alleway | | 1 | | | 1 | 5 | |
| William Webster | 1 | | 1 | | | | |
| Ann Jones | | | 1 | | 1 | 1 | |
| Mary Sunksout | | 1 | 1 | | 3 | 3 | |
| John Cheavis | | 1 | | | 1 | | |
| John Powell | | 1 | | | 2 | | 9 |
| Herbert? Warner | | 1 | 1 | | 2 | 2 | |
| Herbert? Hall | | 2 | 4 | | 2 | 2 | 3 |
| William Cooper | | 1 | 2 | | 1 | 3 | 6 |
| ___ Countiee | | 1 | | 1 | 2 | | |
| Yarnall Plumer | | 1 | 1 | | 1 | 2 | |
| Thomas Plumer | | 1 | 4 | | 2 | 1 | 1 |
| Ann Callahan | | 1 | 3 | | 2 | | 2 |
| Edward Surat? | 2 | 2 | 2 | | 1 | 2 | |
| Robert Dwiging | | 2 | 2 | | 1 | 3 | 2 |
| Nixson Milington | 1 | 1 | 1 | 1 | 1 | 1 | 3 |
| Joseph Morley | | 1 | | | | | 10 |
| ___ Millington | | 1 | 3 | | | 3 | 2 |
| ___ Callihorn | | 1 | 4 | | 3 | | |
| ___ Harris | 1 | 1 | | | 2 | 2 | |
| ___ Williams | | 6 | | | 1 | | 3 |
| ___ Stacy | - | 1 | | | 1 | 1 | |
| ___ Rue | | 1 | | | 1 | 2 | |
| ___ Williss | 1 | 1 | 5 | | 1 | 2 | |
| ___ Nickers | | 1 | | 1 | 2 | 2 | 9 |
| ___ Nickers | | 1 | 1 | | 1 | 2 | |
| ___ Palmer | | 1 | 2 | | 1 | 4 | 2 |
| ___ Roberts | | 2 | | 1 | 2 | 4 | 1 |
| ___ Forster | | 3 | 2 | | 3 | | 2 |
| ___ Buley | | 2 | 2 | 1 | 1 | 4 | 9 |
| ___ Mattorn | | | 1 | | 2 | | 1 |

160

|                      | MALES        |              |              | FEMALES      |              |              |        |
| -------------------- | ------------ | ------------ | ------------ | ------------ | ------------ | ------------ | ------ |
| Head of the Household | over 50     | 16 to 50     | under 16     | over 50     | 16 to 50     | under 16     | Blacks |
| ____ Norton          | 1            | 1            | 2            |              | 2            | 1            |        |
| ____ Pattin          |              | 1            | 3            |              | 1            |              |        |
| ____t Griffeth       |              | 1            | 2            |              | 2            | 2            |        |
| ____ Norton          | 1            |              |              |              |              |              | 4      |
| ____ Warner          | 1            | 1            | 3            | 1            | 2            |              |        |
| ____ Batey           |              | 1            |              |              |              |              |        |
| ____ Maxwell         |              |              |              |              |              |              | 19     |
| Bennet? Lloyd        |              |              |              |              |              |              | 58     |
| ____ Dimmond         |              | 2            | 1            |              | 2            | 1            | 9      |
| ____ Renolls         |              | 1            | 1            |              | 2            | 2            |        |
| ____ ilder           |              | 2            |              |              | 1            | 1            | 7      |
| ____ Miller          |              | 1            |              |              |              |              |        |
| ____ Berwick         |              | 1            |              |              | 1            |              | 1      |
| __r Cottner          |              | 1            | 1            |              | 1            |              |        |
| ____ Blackwell       |              | 2            |              |              |              |              | 6      |
| ____ arron           |              | 1            |              |              |              |              | 2      |
| ____ Sware           |              | 1            |              |              | 1            | 1            |        |
| ____ Bordly          |              | 3            | 2            |              | 3            |              | 16     |
| ____ Cole            |              | 2            | 2            |              | 1            | 2            |        |
| ____ Williams        |              |              | 1            |              |              |              |        |
| ____ Warner          |              | 1            |              |              |              |              |        |
| ____ Foster          |              | 1            |              |              |              |              |        |
| ____ Ozemon          |              | 1            |              |              |              |              |        |
| ____ Roberts         |              | 1            |              |              | 3            |              | 4      |
| ____ Sylvester       |              | 1            | 1            |              | 1            |              | 3      |
| ____ Wrench          |              | 1            |              |              | 1            | 1            | 4      |
| ____ Gannon          |              | 1            | 2            |              | 1            | 6            |        |
| ____ Grace           |              | 1            | 2            | 1            | 1            | 2            | 3      |
| ____ Long            | 1            | 1            | 2            |              |              | 2            |        |
| ____ North           |              | 1            |              |              |              |              |        |
| ____ Robertson       |              |              |              |              | 1            |              | 6      |
| ____ Curry           |              |              |              |              | 4            |              | 5      |
| ____ Lane            | 1            | 1            | 1            | 1            | 1            | 2            |        |
| John Plummer         |              | 1            | 1            | 1            | 1            | 2            | 1      |
| Robert Pickiran      |              | 2            |              |              | 4            |              | 10     |

## Middlesex Hundred of Baltimore County

As Taken by Henry Rutter, Sept. 13, 1776
[Held by State Archives: Contributed by George Horvath, Jr.]

Column 1 - Free men 16 yrs and upwards
Column 2 - Free women 16 yrs and upwards
Column 3 - Boys under 16 yrs
Column 4 - Girls under 16 yrs
Column 5 - Men Servants 16 yrs and upwards
Column 6 - Women Servants 16 yrs and upwards
Column 7 - Servant Boys under 16 yrs
Column 8 - Servant Girls under 16 yrs
Column 9 - Total White
Column 10 - Male Mulatto Slaves, 16 yrs and upwards
Column 11 - Female Mulatto Slaves, 16 yrs and upwards
Column 12 - Male Mulatto Slaves, under 16 yrs
Column 13 - Female Mulatto Slaves, under 16 yrs
Column 14 - Total Mulatto Slaves
Column 15 - Free Negroes, male, 16 yrs and upwards
Column 16 - Free Negroes, female, 16 yrs and upwards
Column 17 - Free Negroes, male under 16 yrs
Column 18 - Free Negroes, female under 16 yrs
Column 19 - Total Free Negroes

| | 1 | 2 | 3 | 4 | 5 | 6 | 7 | 8 | 9 | 10 | 11 | 12 | 13 | 14 | 15 | 16 | 17 | 18 | 19 |
|---|---|---|---|---|---|---|---|---|---|---|---|---|---|---|---|---|---|---|---|
| Samuel Maryman, Sr. | 1 | 2 | 2 | 1 | - | 1 | - | ? | 7 | 3 | 1 | 1 | - | 5 | 1 | - | - | - | 1 |
| Paul Addows | 1 | 1 | - | - | - | - | - | - | 2 | - | - | - | - | - | - | - | - | - | - |
| Jean Gardner | - | 2 | - | 1 | - | - | - | - | 3 | - | - | - | - | - | - | - | - | - | - |
| William Miller | 3 | 2 | 2 | 5 | - | - | - | - | 12 | - | - | - | - | - | - | - | - | - | - |
| Gorg Sauerpry | 4 | 1 | 2 | 2 | 3 | 1 | - | - | 13 | - | - | - | - | - | - | - | - | - | - |
| Robard Right | 2 | - | - | - | - | - | - | - | 2 | - | - | - | - | - | - | - | - | - | - |
| Wm. Hoppern | 1 | 1 | - | 4 | - | - | - | - | 6 | - | 1 | - | 1 | 2 | - | - | - | - | - |
| Sollomon Wooden | 1 | 1 | - | 1 | - | - | - | - | 3 | - | - | - | - | - | - | - | - | - | - |
| Stephen Wooden | 1 | 1 | 3 | 2 | - | - | - | - | 7 | - | - | - | 3 | 3 | - | - | - | - | - |
| John Wooden | 3 | 3 | 3 | 2 | 4 | - | - | - | - | 1 | 1 | 3 | 1 | 5 | - | - | - | - | - |
| Thomas Beach | 2 | 2 | 3 | 1 | - | - | - | - | 8 | - | - | - | 1 | 1 | - | - | - | - | - |
| Nathanel Weston | 1 | 1 | - | 1 | - | - | - | - | 3 | - | - | - | 1 | 1 | - | - | - | - | - |
| John Gardner, Farmer | 1 | 2 | - | 4 | - | - | - | - | 7 | - | - | - | - | - | - | - | - | - | - |
| Wm. Hannah | 2 | 1 | - | 1 | - | 1 | - | - | 5 | - | - | - | - | - | - | - | - | - | - |
| Stephen Hale | 1 | 2 | 2 | 2 | - | - | - | - | 7 | - | - | - | - | - | - | - | - | - | - |
| Andrew Buckmon Qtrs. | - | - | - | - | - | - | - | - | - | 5 | 3 | 6 | 6 | 20 | - | - | - | - | - |
| Edw. Puntry | 1 | 1 | - | 7 | - | - | - | - | 9 | - | - | - | - | - | - | - | - | - | - |
| Edw. Lowry | 2 | 1 | - | 1 | - | - | - | - | 4 | - | - | - | - | - | - | - | - | - | - |
| Leonard Helloms | 1 | - | 3 | 2 | - | - | - | - | 6 | - | 1 | - | 1 | 1 | - | - | - | - | - |
| Maybery Helloms, Jr. | 1 | 1 | 1 | 4 | - | - | - | - | 7 | - | 1 | 2 | - | 3 | - | - | - | - | - |
| Wm. Hall | 1 | 1 | - | - | - | - | - | - | 2 | - | - | - | - | - | - | - | - | - | - |
| Jonathan Weeb | 2 | 1 | 1 | - | - | 1 | - | - | 5 | - | - | - | - | - | - | - | - | - | - |
| John Conner | 1 | 1 | - | - | - | - | - | - | 2 | - | - | - | - | - | - | - | - | - | - |
| Wm. Lux | 4 | 3 | - | 2 | 8 | 1 | 1 | - | 19 | 12 | 3 | 6 | 2 | 23 | - | 1 | - | - | 1 |
| Rosanner Hill | 4 | 1 | - | 1 | - | - | - | - | 6 | - | - | - | - | - | - | - | - | - | - |
| Maybery Helloms, Sr. | 1 | - | 1 | 1 | - | - | - | - | 3 | 2 | 4 | - | 1 | 7 | - | - | - | - | - |
| Thomas Eysom | 1 | 1 | - | - | - | - | - | - | 2 | - | - | - | - | - | - | - | - | - | - |
| Mary Ridgly | - | 2 | 2 | 1 | - | - | - | - | 5 | 1 | 2 | 3 | 1 | 7 | - | - | - | - | - |
| --- Stohs | 1 | 2 | - | - | - | 2 | - | - | 5 | - | - | - | - | - | - | - | - | - | - |
| Dorryty Aldermos | - | 1 | - | 1 | - | - | - | - | 2 | - | - | - | - | - | - | - | - | - | - |
| Thomas Wright | 1 | 1 | - | - | - | - | - | - | 2 | - | - | - | - | - | - | - | - | - | - |

## Middlesex Hundred of Baltimore County

| Name | | | | | | | | | | | | | | | | | |
|---|---|---|---|---|---|---|---|---|---|---|---|---|---|---|---|---|---|
| Robt. Alexander | 1 | 2 | 5 | 1 | - | - | - | - | 9 | 1 | 3 | 3 | - | 7 | - | - | - | - | - |
| Wm. Gibson | 1 | 1 | - | - | - | - | - | - | 2 | - | - | - | 1 | 1 | - | - | - | - | - |
| Alex. Lawson | - | 1 | - | - | - | - | - | - | 1 | 2 | 1 | 2 | 1 | 6 | - | - | - | - | - |
| --harles Ridgley | - | - | - | - | 1 | - | - | - | 2 | 4 | 2 | 3 | 2 | 11 | - | - | - | - | - |
| Samuel Heeth | 1 | 1 | 1 | 1 | - | - | - | - | 4 | - | - | - | - | - | - | - | - | - | - |
| John Ross | 1 | 1 | - | - | 2 | 1 | 1 | - | 7 | - | - | - | 1 | 1 | 1 | - | - | - | 1 |
| The Poor at the Poor House | 9 | 17 | 3 | 6 | - | - | - | - | 35 | - | - | - | - | - | 2 | - | - | - | 2 |
| Edw. Hanson | 2 | 1 | - | - | 2 | - | - | - | 5 | 2 | - | - | - | 2 | - | - | - | - | - |
| Henry Penny | 1 | 1 | 1 | 3 | - | - | - | - | 6 | - | - | - | - | - | - | - | - | - | - |
| Wm. More, Mills | 1 | 1 | 1 | 2 | 4 | 1 | - | - | 10 | - | - | 2 | - | 2 | - | - | - | - | - |
| Marget Hopper | - | 1 | 4 | 1 | - | - | - | - | 6 | - | - | - | - | - | - | - | - | - | - |
| James Grunner | 1 | 2 | 1 | 2 | - | - | - | - | 6 | - | - | - | - | - | - | - | - | - | - |
| John Spiser | 2 | 3 | 1 | 1 | - | - | - | - | 7 | 2 | - | - | - | 2 | - | - | - | - | - |
| Allender Shaw | - | - | - | - | - | - | - | - | - | - | - | - | - | - | 2 | 4 | - | - | 6 |
| Mount Royal Fordge | 3 | - | - | - | 1 | - | - | - | 4 | 11 | 3 | 4 | 5 | 23 | - | - | - | - | - |
| Henry Rutter | 2 | 2 | 4 | 3 | 2 | - | - | - | 13 | - | - | - | - | - | - | - | - | - | - |
| Wm. Phillips | 1 | 2 | 1 | 3 | - | - | - | - | 7 | - | - | - | - | - | - | - | - | - | - |

# INDEX

Abbet, Thomas 38
Abet Sarah 38
Abington, Bob 73
  Elizabeth 73, 75
  Henry 73
  John 73
  Lucy 73
Able Mary 123
Ableider, Geo. 55
Ackman Phil. 38
Acorn Thos. 156
Acton, Ann 120
  Elizabeth 120
  Henry 120
  Hister 120
  Mary 120
  Smallwood 120
Adames Peter 44
  Salathan 44
  Thomas 44
Adams, Alex. 63
  Ann 77
  Bettey 49
  Cassandra 77
  Edward 63
  Eliza. 66, 118, 133, 136
  James 118
  Jane 127
  Jesse 77
  John 63, 99, 118
  Joseph 137
  Joshua 5
  Lucy 133
  Margaret 121
  Mary 49, 66, 118
  Maryan 77
  McNamar 38
  Richard 136
  Robert 127
  Susanna 118
  Thomas 85, 133
  Walter 118
  Winefred 137
Addison Anthoney 140
  Elizabeth 126
  John 126
  Mrs. 140
  Rebecca 126
Addows Paul 162
Adkey Nathan 141
Adkins Eliza. 66
  Rachel 38
Adley Eliza 70
  William 38
Ahare John 63
Airey Thos. 53
Aisquith Wm. 32
Alby Ann 73
  Cassandra 73
  Joseph 73
Alder Chris. 54
  Eliza. 126
  Frederick 54
  George 126
Aldermos Dorryty 162
Aldmand Sarah 111
Aldren Eliza. 159
Aldridge Eliza. 127
  Jacob 127
Ale Robert 78
Alexander Mary 32
  Robert 73, 163
  William 50
Alexson, Alex. 38
All Andrew 139
  Hannah 110
  Margret 110, 139
Allen Ann 33
  Archabald 84
  Dorithy 132
  Elisabeth 84
  John 132
  Moses 159
  Mrs. 138
  Preseller 35
Alleway Wm. 160
Alley Wm. 151
Allham Daniel 100
Allien Joseph 22
Allin Richard 32
Allingins Joe. 21
Allison Addam 19
  Charles 81
  Elisabeth 77
  Ellenner 77
  Hendery 77, 83
  John 83
  Maryan 77
  Mathew 83
  Osiller 83
  Rachel 26, 83
  Silvester 77
  Wm. Lame 87
Allnutt Ann 80
  Daniel 80
  Ellender 80
  James 80
  Jean 80
  Jesse 80
Allnutt John 80
  Joseph 80
  Lawrence 80
  Mary 80
  Mary Ruth 80
  Rebeca 80
  Sary 80
  Susanna 80
  Talbart 80
  Virlinder 80
  William 80
Allway Thos. 148
Alter Cath. 62
  Elizabeth 62
  Margaret 56
  Mary 62
  Susanna 56, 62
Althard Cath. 58, 62
  Larance 58
Ammons Ann 94
  Margaret 94
  Mary 94
  Thomas 94
Amos John 97
Anderson Absol. 12
  Amous 117
  Charles 114, 117
  Daniel 114, 117
  Elizabeth 91
  George 87
  Grace 117
  James 3, 32, 117, 141
  Jane 87
  Jenny 87
  John 91, 141
  Margaret 114
  Mary 70, 87, 91, 114, 117
  Prissiller 114
  Rachel 70
  Richard 117
  Robert 63, 91
  Sarah 114, 117
  Wm. 3, 12, 91, 117
Anderton John 49
Andrews Isaac 45
  John 91
  Joseph 44
  Keziah 46
  Nathal 46
  Rubin 46
  William 5
Angel William 38
Antel Ann 109
Antel Blanch 109
  Hannah 109
  John 109
  Sarah 109
  Thomas 109
Applegirth Al. 152
  George 154
Armigod Danl. 18
  William 19
Armond Eliza. 87
  Hanna 87
  Isaac 87
  Thomas 87
  William 87
Armstrong Alishea, 112
  David 94
  Ezebel 100
  Ford 112
  Hannah 112
  John 100
  Joseph 112
  Josua 112
  Margret 112
  Mary 32, 91, 94, 112
  Robert 94, 100
  Sarah 94
  Sollaman 112
  Susanna 104
  William 100
Arescott Rich. 141
Arnett Ann 52
  Isabella 107
  James 52
  William 107
Arnold Ann 81
  Catharina 56
  Christopher 138
  Cumfort 112
  Daniel 60
  Eliza. 81, 94
  Ellenner 78
  Ephraim 94
  Frederick 60
  George 54
  John 26, 60, 81
  Joseph 78
  Marah 113
  Mary 81, 138
  Sarah 94
  Wm. 27, 81, 94, 112
Ars John 117
Asbeld John 69
Ashcraft Thos. 152
Ashen Ellender 78

Ashen James 78
John 78
Samuel 78
William 78
Ashley Thos. 106,141
Ashton Rev. John 12
Asker Jane 101
Atchinson Efrom 77
John 77
Lody 77
Ruth 77
Athers Ann 135
Athey Benj. 129
Edea 129
Hezekiah 130
Lucy 138
Owen 138
Rebecca 130
Atkins Joseph 63
Atkinson Aaron 156
Ann 103
Elizabeth 103
Frances 103
Greenberry 103
Joseph 157
Mary 103
Atterson Arter 38
Atwell & Attwell
Benj. 21, 23 Dan 6
John 23, 26
Joseph 23
Robt 23, 28
Samuel 29
Wm. 23
Aubrey Wm 63
Auld Daniel 154
Hugh 154
John 154
Philip 155
Auldery Thos. 156
Aulenn Eliza 32
Aunnar Ann & Wm. 122
Austin _ _ 156
Absalom 141
Alexander 63
Amelia 66
Amos 63
Ann 156
Charity 66
Hezek. 63,66
James 63
John 63
Mary 66
Thomas 63
Wm 156
Zechariah 63

Ayres Abraham 102
Betheah 102
Elizabeth 102
Milbie 102
Thomas 102
Azel Martha 99

Babe Ann 103
Mary 103
Patrick 103
Sarah Hail 103
Backster Betty 83
Gabriel 83
Backus Andrew 54
George 51
Badfoot Bashual 63
Badley Christ. 38
Ezekal 38
Nathan 48
Richard 38
William 48
Badolph Phillip 54
Baeghtle Isaac 55
Baiford Thomas 4
Baghtel Saml 55
Bagwell Thos 32
Baily Nehemiah 106
Baker Agnes 17
Bartain 81
Francis 160
Jenny M 108
John 38, 85
Josaway 117
Mildred 70
Nicolis 117
Philip T 69
Saml H 69
William 69
Baldin Eliza 124
James 124
Bakes Charlote 56
William 60
Baley Ann 70
Edward 63
Monjoy 63
Samuel 63
Susanna F 70
William 63
Ball Allen 30
Allison 20,30
Benjamin 38
Elizabeth 137
Hilleary 137
James 154
Priscilla 38
Richard 130

Ball Sarah 136
Thomas 154
Ballson John 15
Bancks Ann 38
Bandure Christian 58
Bannerman Betsey 75
Banning Henry 159
imeah 159
James 105
Barbary Ann 84
Barber Ann 70
Barney 63
Dorothy 66
Elizabeth 66
John 63
Mary 66
Thomas 69, 141
Barclay Eliza 87
John 87
Bardon Cath 62
Jacob 54
John 59
Margaretha 56
Barisood Adeath 159
Barker Eliza 79
John 23,31
William 23,32
Barkes Andrew 60
Eliza 62
Jane 62
John 54
Margaretha 56
Barkley James 43
Barlow Ann 82
Bettey 83
Elisabeth 82
John 82
Mary 82
Susanna 82
Zachariah 75,82
Barnard Eliza. 89
James 87
Jane 87
Leavin 36
Mark 87
Sarah 89
Thomas 87
Barneclew And. 150
John 150
Barnes Annah 112
Benjamin 112
Elizabeth 112
James 154,112
Joshua 90
Mary 90
Nehemiah 106

Barnes Prime 63
Rachael 106
Sarah 48, 112
Thos. 90, 149
Barnet Chas. 148
Barney Wm. 154
Barns, Asyl 113
Averilla 115
Bennet 113
Bethia 110
Eliza. 112,113,115
Ezekiel 94
Ford 112, 113,115
Gregary 115
Hannah 94
Hestor 113
Hosea 113
Job 94
John 112,115
Joseph 108,116
Margret 112,113
Mary 94,115
Rachael 94,112,115
Ruth 94,113 Rich. 115
Sarah 94,112,115
Thomas 47
Viariner 115
William 112
Zachariah 109
Barnsbury Wm. 17
Barratt Isaac 73
Mary 73
Ninian 73
Richard 73
Barren Jane 122
John 122
Barret Ann 136
Richard 136
Barrett Ann 70,75
Eliza. 75,156
Isaac 75
John 75
Mary 70
Thomas 69
Barrot Robt. 136
Sarah 136
Barrow James 152,157
Thomas 157
Barry Mordecai 4
Thomas 60
Bartlet John 158
Richard 158
Bartlett _ 159
George 142
Jack 107
James 150

Barwick James 33,36
Joshua 36
Margrett 36
Basford John 4
Stephen 5
Thos. F. 6
Basil John 2
Basset Thos.51
Bateman James 141
John 141
Michael 141
Bates Joseph 93
Batey Benj. 38
Batsey Rich.155
Battee Ann 7
Battie Agnes 27
Batts Eliza.66
Bauer Ann 57
Eve 57
Mary 28
Sebastian 60
Bauman Eliza.58
Jacob 58,60
John 59,60
Martin 55
Simon 58
Baumward Henry 55
Philip 60
Baward Leonhard 60
Mary 57
Peter 60
Baxter Thos.149
William 149
Bay Alex.89
Eliza.89
Hugh 89
Jennet 89
Sarah 89
William 89
Bayles Ann 112
Augustus 111
Benjamin 111
Debrow 111
Elis 111
Eliza.111
Feaby 111
Feby 111
Hanah 111
James 112
John 111
Mary 111
Mehetabet 111
Nathaniel 112
Saml.111,112
Sarah 111,112

Bayley ___ 115
Aquillia 115
Averilla 115,116
Bennidick 115
Charles 115
Eseakel 115
Josias 116
Margret 115
Mary P. 70
Sarah 115
Baynard Gedion 36
John 33
Mary 33
Thomas 37
Bayne Ann 119
Charity 119
Eliza.119
Henrietta 119
Mary 126
Saml. H. 119
Thomas 119
William 126
Winefred 137
Baynes Joseph N.124
John 124,
Mary 124
Bazill, Ralph 1
Beach Thomas 162
Beacor George 108
Beaghtle Ann 57,6
Barbara 61
Elizabeth 61
Ester 61
Jacob 59
Magdalana 57
Martin 59
Susanna 61
Beaker Christiana 57
Eliza.61
John 59
Peter 55
Susanna 61
William 58
Beall Agnes 127
Alarina 73
Alexander 63
Amelia,121
Andrew 121
Ann 66,121,140,
Cassandra 73,120
Catherine 122, 124
Clement 73
Edward 66
Eleanor 66,120,122
Elenor 73, 126
Eliza.66,73,120,139

Beall Erasmus 63
Frances 128
Geo.63, 121
Henry 63
Hezekiah 63
James 120,140
Jane 73
Jemima 73
Jeremiah 123
John 69,122,128,134
Joshua 121
Josia 125
Josiah 63
Lucy 66
Mannen 128
Margaret 73,121
Mary 70,73,120,134
Ninian 122,124,140
Normand 73
Orasha 74
Patrick 126
Perry 73
Priscilla 73,128
Rebecca,120, 123,133
Rebeckah 74
Richard 73,123,133
Robert 71,72,74
Roger 132
Ruth 70,132
Saml.73,120
Sarah 73,120,123
S.Sebert 65
Shadrick 127
Tabitha 128
Thos.63,116,122,128
Violinda 66
William 80
Wilobe 73
Zachariah 74
Bean Ann 132
Ebsworth 132
George 132
John 132
Josias 132
Susanna 132
Beanes Christ.122
Jane 122
Beans Jane 123
Sanuel 123
Sarah 125
Beanes Wm.125
Beasley Eliza.66
Moses 63
Beaten ___ 159
Beaty Arch.103

Beaty Jane 103
Hannah 103
William 103
Beard Ester 57
Jean 83
Georg 38
Hester 3
James 32
John 7,32,38,87
Matthew 4
Michael 55
Richard 7
Ruth 61
Stephen 7
Susanna 58
Thomas 38
Wm. 55,59,80
Beavor Eliza.93
Beb John 99
Beck Adam 60
Ann 98,103
Bethsheba 98
Caleb 98,103
Daniel 103
Elizabeth 113
Hannah 98
James 98, 129
Jeffery 147
John 103
Joshua 98
Martha 103
Rebecca 129
Sophia 98
Becks Mary 62
William 51
Beckwith Ann 82
Emanuel 52
Mary 82
William 82
Becraft Benjamin 69,73
Deborah 73
Mary 73
Fetter 73
Bedelhall John 108
Beeding Edward 81
Jacob 81
John 81
Joseph 81
Solomon 81
Tabitha 81
Beegding Hennary 80
Beek Anthoney 124
Elizabeth 124
Beeker Elisabeth 61
Magdalena 58

| | | | |
|---|---|---|---|
| Been Thomas 69 | Bennet Abram 100 | Berry Sarah 104 | Blackmore Eliza.66,81 |
| Degarley Ann 73 | Aquila 100 | Bert Henry 32 | Ellenner 81 |
| Elizabeth 73 | Benjamin 100 | Bestpitch Levin 38 | James 63,81 |
| Henry 73 | Gean 100 | William 38 | Loyd Beall 69 |
| Hezekiah 73 | John 100 | Betts Hezekiah 141 | Mary 81 |
| Beggarly George 130 | Joshua 98 | Solomon 141 | Rachel 66 |
| Margaret 130 | Leaven 100 | Beverly George 54 | Saml.63,81 |
| Beggerly Abigail 129 | Mary 100 | Biards Casander 117 | Sary 77 |
| Ann 85 | Peter 100 | James 117 | William 77,81 |
| Charles 85 | Sarah 100 | Jane 117 | Blackstone Eliza.99 |
| Isaac 85 | Bennett Jacob 107 | Rachel 117 | James 99 |
| John 129 | James 32,150 | Biars Ephraim 117 | John 99 |
| Samuel 85 | Jean 141 | Bibber Isaac 32 | Thomas 99 |
| Bell Eliza.56,62 | John 105 | Biddle Jost 55 | Blades John 52 |
| Frederick 60 | William 12 | Biggs Hammator 85 | Blair John 53 |
| Juley 62 | Bennington (Han)iah 87 | Henry 132 | Bland Joseph 34 |
| Margaretha 62 | | Sarah 132 | Blervet Charles 141 |
| Peter 54,60 | Henry 87 | Samuel 85 | Blesset William 38 |
| Belmear Francis 12 | Kessia 87 | Bigner Robt.130 | Bley Barbara 56 |
| Belsher Ann 108 | Mary 87 | Margaret 130 | Christiana 62 |
| Bennet 108 | Priscilla 87 | Billings Wm. 49 | John 59 |
| Daniel 108 | Tom 87 | Billmore Eliza.58 | Rudolph 54 |
| Jacob 108 | William 92 | John 58 | Blockley Eliza.66 |
| James 108 | Benny James 151 | Billingslea Arsena 92 | Mary 66 |
| John 108 | Benson Mary 141 | Francis 92 | Nehemiah 63 |
| Susannah 108 | Nichlas 152 | Samuel 92 | Thomas 63 |
| Michal 108 | Perry 152 | Sarah 92 | Bloodworth Rebecca 106 |
| William 108 | Thomas 12 | Sias 92 | Timothy 106 |
| Belshoober Cath.62 | Benton Benj.63 | Walter 92 | Bloodsworth Robt.45 |
| Henry 60 | Eliza.66 | William 92 | Bloyce David 63 |
| Jacob 54,60 | Erasmus 63 | Binlie John 59 | Mary 66 |
| John 60 | Franson 147 | Bird Magor 50 | William 63 |
| Mary 56 | Hezekiah 63 | Bisbend Eles 70 | Bloys Ann 74 |
| Melker 54 | John 141 | Bisbind James 69 | Charles 74 |
| Beltshoover Eliza.56 | Joseph 63 | Bishop George 60 | Davis 74 |
| Belt Alley 77 | Mordecai 63 | Jacob 58, 60 | Elizabeth 74 |
| Ann 70 | Nathan 63 | John 7 | Jonathan 74 |
| Benjamin 128 | Ninson 141 | Margaret 57 | Mary 74 |
| Carlton 85 | William 141 | William 55 | Mordeca 74 |
| Eliza.57, 77 | Bentz Cathrin 62 | Bittier Daniel 60 | Rebeckah 74 |
| Esther 70 | Christian 55 | Black Betty 34 | Sarah 74 |
| Higinson 77 | Christopher 60 | Blackbourn Wm. 106 | William 74 |
| Joseph 69,73 | George 60 | Blackburn Eliza.56 | Zachah 74 |
| Leonard 63 | John 60 | John 60 | Zadock 74 |
| Mary 85 | Magdalena 57 | Susanna 62 | Bluch William 53 |
| Molley 85 | Beotpich John 51 | Blackford Thos.108 | Blume Cathrin 57 |
| Rebecca 66 | Jonathan 51 | Blacklock Charity 125 | Henry 55 |
| Thomas 55 | Berkley Eliza.131 | Eliza.66 | Blunt Edward 21 |
| Watson 85 | Henry 131 | Mary 66 | Labin 148 |
| William 63,69 | Berry Ann E.104 | Richard 63 | Boarman Joseph 130 |
| Bence Barbara 121 | Benjamin 121 | Thomas 125 | Mary 130 |
| George 121 | Cornelius 6 | Blackmore Abriller 81 | Boayer Elizabeth 100 |
| Bendal Joseph 109 | Deborah 121 | Amma 81 | Bodkin Charles 87 |
| Bendon Joseph 102 | Eliza.104 | Ann 81 | James 87 |
| Beneham Ann 118 | John 140 | Dawson 77 | Janey 87 |

Bodkin John 87
  Margrett 87
  Molly 87
  Nancey 87
  Rachell 87
  Richard 87
  Robert 87
  Sally 87
  Thomas 87
  William 87
Body __ 103
Bolton George 141
Boman Affnea 110
  Christian 110
  David 110
  Ellener 110
  Elles 110
  Henery 110
  Henry 110
  John 110
  Margret 110
  Mary 110
Bond Amelia 91
  Ann 91
  Clarissa 125
  Charlote 93
  Dennis 93
  Elizabeth 91,93
  Finley Dr.91
  Jacob 93
  James 91
  John 93
  Martha 93
  Pricilla 93
  Ralph 93
  Samuel 125
  Sarah 91
  Thomas 93
  William 91
Boner Brise 115
  Cathran 113
  David 113
  Eliza 115
  Elisabeth 115
  John 109,113
  Margret 115
  Mary 115
  Nathan 113
  Robert 115
  William 115
Bonersill McKeel 38
Bonewill Georg 38
Bonifant Mary 119
Bonifield Saml.129
  Sarah 129

Bonner Ann 114
  Arther 114
  Barney 114
  Charles 114
  Charles 114
  Christan 114
  John 114
  Martha 114
Bonnifield Arnold 63
  Dorcas 66
  Elizabeth 66
  Gregory 63
  Henry 63
  Martha 66
  Sarah 66
  William 63
Bonithan Martha 121
Bonser Christ.70
  James T. 69
  John T. 69
  Joseph 69
Booghman Geo.55
Booke Geo. 54
Boogh Cath.57
Booth John 47
Boots Jacob 141
  Nathaniel 141
  Samuel 141
Boovey Thos.92
Booz Geo.46
  James 46
Booze George 46
Bores Ann 70
Borough 70
  Elizabeth 70
  John 69
  Margaret 70
Borough Margaret 86
  Sarah 70
  Simon 69
  Volendine 69
Borrough Volen.69
Boucher John 121
  Mary 121
Boudle Henry 49
  John 49
Boudy Hannah 103
  Ruth 103
  Sophia 103
Bouer Abraham 55
  Moritz 55
Bouff John 152
Boulton Cath.122
  George 122
Bouman Susanna 62

Bourgess Eliza.57
Bourn Ann 130
  David 130
  Jemimah 130
  William 130
Bostick James 33
Boswell David 118
  Edward 132
  Eliz.120,132,133
  George 120
  John 129,133
  Mary 134
  Nicholas 130
  Peter 120,134
  Rachell 130
  Rebecca 129
Botfield Zadock 157
Bothe David 91
  Rachel 91
  Sarah 91
Bots Ann 116
  Charity 112
  Eliz.112,116
  George 112
  Isaac 112,116
  James 116
  John 112,116
  Margret 112
  Mary 112
  Rachel 112
  Ruth 112
  Sarah 112,116
Botts Aron 83
  Francis 83
  Margaret 83
  Susannah 83
Bowan John 84
Bowdel Wm. 157
Bowdy John 94
Bower Cath.63
  Magdalana 63
  Margaret 63
  Susanna 63
Bowers Jean 77
Bowie John 30
Bowlear Peter 110
Bowling John 140
  Mary 139,140
  William L.139
Bowman Ann 57
  Magdalena 56
Boyd Abraham 121
  Barbara 121
Boyer Henry 59
  John 58,59

Boyer July 57
  Margret 57
  Michael 55
Boyls Ebeth 109
  Jane 109
  Mary 109
  Mathew 109
  Thomas 109
Braddsetz James 154
Bradey Michael 106
  Noren 106
Bradford Elianor 133
  Eliz.93,107
  George 93
  Henry 133
  Martha 93
  Mary 93
  Samuel 93
  Sarah 93
  William Capt.93
Bradley Thomas 150
Brady Rebecca 119
Bramble Adam 46
  Aron 49
  Bettey 46
  Edmon 38
  John 45, 46
  Levina 38
  Lewis 45
  Thomas 49
Bramley Eliz.70
Brandon Abraham 78
Branen Eliz.70
  Gorge 69
  Jeremiah 69
  John 69
  Mary 70
  Samuel 69
  Thomas 69
Brannan Caleb 106
Brannen Lawrence 78
Brannon Darkes 116
  Ellender 116
  Hannah 116
  Jane 116
  John 116
  Joseph 116
  Mary 110
  Patrick 116
  William 116
Brascup Thomas 159
Braum John 55
Braun Catharina 57
  Cathrin 63
  Edward 54

|  |  |  |  |
|---|---|---|---|
| Braun George 58 | Bright Fannah 83 | Brown Gustus 114 | Brukes Susanah 115 |
| Magdalena 63 | Francis 148 | H. 20 | Bucey Eleanor 66 |
| Bread Eliz.62 | Jonis 34 | Hannah 138 | John 63 |
| Breat Henry 60 | Margaret 83 | Isaac 32 | Joshua 63 |
| Bredinge John 35 | Soloman 32 | Jacob 99,112 | Samuel 63 |
| Breeding Eliz.85 | Brinsfield James 49 | James 63,77,94 | Buchanan Eliz.10 |
| James 85 | Brion John 147 | 101,102,108,137 | Buckler Bond 90 |
| Mary 85 | Brite George 34 | Jane 116 | Charity 90 |
| Susanna 85 | Broadie John 63 | John 24,25,50,99 | Martha 90 |
| Thomas 85 | Brodess Edw.51 | 100,107,122,132,141 | Sarah 90 |
| William 85 | Tabitha 51 | Martha 106,107 | Buckley Henry 157 |
| Breerton Thos.32 | Thomas 50 | Mary 99,102,112,132 | James 99 |
| Breashears Ann 135 | Brodie Wm. 63 | Peter 152 | John 75,92,99 |
| Frances 129 | Broga Danl.123 | Philip 5 | Sarah 99 |
| Ignatius 129 | Mary 123 | Richard 16 | William 99 |
| Jemima 128 | Brogden John 13 | Robert 100 | Buckmon Andrew 162 |
| Jeremiah 128 | Samuel 7 | Ruth 122 | Budd Sarah 105 |
| John 135 | Capt. Wm. 13 | Samuel 141 | Buddicum Chas.119 |
| Mary 135 | Broks Sarah 38 | Sarah 38,92,100,107 | Bull Bennett 91 |
| Brendlinger And.59 | Bromajim John 47 | 110, 116 | Edward 91 |
| Christianna 61 | Bromwell Mary 152 | Thos.99,102,107 | Eli 91 |
| Conrad 55 | Brook Asa 73 | William 63,7,54,92 | Esther 91 |
| Eliz. 61 | Isaac 63 | 122,141 | Jacob 91 |
| George 59 | John 63 | Browning George 106 | Jerrett 91 |
| Mary 57 | Mary 73 | Martha 106 | Jesse 91 |
| Rosina 57 | Robert 73 | Mary 106 | Mary 91 |
| Sarah 61 | Samuel 73,Thos.73 | Milcah 106 | Renis 91 |
| Bresheares Benj.23 | Walter 73 | Thomas 106 | Sarah 91 |
| Waymark 25 | Brooke Mary 124 | William 106 | William 91 |
| Zadock 24 | William 124 | Brubly Joseph 77 | Buley _ 160 |
| Breshears Nathan 26 | Brookes Eliz.10 | Bruce Ann 94 | Stephen 46 |
| Breshearse Chas.29 | Brooks Amelia 70 | John 94 | Bulgar Daniel 69 |
| Dowel 24 | Ann 119 | Robert 94 | Bulger Margaret 128 |
| Wilkinson 29 | George 69 | Brucebanks Abraham 106 | Richard 128 |
| Brett Damina 33 | Joseph 69 | Ann 102,106 | Burch Anna 134 |
| Brewer Eleanor 11 | Mary 70 | Bennett 106 | Benjamin 106 |
| Henry 11 | Thomas 69 | Blanch 106 | Eliz.134 |
| Joseph 11 | Brotan Eliz.70 | Edward 102,105 | Holford 77 |
| William 11 | Brote Eliz.57 | Francis 102 | John 106 |
| Breyner Lawrence 55 | Henry 56 | Isabella 105 | Jonathan 134 |
| Brice Alice 87 | Broth Rich.93 | Jackson 106 | Oliver 122 |
| Barnett 87 | Browhon Patrick 38 | Jane 102,106 | Verlinda 122 |
| James 87 | Brown Abirilah 100 | Mary 106 | Zepheniah 163 |
| Bride Henry 32 | Amelia 107 | Susanna 105 | Burchfield Adam 101 |
| Bridges Danl.154 | Ann 92,99, 126 | William 102 | Frances 101 |
| William 155 | Aquila 148 | Bruer Eliz.113 | Hannah 101 |
| Brierwood John 52 | Benjamin 126 | Jacob 113 | Prisilla 101 |
| Brigg Mary 70 | Edward 138,148 | James 113 | Burge Alise 51 |
| Brigges Rich.74 | Elianor 122 | John 113 | Burger Catharina 56 |
| Briggs Ann 78 | Elijah 51 | Marah 113 | Burgess Benj.10 |
| Catron 78 | Eliz.99,100,107, | Sarah 113 | Eliz 62 |
| Mary 78 | 110, 122 | William 113 | Fanny 62 |
| William 78 | Freeborn 112 | Bruffit Garner 51 | Francis 55 |
| Bright Ann 148 | George 38, 108 | Brughin Eliz.61 | John 3 |
|  |  |  | Martha 136 |

Burgess Mary A.62
Richard 8
Sarah 10
William 156
Burk David 141
James 149
John 79
Mary 47
Burks Jane 32
Burless Saml.32
Burn Adam 84
Sary 84
William 84
Burne John 32
Burnes Simon 32
Burningham Chris.32
Burns Ann 93
George 93
Mary 100
Mathew 100
Burque Eliz.129
Ezekiel 129
Burrell Thos.141
Burris Rich.90
Burten Jane 117
Mary 117
Burtler And.80
Eliz.80
Ellennder 80
Susanna 80
Bushan Mary 121
Robert 121
Bushanall Jeremiah 141
Busheard Jonathan 17
Bushoope Robart 36
Bushope Wm. 36
Buskhad Francis 14
John 14,15,22
Matthew 15
Nehemiah 14
Samuel 14
Seaborn 14
Thomas H.14
Bustles John 141
Butler Eleanor 9
James 23
Margret 112
Thomas 141
William 89
Button Mrs.32
William 52
Bryan Anna 136,137
Diana 136
George 136
Philip 63

Bryan Rachel 120
Thomas 137
William 136
Byrn Catherine 81
Charles 80
Clementena 81
Martha Ann 81
Mary 81,141
Matthias 81
Patrick 81
Verlinder 81
Brynham Margarett 32
Bryon Mary 90
Byron Lambreth 52

Cadigin James 93
Mary 93
Sarah 93
Cadle Benj.6
James 6
Samuel 6
Cahill John 34
William 34
Cain Eli 149
Caine Daniel 149
Edward 100
Cash Calan 72
Caldwell Jane 62
Lorey 62
Mary 56
Calicoe Eliz 128
Ignatius 128
Calihon Daniel 91
Callaghan Danl.54
Callaghane B.151
Charles 151
Callahan Ann 160
Mary 104
Callender Ann 94
Jane 94
Robert 48,94
Thomas 94
William 38,94
Callihan Mical 101
Callihorn __160
Elianor 135
John 135
Calling James 128
Sarah 128
Callister Athilda 48
Ezekiel M. 48
Jeremiah M. 48
Cambell Ann 101
Camblo Danl.74
Cammel Gollings 69

Cammel John 69
Martha 70
Zacharas 38
Cammell Ann 70
Judah 32
Cammeron John 110
Campbell Ann 82
Benjamin 54
Catherine 103
Daniel 103
Elizabeth 129
Eneas 82
Hester 82
James 122,129
Jeremiah 103
Lidia 82
Margrate 82
Margarethe 62
Mary 56
Patrick 93
Camp George 94
Camper Thos.155
William 154
Campton Richard 114
Canady Ann 66,130
Judea 66
Timothy 130
Cane Sarah 38
Canfield Ann 99
Cannabal Michael 110
Cannon Bettey 45
Elizabeth 45
James 45
Sarah 104
Susannah 45
William 45
Cantor Isaac 38
Canter Sarah 38
Canting Eliz.91
Mary 91
Patrick 91
Thomas 91
Cantler Casander 113
Elisabeth 113
Ellabeller 113
Mary 113
William 113
Cardeff Ann 159
Robert 155
Cardon Danl.M.54
Cared Walter 28
Carleton Joseph 130
Carlile John 107
Margaret 107
Carman John 43

Carmichael Walter 141
William 141
Carmon William 142
Carnes Aray 66
Arthur 63
Margaret 120
William 63
Carns Henrietta 133
Mary 120
Peter.133
Richard 120
Carol James 93
Mary 93
William 93
Carr Ann 126
Benjamin 18,31
John 25,28
Overton 126
Walter 26
Carrel John 109,156
Carrill Grace 33
Carrol Denny 154
Eliz.94,131
James 154
Joseph 128
Keziah 128
Carroll Danl. 75
Ellr.Mrs. 75
Elizabeth 75
John 75
Mary 75,121
Carsey Ann 82
Daniel 82
Ealce 82
Eales 82
Elisabeth 82
Sary 82
Carson Mary 142
Robert 141
Carsons John 22, 30
Carter Arthur 149
Pegey 75
Richard 149
Sarah 7
William 69
Carthew Edmond 72
Cartie Samuel 107
Cartwright Barbary 83
John 83
Samuel 80
Thomas 83
Carty Ann 103
Hannah 103
Marget 100
Susanna & Wm. 103

| | | | |
|---|---|---|---|
| Carvill Alex.8 | Cecil Eliz.128 | Chauncey Sarah 101 | Christie Gabriel 106 |
| William 8 | James 128 | Susan 99 | Christman Eliz.61 |
| Carwan Thomas 47 | Celly Mary 99 | William 101 | Magdalena 57 |
| Cary Michael 55 | Volintine 99 | Chavies Thos.141 | Paul 55 |
| William 137 | Cemp Joseph 22 | Cheavis John 160 | William 58 |
| Case Charles 128 | Quinton 22 | Cheney Joseph 12 | Chue Daniel 69 |
| Elizabeth 79 | Certain Wm. 141 | Martha 128 | Church Abraham 38 |
| Hester 80 | Chafinch John 35 | Samuel 12,128 | Jonathan 128,133 |
| Israel 78 | Chaice Frederick 47 | Zachariah 5 | Sarah 133 |
| Jean 79 | Chamberlain Clem.132 | Chens Ann 123 | Churnman John 106 |
| John 78 | Mary 132 | Richard 123 | Cicil Anne 74 |
| Margaret 78 | Chamberland Chas.32 | Cheshire John 52,63 | Elinor 74 |
| Martha 128 | Chambers Ann 8 | Mary 52 | James 74 |
| Casey James 76 | Philip 9 | Sarah 66 | Jemima 74 |
| John 118 | Richard 147 | Chesney Mary 110 | John 74 |
| Cash Caleb 73 | William 103 | Richard 110 | Mary 74 |
| Dawson 73 C.72 | Champain Hugh 8 | William 110 | Samuel 74 |
| Elenor 73 | Chandley Fran.104 | Cheston Joseph 32 | Sabret 74 |
| Mary 73 | James 115 | Chew Cassandra 70 | Thomas 74 |
| Rachel 73 | Susannah 115 | John 16,22 | William 74 |
| Ruth 73 | William 104 | Nathaniel 22 | Ciseel Mary 124 |
| Caslick Edw,157 | Chanee Aron 33 | Richard 24,96 | Philip 124 |
| Casner Christian 70 | Chanell Eleey 34 | Samuel 14 | Cisell Mary 134 |
| Michael 69 | Elianor 123 | Thomas 95 | Thomas 134 |
| Cassell Henry 125 | Chaney Hezekiah 123 | Cheyney Benj.17 | Cissell Eliz.124 |
| Mary Ann 125 | Chaniee Rich.36 | Charles 17 | John 124 |
| Cassey Mary 103 | Chappell James 110 | Joyce 137 | Susanna 124 |
| Cassill John 135 | Mary 110 | Sarah 137 | William 124 |
| Rebecca 135 | Chaplain John 4 | Thomas 15 | Clagett Ann 66 |
| Caster Eliz.66 | Chaplen Mary 56 | Chezum Daniel 152 | Elizabeth 66 |
| Margret 66 | Chaplin Ann 56 | Childs Henry 20 | Harriet 134 |
| Mary 66 | Moses 54 | Jemima 24 | Hector 118 |
| Thomas 64 | Chapman 156,159 | Samuel 20 | Horatio 118 |
| Vincent 64 | John 118 | William 20,24 | John 63,64 |
| William 64 | Sarah 118 | Chiliten Wm.85 | Judson M. 118 |
| Castiedine Alice 106 | William 95 | Chilrood John 35 | Martha 66 |
| John 106 | Chapple Geo.64 | Chilton Ann 83 | Mary 118,134 |
| Mary 106 | Henry 64 | James 83 | Nathan 63 |
| Sarah 106 | John 64,151 | Jesse 83 | Ninian 63 |
| Caterine England 93 | Rebecca 66 | John 83 | Rich.Keene 63 |
| Cato Christian 125 | Sarah 66 | Mark 81 | Richard 134 |
| William 125 | Thomas 64 | Mary 82 | Sarah 66 |
| Caton Eleanor 137 | Uphane 66 | Sary 83 | Thomas 63,118 |
| Stephen 137 | Virlinda 66 | China Richard 105 | Walter 64 |
| Catter Edward 105 | William 64 | Thomas 105 | William 134 |
| Cattle John 32 | Charles George 55 | Chips Jacob 58 | Zadock 64 |
| Caulty John 154 | Chatham Eliz.141 | John 21 | Claridge Eliz.51 |
| Caultz James 152 | Chauncey Benj.98 | Margret 58 | Clarion Mary 70 |
| Cavender David 50 | Cathrin 99 | Chisholm Thos.108 | Clark Baless 74 |
| Thomas 50 | Elizabeth 99 | John 108 | Benedict 64 |
| Cavillare Chas.141 | George 98,101 | Chitton Thos.83 | Elizabeth 66 |
| Cavinder Nath 142 | John 100 | Saffiah 83 | George 64 |
| Cawill John 8 | Margret 98 | Choislin Thos.108 | Grace 66 |
| Caywood Benj.134 | Martha 101 | Chrisp John 156 | Hannah 66 |
| Elianor 134 | Mary 99,101 | Christian John 101 | Harmon 64 |

Clark Hennerietta 74
Henry 74
James 38,54
Jane 57,62,121
John 66,104,118
Johnson 74
Justson 74
Leonard 64
Lesson 74
Margretha 62
Mary 66
Nancy 74
Nester 79
Patrick 100
Rebecca 66
Richard 151
Robert 48
Samuel 60
Sarah 30
Seven 74
Thomas 64
Thomson 74
Walter 74
William 74
Clarke Eliz 108
John 29,112
Clarkinson Joseph 47
Clarks Richard 32
Clarkson Edw.119
Elizabeth 135
Harry 119
Joseph 137,138
Martha 119
Sarah 119,125
Thomas 125,135
Clarvoe John 119
Henry 119
Mary 119
William 119
Clasby Thomas 55
Claxen Notley 132
Violetta 132
Clayland John 160
Clearwaters Eliz.76
Lettes 76
Silvester 76
Cleckett Ninian 79
Clements Christ.91
Clemmer Francis 36
Cievley Henry 69
Closson Peter 110
Clowes Cathron 111
Elisabeth 111
George 111

Clowes Gorg 111
John 111
Club Keziah 137
Samuel 137
Clubb Mary 124, 134
Mathew 124
Samuel 134
Cole Eliz. 109
Ephram 109
Ezecal 109
James 109
Jane 109
John 16, 109
Samilia 109
Sofiah 109
Sophia 109
Thomas 109
Coale Ann 95
Cassandria 95
Elizabeth 95
Frances 95
Isaac 95
Margrett 95
Philip 95
Richard 95
Samuel 95
Samuel 95
Sarah 95
Skipwith 95
Susannah 95
William 95
Coap John 38
Jonathan 38
Joseph 38
Mary 38
Coarts Chas. 77
James 77
Notley 77
Coborn 159
Ann 157
Anney 158
Cocendofer Christ. 63
Hannah 66
John 63
Mary 66
Michael 63
Cocklin Thomas 50
Codonia Peter 100
Coe Mary 139
Phebe 139
Samuel 139
Coger Samuel 148
Cohee John 142
Cohon Peter 38

Cokendofer Fred.69
Colbo John 74
Colbrock Harriott 70
Cole Barnett 79
Diannah 46
Jonathon 92
Joseph 124
Rachel 46,124
Susannah 79
Tunons 79
William 79
Coleman Chas.9
Darias 142
John 91
Margaret 91
Michael 107
Rose 91
William 142
Collage Rich.14
Collard Agnes 133
Samuel 133
Collener John 160
Collens Eliz.71
Griffith 23
John 71
Mary 71
Sarah 71,94
Colierage Wm. 114
Colleson Geo. 155
Colliar Eliz.78
James 76
Jean 76
John 76
Rachel 76
Thomas 147
William 76
Collilis Robt.35
Collings Cassandra 66
Elizabeth 66
Hezekiah 69
James 64
John 64,75
Jemima 66
Joshua 64
Mary 66
Nathan 64
Rachel 66
Sarah 1
Thomas 64
Zechariah 64
Collins Ann 103,130
Cassandra 102
Catherine 104
Edward 103

Collins Elisha 103
Elizabeth 103
Francis 103,107
Hannah 103
Isabeela 107
Jacob 102
Jimimah 93
John 107,103
John P.107
Mary 102,103
Moses 102
Patience 102
Robert 93
Susanna 102
William 103,130
Collop George 83
Colloson Edw.22
Collwell Martin 156
Colman Roger 141
Colslon James 159
Colson John 53
Colston Casandria 94
Henry 158
John 159
Colter Doctor 32
Colvin William 141
Colyar Ann 66
Elizabeth 66
James 63
John 63
Keziah 66
Lucy 66
Sarah 66
William 63
Condon James 157
John 75
William 157
Coner William 54
Conley Thomas 69
Conn Elizabeth 123
George 121
James 128
Jane 122
Joseph 123
Mary 72,106
Rachell 133
Ruth 128
Sarah 121
William 122,133
Connaly Jane 95
Conally Sarah 104
Connar Jane 102
Connaway Dennis 150
Connely William 35

| | | | |
|---|---|---|---|
| Connelly Jesa 35 | Cooper Owin 33 | Cortny Semelia 108 | Crafford Bazell 124 |
| Conner Eleanor 70 | William 100,160 | Thomas 108 | Elizabeth 123 |
| Frances 84 | Coppper John 50 | Cossey Margaret 131 | James 122 |
| James 32 | Coox Thomas 33 | William 131 | Margaret 124 |
| John 69, 162 | Comberford Mary 156 | Cossin Asel 141 | Mary 122 |
| Mary 84 | Combest Aquila 102 | Costin James 151 | Craford John 111 |
| Paul 69 | Cassandra 104 | Henry 151 | Craft Aleas 39 |
| Richard 84 | Charity 102 | Cotagrave John 95 | Chas. 38,39 |
| Sech 141 | Elizabeth 102 | Cotten John 112 | Elisabeth 57 |
| Connerly Thomas 32 | Francis 104 | Cothlon Hannah 116 | Frederick 55, 58 |
| Connerway Dennis 53 | Israel 102 | John 116 | Jonathan 39 |
| Connicken Jane 107 | Jacob 102,104 | Mary 116 | Sarah 39 |
| Connier Mary 32 | John 102 | Coulson Mary 100 | Crage John 113 |
| Connoly Joseph 92 | Martha 102 | Countiee ___ 160 | Cragg John 13 |
| Connor Cattrine 82 | Mary 102,104 | Counton Mary 35 | Craig Adam 133 |
| Connoway John 5 | Sarah 104 | Coursey Thomas 142 | Ann 133 |
| Conrad Catharine 56 | Susanna 102 | Covey John 51 | Cramphin Eliz.133 |
| William 54 | Thomas 102 | Cowan Eliz.110 | Jeane 66 |
| Conry Margaret 96 | Utice 102 | Thomas 64 | Precilla 134 |
| Conwell Arthur 64 | Comegys John 141 | Coward John 43 | Thomas 134 |
| Cope Sarah 45 | Sarah 141 | Cowen Edward 116 | Cranford Benj.26 |
| Copeland Geo. 101 | Comer Wm. 142 | John 106 | Crandel Addam 26 |
| Frances 101 | Comton John B.33 | Judy 116 | George 23 |
| John 101 | Corbert Isaac 141 | Mark 106 | Joseph 26 |
| Mary 101 | Corbet Margaret 104 | Mary 106,116 | Thomas 26,28 |
| Coppage Philemon 141 | Cord Aquila 98,102 | Rachel 116 | William 25,28 |
| Copper Gustavis 52 | Amos 102 | Sarah 106 | Craton Thomas 32 |
| Cooben William 37 | Ashberry 101,106 | Stephen 116 | Crawford Alex.133 |
| Cook Cassandria 94 | Elisabeth 115 | Susannah 116 | Bazell 133 |
| Daniel 94 | Greenberry 102 | Thomas 116 | Elizabeth 133 |
| Easter 94 | Hannah 102 | William 116 | Hannah 95 |
| Edward 123 | Jacob 115 | Cowin Isabella 109 | James 95 |
| Elesabeth 38 | John 59 | Cowing Ann 110 | John 95 |
| Eliner 49 | Mary 106 | Cowley Eliz.106 | Mary 133 |
| Grace 94 | Neomie 115 | James 24 | Mordecai 95 |
| James 94 | Roger 109 | Sarah 31,106 | Ruth 95 |
| John 51, 94 | Sarah 102 | Thomas 26 | Susannah 95 |
| Joseph 123 | Susanna 102,115 | Cowman John 2 | Thomas 133 |
| Mary 48 | Corker Owen 87 | Joseph 9 | Crecraft John 124 |
| Martha 123 | Patrick 107 | Cox Abraham 118 | Mary 124 |
| Precilla 123 | Corkrey Wm. 55 | Charles 105 | Creggett Jemima 32 |
| Robert 94 | Cormoway Eliz.99 | Elisabeth 120 | Creily Catherina 56 |
| Sarah 94, 131 | Michael 99 | Israel 109 | Elisabeth 58 |
| Thomas 36 | Corner Adam 157 | Jesse 118 | Francis 54 |
| William 33 | Elizabeth 70 | John 115,142 | Herman 54 |
| Zeabulon 48 | Febe 70 | Joseph 38 | John 66 |
| Cooke William 73 | Margaret 70 | Mary 114,115,118,109 | Magdalina 62 |
| Coolley John 108 | Mary 70 | Nathaniel 53 | Crellin James 77 |
| Coomes Joseph 131 | Susanna 70 | Rachel 109,114 | Crick Elizabeth 149 |
| Con John 113 | Cornesh Rebec 156 | Rhoda 150 | Crime Adam 58 |
| Coonet Prudence 133 | Cornish John 53 | Sarah 115 | Catharina 56 |
| Cooney Laughron 90 | Cortny Hollas 108 | William 109,114 | Mary 58 |
| Cooper Benj. 133,150 | John 108 | Zachariah 118 | Michael 60 |
| John 36, 155 | Jonas 108 | Crabb Jeremiah 6 | Crips Edward 83 |
| Mark 36 | Sarah 108 | Crafford Adam 123 | Mary 83 |

Cromwell James 103
  Joseph 94
  Susannah 94
  Vinisha 94
Croney James 151
  Litt 150
Crooks Andrew 87
  Eliz Kerby 87
  Henry 87
  Jane 87
  Margrett 87
  William 87
Croscil 112
Cross Robert 2
Crow James 127
  Mary 127
Crown Arter 72
  Catharin 72
  Elisha 121
  Eliz 121,66,72
  Henry 99
  Joseph 72
  Josiah 64
  Lancelot 64
  Mary 66
  Sarah 72
  Thomas 72
Crues Mary 112
  Nicollous 112
Cruit Cassandra 102
  Francis 104
  John 102
  Nathan 102
Crumback July 56
Crummel Neger O. 112
Crusan Eliz 112
  Garret 112
  John 112
  Mary 112
  Michael 112
Cruse Catharine 114
  Elizabeth 114
  Richard 114
Crutchley Joseph 21
  Richard 30
Crytzer Christ 58
Cryer John 156
Culber Levy 117
Cullin James 55
Cullins Isaac 51
Cullon David 23
Culver Ann 108
  Ben 108,112
  Johannah 112

Culver Mary 112
  Robert 112
Cummings Eliz 153
  Mary 152
  Thomas 153
Cummins Andrew 117
  Benjamin 117
  Casandra 117
  Hannah 108
  James 50,108
  John 117
  Paul 108
  Phillip 117
  Samuel 108,117
  Sarah 117
Cumphen Bearlander 72
  James 72
  William 72
Cunningham John I.T. 87
  Thomas 142
Currenton John 78
Currey William 34
Curry Brian 99
  John 17
Vionah 100
Curswell Esabeellah 111
  James 111
  Mary 111
  Robert 111
  William 111
Curtain Catherine 118
Curtin James 32
  John 81
Cussans John 117
Cuthbert Wm. 91
Cutler Jacob 31

Dacon Francis 99
  Mary 99
Daffin Chas 153
  Joseph 39,53
Dailey James 142
  John 142
Daley Eliz 70
  John 69
Dallam Eliz. 95
  Frances 95
  John 95
  Josias W. 105
  Magrett 95
  Richard 95
  Samuel 95
  Sarah 105
  Winston 95

Dalley John 107
  Mary 107
Dally Jeremiah 107
Daniel John 39
Dansichlor Eliz. 101
Darbay Asa 77
Darbey John 50
Dare Ann 27
Darnal Isaac 131
  Susanna 131
Darnell Benj 25
  Henry 19
  Phillip 19
  Richard 19
Darnold Cornelas 79
  Ezekil 79
  Hennary 79
  John 79
  Marion 79
  Prissillar 79
  Rebeca 79
  Rubin 79
  Thomas 79
  William 79
Darton Margret 57
Daruse Abraham 55,59
  Cathrin 62
  Elisabeth 57
  John 59
Datford Sarah 133
  William 133
Dave Charles 69
Daverson Agnis 114
  Daniel 114
  Elisabeth 114
  John 114
  Sarah 114
David Reed 115
Davidge Eliz. 151
Davidson Eliz. 125
  James 8
  John 125
  Thomas 47
Davies Jane 122
  John 122
  Mary 126,136
  Robert 126
Davis 156
  Ann 84
  Anna 82
  Aza 84
  Azariah 84
  Bexly 77
  Cassandra 84

Davis Catherine 56
  Cresey 84
  Daniel 3
  Darkis 82
  Efrom 82
  Eliz 62,77
  Hennary 84
  Isaac 92
  James 47
  Jane 92
  Jaramiah 82
  Jean 156
  John 75,142,149,151
  Joseph 77,82
  Levisa 84
  Margrit 49
  Mary 82,100
  Maryan 77
  Moses 84
  Nansey 82
  Nathaniel 151
  Poly Carp 77
  Rachael 96
  Robert Pain 11
  Rohdom 84
  Samuel 91,84
  Susanna 84
  Thomas 151
  William 2,32,80,
    84,153
Daubt Margrett 87
  Robert 87
  Roger 87
  Samuel 87
Daugherty Geo 106
  John 106
  Margaret 106
  Mary Ann 106
  Samuel 106
  William 106
Dawney Eliz. 57
  James 55
  Rosina 57
  Samuel 55
Dawson Ann 135
  George 153
  Hugh 154
  Impey 154
  Jacob 32
  James 159
  John 50,53,158
  Joseph 53
  Margaret 155
  Mary 140
  Daws Elisha 97

| | | | |
|---|---|---|---|
| Dawson Ralph 155 | Deibelbeis Mich 55, 60 | Dick Robert 121 | Dilles Wm. 55 |
| Robert 154 | Cathrin 62 | Dickerson Brit. 32 | Dilling Cath. 116 |
| Sarah 107, 155 | John 60 | William 133 | Edward 117 |
| Thomas 140, 142 | Deibely Ann 57 | Dickinson John 51 | Gorge 117 |
| William 53, 155 | Deibley Cath. 61 | Dickson Ellenner 82 | Hannah 117 |
| Day Ann 136, 140 | Frederick 59 | Hannah 82 | John 117 |
| Bazel 72 | George 59 | John 34 | Larrance 116 |
| Elizabeth 73 | Jacob 55 | John 82 | Marther 117 |
| Ezekel 72 | Margret 61 | Mary 82 | Robert 117 |
| Katherine 66 | Delany Ann 103 | Obadiah 36 | Dillion John 35 |
| John 64 | Elizabeth 103 | Ruth 82 | Dimbleton Jane 61 |
| Joshua 93 | Isaac 103 | Sarah 73 | Dingle John 53 |
| Lenerd 72 | John 103 | Susannah 73,82 | Dinney Oliver 103 |
| Mary 67 | Joshua 103 | William 82 | Disney James 2,8 |
| Mathew 136, 140 | Mary 103 | Zachariah 82 | William 8 |
| Samuel 72 | Sarah 103 | Diction Drusilla 98 | Ditty Thomas 23 |
| Sarah 67, 72 | Delihay James 47 | Frances 98 | Dixon Ann 70 |
| Susanah 72 | Delozier Edw. & Ann 129 | Hannah 98 | Benj 36 |
| Tobitha 72 | Dement George 118 | Johannah 101 | James 75,77,142 |
| Deacon Wm. 107 | Demster 142 | John 98 | John 156 |
| Deakins Eliz. 120 | John 142 | Marget 101 | Richard 75 |
| William 120 | Rachel 142 | Morris 98 | Robert 37 |
| Deal James 90 | Dene Christopher 142 | Peter 101 | Sarah 75 |
| John 17, 28 | Denike Samuel 46 | Sarah 98,101 | Simon 69 |
| Mary 90 | Dennair Mary 80 | Susan 98 | William 69 |
| Richard 18 | William 80 | William 101 | Dixson Isaac 159 |
| Thomas 27 | Denney James E.159 | Dibelbies Marg 57 | William 157 |
| William 28, 90 | John 51 | Diemer Johanna 100 | Doalman Thos. 105 |
| Dean John, Capt. 142 | Mary 158 | John 100 | Dodd George 150 |
| Uriah 46 | Dennis Ignatius 136 | Rachel 100,101 | James 150 |
| Deane Bettey 46 | Lucrecia 136 | Dietz Cath.56 | John 150 |
| Henry 45 | Dennison James 104 | Ernst 54 | Mark 150 |
| James 45 | Denny Joseph 154 | John 59 | Thomas 151 |
| Richard 46 | Peter 149 | Digges Cath.129 | Dodo Joseph 142 |
| Death Geo. S. 111 | Dent Ann 118 | Wm. 125, 129 | Dodson Geo. 50 |
| James 111 | Cloe 118 | Dignum Lucy 75 | Thomas 22,152 |
| Deaver Ann 109 | Elizabeth 118 | Dile Adam 54 | Doleman Sarah 113 |
| Aquillar 117 | George 48,118 | Doruse 60 | Dolvin Daniel 151 |
| David 109, 116 | Jane 118 | Elisabeth 63 | Domer Ann 56 |
| Hannah 102 | Mary 118 | Fronica 57 | Frederick 60 |
| James 109, 101 | Richard 118 | George 55, 60 | Michael 54, 60 |
| John 101 | Thos.118,140 | Henry 60 | Donaldson Moses 12 |
| Martha 102 | Walter 118 | John 60 | Donboch Caitron 69 |
| Mary 109 | Denton James 80 | Margaretha 62 | Drusilla 70 |
| Micajah 102 | Deochurume Lues 147 | Mary 56 | Elizabeth 70 |
| Rebeccah 109 | Dermott Cath 89 | Peter 60 | Frederick 69 |
| Samuel 116 | James 89 | Dillehay Wm. 37 | Mary 70 |
| Sarah 102 | Mary 89 | Dilles Dorethea 61 | Michael 69 |
| Sahar 116 | Deudney Aleas 39 | Catharine 57 | Donelley Elisabeth 56 |
| Thomas 99 | Deven Hugh 111 | Elisabeth 61 | Donn John 105 |
| Deavinish Eliz. 142 | Mary 111 | John 55, 59 | Donohue Daniel 116 |
| Deavour Mary 110 | Devenpoto Wm.16 | Magdalena 61 | Margret 114 |
| Deen Charles 39 | Devur Derby 94 | Margret 57 | Donovan Anos 108 |
| Henry 39 | Dick James 13 | Mary 61 | Rachel 108 |
| Deford James 142 | Mason 121 | Sophia 1 | William 103 |
| William 142 | | | |

| | | | |
|---|---|---|---|
| Donnovan Danl. 112 | Dowel Phillip 78 | Drascel Eliz. 57 | Dugless Danl. 93 |
| Elisabeth 112 | Prissiller 78 | Draxeixel Mag. 61 | Lindy 93 |
| Ephram 112 | William 159 | Draxel Abraham 58 | Sarah 93 |
| Hanah 112 | Dowell Eliz. 76 | Daniel 58 | Duglis Joseph 59 |
| Jacob 112 | John 76 | Peter 58 | Samuel 59 |
| John 112 | Mary 76 | Draxser Cath. 61 | Duis Francis 64 |
| Joseph 112 | Peter 76 | Drew Ann 99 | Duke Thomas 100 |
| Martha 112 | Richard 16 | Anthony 98,99 | Duklis William 58 |
| Thomas 112 | William 76 | George 99 | Dulany Bridgett 73 |
| Dooley Mary 90 | Dowling Joseph 156 | Henry 98 | Duley Ann 122 |
| Samuel 106 | William 156 | James 98 | Margaret 66 |
| Door John 25 | Downden Michel 80 | Letitisha 95 | William 122 |
| Doose Ann 57 | Downes Ann 129 | Mary 98 | Duly Henry 122 |
| Christian 58 | H. 150 | Mr. 32 | Mary 122 |
| Dorbey Mitchell 106 | Hynson 150 | Phillip 98 | Thomas 64 |
| Dority John 27 | Jonathan 149 | Rebecca 99 | Dunbarr Mrs. 32 |
| Dorley John 47 | Levin 151 | Sarah 98 | Duncan Thomas 87 |
| Dorroty Ezekel 39 | Downey Joseph 55 | Driskin Ann 91 | William 87 |
| Dorter Jonathan 159 | Patrick 142 | Mary 91 | Duncastle Sarah 70 |
| Dorsey Benedict 104 | Tabitha 142 | Driver Christ. 36 | Dunken James 54 |
| Eassard 104 | Thomas 142 | Edward 83 | Dunkin Robert 142 |
| Elizabeth 131 | Valentine 142 | Martin 52 | Dunley Mary 66 |
| Frances 104 | William 55,148 | Mathew 36 | Dunn George 55 |
| Frisby 104 | Downing Francis 87 | Drown Gran. 133 | John 130,159 |
| Greenberry 104 | Henry 126 | Thomas 133 | Mary 130 |
| John 104,131 | James 128 | Druce Eleanor 4 | Susanna 57 |
| Mary 104,105 | Jemimah 122 | Druiry William 25 | Thomas 101 |
| Milcah 104 | John 87 | Drury Charles 25 | Durben Thomas 109,113 |
| Sally F. 104 | Joseph 122 | Mary 25 | Durbin Amos 116 |
| Sophia 104 | Michael 64 | Ducker Cassandra 6 | Ann 116 |
| Dougal Ann 130 | Molley 87 | Duckett Ann 66 | Avariller 108,117 |
| Thomas 130 | Puck 87 | Samuel 64 | Cassandra 105 |
| Doughoty John 158 | Rebecca 87 | Dudley Abner 142 | Daniel 105 |
| Douglass Ann 67 | Ruth 87 | Dudney Mary 39 | Delila 108 |
| John 64 | Samuel 87 | Dudweiler Henry 54,60 | Elisabeth 116 |
| Robert 64 | Sarah 126,128 | Mary 56 | Francis 116 |
| Dove John 21 | Susanna 87 | Duglace Ann 85 | John 105 |
| Martha 136 | William 87 | Charles 85 | Mary 105,116 |
| Samuel 136 | Downs Benj. 131 | Elisabeth 85 | Rebecca 105 |
| William 17 | Dennis 91 | George 82 | Sarah 105 |
| Dowden Archabald 77 | Henry 131 | Heza 85 | Durell Larrence 35 |
| Elisabeth 80 | Mary 131 | John 85 | Durham Alizanah 90 |
| Jean 75 | Winefred 131 | Rebeca 85 | Aquila 93,94 |
| John 75,77 | Doxse Elenor 74 | Mary 85 | Ann 93 |
| Jonnas 77 | Martha 74 | Samuel 82,85 | Benjamin 90 |
| Martha 77 | Dr ne Sarah 44 | Sue 82 | Cleminey 90 |
| Mary 75 | Draocel George 55 | William 82 | Daniel 90 |
| Michael A. 75 | Draper Ann 85 | Dugless Wm. 33, 142 | Elinor 93,94 |
| Richard 77 | Elisabeth 85 | Dugles John 55 | Elizabeth 90 |
| Sary 77 | Ellener 85 | Martha 61 | Hannah 90,94 |
| Thomas 75,77 | John 85,101 | Mary 61 | James 94 |
| Dowel Allay 78 | Nemiah 35 | Rachel 57,61 | John 90 |
| Bachelder 78 | Samuel 33 | Robert 55,59 | Joshua 90 |
| Elisabeth 78 | William 34,81 | Samuel 55 | Lee 93 |
| John 21 | Drapir Gudall 33 | Dugless Bennet 93 | Loyd 93 |

Durham Mary 93
Mordicai 94
Pricilla 90
Samuel 32,93
Sarah 90
Susanah 93
Thomas 93
Durkins Ann 157
Dusiner Philip 55
Dusinger Cath.61
  Ann 57
Dutton Ann 93
Duvall Alice 127
  Ann 118
  Benj.118,128
  Elianor 134
  Ephraim 10
  John 128
  Lewis 127
  Mary 128
  Moreen 118
  Nancy 119
  Sarah 128
  Thomas 128
  William 134
  Zachariah 13
Duzan Abraham 102
  Alexander 107
  Ezekiah 102, Eliz.102
  Ezekial 102
  John 102
  Nathaniel 102
  Peter 102
  Rachael 102
  William 102
Dwericks Valentine 142
Dwiging Robert 160
Dyar Ann 136, 139
  Anna 134
  Clem. 134
  Henrietta 137
  Henry 136
  Susanna 139
  Thomas 139
Dyer Jonathan 77
  Peter 142
Dyson Aquila 79
  Anna 75
  Barton 75
  Basil 85
  Bennett 79
  Darkes 79
  Dorraty 79
  George 85
  Jamima 85

Dyson Jean 79
  John 79
  Lydia 79
  Margaret 85
  Martha 75
  Mary 79
  Mash 78
  Matdox 79
  Philip 78
  Rebeca 78
  Samuel 79
  Sary 79
  Thomas 79
  William 75
  Zaphaniah 79

Eales Eliz.122
  Thomas 122
Eagle James 99
Eareckson James 142
Earle Richard 149
Earley Benj.64
  Elizabeth 67
  Rachel 67
Early Sarah 67
Earp Caleb 69
Earvin Emmillis 36
Easterley Eliz.32
Easton William 23
Eaton John 158
  Richard 158
Eavins Jonathan 142
Eber Joseph 58
Ebrey Mary 56
Eccleston Hugh 51
  Thomas F. 52
Eddings John 18
Edelen Ann 85
  Bartholomew 85
  Catherine 118,137
  Charles 137
  Christ.136,139
  Edward 118
  Elizabeth 139
  James 118
  Jane 125
  John 125
  Joseph 118
  Margarett 118
  Mary 134,136
  Monica 85
  Philip 134
  Precilla 126
  Richard 130,136
  Salome 118

Edelen Saml.118
  Sarah 118,130
  Susanna 135
  Thomas 126,135
Edelin Thomas 85
Eden Benj.100
  Elizabeth 100
  Jeremiah 100
  Mary 100
  Sarah 100
  William 100
Edgar Adam 153
  James 46
  John 46
  Mary 46
  William 46
Edleton Elinor 93
Edmonston Dorety 127
  Ninian 127
Edmonstone James 129
  Ruth 129
Edwards Ann 159
  Edward 5
  James 110
  Joseph 101,110
  Margaret 110,129
  Mary 110
  Thomas 110
Eggate Valentine 142
Eiteneiger John 59
Ekenbergh Eliz.58
  Jacob 59
  John 59
  Margret 61
  Michael 55
Ekenborgh Cath.57
Ekin Delieca 87
  Jane 87
  Jusch 87
  Nelly 87
  Samuel 87
Elaxandrio Robt.33
Elburd Wm. 39
Elder Amelia 67
  Eleanor 67
  Hannah 67
  Hadassy 67
  Johannah 67
  Mary 104
  Sarah 67
  Tressia 67
Elebin Mary 94
Elemont Eliz.74
Elett John 39
Elke Benjamin 60

Elgin Anabella 82
  Ann 82
  Christopher 82
  Cloe 82
  Jesse 82
  John 82
  Mary 82
  William 82
Elles Ann 84
  Charity 84
  Christopher 84
  Elisabeth 84
  John 84
  Mary 84
  Prisila 84
  Rule 84
  Shadrack 84
  William 84
  Zachariah 84
Ellett Ann 80
  Benj.80
  Elisabeth 80
  John 80
  Joseph 80
  Kassa 80
  Kissiar 80
  March 80
  Mark 80
  Marthe 70
  Richard 80
  Thomas 39
Ellgin Mary 81
Elliott James 7
  John 3
  Matthew 1
  Rebeckah 142
  Richard 2
  Robert W. 1
  Ruth 2
  Sarah 6
  Thomas 1,32
Ellis Ann 75
  Anna 76
  Cassandra 76
  Charles 75
  Eleanor 105
  Ellis 95
  Hannah 76
  Henry 32
  James 75
  Margaret 75
  Martha 75
  Mary 76
  Nicolaus 55
  Robert 136

Ellis Solomon 75
  Thomas 76
  Verlinder 75
  Zaphaniah 76
Elson Archibald 128
  Mary 128
Ellson William 64
Ely Hannah 95, 109
  Hugh 95
  Joseph 95
  Malin 95
  Rachael 95
  Ruth 95
  Sarah 95
  Thomas 95
  William 95
Emerson John 129, 151
  Lucy 129
  Richard 150
  Vincent 150
Emery Margareth 56
  John 33
Emory Arthur 147
  Thomas 151
  Will, Capt. 150
Emry Elisabeth 62
  Jones 54
  Magdalena 62
England Cath. 93
Enloes Abraham 32
Ennales Henry 39
Ennalls --- 49
  Andrew S. 53
  Barthow 47, 48
  Elizabeth 52
  Henry 48
  John, Coll. 51
  Joseph 48, 53
  Thomas 48, 52
  William 48
Enness William 14
Ensinger Susannah 96
Essex Elizabeth 82
Eubanks Adam 159
  John 157
  Rebeccah 157
Evants Ann 67
  Benjamin 99
  David 4
  Edmond 89
  Eleanor 67
  Eliz. 102, 120, 131
  Evan 105
  George 64

Evans Hannah 67
  Henry 32
  Henry 97,32
  James 64
  John 64,125
  Margaret 67
  Mary 53,67,125
  Rachel 67
  Robert 32
  Ruth 67
  Samuel 51,64
  Walter 131
  William 102
  Will 150
  Zechariah 64
Evely Ann 57
  Margaret 61
Evens Job 72
  Mary 72,82,157
  Sary 85
  William 30,82
Everest Benj.104
  Cassandra 104
  Charles 104
  Eleanor 104
  Elizabeth 104
  James 104
  John 104
  Joseph 104
  Lydia 104
  Margret 104
  Mary 104
  Richard 104
  Thomas 104
Everett Joseph 34
Evett Margret 109
  Seth Hill 33
  William 109
Evins Henry F. 39
  Mary 39
Evret William 110
Ewart James 133
  Catharine 133
Ewing Alex. 93
  James 93
  Jane 93
  John 93
  Joseph 93
Eyle Frederick 55
Eysom Thomas 162
Fackler Barbara 62
  Catharin 62
  Catharina 56
  Elisabeth 62
  Eve 56
  George 60

Fackler Helfena 56
  Hellina 62
  Jacob 60
  John 54,60
  Magdalena 62
  Margaretha 62
  Michael 54
  Peter 60
  Susanna 62
Fagin John 83
Fairbanks Anna 154
  Daniel 155
  David 154
  Mary 155
  Phillemon 154
Falconer Wm. 142
Faldo Charles 121
Fanning Thomas 84
Farbush Jean 142
Ferguson Bettey 46
  Daniel 80
  Elias 80
  Elisabeth 80
  Ellenner 80
  John 80
  Lucey 32
  Mary 80
  Molley 46
  Mordecai 80
  Nathaniel 82
  Peggey 82
  Prissilla 82
  Reson 80
Farr Alice 133
  Nicholas 133
Farmer John 111
Farrbairn Wm. 69
Farrell Hugh 32
  Ignatius 120
  Thomas 98
Farris Hugh J.12
Faulkner Abram 156
  Gilbert 148
  Isaac 156
  Thomas 156
Faulks John 69
Fawsett Eliz.102
  Frances 102
  Jonathan 102
Fealds George 85
  James 82
  Joseph 82
  Martha 82
  Mathew 82
  Sary 82

Fealds Wm. 82
Fedmon Batt 34
Fedrick Grace 81
  Milkey 81
Feen Patrick 118
Feigely Christ.61
  Dorothy 61
  John 58
  Peter 59
  Rachel 58
Fell William 100
Felphs Sary 77
Feodorus Felmet 55
Fendall John 151
Fennamoe Wm. 84
Fent Peter 107
Fenwick Ignatius 134
Ferguson Basil 82
  Bershiba 133
  Catherine 128
  Collen 50
  Eliz. 10, 121
  James 128
  John 22,133
  William 121
Ferrel Joseph 71
  William 157
Ferrell Edmond 142
Ferrol Daniel 132
  Margaret 67
  Ruth 132
Fesler Catharine 56
  Mary 62
  Michael 54
  Sophia 62
Feved Peter 54
Fiddaman Ann 153
Fie Baltus 103
  John 103
  Mary 103
Field Stephen 131
Fields Eliz.104
  Joseph 104
  Sarah 104
  Susanna 104
  William 104
Filler Andrew 54
  Henry 59
  Magdalane 56
Finch Thomas 128
Finley Samuel 55
Finna Alender 101
Finnix Andrew 149
Fips John 31
  Roger 31

| | | | |
|---|---|---|---|
| Fish Precilla 131 | Flether Sary 82 | Forgerson Saml.111 | Fox Ann 77 |
| Robert 131 | Flint Thomas 64 | Formar William 51 | Rebeccah 90 |
| Fisher Abraham 35, 137 | Flowers Ralph 28 | Forrage Crister 109 | Sarah 90 |
| Amelia 99 | Floyd Joseph 159 | Forrell James 105 | Foxwell Eliz.43 |
| Asil 99 | Foard Elizabeth 125 | Forster ___ 160 | Isaac 51 |
| Barbara 62 | Susanna 120 | Nathan 21 | John 43 |
| David 59 | William 120,125 | Forsyth Robt.32 | Levi 45 |
| Eliz. 56, 95, 137 | Foghler Christ.55 | Fort Dority 109 | Rachel 43 |
| Henry 59 | Elisabeth 57 | Frances 109 | Roger 45 |
| Isabella 95 | Henry 39 | Mary 109 | Foy Michael 32 |
| Jacob 54 | Simon 55 | Nancy 109 | Fraisear Joseph 14 |
| James 95 | Folkner Ann 99 | Peter 109 | William 14 |
| John 39, 59, 95 | Robert 99 | Forward Jacob 106 | Frances Eliz.74 |
| Magdalena 62 | Follen Barnebay 45 | Forwood Constance 99 | Hessa 74 |
| Mary 95 | Daniel 45 | Faithful 99 | Jacob 74 |
| Sarah 95 | Fooss Eliz.154 | Gean 99 | John 133 |
| Susanna 27, 56 | Foot Thomas 54 | Jacob 99 | Joseph 74 |
| Thomas 95, 99 | Ford ___ 104 | Foster Betsey 87 | Lucy 74 |
| William 27, 31, 94, 95, 99 | Alexander 104 | Elesabeth 39 | Franklain Wm.22 |
| | Benjamin 104 | Fedelious 87 | Franlin Ann 83 |
| Fisler Michael 59 | Blanch 107 | John 87 | Barker 83 |
| Fitchgaret Margt. 110 | Charles 160 | Joseph 35 | Benedicter 83 |
| Mary 110 | Daniel 142 | Keatty 87 | Jacob 27 |
| Fitchgarrel Margt. 84 | Elizabeth 107 | Peggey 87 | John 21,28 |
| Fitzgarrell James 103 | George 104 | Phidelis 87 | Joseph 83 |
| Fitsimons Patrick 99 | Hannah 107 | Rebecca 87 | Mary 27 |
| Fitzgarrell Mary 106 | James 107,116 | Founton And.37 | Maryan 83 |
| Thomas 106 | Jean 75 | John 34 | William 83 |
| Fitzgerald Rich. 92 | John 122 | Merey 37 | Zaphaniah 83 |
| Fitzhugh Wm. 24 | Joseph 104 | Samuel 34 | Fraser Danl.135 |
| Fitzjerrel Rebecca 154 | Isaac 142 | Thomas 33,37 | Elizabeth 135 |
| Fitzpatrick Michael 104 | Joseph 28 | William 34 | George 124 |
| Fitzsimmonds Patr. 106 | Joshua 104 | Fouthner Eliz.156 | Hannah 124 |
| Flames John 148 | Marabel 104 | Fowler Margt.32 | Henry 135 |
| Flanagin Eliz. 104 | Mary 104,107 | Fowler Absolom 150 | Verlinda 135 |
| Fleeger Agtious 55 | Olive 116 | Ann 82 | Frasher Andrew 77 |
| Leonhard 58 | Ralph 81 | David 115 | Frasier Eliz.61 |
| Fleetwood Ann 116 | Sarah 104 | Drucilla 126 | Isabella 61 |
| Benjamin 116 | Thomas 107 | Eliz.82,115,126 | Frazeer Wm. 32 |
| Hannah 116 | William 104 | Elisha 64 | Frederick Eliz.67 |
| Fleming David 157 | Fore Cathrin 57,62 | Frances 107 | George 64 |
| Fletchall Ann 77 | Elisabeth 62 | Hennaritter 82 | Margaret 67 |
| Cintha 77 | Felix 59 | Isaac 126 | Mary 67 |
| Elisabeth 77 | Henry 55,59 | Jeremiah 126 | Molley 67 |
| John 77 | Jacob 59 | John 115 | Nicholas 64 |
| Thomas 77 | Michael 55 | Joseph 115 | Uney 67 |
| Fletcher Sarah 72 | Susanna 62 | Martha 107 | Free Catherine 133 |
| Flether Abraham 82 | Foreman Arthur 142 | Mary 67,107 | Charles 122 |
| Betty 82 | John 142 | Patrick 115 | Elianor 122 |
| Elias 82 | Forgerson Abigill 111 | Peregrine 107 | Nicholas 133 |
| George 82 | Andrew 111 | Rachel 67,107 | French Bazel 20 |
| Hannah 82 | Annah 111 | Rebecca 67 | Benjamin 20 |
| John 82 | Benjamin 111 | Samuel 5, 107 | Otho 3 |
| Pressella 82 | David 111 | Thos.8,4,64,127 | William 3 |
| Rachel 82 | Elisabeth 111 | William 115,107 | Frew Alexander 85 |

Frew James 89
Rose 89
Friend Cath.61
  Christopher 59
  Dorethe 57
  Elisabeth 57,61
  David 55
  George 55
  Philip 55,58
Frisby Hariot 101
  Mary 101
  Thomas P.101
Fry Christian 135
  Leonard 135
Fulk Mary 111
Fuller Andrew 56
  Ann 58
  Elizabeth 118
  James 118
  Ester 57
  Frederick 58
  William 118
Fulton Alex. 90
  Casandra 90
  Hannah 90
  James 64,90
  John 90
  Letitia 90
  Mary 67
  Pricilla 90
  Rachel 90
  Robert 64
  Susannah 90
  William 90
Funck Ann 57
  Barbara 57
  Elisabeth 61
  Henry 55
  John 55
Funk Ann 130
  Jacob 130
  John 59
  Henry 59
  Martin 55, 59
Furnear Henry 58
Furney David 60
  James 54
Furrough Jesse 39
Fyffe Abija 79
  Daniel 79
  Dursiller 79
  Elisabeth 79
  Ellenner 79
  James 79
  John 79

Fyffe Jonathan 79
  Samue 79,Joseph 79
  Sary 79
  William 79

Gabriel Anthoney 130
Gafford Charles 143
  John 143
  Sarah 143
  Valentine 143
Gaghin Sophia 32
Gaither Amos 6
  Ann 4
  Benjamin 12
  Edward 6
  Nachel Capt.12
Gale Edward 120
Gales Sarah 127
  Thomas 127
Galeworth John 136
  Sarah 136
Galiham Rosey 119
Gallion Abariller 101
  Alexander 95
  Betty 109
  Christian 101
  Cumfort 109,115
  Elizabeth 95,115
  George 101
  Gilbert 109,115
  Gregory 95
  Henrietter 103
  James 95,103,109,115
  John 95,104,117
  Joseph 95
  Martha 101,103,104
  Mary 101,103,115,117
  Mathew 117
  Nathan 101
  Phebe 101
  Prisilla 101
  Rachael 101,103,115
  Ruth 109,115
  Samuel 115
  Sarah 95,101,115
  Thomas 109,115
  William 95,103
Galloway Benj.30
  John 21
  Joseph 16
  Samuel 9,13,17
Gallhover Christ.60
Gambell John 39
  Sarah 39
Games Stephen 143

Gantt Ann 125
  James 125
Gardener Elexander 117
  John 28
Gardif Christ. 39
Gardner Geo. 22, 29
  Jean 162
  John 162
  Richard 155
Gare Hannah 57
  Mary 56
Garland Cathrin 100
  Francis 106
  Henry 101
Garment Abeija 59
  Mary 61
  Rebecca 57,61
  William 55
Garnett Wm.143
Garrett Amos 101,104
  Francis 104
  Milcah 104
Garrettson Alley 99
  Aquila 106
  Benjamin 99
  Bennett 105
  Eliz.103,106,107
  Francis 105,107
  Freeborn 100,106
  Garrett 99,103,105
  James 105
  John 102
  Martha 102,107
  Mary 105,107
  Richard 100,106
  Sarah 103
  Susanna 103
Garrin Daniel 69
Garrner Joseph 37
  Parrish 33
Garroot John 34
  Katharine 67
Garvin Eleanor 32
Gary Gideon 6
Gassaway Dinah 10
  Nicholas 10
Gates Ann 119
Gath Eliz.107
  Hannah 107
  Martha 107
  Mary 107
  Thomas 107
Gatten Anna 86
  Azariah 83
  Benj. 76
  Eliz.76,83,86

Gatten Elisha 83
  James 83,86
  John 76,86
  Mary 83
  Phillinder 76
  Rebeca 83
  Richard 86
  Susanna 86
  Thomas 86
  Virlinder 86
  Zachariah 86
Gatton Azariah 132
  Elizabeth 132
  Mary 132
  Notley 132
Gattwith Jonas 17
Gattwood John 25
Gawley William 100
Geats James 75
Gellhoober Dewalt 55
  Christopher 60
  Mary 57
Gellhover Henry 60
Gellin Margaretha 56
Gelon James 158
Gelsin Joseph 54
Gentle Darkey 72
  Dianna 78,122
  Elizabeth 72
  Ellender 78
  George 78,81
  John 78
  Mary 78
  Rebecka 72
  Samuel 78
  Sary 78
  Stephen 78
  Thomas 122
  William 78
George Joseph 54
  Thomas 55
German Sarah 124
  Stephen 124
Gessinger Cath.62
Gest Basel 30
Gestes George 142
Gettry John 55
  Robart 55
Gibbins John 32
Gibbs Ann 135
  John H. 135
  Thomas 10
Gibson John 75,160
  Joseph 10
  William 163
  Woolman 160

Giden Elizabeth 58
  Henry 58
  Peter 55
Gidigh Jacob 58
Giedig George 60
Gies Magdalena 56
Ciest Samuel 11
Gifteth Hannah 117
Gifrin James 47
Gilbert Amous 117
  Aquiller 117
  Chas.108,116,117.
  Elisabeth 116,117
  Fanny 109
  Gidian 117
  James 109,117
  Joseph 30
  Maren 116
  Martha 109,116
Gilbert M. 116
  Mary 109,110,116,117
  Mathew 117
  Michael 109,110,117
  Parker 117
  Prissiller 117
  Samuel 110
  Sarah 109,117
  Susannah 92
  Thomas 109
  William 117
Gilder Ann 120
Giles Ame 109
  Ann 100
  Carolina 57
  Elizabeth 97
  Hannah 97
  Jacob 100,106,109,110
  James 100
  Johanna 100,110
  Nathaniel 57
  Sarah 97
  Susanna 100
Gilham Benj. 64
  Elizabeth 67
  Jacob 64
  John 64
  Margaret 67
  Mary 67
  Thomas 64
Gilks Mary 76
Gill Ann 67
  Betty 118
  John 64,114,118
  Joseph 64
  Samuel 64

Gill Sarah 67
  Thomas 64
  William 64
Gilles Aurthur 87
Gilligan John 75
Gillisson Jane 89
  John 89
  Mary 89
  Noble 89
Gillom John 81
Gillum Thomas 81
Gilpin Ann 135
  Benjamin 135,136
  Sarah 136
Gimlish Ariat 72
  Charlot 72
  Frances 72
  Macket 72
  Mary 72
  Michel 72
Ginkinks Edw. 76
Gipson Robt. 116
Gitig Henry 59
Gittings Amelia 67
  Ann 67
  Benjamin 64
  Cavia 67
  Cassandra 67
  Colmore 64
  Eliz. 67,72
  Erasmus 64
  Henry 72
  Jeane 67
  Jeremiah 64
  Kinsey 64
  Levy 86
  Liley 67
  Sarah 67
  Virlinda 67
  William 72
Givens John 2
Gladston Nathan 34
Glain Margret 109
Glandin Nathan 143
  William 34
Glanding John 49
Glasgow Thos. 120
Glayden Geo. 4
Glaz Charity 74
  Elenor 74
Glaze Dorcas 67
  Joseph 64
  Ruth 67
  William 64
Gleabsalter Danl. 55

Glen Joseph 87
  Mary 87
  Robert 87
Glieve Geo. 152
Glover John 8
Glovver Mary 109
Gloyd Danl. 127
  Joanna 127
Gneadig Eliz. 56
  Henry 60
  Isaac 54
  John 60
  Mary 62
  Susana 62
Godding Eliz. 50
Godfrey Joseph 64
Goldrope John 135
  Mary 135
Goldsborough Howes 157
  Robert 51,157
Goll Baltzer 54
  Elizabeth 56,62
  Jacob 60
Good George 55
Goodhand James 147
  Letitia 148
  Marmaduke 148
  Nathaniel 148
Gooding James 143
Goodings Ann 116
  Margrit 116
  Moses 116
Goodman Ann 72
  Betsy 72
  Charles 93
  Charlot 72
  Humphry 72
  Jeramiah 72
  Kesiah 72
  Patsey 72
  Rebeckah 72
  Samuel 72
  Tomma 72
Goodrick Benj. 71
  Ellender 71
  Elizabeth 71
  John 71
  Rachel 71
Goodwin Preston 34,37
Gonins George 99
Gordin Eliz. 93
  Eannah 93
  Margaret 93
  Peter 143

Gordin Philip 93
  William 93
Gordon ___ 159
  Agnis 87
  Alexander 103
  Ann 126
  Catherine 103
  Charles 121
  Drucilla 124
  Eleanor 102
  Eliz. 87,121
  Henry 87
  James 39,87,102,103
  Jane 87
  John 87,126
  Joseph 72,102
  Josiah 123
  Lucy 123
  Margrett 87
  Mary 87,103
  Rebecca 87
  Sarah 87
  Thomas 124
Gorman Abraham 32
Gorrel Abraham 117
  Esther 116
  Hannah 116
  Issabellah 116
  James 116
  John 116
  Joseph 116
  Thomas 116
  William 116
Gossage Chas. 156
  Daniel 52
  John 158
Gotee Andrew 46
  John 46
Gott Ann 19
  Anthony 28
  Ezekiel 19
  Joseph 26
  Richard 28
Gould Benjamin 143
  Richard 143
Gouldsmith Rosa. 9
  Vincent 9
Goute George 39
  Shadrick 39
  Sophiah 39
Goutee Jabus 51
Gover Cassandria 95
  Eliz. 95,114,124
  Garrat 114
  Gittings 95

Gover Hennery 114
John 124
Mary 21,114
Phillip 114
Prissilla 93,114
Robert 111,114
Sam 114
Samuel 93
Gozlin Wm. 32
Grace Aaron 107
Ann 107
James 138
John 107
Mary 159
Nathaniel 152,155
Peter 107
Rebecca 107
William 154
Gragg Joshua 64
Graham Chas.43
Elizabeth 130
John 39
Moses 130
Grainger Martin 149
Granger Edward 49
William 48
Grant Ann 115
James 114
Richard 123
Sarah 123
Gravel Benj.7
Graver Eliz.70
Jacob 63
Katherine 70
Margaret 70
Philip 69
Graves Cass.67
Chloe 67
Eleanor 129
Elener 143
Elizabeth 67,124
George 64
Humphrey 64
Jeane 67
John 64
Joshua 64
Lewis 123
Matthew 143
Peregrine 64
Solomon 124
Thomas 64,143
Gray Ann 62
Archable 39
Eliz.23,131
Gilbert 123

Gray John N. 3
Leonard 131
Robard 56
Robert 106
Thomas 32
William 143
Greaber Jacob 58
Greandland Rich.116
Greanwhich Beck 148
James 149
Pichael 149
Sheary 148
Greegbaum Philip 54
Gregg Hannah 67
Green Ann 61,84,94
Bazell 126
Benedict 84
Catherine 139
Cloe 84
David 84
Dianna 83
Elianor 126
Elijah 6
Eliz.117,129
Francis 84
George 55
Henry 94
Isaac 83
James 129
Jamima 83
Jean 84
John 83,94
Joshua 94
Margaret 84
Martha 83
Mary 57,82,84
Peter 105
Phil 151
Phillip 84
Ralph 51
Richard 29,39
Sary 78
Thomas 83,135
Valentine 150
William 83,105
Zariah 34
Greene Edward 36
Greenfield Chas.64
Eleanor 67
Eliza.104,152
Keziah 67
Jacob 98
Mary 58
Sarah 67
Thomas 64,104

Greenfield Walt.64
Greenhout ___ 156
Greenlea Rachel 92
Samuel 92
Greenlief James 46
Greenwell James 127
Elizabeth 127
Greenwood John 51
William 143
Greetree Benjamin 71
Gregory William 143
Grenholt Johnathan 36
Griffen William 23
Griffeth Eliz.113
Fanney 113
Hannah 113
Henry 20
James 113
John 113
Mary 113
William 113
Griffin Averilla 113
Frederick 26
Joseph 39,48
Marshall 20
William 52
Griffind John 36
Griffith Ann 92
Evan 95
Frances 105
Funettah 105
Hugh 20
John 20
Jones 102
Martha 105
Mary 105
Lewes 43
Luke 106
Patience 102
Samuel 105
Sarah 105
Rice 102
William 102
Griffiths David 28
Grigg Richard 148
Grigory Rich.136
Violetta 136
Grimes Ann 77
George 151
Lucy 67
Grindle Eliza.73
Gringul George 64
Grinley Eliz.93
Grinnan Ann 39
Grist Isaac 32

Grooms Mary 114
Grose Peter 55
Gross Eliz. 61
Elsy 61
Ester 61
Humphrey 59
Jeremia 59
Sharlote 57
Susanna 61
Thomas 55
William 59
Grove Abraham 59
Cathrin 57
Christian 55
John 59
Thomas 154
Groves Eleanor 103
George 103
Grumbach Conrad 59
John 59
Grunner James 163
Grymes George 137
Catherine 137
Hestor 137
Margaret 138
Robert 137
Thomas 138
Gwynn Francis 1
Guist Alisabeth 109
Amilia 109
Guppey Henry 87
Jane 87
John 87
Margrett 87
Mary 87
Gussaler Anthony 69
Elizabeth 70
George 69
John 69
Katherine 70
Mary 70
Rebecca 70
Guthry James 59
Robert 59
Gutry Ann 57
Ester 57
Pheeb 57
Mary 61
Richard 59
Sarah 61
Hableton Wm.152
Hackett James 143
John 143
Thomas 143,64
William 150
Hadaway Rich.&Sarah
110

Haddan Larance 40
Haddaway Capt. 153
George 153
James 154
John 153
Robert 154
Susanah 153
Thomas 155
Wm. 153, 154, 155
Hadrick Margaret 130
Robert 130
Haeger Catha. 57
Haes William 85
Hagan Nich. 54
Hugh 60
Hagerty Mary 87
Haggy Elisabeth 56
Hagin Henry 59
Hagon Cathran 116
Hague John 91
Haile Eliz. 53
Hailey William 105
Hailey William 105
Hale Jene 53
Stephen 162  143
Hales William 143
Hall Aquila 101
Ann 83, 122
Anna 128
Avarile 100
Basil 83
Barthia 100
Benedict 101
Cordelia 105
Edward 6, 100,101,107
Eleanor 10
Eliza 100
Elizabeth 13, 83
Charlotta 101
Christopher 95
George 139, 160
Hannah 105
Henry 4
Herbert 160
I. Carvel Dr. 106
Isaac 32
John 16, 100, 101, 152
Jonathan 143
Joseph 47
Josias 108
Margaret 83
Margery 126
Martha 101
Mary 56, 83, 100, 101, 139
Nathaniel 124

Hall Orasilla 100
Parker 105
Philip 128
Rebecca 74,105,117
Richard 83
Ruth 19
Sarah 105
Sillar 83
Sophia 101
Susan 83
Thomas 106
Thomas Henry 6
William 6, 101, 105, 126, 162
Hallett John 108
Halley Eliz.130
John 130,131
Mary 131
Hallum Cath.134
Halsall John 121
Mrs.. 121
Hambelton Geo.117
Lilley 39
Mary 39
Phillip 154
William 134,157
Hamblton Jamis 35
William 33
Hamby Delah 109
Fanney 109
James 109
Samuel 109
Sarah 109
William 102,109
Hamilton Alex.88
Andrew 132
Ann 124
Betsey 88
Edward 90
John 51,88,123,133
Jonathan 88
Margaret 90
Mary 132
Polly 88
Reggy 88
Robin 88
Ruth 132
Sally 88
Sarah 123
Susanna 133
Thomas 124
Hammon William 40
Hammond Eliz.143
John 6

Hammond Nathan 21
Phillip 19
William 32
Hampton Ann 108
David 109
John 108
Thomas 148
Hance Kinsey 64
Hancock Melkiah 128
William 128
Hand John 148
Handley Handy 50
Leavin 49
James 101
Hanford John 52
Thomas 53
Hanna(h) Deliverence 92
Joseph 55
William 92, 162
Hannon Patrick 32
Hanson Abbrilah 100
Benjamin 100
Edward 163
Eliz.99,100
George 150
Hollis 99
John 99,104
Joseph 54
Keziah 99
Luke 100
Mary 100,106
Samuel 106
Sarah 100
Harbet Benj.117
Grace 117
Darkes 80
Elias 80
Ellenner 80
James 80
Jarratt 80
Joshua 80
Mary 80
Harbitt Chas.143
Hardesty Eliz.127
Hennary 82 Edm.127
Robert 127
Hardey Ann 118
Baptist 131
Barbary 84
Benedict 120
Elias 84
Eliz.84,118,127,137
Fielder 84
Goerge 118,131
Henry 136,139

Hardey Ignatious 137
John 131,139
Kenzey 84
Letty 118
Mary 81,84,118, 131,136,139
Rachel 131
Rebeca 84,131
Samuel 84
Sary 84
Thomas Dent 118
Zadock 81
Hare Daniel 108
James 117
Mary 108
Patience 108
Robert 117
Sarah 108
Hargadine Edw.150
John 150
Hargrove Absalom 96
Cassandra 117
Elizabeth 96
Lydia 96
Rachel 117
Richard 96,117
Ruth 96,117
Harmon Margaret 70
Rachel 159
Harnish Philip 55
Harp Ann 67
Erasmus 64
Esther 67
Philip 64
Priscilla 67
Samuel 64
Sarah 67
William 64
Harper David 40
Ezekel 39
John 39
Stella 122
Samuel 149
Thomas 158
William 34,122
Hardin Edward 122
Margaret 122
Mary 49
Harding Anna 84
Elias 84
Mary 84
Walter 84
Hardy Anna 77
Ashford 77

183

Hardy Darcus 77
  Eleanor 67
  George 77
  Hennary 77
  Henry 64
  John 77
  Mary 77
  Martha 77
Harres Ezekel 73
  James 111
  John 111
  William 74
Harrington Alice 153
  Joseph 153
  Mary 154
  Richard 152
Harris & Harriss 160
  Aaron 74
  Ann 74,96
  Benj.34, 64, 96
  Charles 143
  Daniel 96
  Edith 126
  Eliz. 74,96
  George 64,96
  James 77,150,151
  Jeane 67
  John 64,82,120,128
  Joseph 117
  Josias 126
  Katharine 67
  Margrett 96
  Mary 74
  Rachel 67
  Richard 150
  Samuel 28
  Sarah 67,74,96
  Susanna 125
  Thomas 74,96
  Walter 74
  Wm.14,96,125
  Zadock 74
Harriss Elsibeth 35
  James 35
  John 158
  Robert 82
  Vinaford 82
  William 36
Harrison 155
  E. 19
  Henry Capt. 27
  James 152,154
  John 43,47,52,53
  Joseph 153
  Harris 30

Harrison Mary 50
  Priscilla 72
  Rachel 24
  Richard 24
  Robert 153
  Samuel 24,31
  Siller 52
  Thomas 154
  Walter 24
Harrisson James 154
  Jonathan 155
  Joseph 155
Harrod Henry 97
Hart Arthur 46
  Christopher 160
  Henry 45
  Jacob 61
  Jane 105
  Levin 43
  Ludwig 56
  Naboth 45
  Noah 54
  Rachel 56
Harthorn Agnis 112
  Jane 112
  John 112
  Margery 112
  Margret 112
  Margrit 112
  Marthy 112
  Mary 112
  Robert 112
Harvey David 47
  Elianor 120
  Eliz.120,123
  George 120
  Henry 120
  James 120
  John 123
  Mary 120
  Richard 93
  Salathal 51
  Thomas 120
  Virlinda 120
  William 40
Harvin Elias 137
  Mary 137
Harwood Ann 8,157
  Elizabeth 74
  Gasaway 84
  John 84
  Mary Ann 74
  Mary Eliza.74
  Mary 84,157
  Richard 8, 16

Harwood Robert 157
  Samuel 74,157
  Thomas 8,24,74
  William 3
Hasleitt Wm. 36
Hastings Geo. 143
Hatfield Francis 121
Hapstone Mary 110
Hatt Samuel 69
  Susanna 70
Hatton Joseph 139
  Mary 139,140
  Nathaniel 140
Haukins Averil.110
  Elisabeth 110
  Joseph 110
  Lidia 110
  Margret 110
  Nancy 110
  Richard 110
  Robert 110
  Sarah 110
  William 110
Haunze Mary 106
Haushalter Mich.55
Hausholder Eliz.62
Haut Barbara 58
  Catharina 57
  Margaretha 62
  Peter 54
Haviner Dominicar 137
  Mary 137
Havis James 137
  Catherine 137
Hawkins Eliz.67,139
  George F. 134
  James 139
  John 64,95,96,97
  Lurana 95
  Matthew 143
  Richard 95
  Samuel 96
  Sarch 96
  Susanna 134
  Thomas 64,96
Hayard Allen 47
Hayes Wm. 26
Hayman John 32
Haynes James 27
Hays John 93
  William 32
Hayward Addling 47
  Francis 47
  John 48
  Leavin 53

Hazwell Anna 134
  William 134
Head William 85
Heaflybauer Geo.60
  Jacob 60
Heard Bennet 79
  Margret 57
Hearn Hannah 103
  James 103
  Mary 103
Heaton James 95
  John 95
  Margrett 95
  Rebecca 95
  Sarah 95
  Thomas 95
Hederick Chas.60
Hedley Ann 67
  Jacob 64
Heeth Samuel 163
Helflybauer Cath. 56
Heinsman Catha. 62
Heiser Ann 56
  Catha. 62
  Elisabeth 62
  Jacob 59
  William 59
Heked Jonathan 58
Hellen Alex. 59
  David 54
  George 59
  Peter 59
  Thomas 59
Hellin Ann 62
  Jane 62
  Susanna 56, 62
Helloms Leonard 162
  Maybery 162
Helms Geo. 32
Hemsley Wm. 149
Henderson Geo. 100
  Richard 100
  Sarah 100, 121
Hendley Joseph 95
Henley James 76
Henman John 64
Hennahon Patrick 81
Hennary John 81
Hennes Benj. 64
  David 64
  Elizabeth 67
  Henry 64
  John 64
  Mary 72
  Sarah 67
Hennesy Andrew 149
Henry Andrew 100
  Ann 133

| | | | |
|---|---|---|---|
| Henry Daniel 79 | Hewing John 22 | Higdon Thomas 71 | Hinton Joseph 123 |
| Eliz.79,87 | Hews Christopher 157 | Higens Diana 49 | Mary 123 |
| Isaac 87 | Hibbey John 78 | Higgens Ann 72 | Thomas 124 |
| John 40,97,134 | Hickey Chas. 64 | Elender 72 | Himes Nathaniel 105 |
| Jonathan 54 | Hickingbottom Joel 32 | Elizabeth 72 | Hitchcock Hannah 106 |
| Martha 134 | Hickman Ann 81 | Joseph 72 | Hitler Catherin 57 |
| Mary 87,134 | Arthur 78 | Martha 72 | George 55,59 |
| Robert 87 | Betty 78 | Higgins Marg.151 | Hittler Barbara 57 |
| Samuel 87 | Elihu 83 | Pricilla 127 | Elisabeth 57 |
| Thomas 133,134 | Elisha 75 | Sarah 39 | Eve 61 |
| Henson Jacob 114 | Gilbert 82 | William 127 | Margret 61 |
| Patrick 84 | Henry 75 | Highskil Cath.56 | Hix Andrew 59 |
| Samuel 77 | Jean 78,81 | Frederick 54 | Joseph 59 |
| Henwood Ann 81 | Jesse 75 | John 60 | Mary 61 |
| Azariah 81 | Joshua 75 | Hignutt Danl.35 | Susanna 57,61 |
| Charles 18 | Joshuah 83 | Hileary Eleanor 120 | Timothy 59 |
| Mary 18 | Lidia 82 | John 120 | William 59 |
| Herbert Marg.139 | Margaret 78 | Mary 120 | Hobs William 34 |
| Herbin Edw. 131 | Mary 78,83 | Thomas 120 | Hocker Dianner 85 |
| Lydia 131 | Nansey 75 | Hill Abill 25 | Elisabeth 85 |
| Herman Cathaina 62 | Prisilla 82 | Ann 107 | Margaret 85 |
| Elisabeth 56 | Richard 81 | Aurilla 114 | Susanna 85 |
| John 58 | Rossel 78 | Elisabeth 114 | William 85 |
| Mary 62 | Sarey 75,85 | Giles 64 | Hoddel Jacob 54 |
| Herns Elizabeth 125 | Solomon 75 | Harmin 114 | Hodges Giles 90 |
| Henry 125 | Stephen 81 | James 32,95 | Hodson Ann 39,47 |
| Heron Elizabeth 50 | William 78,81 | John 64,72,114,122 | Henry 50 |
| John 124 | Hicks Denward 49 | Jonathan 72 | Hoopes 50 |
| Mary 124 | Jesse 90 | Joseph 27,29,72 | John 50 |
| Herring Edward 143 | Joseph 50 | Kesiah 72 | Thomas 39 |
| Herrings Thos.99 | Mary 39 | Margret 114 | Hoerligh Ann 56 |
| Herry Andrew 60 | Tabitha 39 | Martha 95 | Catharina 62 |
| David 54 | Thomas 39 | Mary 95,122 | Josh 54,60 |
| Dorothea 56 | Hiensman Margar.57 | Moses 107 | Peter 54,60 |
| Jacob 54 | Hieser William 54 | Nathan 34 | Hoffman Christ.61 |
| John 54,60 | Hiffner Alberdus 55 | Rosanner 162 | Dorathea 57 |
| Martin 54,58 | Catherin 57,61 | Samuel 114 | George 58 |
| Mary 62 | Conrad 59 | Sarah 27,72,95 | Hoges John 111 |
| Hess Barbary 70 | Elisabeth 61 | Shem 95 | Hoggin Catherine |
| Jacob 69 | Frederick 59 | Solomon 52 | Elizabeth 119 |
| Heterick Chas.54 | Jacob 55 | Sophia 67 | John 119 |
| Elisabeth 62 | John 55 | Thos. S. Capt 33 | Peter 119 |
| Susanna 56 | Margret 61 | William 95, 107 | Rebecca 119 |
| Hett Rachel 2 | Mary 61 | Hills Eliz. 153 | Richard 119 |
| Heugh Ann 67 | Peter 59 | Hilragle Christ. 121 | Soloman 119 |
| Andrew 64 | Valentin 59 | Polsin 121 | William 119 |
| Elizabeth 67 | Higdon Ann 129 | Hincks Thos. 39 | Holbrook Alax.35 |
| Harriot 67 | Benjamin 129 | Hindman Wm. 159 | Holding John 143 |
| Jeane 67 | John 64,71 | Hinds Danl. 37 | Richard 143 |
| John 64 | Joseph 64 | John 143 | Hollan Connar 40 |
| Margaret 67 | Katharine 67 | Hindson Chas. 36 | Michal 40 |
| Mary 67 | Margaret 71 | Hines Henry 118 | Holladay Henry 157 |
| Sarah 67 | Mary 67 | Hinkle Ann 57 | John 25 |
| Heughes John 81 | Peter 64 | Henry 55 | Holland Francis 103 |
| Hevens Luke 48 | Rachel 71 | Hinsman John 60 | Hannah 103 |
| Thomas 48 | Susanna 67 | Hinson Mrs. 32 | Joel 80 |
| | | Hinton Ann 124 | |

Holland John 103
Lydia 80
Rasmis 39
Holliday Benj.13
Elizabeth 118
James 118
Mary 12,108,118
Sarah 25
William 118
Hollingsworth James 143
Jesse 32
William 143
Hollis Abirila 98
Amos 98
Benjamin 98
Cathrin 98
Clark 33,101
James 98
Martha 98
Sarah 101
William 98,101
Holmes James 92
John 43
Joseph 118
Mary 92
Holmod Anthony 72
George 72
Jane 72
John 72
Loveday 72
Sarah 72
Susanah 72
Holton John 11
William 32
Homes Ann 114
Merear 116
Honnos Cavea 74
Hoober Adam 59
Christ.56,62
Christopher 59
Dorothea 62
Henry 59
Jacob 54
William 59
Hoobes Jacob 54
Elesebeth 35
Hoobs Leblun 35
Hood Andrew 88
James 88
Jennett 88
Margrett 88
Robert 88
William 6
Hooder Julianna 56
Hools Joseph 78

Hooper Henry 47,50
John 49,51
Roger A. 50
Shadrach 149
William 52
Hopkins ___ 159
___ard 159
Ann 77,78,96
Charles 96
Dennis 157
Elizabeth 29,96
Ephraim 96
Francis 157
Gerrard 2,12,96
Hannah 96
James 153
Jarrard 29
John 39,96,152
Johns 12
Joseph 12,96,153,157
Lambath 157
Lear 77
Leven 81,96
Mary 96
Phillip 96
Rachael 96
Richard 16
Samue 96
Sarah 96
Stephen 81
Susannah 96
Thomas 143,153
William 29,45,56,152
Hoppar Henry 40
Hopper John 124
Marget 163
Sarah 124
Hoppern William 162
Horepening Mary 57
Horn Elizabeth 148
Horne Mathew 54
Horner Casandrew 108
Elisabeth 108
James 108
Mary 108
Mary G. 108
Moses 45
Thomas 102, 108
Horney James 35
Jiffery 35
John 153
Thomas 153
Horsley Rich. 143
Horsman Henry 40
John 40
Luke 40         186
Horten John 108

Hortley John 81
Horton Elisabeth 108
James 108
Mary 108
Ruth 108
Sarah 108
William 108
Hoshorn Eliz.105
Hosier John 102
Hoskins Elisha 126
George 128
John Allen 132
Josias 127
Mary 128
Susanna 132
Hoskinson Chas.76
George 81
Heugh 76
Josiah 76
Margaret 76
Mary 78
Hoskison Ruth 85
House Ann 67
John 69
Margaret 70
Householder Barb.61
Cathrin 61
Elisabeth 56,61
George 58
John 58
Margret 57
Margretha 58
Simon 61
Housle Eliz.71
Jonathan 71
Leviah 71
Lucy 71
Malmaduke 71
Mary 71
Proscoolah 71
Robert 71
Samuel 71
Sarah 71
Houton Ann 32
Howard Aquila 90
Ann 90
Benjamin 90
Denune 2
Dorsey 90
Elizabeth 90
Hannah 28,90
John 110
John Dutton 90
Joseph 2,9,35
Lemuel 90

Howard Martha 90
Mary 90
Mary Dutton 90
Nashet 4
Ruth 90
Sarah 90
Sary 84
Susannah 90
Thomas 84
Howe Eliz.135
Thomas 135
Howel Joseph 80
Samuel 110
Howell Abraham 104
Ann 104
Elizabeth 104
John 104
Mary 104
Mary Ann 125
Thomas 125
William 104
Howes James 152
Howlet James 88
Margrett 88
Howlett Andrew 87
Ann 87
Elizabeth 87
John 87
Margrett 87
Mary 87
Howley Wm. 83
Howman Benj.83
Elisabeth 83
Isaac 83
Jesse 83
Martha 83
Stayson 83
Hoxter Ann 149
John 149
Hoy Roger 99
Hoze Elisabeth 62
Frederick 55,60
Henry 60
Jacob 54,60
Juliana 62
Magda.56,62,63
Peter 54,60
Salmey 56
Susanna 62
Hubard Belt 88
Joe 88
Hanna 88
Ruth 88
Hubbard Geo.97
Humphra 40

Hubbard John 49
Joseph 151
Hubbart Bettey 50
Hudson John 35
Walter 143
Hues Ann 124
Huet John 23
Huffington John 40
Hufman Barbara 72
  Elizabeth 72
  Hannah 72
  John 72
  Joseph 72
  Martain 72
  Mary 72
Hugar Ann O.125
  William 125
Hugh Sarah 67
Hughe John 40
Hughes Amelia 67
  Edward 64
  J. H. 106
  Nathan 104
Tughs Ames 115
  Ann 99
  Daniel 33
  Edmon 40
  Elie 117
  Everitt 99
  James 40,43,99,116
  Jane 116
  John 91,99,116
  Joseph 126
  M. 20
  Nathaniel 116
  Phebe 126
  Phillemon 53
  Precilla 39
  Scott 99
Hugins Hezekiah 40
Hughins James 36
Hughston Alex.89
Hull Daniel 154
Humes Susannah 157
Humphrey Eliz.136
  Henry 136
  Sarah 136
Humphreys John 66
  Richard 96
Hunt James 120
  Peter 155
  Ruth 120
  Thomas 143
Hunter James 13
  Joshua 83

Hunter Margaret 12
  Martha 83
  Mary 83
  Sary 83
Huntly Robert 107
Hurd William 33
Hurdle Ann 67
  John 64
  Leonard 64
  Priscilla 67
  Richard 64
  Susanna 67
  William 64
Hurley Alex.64
  Ann 138
  Constantine 40
  Daniel 138
  Durbey 40
  Edward 40
  Elijah 40
  Jacob 40
  Jan 40
  Jane 138
  John 40
  Joseph 138
  Judy 109
  Matthew 40
  Moses 40
  Rachell 139
  Sophiah 40
  Thomas 40,138
  William 64,139
Hurly Cornelius 138
  Mary 138
Hurnman Alex.83
  Ann 83
  Jacob 83
  John 83
  Samuel 83
  Thomas 83
  William 83
Hurst George 3
Husband Ann 111
  Elizabeth 95,96
  Hannah 95,111
  James 95
  Joseph 111
  Josua 111
  Mary 95,96,111
  Meleson 95
  Rachel 96
  Sarah 111
  Susanna 95,96
  William 95
Hust Archabel 40

Hust James 40
  Joseph 40
  Samuel 40
Husterfield, Chas.110
Hutchings Risden 150
Hutchins James 148
Hutchison Ann 124
  William 124
Hutsen Jane 57
Hutson Chas. 59
  George 55
  Isaac 59
  Sarah 61
Hutton Henry 18
  James 17
  Joseph 18,24
  William 18
Hutts Andrew 80
Hyat Christopher 127
  Elizabeth 127
  Martha 127
  William 127
Hyfield Chas.100
Hyser Martain 81
Hyton Ann 129
  Joseph 129

Iiames John 13
  Thomas 13
Iiams Jacob 4
  John 7
  Plummer 9
  William 9
Inch Jane 10
Ingram Saml.93
Ingrum John 34
Insley Andrew 45
  Bettey 44,45
  Elizabeth 46
  Gabril 45
  Jacob 44
  Joseph 45
  Solomon 46
  Vallintine 44
Ireland John 150
Irvine Alex.159
Isaac Jacob 128
  Jane 128
  Richard 121
  Sarah 121
Isgate Thomas 157

Jackling And.91
Jackson Abraham 32
  Alexander 134

Jackson Ann 67
  Bennett 78
  Casandra 93
  Deborah 134
  Ellenner 78
  Elizabeth 134
  Isaac 157
  Jafaras 78
  James 64,156
  John 64,78
  Mary 67
  Robert 21,51
  Samuel 93,143
  Sarah 99
  Sary 78
  Stafford 143
  Susanna 67
  Thomas 99
  Wm. 64,134,160
Jacob Barbara 57
  Cathrin 61
  George 59
  Henry 59
  Martin 55
  Mary 57
Jacobs Edward 76
  Henry 143
  Jeremiah 76
  John 1,76
  Mary 2
  Rachel 76
  Rebeca 76
  Richard 1
  Ruth 76
  Samuel 9
  William 1,32
  Zachariah 76
James Elizabeth 91
  Esther 91
  George 32
  Henrietta 67
  Jemimah 94
  Jeremiah 94
  Jervis 91
  John 96,135
  Joseph 91
  Mary 91,94,96
  Mather 94
  Michael 94
  Robert 96
  Sarah 96
  Thomas 91,94,96
  William 91,96
Jameston Ann S. 122
  Richard 122

Jams Daniel 115
Janes Ann 122
Edward 122
Jane 122
William 122
Willie 64
Jarboe Elizabeth 139
James 135,139
Martha 135
Jarman Stephen 149
Jay Elizabeth 96
Hannah 96
Joseph 96
Martha 96
Samuel 96
Sarah 73
Stephen 96
Thomas 96
Jeanes Henry 64
Mary 67
Jefferry James 88
Martha 88
Nancey 88
Jeffers George 149
John 150
William 147
Jefferson Eliz.132
Francis 155
George 155
Luke 132
Thomas 154
Jeffery Wm. 106
Jenkins Ann 124
Bartholomew 137
Enoch 121
Frances 121,123,124
Henrietta 125
Job 129
John 97,123
Martha 104,126
Mary 104,121,137
Precilla 137
Richard 125
Samuel 104
William 124
Zachariah 126
Zadock 137
Jennens Ann 71
Elizabeth 71
John 71
Margaret 71
Mary 71
Rachel 71
Sarah 71
Jenney Wm.24

Jennings Wm.11
Jess Mary 57
Jewel & Jewell
Amay 81
Ann Tabitha 81
Arnay 83
Bassel 81
Betty 81
David 82
Elisabeth 83
Elisha 82
George 82
John 83
Jonathan 82
Mary 82
Rebecah 81
Richard 90
Sary 83
Smallwood 82
William 81,92
Jewry Richard 98
Jiams William 2
Jimmison Ellex.112
John 112
Marthie 112
Mary 112
Sarah 112
William 112
Jingrims Thomas 69
Jinkins Eliz.70
Jinnings Lucy 70
Johnjones John 82
Johns Ann 110
Aquillar 32
Cassandrew 110
Elisabeth 110
Frances 110
Hannah 96
Hosea 96
Mary 29,67
Nathaniel 110
Richard 64,108
Ruth 110
Sarah 67
Skipwith 96
Susannah 6
Thomas 64
William 110
Johnson Adam 105
Amelian 99
Ann 67,105
Aquila 106
Archibald 104,105
Bartholomew 81
Eliz.76,88

Johnson Ezekie 43
Frances 105
George 143
Hance 143
Henry 33,45
Horasha 76
Isaac 76,88
James 43,88,150
John 33,81,93,143
Joseph 40,81,106
Josias 105
Levi 45
Lisbell 81
Margery 139
Martha 106
Mary 76,88,99,105
Monica 131
Nathan 40
Prissilla 106
Rebeca 81
Samuel 99,106,109
Sarah 56,67,88
Sophia 106
Thomas 88,105,139
William 32,43,106
Johnston Ann 67
Armstrong 96
Eleanor 67
Elizabeth 67
Esther 67
John 64
Joseph 64
Mary 70
Precious 67
Sarah 67
William 64
Virlinda 67
Jolley Ann 96
Cassandria 96
Edward 96
Elizabeth 96
John 96
Sarah 96
William 96
Jones Abner 148
Abraham 73
Ann 132,135,160
Anna 128
Aquila 88
Benjamin 92,135
Casandra 92
Catherine 126
Charles 64,125
Charity 67,125
Curvil 92

Jones Daniel 83
Edward 135
Eleanor 67
Elianor 119,122,135
Eliza.7,67,83,84
92,135
Frances 41
Gilbert 92
Henry 1,64,132
Henrietta 67
Hugh 4
Isaac 7,41,92
Jacob 45,92
James 40,83,150
Jeane 83
John 64,143,135
Jonathan 19
Josiah 128
Joseph 5,82,84,96
103,128
June 103
Keziah 67
Levin 40,41
Lewis 19,83
Lurinah 155
Magdeline 92
Malintha 67
Martha 132
Mary 40,50,67,77,
80,96,101,125,
135
Mary Ann 67
Margaret 84,128
Morgan 14,50
Notley 122, 135
Patience 96
Philip 84,125
Rachael 96
Richard 132
Robert 99,143,155
Ruben 96
Samuel 126
Sarah 4,40,67,
131,137
Sary 84
Silvester 131
Stephen 92
Susanna 80,84,67
119,136
Thomas 80,119
William 35,40,92,
118,119,125
Wm. Kirby 151
Joy James 24
Joyce Elijah 94

| | | | |
|---|---|---|---|
| Joyner Dobs 148 | Mary 75, 101 | King Benjamin 71 | Klebsadler |
| William 147 | Sarah 101 | Charity 71 | Catherina 57 |
| Joys Elizabeth 29 | Kelly Ann 32 | Edward 71 | Klaber, Catrin 57, |
| Richard 21 | Bush 75 | Elianor 136 | 63 |
| Judd Ann 108, 117 | Elisabeth 32 | Elizabeth 71 | Christiana 57 |
| Daniel 108, 117 | James 151 | Jane 127 | Elizabeth 57 |
| Elisabeth 108 | Kenney 75 | John 136,137,139 | Frances 57 |
| Hanah 108 | Ritchard 60 | Kersey 139 | Henry 55, 58 |
| James 108 | Spencer 32 | Mary 67,71,92,137 | Herman 55, 59 |
| Jane 117 | Tom 75 | Rebeckah 71 | John 55, 58 |
| Joshua 108 | Kemp Benj. 153 | Richard 127 | Ludwig 59 |
| Rachel 108 | John 143, 153 | Samuel 64 | Mary 63 |
| Saran 117 | Magdalain 153 | Sarah 71 | Kline Cathrin 63 |
| William 108, 117 | Thomas 153 | Thomas 1 | Elisabeth 63 |
| Judey Martin 32 | Kenard Ann 99 | Kinghton Wm. 30 | John 58 |
| Jurdam Batt 34 | George 99 | Kingsbeary James | Jost 55 |
| Juvel William 37 | Hannah 99 | 32 | Magdalena 63 |
| Kady John 99 | James 99 | Kingsberry | Mary 63 |
| Kagan Margaret 70 | Mary 99 | Demillion | Michael 54 |
| Kann John 60 | Michael 99 | 138 | Peter 59 |
| Susanna 56 | Kendel James 27 | Elizabeth 138 | Susanna 63 |
| Karr John 88 | Kennerson John 69 | Kingsbury Gabriel | William 58 |
| Rachell 88 | Kennett Matthew 64 | 148 | Kling Mary 57 |
| Stephen 64 | Kenny Easter 97 | Kinord Richard 35 | Knepsin Mary 56 |
| Katz Catha. 56, 62 | Mary 97 | Kinsberry Susanna | Knight Abraham 88 |
| Elisabeth 62 | Kent Christ. 91 | 136 | Aquiller 115 |
| Jacob 54 | Emanuel 143 | Kiphart Eliz. 70 | Aquillia 88 |
| Keath George 136 | Rosannah 91 | George 69 | Cassandra 88 |
| Monica 136 | Kern Susanna 61 | Jacob 69 | David 117 |
| Keech Clotilda 119 | Kerns Edward 32 | John 69 | Debrow 115 |
| Edward 119 | Kersey John 153 | Katherine 70 | Eliz. 98, 115 |
| John 119 | Kickman William | Leonard 69 | Ellender 108 |
| William 119 | 143 | Phillip 69 | Ezekel 117 |
| Keen Ann 114 | Killin Margareth | Susanna 70 | George 115 |
| Aquila 114 | 62 | Kirbey --- 159 | Hanna 88, 115, |
| John 114 | Kellener John 41 | Elizabeth 158 | 116 |
| Rebeckah 114 | Killer Fred. 60 | Mary 132 | Isaac 116 |
| Sarah 114 | Killey Batt 35 | Richard 132 | James 88 |
| Timmothy 114 | Kiltey Frances 80 | Kirby Benj. 149 | Jane 116 |
| William 114 | Kilty Capt. John | Mary 159 | John 74, 117 |
| Keene Mary 52 | 19 | William 31 | Jonathan 108 |
| Thomas 52 | Kimble Eleanor 102 | Kirck Wm. 85 | Light 115, 116 |
| Kees Francis 50 | Francis 102, 104 | Kirk Arthur 32 | Margret 115 |
| James 53 | George 102 | Georg 41 . 32 | Martha 115 |
| John 53 | Giles 102 | Levin 41 | Mary 110,115, |
| Kehn Daniel 58 | James 102,104,106 | Kirns Eliz. 113 | 116,117 |
| Margret 58 | Jamima 106 | Margret 113 | Michael 88 |
| Keithley James 152 | John 102 | Mary 113 | Rachel 116 |
| Keizer Ann 67 | Josias 102, 103 | Matthew 113 | Sally 88 |
| Elizabeth 67 | Margaret 102 | Kirtze Nicholas 69 | Sarah 110, 116 |
| Jacob 64 | Rowland 104 | Kiser Margaret 70 | Susannah 115 |
| John 64 | Saml. 106 | Susanna 70 | Thomas 88, 116 |
| Margaret 67 | Sarah 104, 106 | Kissick Jane 130 | William 115, 116 |
| Rebecca 67 | Stephen 102 | Robert 130 | Knighton Jane 3 |
| Stophel 64 | Susanna 102, 106 | Kiteley Rachel 94 | Knott John 48 |
| Susanna 67 | Wm. James 102 | Kizer Christine 70 | Koenig Catharin |
| Kell George O. 91 | Zachariah 106 | Elizabeth 70 | Elisabeth 61, 57 |
| Keller Lawrence 58 | Kimmey Henry 41 | Frederick 69 | Jost 59 |
| Kelley Fred. 75 | Kindrick Sarah 136 | John 69 | Magdalena 61 |
| James 101 | Thomas 136 | Katharine 70 | Mary 61 |

Koenig Mathias 59
Peter 59
Koenigh Christian 55
Kogh Catharina 56
Elisa. 62
Marg. 62
Kooke Peter 60
Kor Darkus 71
Korepening John 54
Lowe Dewalt 56
Elisabeth 57
Henry 56, 58, 60
Mary 57
Kraus Dorothy 70
Jacob 69
John 69
Katherine 70
Peter 69
Susanna 70
Theodoris 69
Krumbach John 54
Kunes John 55
Kurtze Peter 69

Laine Francis 33
William 52
Lake Henry 44
Lalar Hennary 84
Lamb John 47
Lambath John 19, 25
Stephen 15
Lambeth Ann 72
John 72
Lucy 72
Mary 72
Samuel 72
Lambden Thomas 97
Wrightston 153
Lambert Robert 144
Lambson Robert 153
Lamden Elizabeth 155
Lamdin Francis 143
Lamford James 96
Lammar Nathan 34
Lampper Charity 111
John 111
Margret 111
Soffiah 111
William 111
Lanabach Baltzer 56
Lanagin James 99
Lancaster Cath. 104
Susanna 104
Thomas 104
Lanch Samuel 147
Landard Johnana 82
Lane Benjamin 17
Gabriel 17
Harrison 20

Lane John 16, 25, 28
Thomas 17, 20
Samuel 26. 28
Lanebach Elisa. 57
Jacob 60
Lang John 90
William 144
Lange Peter 86
Langfitt Frances 41,50
Jarvis 41
John 41
Levin 41
William 41
Langton Ann 67
Eleanor 67
Elizabeth 67
James 65
John 65
Thomas 65
William 65
Langurl Wm. 41
Langwell Eliz. 128
Robert 128
Lanham Aaron 65
Ann 118
Archibald 127
Azariah 137
Catherine 133
Charity 133
Edward 120,134
Eleanor 67
Elias 118
Elisha 119
Elizabeth 67,129,135
Jesse 135
Jane 127
Jemimah 119
John 118
Josias 129
Letty 118
Lucy 135
Margaret 135
Mary 130
Nathan 122
Robert Poor 120
Samuel 133
Sarah 122,126
Shadrick 122
Soloman 135
Susanna 134
Thomas 135
Walter 65
William 69,133
Lankford Jas.F.73
Lannabach Catha.63
Elisabeth 63
Mary 63
Susanna 63
Lanner Thomas 79

Lansdale Cath. 119
Charles 119
Elizabeth 119
Harry 119
Richard 127
Susanna 119
Larance Alex. 113
John 113
Margret 113
Larkin Ann 32
Larnan Ann 80
Larramoor Cath. 155
Jenney 155
Larramore Mary 155
Larrew Abraham 74
Elizabeth 74
Frances 74
George 74
James 74
John 74
Martha 74
Larrow Jane 74
Michel 74
Lary Laurance 104
William 144
Laskin Wm. 14
Lashlee Aaron 86
Arnold 86
Elizabeth 74
John 86
Lucy 130
Margry 86
Mary 86
Moses 86
Rachel 86
Rebackah 86
Robert 86,130
Thomas 74
William 86
Lashley Robt. 130
Laton Danl. 41
James 41
Latimore John 89
Lattimore Eliz. 118
Lauder Ann 107
Laughlin Eliz. 22
Mary 96
Rachael 96
Sarah 96
Thomas 22
William 96
Lauman Cath. 61
Elisabeth 57,61
Lavey Sarah 30
Lavie John 28
Law Patrick 121

Lawder Mary 83
Lawrence Henry 32
John 149
Mary 154
Lawson Alex. 163
Samuel 52
Layton Mary 49
Lazenby Joshua 84
Margery 84
Robert 84
Thomas 84
Leach Ann 118
Leadnenham Edw. 155
League Aquila 103
Leatch Catron 86
James 86
John 86
Mary 86
Lecompt Chas. 37,51
James 37,51
John 50
Leavin 50
Samuel 50
Thomas 34
Wm. 49,51
Lecount Anthoney 158
Ledenham Nath. 152
Lee Ann 102
Cleo 126
Dan 71
Daniel 71
Edward 3
Eliz. 67,71,96
Emelia 71
George 126
James 71,96,112
John 11,54,71,73, 102
Lewis 8
Lucy 67
Oinson 144
Rachel 144
Ruth 67
William 144
Leech Jeremiah 69
Leeds John 155
Leek William 144
Lees John 32
Legg Edward 124
John 149
Mary 124
Matthew 149
William 149
Leidy John 54
Margaret 58
Samuel 60
Susanna 56

| | | | |
|---|---|---|---|
| Leiper Dr. And. 15 | Lewis Thos.64,136 | Linthicum John 5 | Loney Wm.106,107 |
| Leiser Adam 55 | Walter 91 | Thos.Francis 4 | Long Ann 67 |
| Cathrin 57, 62 | Wm.51,55,64,135 | Lintrage Saml.81 | Charles 64 |
| Christianna 62 | Lewos John 72 | Linzy Edward 144 | Christopher 92 |
| George 60 | Leyder Abraham 56,59 | Liphard Augustine 55 | Ellender 112 |
| Henry 60 | Andrew 61 | Catharina 57 | Elisabeth 62 |
| Margret 62 | Cathrin 57,63 | Elisabeth 61 | James 64 |
| Mathias 58 | Christian 55 | Henry 59 | Jane 56 |
| Peter 60 | Eliz.62,63,57 | Lister Joshua 35 | John 51,60,64,120 |
| Susanna 62 | Eve 63 | Litten Alisabeth 111 | Margaretha 62 |
| William 60 | Jacob 61 | Ann 111 | Mary 67 |
| Leith Peter 26 | John 59,61 | Clemency 111 | Thames 58 |
| Lekron Dorethea 57, 61 | Judith 63 | Hannah 88 | Thomas 64 |
| Jacob 60 | July 57 | John 88 | Venia 120 |
| Margret 61 | Julyanna 63 | Mary 88,111 | Longdon Abell 130 |
| Simon 60 | Magdalene 62 | Ruth 111 | Margaret 130 |
| Lemmon Eliz. 110 | Mary 62 | Samuel 111 | Longe John 34 |
| Lemmons Marshal 95 | Susanna 62,63 | Sarah 111 | Thomas 34 |
| Lemon James 158 | Leydor Jacob 56 | Susannah 111 | Longenston Danl.79 |
| Lenard Jonathan 152 | Leyor James 54 | Little Ann 98 | Longly Edw.125 |
| Sarah 153 | Leyfine Thomas 54 | Cathrin 98 | Lookket John 114 |
| Lennard John 159 | Lilley Wm.33,96 | George 98 | Love Ann 79 |
| Thomas 158 | Lillis John 118 | Nathan 97 | David Rev.10 |
| Lestenbarro Henry 84 | Linch Daniel 101 | Littleton Ann 110 | Elisabeth 79 |
| Letherman Cath. 58 | John 95 | Mark 48 | James 96 |
| Letman Jane 128 | Mary 101 | Southy 48 | Leonard 79 |
| John 128 | William 96 | William 48 | Levy 79 |
| Lettlemore Rich 119 | Lincoler John 55 | Lively Eliz.32 | Margarett 96 |
| Letton Eliz. 3 | Lindsey Saml.134 | Lloyd Edw.160 | Sary 79 |
| John 11 | Sarah 134 | Locker Amelia 119 | Thomas 79,96,152 |
| Levell Wm. 156 | Linenberry Benj.86 | David 119 | Lovejoy Alex.126 |
| Leventon Mary 34 | John 86 | Eliz.80,119 | Mary 126 |
| Levin Major 41 | Nicholas 86 | Ellenner 80 | Lovell Eliz.102 |
| Lewin Eliz. 16 | Lines Cornelus 41 | Isaac 119 | Frances 102 |
| Samuel 16 | Lingan James 69 | James 119 | John 102 |
| Lewis Abraham 80 | Joseph 69 | Jesse 80 | Mary 102 |
| Ann 80, 81 | Nicholas 86 | John 80 | Peter 102 |
| Benedict W. 64 | Lingart James 41 | Joseph 81 | Lovitt Charles 32 |
| Eliz. 80, 136 | Lingoe John 64 | Lusey 81 | Lovlis Barton 78 |
| Ellennder 80 | Rachel 67 | Patrick 80 | Benjamin 78 |
| George 80 | Thomas 64 | Phillip 119 | Eleanah 78 |
| Glod 41 | Lingurl Wm. 41 | Shaderick 81 | Reson 78 |
| Hyrom 81 | Link Andrew 58 | Thomas 119 | Sary 78 |
| John 64, 80, 91 | Elisabeth 62 | Virlinder 81 | Zadock 78 |
| Keley 11 | Mary 56 | Lockton Michel 81 | Lovvel John 109 |
| Levin 41 | Linkom Richard 155 | Lockwood Wm. 2 | Low Charles 65 |
| Margaret 80 | Linn Barbra 82 | Logue Cathran 114 | Deborah 97 |
| Martha 70 | Linnenbery Christ.70 | Charity 114 | Henry 156 |
| Mary 67, 80, 91 | Elizabeth 70 | Elisabeth 114 | James 155 |
| Rebecca 91 | Mary 70 | Mary 114 | Rachel 157 |
| Richard 81 | Rusener 70 | William 114 | Lowderman Geo.32 |
| Samuel 80 | Linningham Peatrick 50 | Loney Amos 106 | Lowe Ann 120,134, |
| Sarah 91, 135 | Linthicum Burton 4 | Frances 106 | 138,139 |
| Shadrick 44 | Elizabeth 5 | Mary 107 | Barbary 120 |
| Susanna 80 | Francis 11 | Moses 106 | Elienor 121 |

Lowe Eliz. 120
Henry 120, 139
John 132, 134
Lloyd M. 120
Mary 132
Michael 120
Richard 138
Sarah 72, 138
William 72, 138
Lowman Eliz. 99
Lowndes Christ. 120
Elizabeth 120
Lowrey John 78
Lowry Edward 162
James 126
Joseph 155
Thomas 155
Lucais John 36
Michill 36
Lucas Adam 125
Ann 122
Basil 32
Catherine 128
Charles 76,81
Elijah Capt.32
Ignatius 128
Jamima 81
John 149
Kissiah 81
Lindoes 81
Mary 76,81
Nancy 81
Nansy 76
Precilla 131
Richard 81
Sarah 125
Susanna 81
Thomas 81
William 76,122
Luckett Charity 85
John 84
Leven 85
Moley Ann 84
Phillip H. 84
Susanna 85
Virlinder 85
Wm. Capt.85
Lunan Ormand 106
Lusby Cath 12
Samuel 136
Susanna 136
Lux William 162
Luth Alex. 32
Lyles Sarah 125
William 125

McArdell Isaac 60

McArdell Patr.58
Thomas 58
William 60
McBew James 122
Susanna 122
McBrayerta Mich.97
McBrid Hugh 41
McBride Alex.105
Archibald 32
McCain Wm.Geo.9
McCainley Francis 6
McCallester And.41
Easter 41
Sarah 41
William 41
McCallister John 41
Sutt. 150
McCallster Alceabeth 41
McCann Arthur 97
McCanna Patr. 79
McCarnon Danl. 156
McCartee Hannah 102
Sarah 102
William 107
McCarty Flurrance 84
Levy 109
McCauley Sarah 6
Zachariah 6
McClam Betsey 88
James 88
Mary 88
McClain Alex.6
McClane Geo.130
John 130,144
Mary 130
Precilla 130
McClannahan Saml.144
McClasby Stephen 54
McClean Cath.106
Mary 106
Patrick 106
McClemmey Saml.51
McCloud Sarah 70
McClure Ann 96
McCollester Tabtha 41
McColley Sary 77
McCollister Nath.53
McComas Alex. 93, 100
Ann 94
Aquila 92, 93
Aron 94
Benjamin 100
Edward 93
Elizabeth 93, 94
Hannah 93, 94

McComas James 94
John 92,93
Josiah 94
Martha 94
Mary 92,93,94,100
Nathaniel 94
Salinah 93
Solomon 94
Susannah 94
William 93,94
McComb John 84
McConnal Brian 55
McCormack Eve 67
James 65
John 65
McCoy Alice 144
Janet 75
Katharine 68
McCrackin James 106
Mary 106
Winney 32
McCrary Sarah 41
McCray Zaph.80
McCrown Thos.H.65
McCullough Jane 97
Thomas 97
McCullugh James 84
McDaniel Ann 78
Catherine 136
Daniel 78
Elisabeth 78
Elisha 80
Hennary 78
Jane 139
John 84,139
Leavin 50
Linder 78
Mary 78,80,139
Nancey 87
Reubin 136
Walter 139
Wm. 50,78
McDonald Ann 68,132
Edw.O.73
Elizabeth 68
Jean 121
John 65
Mary 68
Sarah 68
Thomas 65
William 65
McDonale John 65
McDougle Char.& John 127
McDowell Elianor 126
John 126

McFadden Alex.69
McFercen Wm. 69
McGanley Mary 93
McGeomery John 88
McGill Rachell 133
Thomas 133
McGinnis Alethea 68
John 144
Susanna 68
McGirtt James 75
McGlocklanen Mary 85
McGlogian Patr.100
McGomery Wm.88
McGonegill James 144
McGown Ann 99
Margaret 92
McGraw John 46
McHenry Alex.50
McIntoush Alex.82
Ann 82
Benjamin 82
Ellender 82
Lowre 82
Macke 82
William 82
McKay James 55
Timothy 55
McKell Thomas 41
McKenery James 69
John 69
Margaret 70
Mary 70
Thomas 69
McKenn Mich.91
McKenny Joseph 96
McKinsey Elenor 92
Mary 92
Patrick 92
McKisson Arthur 88
James 88
Jane 88
John 88
Sally 88
McLannahan Eliz.144
McLaughlin James 101
McMath Matthew 95
McMurphey Arch.106
McNabb Alice 88
Elizabeth 88
James 88
Jim 88
Keatty 88
Rachell 88
McNeal Arch.158
McNemara John 45

| | | | |
|---|---|---|---|
| McNemara Levin 45 | Mackfaddin Joseph 114 | Maggon Philip 73 | Mahew James 131 |
| Timothey 44 | Mackfail Martha 109 | Maggry Andrew 60 | John 131 |
| McNew Martha 134 | Mackfiel Ann 110 | Magin Ann 56 | Lydia 135 |
| James 134 | Daniel 110 | Magowan Walter 27 | Mary 131 |
| McNulty John 155 | Jane 110 | Magruder Amelia 68 | Samuel 135 |
| McQuay Cath. 155 | John 110 | Ann 67,68 | William 130 |
| Patrick 154 | Mackgyer And. 74 | Aquila 65 | Mahon Thomas 100 |
| McQuillen Rowland 32 | Macklemurray Char. 97 | Archibald 65 | Mahony Anthony 155 |
| McSkiming Enen 144 | John 97 | Brooke 65 | Maikmahn Wm. 34 |
| McSwain Isaac 103 | Margaret 97 | Charity 123 | Mainear Thomas 10 |
| McWilliams Christ. 96 | Patrick 97 | Charles 65 | Major Dosha 105 |
| Elizabeth 96 | Starrat 97 | Charlottee 86 | Jane 105 |
| | Mackmaness Ann 74 | Daniel 65 | John 105 |
| Mabra John 41 | Thomas 74 | Dennis 118 | Malone Thomas 32 |
| Macal Robt. 59 | Macky George 100 | Edward 65,138 | Maloney Jonathan 151 |
| Macantraus Feeby 108 | Macnew Bazell 126 | Elianor 118 | Michael 151 |
| Hugh 108 | Frances 126 | Elias 65 | Maloy Elizabeth 32 |
| Mary 108 | Madding Ann 71 | Eliz. 67,76,86,118 | Mand Daniel 104 |
| Macarty Jacob 109 | Benjamin 71 | Enoch 65,118 | William 144 |
| Maccatee Charity 129 | Catharine 71 | Ezekiel 65 | Mandate Hannah 121 |
| Elizabeth 68 | Elizabeth 71 | George 65 | Manen James 69 |
| Maccatee John 129 | Hezekiah 71 | Hazwell 123 | Manidier Mary 52 |
| Lucy 68 | James 71 | Hezekiah 65 | Manigher Henry 55 |
| Mary 68 | John 71,72 | James 65 | Maninger Eliz. 57 |
| Maccattee Ann 68 | Joseph 71 | Jeane 68 | Manning Anthony 50 |
| Charles 65 | Margra 71 | John 65 | John 52,125 |
| Samuel 65 | Margrett 71 | Josiah 65 | Mary Ann 125 |
| Macceni Sarah 29 | Mary 71 | Lethe 67 | Mansfield Rich. 155 |
| Maccleroy Fargus 32 | Rebeckah 71 | Levin 65 | Mantel Christ. 60 |
| Macconichin Wm. 149 | Sarah 71,72 | Lucy 67 | George 59 |
| Macconikin Elias 149 | Thomas 71 | Margaret 67 | Nicolaus 60 |
| Maccubbin Hellen 68 | Maddocks Eliz. 102 | Mary 67,68,138 | Mantle Barberry 57 |
| Martha 68 | Maddox Catrine 94 | Meek 118 | Christian 54 |
| Mary 68 | Charlotte 94 | Nathaniel 65 | Christiana 62 |
| Nicholas 9,11 | Dorcas 68 | Ninian 65 | Elisabeth 56 |
| Thomas 65 | Elizabeth 71 | Normond B. 65 | Mary 62 |
| Zechariah 65 | Jannet 71 | Patrick 65 | Maradeth Benj. 148 |
| Mackall Benj. 75 | Jacob W. 71 | Priscilla 68 | Marbury Eliz. 125 |
| Elizabeth 74 | John 71,94 | Rebecca 67,86 | Luke 125 |
| Darke 75 | Martha 94 | Richard 65 | Marchel___159 |
| John 75 | Matthew 65 | Sam B. 65 | Ather 158 |
| Mary 75,77 | Rachel 68 | Sam W. 65 | John 158 |
| Rebaca 75 | Thomas 71 | Samuel 65 | Joseph 158 |
| Mackeay Agga 73 | Maffatt Barney 65 | Sarah 67,86 | Marchle James 71 |
| William 73 | Rachel 68 | Susanna 68 | Mary 71 |
| Mackentoush John 128 | Susanna 68 | Thomas 65,138 | Marcum Wm. 99 |
| Pricilla 128 | William 65 | Walter 65 | Marcy Mary 41 |
| Mackette Agness 73 | Maffet Ann 56 | Wm. Beall 65 | Marick John 81 |
| Cloa 73 | Mafford James 88 | Zechariah 65 | Marign Angel 41 |
| Elisha 73 | Magee Sarah 100 | Mahall Eleanor 86 | Marlow Dorithy 124 |
| James 73 | Mager Eliz. 90 | Stephen 65 | Elianor 126 |
| Joseph 73 | Rachel 90 | Mahannah Elener 84 | John 126 |
| Loweser 73 | Thomas 90 | Margaret 84 | Marques Eleanor 70 |
| Mary 73 | Maggal Jane 57 | Mahew Charity 130 | James 69 |
| Mackey Thomas 27 | Maggey Andrew 55 | Elizabeth 131 | Kidd 69 |

| | | | |
|---|---|---|---|
| Marques Mary 70 | Masters Tryphenia 132 | Mecarty Sarah 109 | Messicopp Christ. 80 |
| William 69 | William 65,132 | Mecendlis Ester 114 | George 80 |
| Marr Charles 130 | Mather John 153 | Elizabeth 114 | John 80 |
| Hester 130 | Mathers Rose 35 | John 114 | Margaret 80 |
| John 29 | Mathews Ann 102,105 | Sarah 114 | Mary 80 |
| Marrain John 54 | Bennet 105 | William 114 | Messor Alse 70 |
| Marriott Ellinor 26 | Carvel 105 | Mecool Mary 116 | Thomas 69 |
| Thomas 29 | Elizabeth 105 | Mecurdy Archa 110 | Messy Wm. 54 |
| Marsh Cath. 102 | Francis 105 | Ellender 110 | Metawe Betsey 79 |
| Hannah 102 | Isiah 105 | Margret 110 | Metler Jacob 58 |
| Lloyd 102 | John 105 | Medcalf James 30 | Margaretha 62 |
| Mary 102 | Leven 105 | John 27 | Mettler Henry 60 |
| Thomas 144 | Mary 105 | Thomas 17 | Magdalene 56 |
| Marshall John 49 | Milcah 105 | William 30 | Sebastian 60 |
| Mary 132 | Neomy 105 | Meddis Thomas 41 | Metz Cathrin 57 |
| Richard 153 | Roger 105 | Medly George 76 | Christian 55 |
| Marshel Feby 110 | Matthews ___ 156 | Medowel Mary 114 | Metze Christian 60 |
| Henery 110 | David 158 | Meeds Francis 144 | Meyer Abraham 59 |
| John 110 | James 92 | Thomas 144 | Augustin 60 |
| Martain Virlinder 82 | Thomas 156 | Meeting Thomas 32 | Christian 59 |
| Marten Edward 114 | Mattinly Clement 136 | Megare Alex. 54 | Felix 55 |
| John 78 | Frances 136 | Megay Alee 100 | Francis 55 |
| Margret 114 | Mattorn ___ 160 | George 100 | Henry 59 |
| Mary 114 | Maxley Ann 83 | Hugh 100 | Jacob 55 |
| Samuel 78 | Daniel 83 | James 100 | John 55 |
| William 112 | Elisabeth 83 | John 100 | Miars John 41 |
| Marthers Darby 36 | John 83 | Robert 100 | Michael Eberhard 58 |
| Martin Amelia 118 | Susanna 83 | Sarah 100 | John 54 |
| Elaxander 116 | Maxwell Alex. 144 | William 100 | Mary 58 |
| Isaac 115 | May Ann 75 | Meggs John 157 | Michel Mary 56 |
| James 59 | Benjamin 128 | Megill Elisabeth 117 | Middleton Belt 128 |
| John 132 | Elizabeth 128 | John 117 | Mary 134 |
| Martha 116 | John 92 | Mary 117 | Ruth 128 |
| Mary 132,134 | Mayer Charles 149 | William 117 | Smith 134 |
| Michael 134 | Maynard Foster 158 | Meginias Alleyfar 78 | Theodore 65 |
| Rozia 118 | Samuel 21 | Catarin 78 | William 160 |
| Rosina 57 | Mayo Joseph 7,11 | Mary 78 | Milbey John 144 |
| Samuel 59 | Mead Saml. 25 | Neal 78 | Milbourn Mary 104 |
| Smith 118 | Meads John 151 | Thomas 78 | Sarah 104 |
| Susanna 118 | Meake Adam 113 | Meginis Mary 109 | Milburn Wm. 144 |
| Thomas 52,118 | Andrew 113 | Meglin Marg. 56 | Miles Ann 140 |
| William 55 | Esther 113 | Meguire Marg. 61 | Elisabeth 81 |
| Martus Henrietta 68 | John 113 | Melarve John 82 | James 81 |
| Maryman Samuel 162 | Martha 113 | Merick Elianor 123 | John 81 |
| Mashman Susanna 102 | Mearet Margaret 78 | John 123 | Mary 25,81 |
| | Mears Fisher 41 | Merideth John 43 | Nicholas 81,140 |
| Mason Abraham 33 | Osborn 120 | Rebecca 44 | Thomas 21,25 |
| Isaac 151 | Mecan Chas 112 | William 43 | William 25 |
| John 33 | Daniel 112 | Meridith Thomas 144 | Millar Sarah 41 |
| Sarah 136 | Elisabeth 112 | Merrick Isaac 36 | Milley Jacob 69 |
| William 148 | John 112 | Merrill Silvanus 32 | Millican Ruth 136 |
| Massey Isaac 97 | Patrick 112 | Mesick John 44 | Samuel 136 |
| Wm. Clark 144 | Mecarty Eliz. 109 | Messack James 41 | Millington ___ 160 |
| Masters Barsheba 68 | Mary 109 | Messay Evey 70 | Nixson 160 |
| John 65 | Owing 108 | Messer Elisabeth 57 | Miller Agnis 114 |
| Margaret 68 | | | |
| Mary 132 | | | |

Miller Andrew 54, 58
 Barbara 58
 Cath. 57, 62
 Christiana 56
 Eliz. 62, 130, 133
 Eve 62
 Fronica 56
 George 58, 60
 Hannah 97
 Henry 55, 60
 James 121, 151
 John 97
 Joseph 97
 Margaretha 62
 Margret 58, 114
 Martha 97
 Mary 56, 62, 97, 114
 Peter 130
 Philip 133
 Salomon 58
 Samuel 114
 Sarah 114
 Thomas 82
 Thomisdike 114
 William 162
Mills Edward 52
 Frederick 29
 Jacob 65
 James 47
 John 114
 Right 52
 Robert 114
 Susannah 114
 Thomas 32
Milwood Wm. 157
Minnis Dorithy 138
 John 138
Minish Elesabeth 41
Mires Adam 65
 Conrod 84
 Hannah 98
 James 98
 John 84, 98
 Leamah 98
 Margaret 84
 Mary 84
 Mirey Fred. 69
Misler Abraham 44
Mitchel/Mitchell
 Ann 113, 115
 Aquilla 113
 Asel 113
 Averrillah 114, 115
 Barbara 73
 Barker 113
 Barnet 115

Mitchel Bath.73
Clemmency 113
Edward 113
Eliz 93,108,113,
  115,125,134
Elaxanders 115
Frederick 108
Gaberil 108
Hannah 113
James 112,113,115
Jane 115
John 93,108
Joseph 125
Kent 113,115
Micajah 114
Moredeca 73
Lucy 73
Martha 113,114
Mary 108,150
Notley 73,134
Rachel 108,113
Ritchard 115
Robert 93
Sarah 10,73,93,
    113,115
Shadick 113
Shurlotter 113
Thomas 113,115
William 93,113
Moaks Ruth 32
Moaner Timothy 144
Moberey Arron 36
Mockby Ann 68
 Dennis 65
 John 65
 Joice 68
 Zechariah 65
Mohan Edw.115
 Elisabeth 115
 James 115
 John 115
 Judy 115
 Margret 115
 Mary 115
 William 115
Mohon Ann 117
 Cathron 117
 Jane 117
 John 117
 Martha 117
 William 117
Mold Walter 144
Molds Dannil 148
Molix Jimmimey 50
Moll Benj.55

Moll Elisabeth 56
 Henry 55,59
Molten Mrs.32
Molten Ann 113
 John 115
Molton Mathew 108
Monday James 92
Monger Mary 56
 William 69
Monroe John 106
Monrow Eliz.50
Montgomery Margaret 118
Montgomry James 60
 William 60
Mooberry Frances 103
 William 103
Mookin Mark 43
 Mary 43
Mookins Ezekiel 46
Mooney Patr.144
Moor Elijah 41
 Thomas 41
Moors Samuel 46
Moore Andrew 65
 Benj.73,137
 Christopher 51
 Elizabeth 73
 Enesent 122
 Hester 139
 James 137
 Jeremiah 122
 Mary 151
 Sarah 73
 Susannah 46
 Thomas 45, 139
 Wm. 163
Morain Mary 49
 Moses 48
More James 144
 Martha 79
 Mary 79
 Nathon 79
 Samuel 79
 William 33
Moreland Henry 144
Morgan Cassandria
 96
 Druzillah 94
 Echsah 94
 Eliz. 35, 96, 131
 Hugh 94
 James 32, 34
 Joel 96
 John 96
 Lucy 94
 Lydia 96
 Margret 96

Morgan Marmaduke 1
 Mary 96
 Nathaniel 54
 Rachael 96
 Robert 96
 Ruth 96
 Sarah 94,96
 Solomon 34
 Thomas 96,156
 William 41,96
Morgar Joseph 88
Morgin David 54
Morley Joseph 160
Morling Francis 59
Morris Barton 136
 Daniel 126
 Edward 48
 Elizabeth 125
 Giles 103
 Jane 103
 Mary 136
 Richard 103
 Susanna 103
 Thomas 32,125
 Ufam 103
Morrison Ann 88
 John 32,88
 Joseph 93
 Martha 93
 Mary 88,93
 Samuel 15
Morsal James 153
Morse Wm.144
Morrow John 85
Morry James 69
Morton Thos.21
Moses Robt.69
 Margaret 70
Moubrey James 101
 Mary 101
 Robert 101
Mounce Eliz.70
 Jacob 69
 John 69
 Katharine 70
Mountseer Wm. 144
Mowbery Robt.32
Mowen Baltzer 61
 Catharina 58
 Catrin 57
 Daniel 58,61
 George 61
 John 55
 Leonhard 59
 Ludwig 56

Mowen Madg. 63
  Margaret 56
  Mary 57, 63
  Peter 61
  Stephen 55
Muan Thomas 17
Muckelrath Sarah 109
Mudd Ann 125
  Francis 134
  John 119
  Sarah 134
  Thomas 125
  Walter 119
Muffet Elisabeth 62
  Margaretha 62
  William 54
Muir Charles 41
  James 41
  Thomas 53
Mulania James 53
Mulkehy James 65
Mull Catherin 61
  Eliz. 57, 61
Mullican Catherine 123
  Elizabeth 123
  John 123
  Mary 128
  Sarah 123
  Thomas 123
  William 128
Mulliken Belt 12
  Jeremiah 12
  Thomas 12
Mumford John 144
Mungess Benj. 19
Mungle --- 70
  Michael 19
Munnett Wm. 35
Munroe Eliz. 100
  John 100
  Mary 100
  Thomas 100
  William 100
Murdock John 65
  Martha 75
Murfey Alea 111
  Elisabeth 111
  Frances 111
  James 111
  John 111
  Rosannah 111
Murphey Ann 32
  Antoney 69
  Elizabeth 70
  Hannah 102

Murphey Joab 106
  John 45, 144
  Joseph 105
  Katharine 68
  Peter 105
  Rebecca 70
  Sarah 106
  Susanna 105
  Thomas 101
  Timothy 105
  William 69, 105, 106
Murphy Frances 102
  John 102
  Mary 102
  Sarah 102
  Timothy 102
Murray Alex 97
  Archibald 97
  Elizabeth 97
  James Dr. 53
  Jane 97
  John 97
  Mary 97
  Sarah 97
Murrey Judah 118
Murtle Ann 119
  Elianor 119
Muse Thomas 52, 53
Musgrave Benj. 126
  Jemimah 126
Musgrove Frances 110
Mussy Charles 26
Myer Barbara 61
  Elisabeth 57
  Margret 57
  Simon 58
Myers John 4

Nabb Sarah 144
Nalley Saml. 130
  Sarah 130
Nash Thos. 22, 156
Nave Abraham 58
  Christianna 58
  George 55
  Henry 59
  Leonhard 54
  Magdalina 57
  Margret 61
  Michael 59
  Sophia 61
Neagle Rachell 132
Neal & Neall
  Charles Dr. 79
  George 18

Neal Hugh Rev. 151
  Ralph 79
  Thomas 30, 85
  William 151
Neave John 92
  Mary 93
  Sarah 92
  Timothy 92
  William 92
Need Barbara 56
  Catharina L. 56
  Daniel 60
  Jacob 60
  Juley 62
  Mathias 54
  Sharlote 62
Needham Ann 68
  Sarah 68
Neel James 41
Neighbories Saml. 151
Neighbours Thos. 157
Neithsmith John 157
Nelson Aquila 100
  John 100
  Mrs. 32
  Pesilla 100
Nemara John M. 43
Nennom George 2
Nerol John 144
Neronam Danl. 144
  John 144
  Joseph 144
  William 144
Nevel Ann 119
  James 119
  John 100, 119
  Joseph 119
  Margaret 121
  Mary 119
  Richard 119
  Ruth 100
  Thomas 119
  William 121
Nevil James 144
  Sarah 144
  Walter 144
New Mary 73
Newbon Thomas 103
Newcom Robert 159
Newland Thomas 104
Newswanger Isaac 55
Newton James 84
  Mary 84
  Nathaniel 139
Neydin Hestor 118

Neydin Mary 118
  Thomas 118
Nickers ___ 160
Nicodemus Andrew 60
  Catharina 58
  Conrad 56
  Frederick 56
Nicholls & Nickolls
  Ann 68, 75
  Benjamin 75
  Casandra 75
  Daniel 75
  Elizabeth 68, 75
  Henry 65
  Isaiah 75
  James 65
  John 65
  Rebeckah 75
  Samuel 75
  Thomas 65, 75
  William 75
Nichols Ann 68
  Asa 128
  Charity 68
  Elizabeth 68
  Henney Mrs. 156
  Henry 135
  Mary 135
  Mary Ann 68
  Susanna 68
Nicolous Eve 56
  Jacob 54, 60
Nicholson Alice 11
  Daniel 160
  John 1, 13
  Joseph 144, 151
Nighton Keizer 135
  Mary 135
Niles George 76
Nisbet Ann 79
  Barnett 79
  Catron 79
  Charles 79
  Ellenner 79
  Lydea 79
  Mary 79
Nix Elizabeth 158
Nixon John 53
  Jonathan 73
Nixson Jonathan 74
Nobbs Elisabeth 84
  Hennary 84
  John 84
  Nansey 84
Noble Catherine 124

Noble Mark 50,107
Nehemiah 149
Thomas 118
William 47
Nobs Joseph 156
Nohel Catherine 106
Nonlon Thomas 106
Norress William 158
Norman Benjamin 23
  Christopher 41
  Ester 49
  John 31
  Nicholas 31
  Phillip 80
  Thomas 23,52
Norris Alex.91
  Benedict 91
  Benj.Bradford 91
  Daniel 93
  Elizabeth 91
  Hannah 90
  Jacob 92
  Jane 90
  John 31,91
  Lester 105
  Margaret 90
  Martha 91
  Mary 90
  Moliein 53
  Richard 90
  Sarah 91,93
  Susannah 91
  Thomas 31,91
Norton Amelia 119
  Ann 122,132
  Catherine 123
  Chloe 132
  Elianor 135
  Elizabeth 123
  Henry 128
  John 123
  Mary 119
  Neamiah 122
  Robert 132
  Sophia 97
  Stephen 97
  Thomas 123
  William 119,135
Norwood Ann 153
  Edward 159
  Robert 157
  William 158
Notherwood Joseph 51
Nott Jane 97
  Mary 97

Nott Sarah 97
  William 97
Nowell Richard 26
Nowland Mary 97
Nower Alex.93
  Ann 93
  James 93
  Jesse 93
  Phebe 93
  Rachel 93
Nox James 55,58
  June 57
Nuckle Wm. 32
Nugen Ann 92
  Elizabeth 92
  Jane 92
  Robeccah 92
  Sarah 92
Nuols Mary 152
Nussey Johanna 136
Nuton Nimrod 50
  Richard 48
  Willis 50
Nutterwell Danl.105
Nutwell Bennet 114
  Daniel 114
  Minty 114

Obrien Roger 103
Odear Ann 62
  Benjamin 60
  Jane 62
  John 54
  Sarah 56
Odle Baruch 65
Offley Benton 144
  John 144
  Vinson 144
Offutt Ursula 68
Ogden Ann 86
  Charles 86
  David 86
  Dorraty 86
  Heugh 86
  Mary 86
  Ruth 86
Ogdon Robert 124
Ogg Cordelia 99
  Stocke 99
Oggan Peggey 51
Oldson Thos.150
Oliver Esther 107
  Cathrin 100
  James 100,107
  Susanna 107

Olliver Daniel 30
  William 20,30
O'Neal Barton 76
  Janet 76
  John 76
  Joseph 76
  Margaret 76
  Mary 76
  Peter 76
  Phebe 76
Onell Thomas 36
Onely John 9
Onion Henry 5
  John 1
  Stephen 93
  Thomas 93
Oram Levi 41
  Rachel 158
Oramm Wm.158
Ore Mary 101
  Rebecca 101
Oren Precilla 127
  Robert 127
Orme Ann 128
  Eleanor 70
  Lucy 70
  Nathan 128
  Ruth 70
Orne Hezekiah 26
  Michel 81
Orill John 37
_orkston John 159
Orrell Thomas 34
Orrick Thomas 5
Orusan Mary 112
Orsburn Amous 109
  Ann 109
  Aquila 109
  Bennet 109
  Elisabeth 109
  John 109
  Josias 109
  Sarah 109
Osben Hannah 82
Osbond Saml.147
Osborn Ann 82
  Benjamin 82
  David 82
  Gean 99
  James 98,99
  Martha 99
  Mary 82
  Thomas 83
  William 98
Osborne Abariler 99

Osborne Ann 105
  Benjamin 98
  Cordelia 99
  Cyrus 99,105
  Mary 99
  Semelia 98
  Susannah 98,105
  William 99
Osburn Samuel 21
Oster Catharina 56
  Catharine 62
  Elisabeth 56,62
  John 54,59
  Mary 62
  Philip 54
Ott Catharina 56
  Jacob 54,60
  Margaretha 56
  Michael 54,60
Otten John 83
Oure John 109
Overstocks Peter 93
Owen Anne 127
  Benjamin 127
  Elizabeth 78
  John 78
  Lawrence 63
  Thomas 78
Owens Charles 105
  James 9,29
  John 51
  Joseph 5,18,24
  Mary 105
  Owen 49
  Sarah 105
  Thomas 18
Owings John 144
Owins William 34
Ozburn Ann 72
  Archabald 72
  Charlot 72
  Elander 72
  Issac 72
  Lenard 72
  Mary 72
  Potter 72
  William 72

Paca Aquila 107
  William 107
Page Anthoney 123
  Frances 134
  James 134
  Mary 109
  Winefred 123

Pain Elizabeth 90
  John 90
  Pricilla 90
Paine Isaac 34
Palmer ___ 160
  Jariat 77
  Tobitha 77
  William 135
Pane John 135
  Mary 135
Paniel Robert 28
Paris Elizabeth 92
  Kisiah 92
  Mary 92
  Moses 92
  Rachel 92
  Rebeccah 92
  Sabinah 92
  Susanah 92
  William 92
Parker Alethea 139
  Amelia 68
  Ann 25,68
  Daniel 51
  David 65
  Drusilla 122
  Elizabeth 68
  John 101,121,122
  Josias 25
  Margaret 68
  Martha 68
  Mary 68,121
  Sarah 68
  William 65
Parkins Ann 119
  Casandria 137
  Rachell 119
  Samuel 119
  Thomas 137
Parks James 88
  Jane 88
  John 44
  Martha 88
Parmer James 52
Parr Nathaniel 121
Parriott Thos.16
  William 15
Parris Comfort 42
Parrish John 42
  Peter 22
Parsley Thomas 5
Parson Edward 36
Partridge Isaac 52
  Jonathan 52
Pasley John 69

Patee Elizabeth 91
  Peter 91
  Sarah 91
Paten Samuel 54
Patterson George 32
  Gorge 117
Pattison Atthow 52
Patrick Ann 97
  Elizabeth 97
  Hugh 97
  John 97
  Margret 97
  Mary 97
Paul Charles 46
  Daniell 48
  Edward 48
  Elizabeth 70
  Jacob 44,69
  Lewis 47
  Margaret 70
  Mary 44
  Nicholls 69
  Peter 69
Paydan Thomas 114
Peacock Cassandria 97
  John 97,145
  Mary 97
  Robert 145
Pear John 134
Pearce Ann 70
  Benjamin N.69
  Daniel 9
  Joseph 3
  Martha 130
  Martha 130
  Mary 134
  Rachell 130
  Sarah 11
  Thomas 130
  William 3,130
Pearson Abel 109
  Edward 43
  Elisabeth 109
  Joseph 109
  Mary 109
  Samuel 109
  Thomas Capt.10
Peddicoat Nicholas 85
Peifer Elisabeth 57
  George 59
  Joseph 55
Peirce Catharin 72
  John Baptis 72
  Margratt 72
Pely William 42

Pemberton Joseph 18
Penix James 88
  John 88
  Keatty 88
  Sarah 88
  Susanna 88
Penningtton Segar 53
Penny Henry 163
Penrose Cassandra 104
  Isaac 104
  Herriot 104
Perraron Geo. Hy 145
Perrarone Thomas 145
Perrey Mary 35
Periman Eliz.109
  Isaac 109
  John 109
  Martha 109
  Mary 109
Permar James 145
Perry Chas.77
  James 77,133
  Jane 117
  John 101,133
  Marcia 133
  Margret 117
  Mary 87
  Penelope 133
  Peter 117
  Sarah 117
  Thomas 87,117
  William 109,117
Perryman Rich.81
Pervail Gidian 111
  Margret 111
  Mary 111
Peterkin James 37
  Mary 32
Peters Frances 32
  R. 129
  Robert 63
  William 103
Petor Alex.69
  Elizabeth 70
  John 69
  Margaret 70
  Robert 69
  Thomas 69
Pettlehiser Lewis 99
Peyfer Martin 54
Phelps Deborah 4
  James 2
  John 4
  Josiah 2
  Margaret 76
  Richard 3

Phelps Susannah 5
Pheps Thomas 22
Philips Jane 132
  Obeddo 132
  Robert 140
  Sarah 140
Philleps John 41
Phillips Amos 84
  Bethia 110
  Elizabeth P.101
  James 101,109,110
  John P. 101
  Jeane 46
  Jesse 84
  Martha 99,101
  Mary 26
  Pegey 51
  Rachel 46
  Samuel 98,99
  Sarah 110
  Susannah 101
  William 42, 48, 163
Philpott Thos.7
Phips Nathaniel 22
  Thomas 8
Pibus John 27
Pickerson Elizabeth 139
  Ralph 139
Pierce Ann 104
  John 129
  Nicholas 65
  Rachael 104
  Richard 104
  Susanna 129
Pike Aquila 104
  Lewis 48
  Rebecca 104
Piles Osborn 131
  Mary 131
Pindel Ann 18
Pindell John 18
Pinder Edward 145
  William 145
Pine John 32
Pitt Frances 100
  Thomas 47
Plommer Eliz.73
  Jane 73
  Kesiah 73
  Mary 73
  Rebeckah 73
  Sarah 73
Ploughman John 155
Plowman Edward 107
Plug Rose 48

Plumer Thomas 160
Yarnall 160
Plummer Henry 16
John 17,151
Rizdon 144
Plunket Michael 104
Poage Sarah 88
Poland Christian 93
William 63
Pollixiin Ann W.77
Elisabeth 77
Ellennas W. 77
Jemeny W. 77
James W. 77
John W. 77
Mary W. 77
Matthew W. 77
Victory W. 77
Ponder John 145
William 145
Pool Ann 77
Benjamin 77
Elisabeth 77
John 77
Joseph 77
Mary 77
Rachel 77
Sary 77
Tary 77
Samuel 3
Poole Samuel 3
Pooley Sarah 145
Poor Elizabeth 129
John 129
Pope Elizabeth 131
Joseph 131
Margret 62
Nathaniel 131
Samuel 145
Poplin Elisabeth 78
Porter ___ 159
Agnis 110
Arthur 52
Elisabeth 113
Ellender 110
Hewes 153
James 52
Jane 152
John 110,153
Joseph 152
Larnie 34
Margret 110
Robert 35
Saran 110,154
William 113,160

Poselwatte Robet 36
Pots Cathran 115
Elisabeth 115
Jacob 115
John 115
Rynard 115
Powel William 25
Powell John 9,160
William 9
Power Elisabeth 113
Nicholas 84
Nicoles 115
William 113
Prakunie Margret 57
Margretha 57
Parkunier Barbara 61
David 58
Elisabeth 61
Henry 58
Jacob 58
Peter 55,58
Susanna 61
Prather Ann 126
Joseph 126
Martha 127
Nathan 126
Rachell 127
Ruth 126
William 127
Zepheniah 127
Pratt Henry 150,151
Phil.150
Prendergast Electea 92
Thomas 92
Presbury Elisabeth 110
Hannah 103
Preston Elisa.112
Rachel 145
Prewit James 98
Price Ann 123
Banoney 123
Charles 151
David 20
Hannah 93
Ignatius 123
James 93
John 135
Margaret 144,145
Mary 123,135
Robert 93
Thomas 76,148
William 47,145
Prigg Mary 108
Primrose Geo. 145
John 145

Pringle John 69
Prise Mary 109
William 109
Pritchard Benj.115
Elisabeth 115
Harmon 115
James 115
John 115
Obidiah 117
Samuel 115
Sarah 115
Stephen 117
Thomas 103
Pritchard Mary 108
Pritchett Arthur 45
Jobis 45
Margaret 68
Thomas 45
Zebulon 45
Proctor Rich.97
Proud Cath.151
Prusten Edward 76
Pryor Wm. 145
Puesly Lidia 111
Pullin Eliz.62
Mary 56
William 54
Pumphries Eliz.139
William 139
Punteny Ann 100
Aquila 100
Geo. H. 100
James 100
John 100
Joseph 100
Nelson 100
Prisela 100
Samuel 100
Sarah 100
Puntry Edward 162
Purdey Ann 79
Catron 79
Richard 79
Purdie Henry 134
Purdom Henna 79
John 79
Joshua 79
Kesiah 79
Walter 79
Purdy Edmund 10
Henry 11
Thomas 69
William 11
Purkins John 112
Ritchard 108
Purley Ned 75

Purliven Eliz.68
Purse Gabriel 144
Putty Charles 69
Pyfer Margaret 58

Queen Eliz.130
Mary 130
Richard 130
Walter 130
Quere Henry 54
Querrer Oniah 101
Quimby John 145
Quinnily Rich.34

Ragen Andrew 86
Ragg Andrew 42
Ragon Eliz.123
Timothy 123
Ralph Stephen 145
Ramington James 65
John 65
Ramsey Alisabeth 111
Andrew 111
James 111
Jane 111
Mary 111
Thomas 111
William 111
Randel Augustis 21
Richard 15
Randell Eliz.79
Randle John 69
Rankin Ann 12
Rantzell Andrew 121
Catherine 121
Rarrone James 60
Rately Isiah 90
Rathell Saml.150
Ratican Peter 91
Ratliff Rachel 25
Raughlins James 126
Mary 126
Raush George 59
John 59
Nicholous 58
Sabastian 59
Ravenscroft John 69
Rawley James 42
John 42
Rawlings Aaron 3
Cassaway 9
Jonathan 16
Richard 1,16
Samuel 16,31
Stephen 8

Rawlings Wm. 10
Rawls Ann 8
Raws James 35
  Sarah 33
Ray Ann 68
  Cathron 115
  Gorge 115
  James 65
  Jemima 68
  John 121
  Mary 68,115,131
  Robert 115
  Samuel 115
  Sarah 121
  Thomas 65,131
Raybolt Jacob 32
Rayley Water 47
Reab John 54,59
  Peter 59
  Margret 57
  Michael 58
Read William 1
Ready Sophiah 71
Reagar John 130
  Sopnia 130
Reap Eve 61
  John 54
  Mary 61
Reardin Daniel 94
Reaugh John 155
Reardon Osias 102
  John 102
  Mary 102
Reason James 98
  John 98
  Richard 104
Reaves John 137
  Sarah 137
Redden John 131
  Ruth 131
Reddin James 132
  Rebecca 132
Reding Ann 101
  John 101
  Milcah 101
  William 101
Reddish Joseph 154
Redman Clie 139
  John I.S.139
Redman James 105
  John 128
  Margaret 105
  Mary 120
  Rebecca 120
  Sarah 128
Reease Robart 109

Reeb Elisabeth 57
Reeber Mary 61
Reed Charles 33
  Eleanor 12
  Eliz.68,99
  Francis 145
  George 65
  Joshua 42
  Priscilla 68
  Rosanna 52
  Samuel 145
  Sarah 68
  William 33,46,145
Rees Aberam 116
  Abraham 113
  Averilla 115
  Cathron 113
  George 115
  Hector 97
  James 113
  Jane 116
  John 97,113,115
  Joseph 113,116
  Margrett 97,113,115
  Mary 97
  Sarah 115
  Sollimin 115
  Soloman 57
  William 113
Reese Alex.88
  Ann 32,88
  Christian 32
  Hanna 88
  Jese 88
  Margrett 88
  Mary 88
  Nancey 88
  Nelly 88
  Sary 100
  William 88
Regin Tabitha 42
Reigel Adam 38
  Eve 56
Reily Barney 55
Reimal Elias 60
  Elisabeth 57
  George 56
  Jacob 60
  John 60
  Philip 56,60
Reimel Cathrin 57
  Mary 57
Reitenauer Barbara 57
  Cathrin 61
  Dorothy 61
  Eliza.61

Reitenauer Eliz.M.61
  Eve 58,61
  Henry 58
  Jacob 55
  Joseph 59
  Ludwig 55
  Magd.57,58
  Mary 61
  Mathias 55
  Nicolous 58
  Peter 58
  Rosina 57,61
  Susanna 61
Rench Andrew 55
  Daniel 59
  David 59
  Catherin 61
  Catharina 61
  Elisabeth 67,61
  Ester 61
  Jacob 59
  John 55,59
  Joseph 58,59
  Margret 57
  Michael 59
  Peter 55,59
  Susanna 61
Renner Philip 55
Renshaw Casandra 92
  Elizabeth 92
  Jane 92
  Joseph 89,92
  Philip 92
  Samuel 92
  Susanah 92
  Thomas 92
Reyley Elianor 131
  Jeremiah 131
Reyly Christian 133
  Margaret 133
Reynolds Ann 151
Rhodes George 98
Rhoads Hannah 89
  Magdeline 89
  Martha 89
  Mary 89
  Thomas 89
Rian Joshua 76
  Jamima 76
  William 76
Rich John 94
  Peter 36,151
  William 37
Richards Ann 42
  John 83,100
Richardson ___159

Richardson Anne 127
  Benjamin 148
  Daniel 152
  Henry 158
  John 36
  Joseph 6,30
  Peter 154
  Philip 3
  Richard 16
  Robert 154
  Thomas 69,127
Richmond John 26,28
Ricords Wm.145
Riddall Eleanor 106
  John 106
  Mary 106
  Robert 106
  Sarah 106
Riddell Eliz.124
  Henry 125
  John 124
Ridgely Eliz.6
Ridgeway Charity 136
  Elizabeth 136
  Jonathan 136
  Martha 123
  Mary 131
  Richard 131,136
  Robert 123
  William 158
Ridgley Charles
  163
Ridgly Mary 162
Ridgway Isaac 65
  Jemima 68
  Jonathan 65
  Joseph 65
  Robert 65
  Sarah 68
Ried John 14
Riedd James 137
Riefenagh Philip 54
Rigbey Jonathan 158
  Moses 158
  Philmon 158
Rigbie Ann 97
  James 97
  Mary 97
  Nathan 97
  Sarah 97
  Susannah 97
Rigbies J. 88
Rigby John 145
  Thomas 159
Rigdon Charles 108
  John Edw.69
  Mary 70,91
  Sarah 108
  Thomas 69

| | | | |
|---|---|---|---|
| Rigeaway Eliz.83 | Ringrose Aaron 152 | Robinson Andrew 45 | Rogers Rebecca 63 |
| Hathaliah 83 | Rippeth James 145 | Ann 78,90,123 | Robert 94 |
| John 83 | Risoner Eleanor 70 | Charity 78 | Thomas 48 |
| Sary 83 | Elizabeth 70 | Charles 78,139 | Ruth 94 |
| William 83 | Jacob 69 | Carlos 78 | Sarah 94 |
| Rigg Ann 83 | Mary 70 | Eleanor 68 | Rogirs William 33 |
| Benjamin 83 | Risteau Susanna 107 | Eliz.56,62,68,78, | Rohrer Ann 63 |
| Charles 83 | Riston Babtist 132 | 90,122,124,139 | Barbara 62 |
| Hennaritta 83 | Mary 132 | George 32,49 | Catharine 56 |
| Rebeca 83 | Ritcharson Saml.60 | Isaac 124 | Cathrin 63 |
| Riggin Edward 42 | Ritter Ann 57 | Jaen 78 | Christian 55,58 |
| Riggs Ann 78 | Barbara 63 | James 78,88,123,135 | Christiana 57 |
| Azariah 76 | Cathrin 57 | Jane 137,88 | Elisabeth 63 |
| Basil 65 | Elias 56 | John 45,78,58, | Frederick 54,59 |
| Charles 78 | Elisabeth 63 | 122,124 | Fronica 57 |
| Elisabeth 76 | Jacob 56,60 | Keziah 124 | George 59 |
| James 65 | Judith 57 | Lake 45 | Jacob 55,58,59 |
| John 76,77 | Margret 63 | Martin 55 | John 58,59 |
| Mary 68, 78 | Tobias 60 | Mary 68,78,80,88,135 | Mary 63 |
| Maxemilia 68 | Roach Richard 85 | Matthew 4 | Samuel 58 |
| Nansey 76 | Robey Eliz.78 | Molley 45 | Roles Joseph 113 |
| Ophea 76 | John 130,134 | Rachel 68 | Mary 113 |
| Rachel 76 | Margaret 134 | Peter 139 | Matthew 113 |
| Robert 65 | Mary 130 | Richard 90 | Rolle John 152 |
| Ruth 76 | Roberson Abraham 116 | Sary 78 | Rollins Eliz.136 |
| Sarah 68 | Amelia 114 | Stephen 137 | John 119 |
| Thomas 65, 76 | Elisabeth 116 | Susanna 68 | Rollisten Rich.49 |
| Right Henry 69 | Ellender 113 | Susey 73 | Romalls Leon.1 |
| Margartha 62 | Eseakel 113 | Thomas 90 | Roodes Jeremiah 36 |
| Robard 162 | John 42,116 | Virlinda 68 | Roof John 59 |
| Rigney Ann 78 | Sarah 112,116 | Walter 88 | Roofe Margret 57 |
| Lusey 78 | Zachariah 69 | William 78,88,90 | Roofer Margret 57 |
| Terance 78 | Roberts ___160 | Robson Andrew 158 | Rooke Michael 105 |
| Rilay Danais 84 | Arthur 69 | Elizabeth 147 | Root Ann 111 |
| Riley Amos 65 | David 145 | John 158 | Daniel 111 |
| Eleanor 68 | Elizabeth 105 | Robert 159 | James 111 |
| Esther 68 | Even 21 | Thomas 158 | Jean 111 |
| George C. 65 | Henry 25 | Rochester Eliz.145 | John 111 |
| Hugh 65 | James 145 | Francis 145 | Margret 111 |
| Isaac 65 | Jane 134 | Mary 145 | Mary 111 |
| James 65 | Jonathan 134 | William 145 | Richard 111 |
| Martha 68 | Sarah 105 | Rockford Edward 78 | Rose Aquila 93 |
| Patrick 85 | Thomas 31 | Rodgers Cassandra 97 | Constant 93 |
| Sarah 68 | William 11,65 | Elizabeth 97 | Joseph 93 |
| Walter 65 | Robertson Andrw.81 | Joseph 97 | Rebeccah 93 |
| Rimmer James 152 | Daniel 65 | Mary 97 | Sam 50 |
| Rinehard Ann 63 | James 65 | Rachael 97 | Roser John 145 |
| Barbara 56 | Middleton 65 | Samuel 97 | Roseberry James 145 |
| Catharina 63 | Nathan 65 | Susannah 97 | Ross Alexander 65 |
| Eve 57 | Robert 65 | William 97 | Annania 120 |
| George 60 | Samuel 65 | Roe Robt.73,75 | Casandrew 93 |
| Magdalena 58 | Zechariah 65 | Rogers Belinda 54 | David 120 |
| Thomas 55 | Robeson Eliz.73 | John 33,112 | Elenor 93 |
| Rinehart George 54 | James 74 | Joseph R.32 | George 19 |
| Ringgold Jacob 149 | Robins John 100 | Nathan 145 | James 50 |
| Thomas 149 | | | |

Ross John 150, 163
Mary 63, 93
Prudence 63
Robert 44
Sarah 93
Susanna 123
Thomas 44
William 93, 123
Rotherick Eliz.92
Mary 92
William 92
Roughton Robt.14
Roush Catharine 61
Elisabeth 57
James 32
John 145
Magdalena 61
Margret 61
Sara 148
Susanna 61
Row Thomas 36
Rowan Wm. 65
Rowe George 135
Sarah 135
Rowen Daniel 69
Royal Joseph 152
Roylins Hodson 49
Rozer Eleanor 139
Henry 139
Notley 126
Rue___ 160
Jersey 48
Rufe Ruedy 55
Ruff Ann 109
John 101
Sarah 101
Ruhe Elisabeth 56
Rullan Rachel 77
Russel Aaron 65
Russum Luke 48
Ruth John 145
Thomas 145
Rumble John 45
Rumbley Edger 36
Jacob 36
Rumbly Smith 35
Rummage Davis 88
Martha 88
Rummage Geor 88
George 88
Mary 88
Tom 88
Rumsey Harritt 110
John 110
Martha 110

Rumsey Mary 110
Runhel Daniel 69
John 69
Katharine 71
Mary 70
Sarah 70
Valentine 69
Rursum Will 151
Russel Mary 68
Russell Ann 131
Bazell 140
Thomas 85
Rutherford John 65
Rutland Thomas 2
Rutter Ann 116
Esther 116
Henry 163
Richard 116
Sarah 116
Ryan John 121
Sarah 121
William 3, 8, 151
Sackel John 42
Sadler John 93
Sailor Barbara 57
John 55
Magdalena 57,58
Mathias 58
Peter 55
Susanna 61
St.Clair Robert 132
St.Lawrence Eleanor 5
Nicholas 5
William 5
St.Tee James 150
St.Thomas Jenifer Daniel 13
Salome Mary 56
Salter Thomas 123
Margaret 23
Samders Charles 77
Edward 77
John 77
Hennaratter 77
Sandars John 42
Sander Elisabeth 62
Sophia 62
Sanders Eliz.11
James 1,
Levin 44
William 11
Sands Benjamin 153
Sandsbery Middle.65
Solomon 65
Thomas 65

Sansberry, Eliz. 68
Sarah 128
William 128
Sansbury Isaac 123
Mary 123
Sargo John 65
Sasorson Daniel 42
Sauder Christ. 56
Felix 58
Henry 60
Susanna 56
Sauerpry Gorg 162
Saunders Benedict 94
Casandra 94
Charles 150
Charlotte 94
Elizabeth 93
Henry 52
Jemima 138
Joseph 93
Josias 138
Mary 94
Thomas 52,93
Wm.49,51,93
Sate Eliz.95
Savage Barth.90
Gorge 117
Savil Ann 127
William 127
Sawyer Richard 29
Saxton Hester 119
Leonora 119
Scantlin James 110
John 110
Rachel 110
Scarce Nathan 137
Sarah 137
Scarf John 92
Scarfe Eliz.119
John 119
Scarff Wm. 32
Scarlet Stephen 92
Scharbraugh Euclid 88
Hanna 88
Jemmy 88
Mary 88
Rebecca 88
Sally 88
Sammy 88
Thomas 88
Schoffield Eleanor 68
William 65
Scholar John 150
Scholfield Ann 71
Rachel 71
Schoolfield And.69

Schoolfield Issachar 69
John 70
Joseph 69
Maland 70
Sciles Cathrin 61
Elisabeth 57
Jacob 59
John 55,59
Rachel 61
William 59
Scoot James 37
John 37
Scot Ann 62
James 59
John 55,59
Mary 57,61
Milker 59
Samuel 60
Sarah 62
Sukey 110
Scott Absalom 146
Alexander 90
Ann 56,92
Aquila 89,92
Charles 53
Clemmency 89
Daniel 91
David 55
Edward 146
Eliz.89,90,137
Henry 133
James 89,90
John 49,90,135
Margaret 90
Mary 49,89,90,129, 133,135
Martha 61,92
Mrs.131
Ozbel 90
Robert 44
Sarah 90,95
Simon 129
Wm.22,54,146
Zachariah 137
Scotten Lucey 111
Scotter Edward 49
Scougall Eliz.10
Scovin Francis 100
Scrivanor Rich.19
Scrivenor Francis 14
John 26
John 28
Lewis 14
William 24
Searce Casandra 133

| | | | | |
|---|---|---|---|---|
| Searce David 133 | Seymour Joseph 158 | Sheckells Richard 18 | Shitz Cathrin 62 |
| Seares Anna 85 | Shabord Benony 85 | Shees Catharin 61 | Catharina 58 |
| Elias 85 | Middleton 85 | Elisabeth 62 | Conrad 54 |
| Elisabeth 85 | Rachel 85 | Magdalena 62 | Elisabeth 62 |
| Israel 85 | Samuel 85 | Peter 55,58 | Henry 60 |
| James 85 | Sary 85 | Susanna 57 | Lawrence 58 |
| John 85 | Shackall John 24 | Sheid Mary 58 | Margaret 57 |
| Joshua 85 | Shackells Ann 121 | Shehone Ann 68 | Shney Sara 148 |
| Mary 85 | Samuel 121 | Eleanor 68 | Shoaner Geo. 54 |
| Prissilla 85 | Shanahan John 153 | James 65 | Shoemaker Gedean 15 |
| William 85 | Shanks Abner 42 | Joseph 65 | Jacob 66 |
| Sears Peter 42 | Susanna 134 | Lucy 68 | John 59 |
| William 155 | Thomas 134 | Luransh 68 | Joshua 66 |
| Sebis John 55 | Sharadine Moses 146 | Richard 65 | Mary 68 |
| Sebon John 75 | Sharom George 46 | Thomason 68 | Thomas 66 |
| Sedgwick Benj.51 | Job 46 | Shekelworth Phil.86 | Shookard Lidia 56 |
| Sarah 91 | Sharrad John 73 | Luranah 86 | Shoomaker Baltzer55 |
| Seean Eliz.146 | Shaw Allender 163 | Shell Andrew 91 | Catherin 61 |
| Sees Eliz.Reab 57 | Ann 97, 125 | Mary 91 | Christianna 57 |
| Seiman Ann 57 | Armintha 97 | Shenafeild Ann 57 | Jacob 59 |
| John 55,58 | Bazell 127 | Shenafield Cath.61 | Michael 59 |
| Sarah 61 | Benjamin 78 | Henry 59 | Susanna 61 |
| Valentine 58 | Charles 128 | Jacob 59 | Shooman Dorathea 62 |
| Seitz Cathrin 62 | Dorraty 78 | John 59 | Jacob 60 |
| Hannah 62 | James 42,102 | Margaret 61 | John 58 |
| Selbey Agnes 126 | Jane 102 | Susanna 61 | Magdalane 62 |
| Elizabeth 127 | John 129 | William 55,59 | Thames 60 |
| James 126 | Joseph 125 | Shepard John 160 | Shores Eliz.88 |
| Martha 127 | Josiah 124 | Sheppard John 48 | Mary 88 |
| Selbey Nathan 126 | Kiziah 128 | Sheredine Thos.52 | Richard 88 |
| Ruth 126 | Mary 124 | Sheridine Mary 100 | Shors Sarah 44 |
| William 127 | Nancy 49 | Nathan 97 | Short Abraham 2 |
| Solby Benj.2 | Sarah 127,129 | Sherife Cath.129 | Isaac 127 |
| Jorsthan 2 | Susana 127 | John 129 | James 124 |
| Joshua 127 | William 36 | Ruth 129 | Jane 124 |
| Sarah 127 | Shea David 110 | Thomas 129 | Mary 127 |
| Sell John 84 | Elisabeth 110 | Sherman Benj.48 | Richard 79 |
| Seller Alex.59 | Isabel 110 | Sherrived Francis 33 | Samuel 156 |
| Elisabeth 62 | Sarah 110 | Hugh 33 | Shorter Wm.44 |
| Sellman Wm.22 | Thomas 110 | Sherwood David 154 | Sbryock Ann 56,62 |
| Selman John 1,8 | William 110 | Nathaniel 155 | Cathrin 56,62 |
| Jonathan 11 | Shealer Andrew 60 | Phillimon 152 | Catharine 62 |
| Sells Daniel 15 | John 60 | Prudence 157 | Elisabeth 62 |
| Semour Christ.90 | Leonard 55 | Thomas 153 | George 60 |
| Saney John 146 | Margret 51,62 | Shields Thomas 16 | Henry 54,60 |
| Nevil 146 | Shearbert Eliz.29,31 | Chine John 32,118 | Jacob 54,60 |
| William 146 | Pichard 22, 29 | Shinmer John 15 | John 60 |
| Serrell Wm. 146 | Thomas 22,29 | Shinnee Peter 35 | Leonard 54 |
| Seward Thomas 146 | William 30 | Shinton Ann 92 | Margaretha 57 |
| Sewel Dianna 159 | Shearlock James 65 | Elizabeth 92 | Mary 62 |
| John 47 | Jenne 68 | John 92 | Susanna 62 |
| Sewell James 154 | Shearwood Ann 135 | Sarah 92 | Shrieves Ann 135 |
| Marty 154 | Thomas 135 | William 92 | Jeremiah 135 |
| Seymour Henry 158 | Sheaver Wm. 107 | Shirtcliff Dorothey 131 | Shukells Saml.17 |
| John 159 | Sheckells Francis 24 | Joseph 131 | Shumkin Cath.56 |
| | John 19,24 | | |

Sible James 83
Siddel John 159
Sifton John 10
Siles Ann 71
  George 70
  Jacob 70
  John 70
  Susanna 71
Silhard Sophia 62
Silkerd Eliz. 56
  Philip 60
Sillavin Philip 83
Sillhard Fred. 60
Godfry 58
Sillory Jude 90
Silvers Affey 111
  Amons 111
  Benjamin 111
  David 111
  Gashim 111
  James 111
  John 111
  Margret 111
  Mary 111
  Mellison 111
  Rachel 111
  Sarah 111
  William 111
Simms Ann 56,119
  Darius 137
  Edward 119
  Mary 137
Simmonds Thomas 65
Simmons Abigail 17
  Ann 32
  Abram Capt. 27
  Elizabeth 122
  Jeremiah 27
  John 30
  Jonathan 122
  Isaac 24,26
  Mary 127
  Richard 17,127
  Tabitha 127
  Thomas 54
  Van 127
  William 15,17
Simon Catharina 57
  John 59,105
  Magdalana 58
  Peter 55, 59
Simpson Amelia 118
  Ann 32
  Charity 118
  Elizabeth 138

Simpson George 118
  Green 139
  James 136
  John 137,139
  Joseph 118,135
  Levey 118
  Margaret 89
  Mary 140
  Peter 44
  Precilla 136
  Rose 89
  Salome 118
  Solomon 118
  Sarah 135,137
  Tennally 118
  Thomas 118
Sims Alice 88
  Ann 88
  Ann Boyle 88
  Betsey 88
  Frances 88
  James 88
  Jane 88
  Margrett 88
  Mary 88
  Ralph 88
  Robert 88
  Rol 88
  William 88
Simson Elijah 33
  John 35
Sinclare Sawney 152
Sinclear Dunkin 78
  Mary 78
Sinners Charles 148
  James 148
Sisler Ann 62
  Catharina 62
  Henry 60
  William 58
Sisor Joseph 70
Sitze Barbara 57
  Christian 55
  George 60
  Hannah 57
  Henry 60
  John 55
  Peter 60
  Wendle 58
Sitzler Elisabeth 56
Skinner Francis 33
  Mary 106
  Mordica 158
  Phillimon 153
Skryock John 54

Slater Ann 121
  Jonathan 121
Slator Thomas 109
Slee Joseph 53
Slicer James 65
  Nathaniel 65
  Mary 68
  Sarah 68
Slight Joseph 51
Slond Sarah 111
Slone Elisabeth 111
  Henery 111
  John 111
  Mary 111
  Saras 111
Sloven Wm. 70
Small Frances 151
  Elizabeth 108
  John 108
  Robert 108
Smallwood Ann 124
  Benjamin 120
  Derecter 77
  Francis 120
  Martha 120
  Mary 140
  Precilla 120
  Phillip 120
  Richard 120
  Sarah 137
  William 140
Smith Abigail 36
  Adam 54
  Albert H. 16
  Ali 79
  Andrew 97
  Ann 51,57,68,97
  Anthoney 128
  Archabald 79
  Archibald 157
  Arthur 46
  Benjamin 79,117
  Catharina 61
  Cathron 110
  Charles 65
  Christian 58
  Clement 70
  Daniel 145
  David 65
  Deborick 93
  Drusiller 79
  Edward 34,150
  Elianor 118
  Elias 93
  Elisha 158

Smith Elizabeth 16,57
  68,71,105,111,112
  Errhard 59
  Esther 71
  Eve 57
  Francis 49,51
  George 55,58
  Gorge 111
  Hannah 112,137,146
  Henry 55,109,145
  Hugh 112
  Imanuel 55
  Isabel 91
  Jacob 55,58,107
  Jabish 110
  James 60,112,118,
    126,146,158
  Johanah 78
  John 12,32,35,46,
    58,59,65,69,96,
    105,138
  Joseph 146
  Joshua 35
  Josiah 145
  Leander 79
  Leaven 36
  Luis 110
  Magdalane 61,62
  Magdalena 57
  Margaret 71
  Mary 56,62,71,92,
    110,112,115,117,126
  Martha 97,123
  Matthew 65
  Nathan 79
  Nathaniel 112
  Nicholas 47,65
  Orlando 123
  Patrick 70,111
  Philip 21,32
  Preshey 79
  Rachel 91
  Ralph 97
  Rebecca 68,79,118
    132
  Redy 68
  Robert John 7
  Roda 79
  Rosina 57
  Ruth 97
  Salome 61
  Samuel 112
  Sarah 68,97,111
    117,118,138
  Stephen 65

| | | | |
|---|---|---|---|
| Smith Theop.91 | Snodgrass Cathroan 111 | Sparks Julyanna 146 | Spinkes Sarah 138 |
| Thomas 16,35,65, | James 111 | Levi 146 | Spiser John 163 |
| 112,145,146,155 | Margret 111 | Mary 146 | Spratt Sarah 106 |
| Walter 70,118 | Mary 111 | Mathew 123 | Sprigg Amilia 57 |
| William 32,36,46, | Robert 111 | Millenton 146 | Ann 61 |
| 91,107,109,110,112 | William 111 | Nathan 146 | Casber 59 |
| Winston 110 | Soaper Ann 68 | Solomon 145 | Corbin 61 |
| Smithson Arch 90 | Esther 68 | Thomas 122,146 | Hanna 57,61 |
| Casandra 90 | Mary 68 | Vinson 146 | Joseph 55,59 |
| Elizabeth 90 | Rachel 68 | William 145,146 | Lettica 61 |
| Margaret 90 | Soin Catharina 56 | Sparrow Ann 130 | Philip 59 |
| Mary 90 | Sole Samuel 65 | Dinah 10,68,Benj.65 | Samuel 60 |
| Nathaniel 90 | Sollars Abram 29 | Elizabeth 68 | Thomas 9,55 |
| Thomas 90 | Samuel 32 | Jonathan 65 | Spry Francis 145 |
| William 90 | Solomon John 84 | Jonthan West 65 | John 146,158 |
| Smyth William 148 | Solsboury James 35 | Joseph 130 | Spurry John 149 |
| Snail James 146 | John 35 | Luranah 68 | Spyvey Ann 68 |
| Sneed Moses 148 | Nemiah 34 | Mary 68 | Barsheba 68 |
| Richard 147 | Oliie 35 | Rich.L.65 | John 65 |
| Sneider Cathrin 63 | Solsboy Ebenezar 35 | Solomon 65 | Jonathan 65 |
| Snelling Sarah 156 | Soper Alexander 131 | Tidings 68 | William 65 |
| William 157 | Alvan 76 | William 65 | Squiers George 54 |
| Snyder Arnold 59 | Ann 76 | Speaks Eliz.68 | Stacy ___160 |
| Catharina 62 | Elizabeth 138 | Hezekiah 65 | Staford John 36 |
| Cathrin 58 | James 76 | Mary 68,72 | Stains Moses 153 |
| Christian 60 | John 76,131 | William 72 | Staintors Thos.42 |
| Christianna 56, 57, | Leonard 138 | Speight Ann 75 | Stallons Eliz.72,74 |
| 61, 63 | Martha 131 | Elisabeth 75 | Ezable 74 |
| Daniel 60 | Mary 131 | Mary 75 | Griffon 72 |
| Eliz. 61, 62, 63 | Mereen 76 | Robert 75 | Isaac 74 |
| Frederick 60 | Robert 131 | William 75 | Jacob 72 |
| Henry 56, 59 | Sarah 131 | Spencer ___159 | Joseph 74 |
| Jacob 55, 59 | Thomas 76 | Job 89 | Margaratt 72,82 |
| John 55, 59, 60 | Zadock 65 | Jane 115 | Patsa 74 |
| Levy 59 | Sordinge Edward 34 | Joseph 153 | Sarah 74 |
| Margaretha 62 | Southerlin James 49 | Margaret 105 | Susanah 72 |
| Martin 55 | Spain Beaver 89 | Phillimon 152 | Thomas 74 |
| Mary 56,57,61,62,63 | Elizabeth 89 | Ritchard 115 | William 74 |
| Peter 59 | Hana 89 | William 31 | Stalons Wm.81 |
| Susanna 57 | Jacob 89 | Spenser Agnes 117 | Standage Marg.132 |
| Valentine 59 | Nelly 89 | Cathron 117 | Thomas 132 |
| Sneydor Barbara 61 | William 89 | Charles 28 | Standiford Aquila 91 |
| Catherina 62 | Spalding Ann 139 | Elisabeth 117 | George 91 |
| Elisabeth 61 | Henry 139 | Heanary 117 | Hannah 91 |
| Eve 62 | John 139 | James 117 | Mary 91 |
| Henry 60 | Sparks Abner 145 | Jare 117 | Milkey 91 |
| Jacob 60 | | John 117 | Nathan 91 |
| John 60 | Caleb 146 | Lenard 117 | Sarah 91 |
| Martha 56 | Edward 145 | Mary 117 | Standly Margret 113 |
| Mary 61 | Elianor 123 | Roland 117 | William 113 |
| Susanna 61 | Elizabeth 122 | Ruth 117 | Stanton Benson 37 |
| Snowden Eliz.126 | James 146 | Sarah 117 | Elizabeth 157 |
| Mary 126 | John 146 | Thomas 117 | Stapleton David 97 |
| Samuel 126 | John Joyner 146 | William 117 | Edward 97 |
| Thomas 126 | Jonas 146 | Spinkes Francis 138 | Joshua 97 |
| | | | Lydia 97 & Susa.97 |

205

Stareman Alisabeth 117
Starkey John 130
Starling Elijah 44
  Henry 44
Start John 150
  Jonathan 151
Staton Jacob 42
Steal Abraham 109,112
  Casandra 109,112
  Elisabeth 80,109
  James 80,91
  John 80,109
  Joseph 80,109
  Josua 112
  Margaret 80
  Mary 80
  Rebeca 109
  Samuel 80
  Sarah 112
  William 80
Steall Wm. 80
Steaverson John 112
Steck Catherina 56
  Martin 54
  Mary 62
Steddam Eliz.153
Steel Eliz.68,99
  John 1,65
  Martha 68
  Mary 68
  Priscilla 68
  Richard 65
  Sarah 68
  Susanna 68
  William 65
Steele Henry 42
Steidinger Fred.54
  Julianna 62
  Magdalen 58
Steiner John 55
Steitzman Eve 57
Stephans Geo.145
Stephens Edw.53
  Elizabeth 139
  Mary 139
  Patrick 65
  Rebecca 129
  Thomas 139
  Wm.121,129,139
Stephenson John 97
  Jonas 99
  Mary 99
  Rebeca 99

Stertzman Adam 58
  David 58
  Henry 58,59
  July 61
  Margarethe 58
  Margret 61
  Martin 59
  Peter 58
Steuart Bryan 65
  Catharine 3
  Charles 13
  Edward 12
  Robert 3
Stevens Azell 35
  James 147
  John 37,49,151
  Lewis 15
  Wm.36,148
Steward Steppen 30
Stewardweall Wm.69
Stewart___ 156
  Anthony 13
  Charles 10
  David 24
  Elizabeth 103
  James 103,48
  Henry 52
  John 52
  Mary 103
  Stephen 31
  Susanna 103
  Thomas 52
Stiles Eliz.114
Stimpson Dorkus 76
  Solomon 76
Stineseiver Cath.62
  Elisabeth 62
  John 54
  Margaretha 56
  Mary 62,63
Stinson Saml.42
Stoaks Vollintin 42
Stockett Lewis 9
  Rachel 9
  Thomas Noble 9
Stockley Geo.36
Stoddert Benj.133
Stohs --- 162
Stokes Elijah 158
  Robert 107
  Susannah 159
Stolker Geo. 7
Stone John 137
  Elianor 136
  John 27, 137

Stone Joseph 136
  Margaret 137
  Marshall 19
  Richard 133
  Susanna 133
Stonestreet Alice 135
  Ann 129,135
  Bazell 122
  Butlar 70
  Elianor 137
  Elizabeth 122
  Henry 139
  John 135
  Joseph 135
  Mary 139
  Richard 129
Stoops David 146
Story Solloman 18
Strachan Mary 7
Stradlee Thos.C.33
Strannum Mary 71
Street Thomas 45
Styles John 66
  Sarah 68
  Thomas 66
  Virlinda 68
  William 66
Stuard Alex.115
  Ann 57,115
  George 55
  Margret 115
  Mary 115
  William 115
Stuart Ann 4
  David 5
  Elianor 119
  Jane 97
  John 133
  Sarah 133
Stuky Peter 55
Stull Daniel 55
  John 55
  Litha 63
  Madilta 61
  Martha 57
  Mary 57,61
  Susanna 57
Stump Eliz.116
  Esther 116
  Hannah 116
  Henery 116
  John 116
  Mary 116
  Rachel 116

Stump Rubin 116
  William 116
Sturd James 42
Sturgis John 94
Sudler Emory 148
  John 146
  Joseph 146
  Thomas 146
Suger Wm.76
Suillovon John 108
  Margret 108
Suit Mary 123
  Nathaniel 123
Sulivan Niell 42
Sullavin James 108
Sullivan John 16
  Rachel 9
  Thomas 66
Sullivane Danl.48
  James 49
  Thomas 51
Sulliven Nath.108
Summers Ann 120
  Benjamin 74
  Dent 75
  Elizabeth 120
  George 120
  Hezekiah 74
  Lydia 137
  Mary 157
  Montha 68
  Parks 51
  Paul 120
  Rebacka 74
  Thomas 69
  Verlinda 120
  Wm.65,66,74
Sung James 65
Sunksout Mary 160
Surat Edward 160
Surcom Thomas 149
Sutten Edw.112
  William 80
Sutton Elizabeth 101
  Jacob 107
  James 107
  John 65,146
  Jonathan 107
  Mary 101,107,120
  Oliver 107
  Rachael 107
  Rebecca 101
  Reubin 101
  Robert 65

| | | | |
|---|---|---|---|
| Sutton Saml 101 | Swegatt Thos.35 | Tarbert Janey 89 | Tawnihill Wm.133 |
| Solomon 101 | Swegott Henry 36 | Mary 89 | Teasewell John 92 |
| Susanna 107 | Sweier Fred.60 | Tarman H. 20 | Tenant Mable 152 |
| Tabitha 107 | Swgat Benj.34 | Tarr Richard 158 | Tennally Eliz.119 |
| Wm.107,120 | Swink Catherine 119 | Tasker James 15 | Joanna 119 |
| Suttone Ann 99 | Elizabeth 119 | Tate Ann 90 | John 119 |
| Elizabeth 99 | George 119 | Doctor 90 | Lydia 119 |
| Hannah 99 | John 119 | Tayler Warter 109 | Sarah & Thos.119 |
| Marget 99 | Mary 119 | Taylor Abraham 103 | Tracey & Wm.119 |
| Mary 99 | Susanna 119 | Alryhan 110 | Tenssil John 92 |
| Robert 99 | William 119 | Ann 4,83,90 | Terry Denisha 156 |
| Samuel 99 | Swording Sarah 37 | Aquila 103 | Thamson Adam 58,59 |
| Sarah 99 | Sydebothan Wm.133 | Aquiller 115 | John 59 |
| Thomas 99 | Syllavin Sarah 145, | Ashberry 103 | Susanne 57 |
| Swain Bethiah 104 | 146 | Asia 102 | Thomas Amelia 127 |
| Cassandra 104 | Talbert Ann 78 | Benjamin 66 | Ann 89 |
| Elizabeth 104 | Ellenner 78 | Bennet 134 | Barnet 89 |
| Gabriel 104 | Leven 78 | Caleb 5 | Edward 146 |
| Nathan 104 | Lewis 78 | Charlotte 103 | Elianor 128 |
| Swan John 55 | Notley 78 | Cordelia 103 | Eliz.68,98 |
| Swann Ann 79 | Reson 78 | Daniel 90 | Harison 117 |
| Anna 79 | Talbot Ann 136,137 | Delea 90 | Isaac 89 |
| Heza 85 | Daniel 66 | Delitha 83 | John 7,30,89,98,99 |
| Jesse 79 | Edward 66 | Elianor 129 | Joseph 98 |
| Mary 79 | Enock 66 | Eliz.17,72,90,112,146 | Marget 99 |
| Orpha 79 | John 137 | Frederick 50 | Martha 89,98 |
| Thomas 79 | Martha 137 | Griffin 85 | Martin 81 |
| Zephaniah 79 | Mary 125 | Hannah 103,110 | Mary 89 |
| Sward Peter 42 | Nathaniel 66,136 | Isaac 128 | Milky 89 |
| Swarth Cath 112 | Paul 137 | Isabella 105 | Nancey 89 |
| Christian 112 | Sarah 132 | James 101,102,103, | Notley 78 |
| David 112 | Tobias 132 | 105,129 | Philip 5,18 |
| Gorge 112 | William 66 | Jane 110,123 | Rachell 89 |
| Isaac 112 | Talbott Benj.5 | Jesse 102 | Richard 34 |
| Mary 112 | Richard 66 | John 81,83,90,91 | Samuel 116 |
| Peter 112 | Sarah 132 | Joseph 105 | Thurston 89 |
| Samuel 112 | William 132 | Laania 102 | Unity 89 |
| Sarah 112 | Talboy Ann 34 | Margaret 71 | Wm.66,89,127,128 |
| Swearinger Clemmey 81 | Tall Arthur 82 | Martha 103 | 98,159 |
| Lacy 81 | Benjamin 82 | Mary 90,103,110,128 | Thomlinson Thos.152 |
| Leonard 81 | Maryann 82 | Ninian 146 | Thompson Agnes 132 |
| Mary 81 | Pentacast 82 | Rachel 101 | Andrew 89,96 |
| Samuel 81 | Talley Cordelia 107 | Richard 70,108 | Ann 89 |
| Van 81 | Edward Carvel 107 | Robert 105 | Auther 4 |
| Sweatman Susannah 75 | Martha 107 | Ruth 75,89 | David 66,110 |
| Sweatten Siney 48 | Talor James 42 | Samuel 4 | Edwards 42 |
| Sweeny David 88 | Tanar Vinson B.42 | Sarah 90,102,105,134 | Elianor 124 |
| Henrietta 88 | Tannar Benj.148 | Stephen 101 | Eliz.89,110 |
| Major 70 | Tanner Phillen.147 | Susanna 68 | James 110 |
| Mary 88 | Tanquain Abram 24 | Thomas 146 | Jery 110 |
| Olive 88 | Tannehill Anne 74 | Wm.66,72,89 | John42,49,82,124, |
| Richard 88 | Rebeckah 74 | Tawnihill Eliz.133 | 126,136,146,110 |
| Sarah 88 | Sarah 74 | James 132 | Joseph 42,81 |
| Sweeting Rich.42 | William 74 | Jeremiah 133 | Martha 89 |
| Swegatt James 35 | Tarbert James 89 | Lottie 133 | Mary 75,89,110,126 |
| | | | 140 |

Thompson Nancy 81
 Nathan 104
 Rachel 127
 Richard 146
 Robert 132
 Samuel 146
 Sarah 89,136
 Susanah 81
 Thomas 89,119,127
 Wm. 81,140,146
Thomsan John 55
Thomson Alex.92
 Ann 92
 Caterine 93
 Daniel 92
 Edward 108
 Elizabeth 92,93
 Hanna 61
 Jamime 108
 John 92
 Mallon 108
 Margaret 92
 Martha 108
 Mary 92,93,108
 Sarah 92
 Thomas 92,93
 William 108
Thoritan Elis.113
Thorn Alice 102
 Amelia 135
 Benjamin 135
 Casandra 121
 Catherine 102
 Elianor 121
 Ephraim 121
 Thomas 121
Thornton Wm. 10
Thrasher Eliz.71
 John 71
 Margret 71
 Mary 71
 Sarah 71
 Thomas 71
 William 71
Threlkield Henry 70
Threlkild John 70
 Mary 71
Thrift Wm. 7
Thurston Hannah 92
Tibbels John 157
 Thomas 159
Tickel David F.42
 William 42
Tidings John 8
Tiffendale Mary 80

Tigner Wm.43
Tilbrook John 92
Tile Jacob 60
Tilghman Edw.146
 Elijah 42
 Mathew 155
 Richard 146
Tillard Thomas 17
 William 23
Tilley Eliz.134
 Mary 134
 Robert 134
 Thomas 134
Tillhard Mary 56
Tills Samuel 129
Timons Lawrance 100
Tims John 22
 Joseph 23
 Peter 23
Tinker Wm.32
Tinlan Mary 109
Tippins James 146
Tittle John 146
Tobb Job 44
Todd Benj.44
 David 44
 George 102
 Jabis 47
 Jobe 45
 John 44
 Jonathan 45
 Michael 44
Tolbart Ellenner 81
 Rebeca 81
Tolbert Basil 78
 George 78
 Mary 78
Tolon Ann 139
Tolson Alex.148
Tolston Mary 94
 Sarah 94
Tomlin Ann 120
Tomlinson Hester 76
 Heugh 75
 John 75
 Martha 76
 Mary 75
 William 76
Tommas Elesabeth 42
 John 42
 Joseph 42
Tomson Richard 70
Tongue Thomas 27
Tophouse Francis 17
Topping Eliz.107

Topping James 66
 Jude 68
 Margaret 68
Tootle John 47
Toppon Wm.72
Torresh Wm.156
Touchstone Mary 110
Toulson Eliz.103
Towirs James 35
Townsell Cassandra 101
 Charity 101
 Hester 101
 William 101
Townsend Joseph 66
 Thomas 152
Townshend Ann 125
 Samuel 125
Toyner Asalum 147
Tracey Eliz.127
 Usher 104
 William 127
Tracy Elenor 71
 James 71
 Philip 71
 William 71
Trahern Amelia 129
 Neamiah 129
Trame John 117
Trammill Ann 125
 John 125
Trapp Barbara 56
 Christopher 54
 Elisabeth 62
 Henry 60
 Jacob 60
Trass Hugh M.112
Travers John H.42
 Levin 42
 Matthew 42
Traverse Leavin 51
Tredway Edw.92
 Elizabeth 100
Tregor Nuton 52
Trezare John 150
 Thomas 150
Tribble John 96
Trice Vincent 156
Trigg Alice 123
 Clement 124
 Mary 124
 Samuel 123
Trimble Ann 90
 Esther 90
 Robert 90
Wm.32,90

Tripe Wm. 50
Tripp James 154
Trissoler Eliz.71
 George 70
 Jacob 70
 John 70
 Mary 71
Trott John 19
 Richard 20
 Seibert 20
 Tho'son 20
Trueborn___103
Truelove Ann 103
 Mary 103
Truelock Eliz.105
 Isaac 105
 Moses 105
 Sarbot 105
Truman Ann 68
 Richard 80
Trundle David 72
 Johanah 71
 John 72
 Mila 71
 Rachol 71
 Ruth 72
 Thomas 71
Tucker Alen 74
 Alexander 66
 Benj.66,121,130
 Catharine 74
 Darkis 80
 David 70
 Dianna 122
 Drucilla 130
 Edward 66,80
 Eleanor 68,131
 Eliz.68,74,123
 Henry 74
 Hester 130
 Hezekiah 66
 Isaac 20
 James 23,80,148
 Jemima 74
 John 23,31,66,70,130
 Jonathan 80
 Joseph 66
 Leonard 80
 Levi 73
 Margary 73
 Martha 74
 Mary 6,68,71,80
 Miltrue 80
 Nathaniel 66
 Osborn 66

| | | | |
|---|---|---|---|
| Tucker Racbell 132 | Umbel Cathran 111 | Veares Lien 79 | Vincent Wm. 53 |
| Razin 66 | Isaac 111 | Luranar 79 | Vinn Elizabeth 133 |
| Robey 130 | Mary 111 | Mary 79 | Robert 133 |
| Sarah 74 | Unmell Eliz. 68 | Nehemiah 79 | Vinson John 42 |
| Sary 80 | George 66 | Sary 79 | Nehemiah 51 |
| Sebina 74 | Upright Jacob 70 | Solomon 79 | Stephen 48 |
| Seeborn 20 | Katharine 71 | William 79 | Vinton Daniel 153 |
| Selah 23 | Upton John 131 | Veatch Barshaba 84 | Solomon 152 |
| Susannah 31,74,68 | Keziah 131 | Elijah 84 | Virthworth Sarah 109 |
| Thomas 5,20,70,122,123 | Thomas 131 | Elisabeth 85 | William 109 |
| Walter 66 | Urrvine Cathaina 61 | Grase 86 | Voice Ezabela 147 |
| William 22,66,73,74 | Margaretha 58 | Hensenk 84 | Mary 135 |
| 131,132 | Urwan John 58 | James 85 | |
| Tuile James 151 | Unsel Eliz. 62 | Jamima 85 | Wade Ann 119 |
| Tull Handy 32 | Henry 59 | Jean 86 | George 119 |
| Tully Ann 85 | John 59 | John 84,85 | Robert 129 |
| Elisabeth 85 | Magdalan 56 | Kessiah 86 | Zachariah 119 |
| Ellenner 85 | Unsill John 54 | Nin 85 | Wadkins Amos 99 |
| James 85 | | Ninian 85 | Ann 99 |
| John 85 | Vain Henry 42 | Lander 86 | Eliner 147 |
| Mary 85 | Vallont Bennet 158 | Lurana 84 | John 99 |
| Turk Esau 89 | John 158 | Mary 84 | Purify 99 |
| Turnball John 134 | Nicholas 158 | Matha 85 | William 99 |
| Sarah 134 | Vanbibber Mrs. 32 | Rebeca 85 | Wadlow Francis 91 |
| Turner Ann 47,125 | Vancleave Eliz. 96 | Richard 85 | John 91 |
| Benjamin 125 | Mary 96 | Sary 85 | Moses 91 |
| Catherine 121 | Vanderfer John 150 | Silas 86 | Ruth 91 |
| Edmond 121 | Vandevort John 32 | Solomon 85 | Wagon Patrick 91 |
| Elijah 125 | Vandigraft Rich. 114 | Susanna 86 | Wagoner Conrad 60 |
| George 146 | Vandigrift Eliz. 112 | Thomas 84 | Eliz. 56,62 |
| Jane 127 | George 112 | William 86 | Francis 54 |
| John 24,127 | Mary 112 | Venables Eliz. 130 | John 70 |
| Jonathan 129 | Vanhorn Eseacall 110 | William 130 | Margaretha 56 |
| Margaret 127 | Jessay 110 | Vensieler Alener 100 | Peter 54 |
| Mary 125,129 | Peter 100 | Vermillion Abraham 118 | Sharlote 56 |
| Patience 125 | Richard 114 | Benjamin N. 137 | Valentine 60 |
| Ruth 147 | Sary 110 | Eleanor 118 | Wakeland John 90 |
| Sarah 124 | Vansickleton Cath. 106 | Elizabeth 118,130 | Waker Michael 58 |
| Shadrick 124 | Elizabeth 106 | Giles 131,139 | Walch Mary 85 |
| William 2,20,66,125, | Francis 106 | Henson 137 | Wale John 43 |
| 147 | Henry 106 | James 118 | Wales John 32 |
| Turnner John 34 | Varnel Saml. 25 | Mary 131 | Robert 152 |
| Turton Aquilla 118 | Vaulx Ebennezer 37 | Rachell 118 | Walker 66 |
| Catherine 124 | Vaun Betty 75 | Robert 130 | Ann 114,133 |
| Fielder 118 | Veares Ann 79 | Sarah 131,139 | Benjamin 66 |
| Harrison 118 | Basil 79 | Thomas 131 | Charles 124 |
| John 118 | Brice 79 | Vessel Eleanor 71 | Elender 114 |
| William 124 | Cassandra 79 | Even 70 | Elianor 136 |
| Tush Rachael 104 | Daniel 79 | Vickars Soloman 42 | Elizabeth 68,114, |
| Tuttle Wm. 153 | Edward 79 | Vickers Charles 152 | 128,129,136,150 |
| Tydings Richard 3 | Elisabeth 79 | Vincent Frances 118 | George 66 |
| Tyler David 43 | Elisha 79 | John 118 | Gorge 114 |
| John 43,45,47 | Ellender 79 | Joseph 118 | Henry 136 |
| Tyson Ann 73 | Hezakaih 79 | Mary 118 | Isaac 129 |
| Mary 73 | John 79 | Prudence 118 | James 114 |

| | | | |
|---|---|---|---|
| Walker Jane 104,124 | Walters Wm. 79 | Warner Mordecai 97 | Watkins Stephen 16 |
| John 33,104,136 | Wamigim Thomas,Ann 110 | Ruth 97 | Thomas 9,13,127 |
| Jonathan 66 | Ward Andrew 73 | Samuel 85 | William 95 |
| Joseph 128 | Ann 73 | Sarah 98 | Wats James 84 |
| Margaret 104 | Avis 97 | Silas 97 | William 158 |
| Martha 136 | Benj.24,30,80 | Thomas 18 | Watson Eliz.77 |
| Richard 7,157 | Cassandria 97 | William 157 | Elkanah 77 |
| Susanna 68 | Edward 97,105 | Warren Alley 76 | John 75 |
| Thomas 10 | Elizabeth 105 | Charles 76 | Lucy 77 |
| William 136 | John 15,105 | Elisabeth 76 | Rebecca 77 |
| Vineay 68 | Joseph 18,30 | George 76 | Sally 75 |
| Wallace Alex 66 | Lousey 48 | Johan 76 | Samuel 77 |
| Ann 86 | Margret 97 | Mary 76 | Sarah 75 |
| Anne 68 | Mary 36,73,105 | Sary 76 | Sary 77 |
| Barbara 68 | Matten 80 | Thomas 76 | Watters Benj.148 |
| Charles 66 | Paul 55 | Warring Eliz.123 | John 148 |
| Eleanor 68,86 | Rachel 73 | James 123 | Robert 149 |
| Elizabeth 68 | Richard 97 | Warringfrod Ammina 131 | Wayford John 49 |
| Frances 68,86 | Robert 15 | Ann 131 | Wayman Edmund 5 |
| Herbert 66 | Samuel 18,105 | George 131 | Francis 11 |
| James 66 | Sarah 105 | Joseph 131 | Leonard 6 |
| John 66 | Talbott 105 | Warron Beazil 50 | Thomas 154 |
| Margaret 68 | Summars 51 | Solomon 34 | Weaks Ann 91 |
| Mary 68,86 | Tracy 73 | Warters James 77 | Elizabeth 91 |
| Mathew 82 | William 11 | Wartes Johannah G.110 | John 91 |
| Nathaniel 66 | Warde Elizabeth 75 | Wartus Godfrey 111 | Mary 91 |
| Rhode 47 | Ware James 147 | Waskey Christian 32 | Rachel 91 |
| Richard 47,133 | Warfield Henry 104 | Wason John 19 | Ruth 91 |
| Robert 66 | Mary 104 | Richard 31 | Zachariah 91 |
| Susanna 68,86 | Warham Rachael 104 | Wassin James 55 | Weathers Rachel 135 |
| William 66 | John 104 | Waters Alex.149 | Weaver Ann 131 |
| Zepheniah 66 | Warker Arch.85 | Ann 92 | Casper 115 |
| Wallas John 42 | Cassandra 78 | Bazel 92 | Jacob 131 |
| William 42 | Elisabeth 85 | Deborah 94 | James 101 |
| Wallase Wm.84 | James 85 | Elizabeth 92 | John 101 |
| Wallis Grace 98 | Thomas 78 | Henritte 92 | William 149 |
| John H. 96 | Virlinder 78 | John 92 | Webb Augustus 47 |
| Phanney 98 | William 78,85 | Joseph 137 | Elizabeth 124 |
| Samuel 95 | Warner Aaron 98 | Margaret 137 | John 48 |
| Thomas 98 | Agnes C.98 | Martha 92 | Harry 148 |
| Walsh Mary 8 | Amos 98 | Mary 94 | Rebecca 129 |
| Walter Ann 78 | Asa 98 | Nathan 11 | Thomas 124,129 |
| Catharina 57 | Aseph 97 | Rebeccah 92 | Webster Ann 129 |
| Clement 82 | Catherine 137 | Robert 94 | Catron 43 |
| Daniel 43,83 | Crosdale 98 | Sarah 92 | Eliz.105,106,129 |
| David 78 | Cuthbert 98 | Susanah 147 | Hannah 105 |
| Eliz.62,82,83 | Drusila 85 | Thomas 92 | Mary 105,129 |
| George 83 | Francis 137 | William 128 | Mary Ann 129 |
| John 83 | James 97 | Watkins Eliz.112 | James 95,129 |
| Levy 80 | Hennary 85 | Gassaway 7,26 | Joanna 125 |
| Mary 83 | Herbert 160 | Jane 127 | John 106,125 |
| Michael 54 | Hizekiah 97 | Jeremiah 9 | John Lee 106 |
| Rebeca 82,83 | Joseph 15,57 | John 9,17 | Thomas 129 |
| Sary 78,82,83 | Lemuel 150 | Joseph 7 | Wm. 129,160 |
| Stephen 78 | Ludwick 99 | Richard 10 | Weeb Jonathan 162 |
| Thomas 83 | Mary 85,98,147 | Samuel 8 | Weekly Eliz. 94 |
| | | | Weems David 21 |

Weems James 30
John 24
Richard 27
William 21
Weickle Jacob 60
Weikle Henry 54
Susana 56
Welch Darcas 128
Elizabeth 118
Hannah 113
Jacob 27
James 148
Jason 31
John 15,18
Robert 18
Ruth 113
Thomas 113,128
William 109
Weldon Ann 132
John 132
Welling Ann 119
Thomas 119
William 119
Wells Benj.147
Cassandra 97
Drusillah 97
Elizabeth 97
George 32
Jane 97
John 43
Mary 97
Richard 16,17,97
Samuel 23,26,97
Susanna 29,97
Tobias 147
Welsh Benj 3
Henry O. 8
Richard 10
Robert 3
William 54,59
Wenner Cath.56
Wentel George 60
Wesbbach Elis.58
West Ann 108,116,117
Benjamin 116
Bethiah 104
Elisabeth 116,108,113
Enoch 113
Ephram 116
Geo.Wm.100
Hannah 89,116
Heanary 117
Isaac 108
Jacob 89
James 89,108,117

West John 89,116
Jonathan 89
Lidia 89
Loten 53
Mary 48,108,116,117,158
Marget 100
Margrett 89
Martha 116
Michael 116
Nathaniel 89
Phebe 85
Robert 116
Ruth 89
Samuel 108
Sarah 89,108,117
Sibyl 100
Solomon 49
Susanna 89,100,109
Thomas 95,108
W.Rev.107
Wm.89,100,113,155
Westinecoat Thos.19
Westly Wm. 30
Weston Ann 68
Nathanel 162
Weyand Eliz.62
Jacob 60
Jost 54
Margaretha 56
Weyer Margaretha 56
Whaland Joseph 45
Whalen Daniel 80
Rebeca 80
Whalend Jon 43
Whallen Bridgett 73
Margrett 73
Mark 73
Martin 73
Mary 73
Mathew 73
Michel 73
Thomas 73
Whealand Nicholas 122
Sarah 122
Wheat Francis 126
John 135
Mary 135
Wheatly Wm.37
Wheeler Chas.52
John 43
Mary 47
Solomon 49
Thomas 50
William 53
Whefing Nath.148

Wheeler Eliz.119,133,137
Francis 133
Hezickiah 139
Ignatius 137
James 93
Lydia 127
Richard 127
Sarah 93
Where Ann 57
Catharina 63
Christian 58,59
Christiana 61
Eliz.11,57,58
Henry 60
Magdalana 62
Martin 55
Michael 55
Peter 60
Susanna 61
Wheever Rachell 138
Whitacre Hezek.99
Isaac 99
John 99
Whitaker Alex.76
Benjamin 89
Elizabeth 89
Hester 76
Isaac 89
John 52,89
Joshua 89
Martha 89
Samuel 89
Whitchits Ezek.49
White Abednigoe 123
Absolom 19
Alexander 130
Ann 57,116
Bazil 75
Cathrine 36
Charles 60,103
Eleanor 103,121
Elsia 72
Hannah 130
Isaac 103
Jach 72
James 72,121
John 33,37,43,49,103,147
Jonathan 103
Katharine 71
Ketty 82
Margaret 103,116
Mary 43,72,103,123
Richard 116

White Saml.8,72
Sarah 43,116
Thos.22,43,49
William 103
Whitee Saml.36
Whitehead Tim.73
Whiticer Mary 116
Whitington Jas.21
Thomas 19
William 15
Whitley Bridget 44
David 46
Thomas 44
Whitlow Will G.93
Whitmore Elianor 135
Humphrey 135
Whitnell Soloman 72
Whittaker Robt.7
Whitting Ann 90
Elizabeth 90
Hannah 90
Sarah 90
Thomas 90
Whittington John147
Stephen 47
Whyle James 89
Jane 89
John 89
Kathrine 89
Mary 89
Nathaniel 89
Philip 89
Sarah 89
Whorten ___ 159
Henry 159
Whymer Jacob 54
Wickel Adam 70
Wickes Joseph 147
Matthew 147
Simon 147
Wieghler Felter 133
Wieley Epheram 147
Wigfield Eliz.132,138
Joseph 138
Mathew 132
Radie 138
Thomas 138
Wiggins Benj.147
Cassandra 103
Charles 147
Ebenezer 147
Elizabeth 147
James 103
Mary 103

Wiggons Bezleel 98
Cuthbert 98
Hannah 98
Joseph 98
Sarah 98
Tarace 98
Wilcock John 115
Wilcox Michal 43
Wilcoxon Amos 66
Ann 68
Elizabeth 68,131
Jesse 66
John 66
Josiah 66
Rachel 68
Rebecca 68
Ruth 68
Sarah 68
Thomas 66,131
William 66
Wildey Molley 44
Willighboey Rich.33
Wilimson Elijah 35
Wilkerson Wm. 83
Wilins Thomas 32
Wilkinson John 100
Nathan 151
Thomas 147
Wilkson Henry 33
Wille Pritch 43
Willen Levi 45
Willerd Gotlieb 54
Willet Mary 126
William 126
Willett Griffeth 77
Willey Ezekiel 46
Indey 46
Jane 46
Nellie 46
William 46
William & Williams
Williams ___160
Abigal 90
Andrew 84
Ann 73,75,116
Barnet 113
Basol 86
Benjamin 4
Cassandra 84
Charles 86
Daniel 73,84,107
Deborah 151
Ellenner 84
Elisha 75
Eliz.2,49,73,86,94,
100,113

Williams Elisha 75
Ephrame 113
Eseakel 113
Frances 113
George 60
Hazel 75
James 66,80,113,149
Jarred 75
Jesse 84
John 21,66,75,84,
86,113,116,151
Joseph 1,2,130
Levin 43
Margaret 8,113
Martha 75,113,116
Mary 75,86,99,
113,116
Morras 116
Moses 27
Nancy 86
Phillip 49
Prissilla 84,116
Rezen 84
Robert 43
Sarah 113,130
Sary 84
Stockett 2
Susanna 29,84,113
Thomas 43,75,84,
100,147
William 32,84,86,
97,113,116
Williamson Ann 105
George 147,105
. William 93
Willicoxen Thos.137
Ruth 137
Willighbouy Edw.34
Willis Leavin 52
Williss ___160
Mary 147
Willowbee Absol.33
Solomon 33
Willowbeey Saml.37
Wilmott Ann 9
Mary 132
Samuel 9
Thomas 132
Wilmonton Joseph 116
Wilson & Willson
Abraham 66
Absolom 85
Agnes 89,132
Alianna 114
Andrew 108

Wilson Arch.89
Barbary 124
Bazell 123
Benj.76,98,108
Betsey 89
Casandra 90,114
Cathron 108
Christopher 37,114
Cloe 129
David 124
Edmond 123
Elender 72
Elianor 85,124
Eliz.78,85,98,119
124,136
Folandor 72
Francis 85
George 78,127,147
Hannah 76,98
Henry 72,76,90
Heza 85
Hugh 107
Ignatius 124
Isaac 114
Isable 89
James 72,85,89,108
114,121,124,149
Janima 85
Jane 89,119
Jesse 32
Jobe 45
John 37,76,89,98,
114,121,124,147
Jonathan 36
Joseph 119,129,132
Josiah 85,123
Lanclot 72
Leven 85
Lidia 78
Lidiea 108
Lucy 72,123
Margaret 85,90,98,
107,114,127
Margrett 89
Martha 98,119
Mary 72,78,85,89,
98,114,121,123,127
Mathew 76
Michel 78
Nansey 85
Nathaniel 119,136
Norindo 123
Poter 115
Priscilla 85,90
Rachel 76,107,114

Wilson Rebecca 13,85
124,147
Richard 148
Robert 32,34,89
Ruth 114
Samuel 90,98,114
Sarah 71,98,114
Sary 85
Thomas 72,85,148
Verlander 73
William 30, 70,78,
85,90,94,113,114,
124,127
Wodsworth 85
Zachariah 73
Zadock 72
Winard Abraham 70
Elizabeth 71
Winbargle Geo.70
Jacob 70
John 70
Margaret 71
Susanna 71
Windham Eliz.79
George 79
Robert 79
Windom Charles 42
Windon Mary 58
Windows Thomas 47
Wine John 59
Wingal Eliz.71
Lazuress 70
Wingate Angelo 44
James 47
John 44,47
Molley 44
Robert 44
William 44
Winget Zebulon 43
Wingle John 70
Wings Arther 111
Winman John 89
Winn Ann 139
John 140
Mary 140
Sarah 140
William 139
Winterbottom John 155
Robert 155
Winters Jonathan 153
Winterson John 22
Winwright Evins 43
Wirt Catherine 130
Jasper 130
Wise Adam 54,59

| | | | |
|---|---|---|---|
| Wise Cath.61,62 | Wood Rebecca 105 | Wooton Mary 44 | Wrightson James 153, 154 |
| Christian 59 | Richard 15 | Worker Agnes 76 | |
| Christiana 62 | Robert 73 | George 107 | Wyght Ann 122 |
| Eliz.56,61,62,71 | Sarah 15,68,105 | Jane 107 | John 122 |
| Ester 57 | Stephen 77 | John 76 | Jonathan 121 |
| Eve 56 | Susanna 20,105,113 | Margaret 76 | Sarah 121 |
| G orge 58,60 | Thoma 71 | Rachel 107 | Wyth Daniel 33 |
| Jacob 59 | Thomas 76 | Ruth 107 | |
| John 60,70 | Tochua 113 | William 76 | Yates Joseph 70 |
| Katharine 71 | Walter 76 | Worland Charles 136 | Mary 84 |
| Ludwig 60 | Zadock 73 | Edey 125 | Sarah 95 |
| Mary 61,62 | Zebedee 26 | Elianor 119 | Susannah 95 |
| Samuel 59 | Zephonioh 76 | James 119 | Yeates John 76 |
| Sarah 122 | Woodard Frances 74 | John 119 | Joshua 11 |
| Susanna 62 | Hezekiah 74 | Mary 119 | Yegley Catharina 62 |
| Thomas 122 | Mary 68 | Robey 125 | Christian 60 |
| Wiseam Eliz.71 | Sarah 74 | Stacey 119 | Christopher 60 |
| Wiser Michael 66 | Weneford 74 | Thomas 119 | John 60 |
| Wishler Lawrence 60 | Zachariah 74 | Walter 119 | Michael 54 |
| Withers Aaron 35 | Woodards Benj.43 | William 119 | Yegly Catharina 57 |
| Solomon 36 | Elizabeth 48 | Winefred 136 | Yeoman Ann 32 |
| Witman Andrew 55 | Woodcock John 54 | Worner __156 | Yoe Aaron 149 |
| Wivell Duke 27 | Wooden John 162 | Worrell Thomas 133 | Yokely Eliz.102 |
| William 19 | Sollomon 162 | Worthington Ann 98 | John 102 |
| Wollyhand Fransis 147 | Stephen 162 | Charles 98 | Mary 102 |
| Wolseger Jacob 54C.56 | Woodfield Anthony 28 | H nry 98 | Young Abraham 66 |
| Woltz Charlote 56 | Mariar 79 | John 98 | Agness 101 |
| Elisabeth 62 | Woodgard Ann 84 | Joseph 98 | Benjamin 81 |
| George 54,60 | Woodgerd Dennis 82 | Margret 98 | Eistations 54 |
| Jacob 60 | Elisabeth 82 | Mary 98 | Eleanor 72,125,131 |
| Mary 56,62 | Jene 82 | Prissilla 98 | George 55,70,101 |
| Peter 54 | Jerry 82 | Samuel 98 | Isaac 59 |
| Wood Ama 73 | Jisse 82 | Sarah 98 | Jacob 59 |
| Ann 68 | John 82 | wothers Elijah 34 | James 66 |
| Anna 76,77 | William 82 | John 34 | Jane 72 |
| Bennet 77 | Woodling John 43,44 | Ruban 34 | John 60,72,81 |
| Catherine 129 | Richard 43,47 | Wotten Aquiloe 47 | Kessiah 81 |
| Charity 76 | Solomon 44 | Woulds James 152 | Ludwig 55,59 |
| Charlotte 68 | Woodward Abraham 5 | Wrain Ann 102 | Magdalina 57 |
| Chloe 68 | Ann 104 | William 102 | Magdaline 62 |
| Eli 76 | Benedict 66 | Wraken John 54 | Margaretha 56 |
| Eliz.32,73,76,77,97, 113,116 | Clement 130 | Wright Ann 91 | Margret 57,61,103 |
| | Frances 130 | Charles 108 | Mary 56,72 |
| George 112 | John 66 | Edward 147 | Nancy 81 |
| Hopeful 14 | Martha 68 | Elizabeth 125 | Notley 139 |
| Isaac 116 | Mary 104 | Greenbutt 149 | Peter 66 |
| James 66,76,113,129 | Thomas 66,104 | Henry 50 | Samuel 54 |
| John 15,73,76,105,113 | William 104 | James 148 | Sarah 71,103 |
| Joshua 105 | Woodyard Jesse 81 | John 107 | Thomas 70,108,125 |
| Josua 112 | John 81 | Nathaniel 149 | William 70,81,101, 131,147 |
| Mary 73,76,105 | Woolcott Mathias 156 | Ruth 134 | |
| Morgan 15 | Woodford Roger 52 | Sarah 49 | Youst Casbery 70 |
| Posaurus 113 | Woollen Leavin 52 | Sol.151 | Eleanor 71 |
| Preasha 77 | Wooten Hager 44 | Thomas 91, 134,35 135, 162 | Elizabeth 71 |
| Rache 71 | John 46 | | John 70 |
| | Priss 44 | Turbutt 150 | |
| | Prissilla 44 | | |
| | Thomas 44 | | |

## INDEX

Youst Katharine 71
  Mary 71
  Phillip 70
  Rebecca 71
  Susanna 71
  Tobias 70

Zigler John 32
Zinn Elisabeth 62
  George 54, 59
  Mary 56

Omitted from St. James Parish: Eliz. Brunk, white woman - No other data

www.ingramcontent.com/pod-product-compliance
Lightning Source LLC
Chambersburg PA
CBHW051050160426
43193CB00010B/1131